MW01033525

THE BHAGAVAD GITA
FOR AWAKENING

THE BHAGAVAD GITA FOR AWAKENING

A PRACTICAL COMMENTARY FOR LEADING A SUCCESSFUL SPIRITUAL LIFE

ABBOT GEORGE BURKE
(SWAMI NIRMALANANDA GIRI)

LIGHT OF THE SPIRIT
PRESS
CEDAR CREST, NEW MEXICO

Published by
    Light of the Spirit Press
    lightofthespiritpress.com

    Light of the Spirit Monastery
    P. O. Box 1370
    Cedar Crest, New Mexico 87008
    www.ocoy.org

ISBN-13: 978-1-7325266-0-0
ISBN-10: 1-7325266-0-5

Library of Congress Control Number: 2018961637
Light of the Spirit Press, Cedar Crest, New Mexico

Translation of the Bhagavad Gita used in this book is from
The Bhagavad Gita: The Song of God by Abbot George Burke.
Copyright © 2018 Light of the Spirit Monastery.

1. SEL032000 SELF-HELP / Spiritual
2. REL032030 RELIGION / Hinduism / Sacred Writings

First edition, (December 2018)

Credits: The cover contains an illustration of Krisha and Arjuna on the
Battlefield of Kurukshetra based on a painting by the Rajasthani artist
Bhanwar lal Girdhari lal Sharma

03042021

CONTENTS

BHAGAVAD GITA–THE BOOK OF LIFE

Several thousand years ago in north-central India, two people sat in a chariot in the midpoint of a great battlefield. One of them, the yogi Arjuna, knew that it would not be long before the conflict would begin. So he asked Krishna, the Master of Yoga (Yogeshwara), what should be his attitude and perspective in this moment. And above all: What should he do?

There was no time to spare in empty words. In a brief discourse, later turned into seven hundred Sanskrit verses by the sage Vyasa, Krishna outlined to Arjuna the way to live one's entire life so as to gain perfect self-knowledge and self-mastery.

The battle was ferocious and–as always with war–everyone lost. But when Vyasa wrote his epic poem, the Mahabharata (The Great Indian War), he put Krishna's inspired teachings into it as a precious jewel. Instantly they were extracted, named Bhagavad Gita (The Song of God), and circulated throughout the subcontinent.

That was several thousand years ago, and today the Gita is found in nearly every household in India and has been translated into every major language of the world. Literally billions of copies have been handwritten and printed. (A few years ago a spiritual organization in South Africa printed one million copies for free distribution.) When Rudyard Kipling became a Freemason in Lahore, four scriptures were on the altar, including the Bhagavad Gita.

What is the appeal of the Gita? First of all, it is totally practical, free of any vague or abstract philosophy. During my first trip to India over forty years ago, I heard about a yogi who lived in a small houseboat on the Ganges river in the holy city of Benares (Varanasi). He never spoke or wrote, yet every day for many years people came to him for advice. How did he manage? He had a copy of the Bhagavad Gita, and after he was told the problem or question he would open the book, point to a portion, and the inquirer would have a perfect and complete solution to the trouble.

My own spiritual awakening began by kicking me out of the nest of comfortable religion into a vast world of realities I had no idea how to cope with. I floundered around in the sea of my new horizons until one day I bought a paperback edition of the Bhagavad Gita. I did not read it, I inhaled it. I was not reading the words of a long-dead teacher: my own Self was talking to me in the pages of that little book. Nor did I learn anything from the Gita—I *remembered* that which I had always known. Eternal Self spoke Eternal Truth. The Bhagavad Gita changed my life by giving me Life that has never ended.

Nothing has ever arisen in my life, internal or external, that the Gita has not made clear and enabled me to deal with or understand. Yet is it not dogmatic. At the very end Krishna says to Arjuna: "Now I have taught you that wisdom which is the secret of secrets. Ponder it carefully. Then act as you think best." No threats, no promises, no coercion. It is all in the reader's hands.

Even better: the Bhagavad Gita tells us that we can attain a Knowing beyond even what it tells us. And it shows us the way. It is a wise resolve to read the Gita every day without fail for the rest of one's life.

A practical suggestion

The translation used in this commentary is my own, but I recommend that you obtain other translations of the Gita, for it is impossible to produce a definitive translation of a text written in such a complex language as Sanskrit. I always check at least four translations when looking into the meaning of a verse: those of Swamis Prabhavananda, Swarupananda, Sivananda, and that of Winthrop Sargeant. I sometimes consult those of Sri Aurobindo, Gandhi, and William Judge, as well.

I would like to point out that reading any English-only translation of the Gita, however good, will only be skimming the surface. This is because of the many meanings of Sanskrit words—meanings that were in the mind of Vyasa and that were used for that very reason. In the West we have the idea that spiritual texts have but one meaning, and that may be so for some, but this is not at all the case for Sanskrit texts which are intended to have multi-level messages and subtle nuances. Words which carry several relevant ideas are ideal for the profound wisdom of the Gita and Upanishads, particularly.

In the Gita translation, words in parentheses indicate alternate readings of the actual Sanskrit word preceding them. Those alternate readings are as legitimate as the English term I have used. Brackets indicate words not in the Sanskrit text but inserted by me to clarify the meaning.

Because of this I recommend that you obtain translations of the Gita that contain the Sanskrit text with word-by-word translations as well as the usual verse form. Sargeant's translation is definitely the best for this, but it would be good to have one or two more. In addition you need some Sanskrit dictionaries. I recommend: *A Concise Dictionary of Indian Philosophy* by John Grimes, *The Yoga-Vedanta Dictionary* of Swami Sivananda, *Sanskrit Glossary of Yogic Terms* by Swami Yogakanti and *A Sanskrit Dictionary* by John M. Denton. My own endeavor, *A Brief Sanskrit Glossary,* is certainly helpful, and definitely complements them.

Swami Nirmalananda Giri
(Abbot George Burke)

THE BATTLEFIELD OF THE MIND

Most of us have heard the story of the centipede who, when asked how he managed to walk with so many legs, tangled his legs in the attempt to figure it out and ended up on his back, helpless. This is not unlike the person who attempts to plumb the depths of oriental scriptures. Right away it becomes evident that they consist of incalculable layers, many symbolic in nature. Furthermore, the meanings of the symbols are not consistent, changing according to the levels on which they occur. For example, on one level water symbolizes the mind, on another level the constant flux of samsara, and on another the subtle life-currents known as prana. This being the case, the Western linear mode of thought becomes as entangled and disabled as the fabled centipede. Knowing this to be so, I have decided to avoid subtle symbolism and concentrate instead on the obviously practical side of Krishna's teachings in the Bhagavad Gita. (For an exposition of the symbolism of the Gita, see Paramhansa Yogananda's commentary, *God Talks With Arjuna: The Bhagavad Gita*.) However I do want to take some time and consider the obvious symbolism encountered in the first chapter of the Gita.

We find ourselves on Kurukshetra, a field of impending battle. It is not as vast as our Hollywood-epic-shaped minds might imagine, as can be seen for oneself by a visit to Kurukshetra, not very far from Delhi. At one end is a hillock topped with a huge tree under which there is a great bronze statue of Arjuna, Krishna and their chariot. (When I was there only the tree and a large marble replica of the chariot marked where they sat.) This is the vantage point from which Arjuna, the great warrior, and Sri Krishna, his teacher, looked out over the field. Today its tranquillity is charming, despite the strong feeling in the air that something tremendously momentous occurred there in the distant past. It is both awesome and soothing.

For background information regarding how the battleground came to be thronged with soldiers, chariots, elephants and the other paraphernalia of a deadly war, see the introductory essay, "Gita and Mahabharata" in Swami Prabhavananda's translation *The Song of God*.

Suffice it to say that the two opposing armies are very easy to morally identify. The Kauravas, led by the murderous Prince Duryodhana, are fundamentally evil, although many honorable men have, through various complicated alliances and obligations, found themselves among their ranks. The Pandavas, headed by the virtuous and noble Yudhisthira, the eldest brother of Arjuna, are embodiments of all that is good, among them being the divine Sri Krishna himself who chose to be the charioteer of Arjuna.

The symbolism is not very hard to figure out (leaving aside the complex matter of assigning a symbolic meaning to every person named in the battle narrative). Kurukshetra is the personality–particularly the mind (intellect)–of the awakened seeker for higher consciousness. Such a seeker, determined to end the whirling cycle of birth and death, finds that his aspiration itself has inspired opposition from within his own mind and heart, where good and evil, truth and falsehood, ignorance and wisdom, like the Kauravas and Pandavas, have drawn themselves up in readiness for a conflict that must end in the annihilation of one side or the other. Even more daunting is the fact that much considered good is found lining up in support of negativity, and most of the Pandava side will also be blotted out in the eventual transmutation of the individual into a higher state of being itself, much as the endearing ways of infancy and childhood must be eradicated at the advent of adulthood and replaced with completely different virtues.

In the chariot set betwixt the two armies we find Arjuna and Krishna. Many interpretations of these two pivotal figures are possible, nearly all of them correct, but the words of the Mundaka Upanishad, written long before the Gita, are certainly worthy of our attention.

"Like two birds of golden plumage, inseparable companions, the individual self and the immortal Self are perched on the branches of the selfsame tree. The former tastes of the sweet and bitter fruits of the tree; the latter, tasting of neither, calmly observes.

"The individual self, deluded by forgetfulness of his identity with the divine Self, bewildered by his ego, grieves and is sad. But when he recognizes the worshipful Lord as his own true Self, and beholds his glory, he grieves no more" (Mundaka Upanishad 3:1:1, 2. This is the translation found in *The Upanishads, Breath of the Eternal,* by Swami Prabhavananda.)

These two paragraphs are a perfect picture of the setting of the Gita. Arjuna is the bewildered and sorrowing Atma, the individual Self, and Krishna is the divine Paramatma, the Supreme Self from which the Atma derives its very being and existence. Forgetful of its true nature as part of the Infinite Spirit, the finite spirit passes through countless experiences that confuse and pain it, producing utterly false conclusions that compound and perpetuate the confusion and pain. Only when the perspective of the Divine Self is entered into, can its troubles cease. We can also think of Arjuna as our lower, mortal self, and Krishna as our higher, immortal Self. Krishna and Arjuna thus represent both God and Man and our own (presently) dual nature as mortal and immortal. Keeping this perspective before us, the ensuing dialogue which forms the Gita is to be seen both as God's communication to human beings and the communication of our own divine Self with our human self, liberation (moksha) of the spirit being their sole intention.

With this in mind, we are ready to begin. I will be using my own version of the Gita which is based a great deal on the translation of Winthrop Sargeant: *The Bhagavad Gita,* published by State University of New York Press, which I recommend as an excellent version, especially since it gives a word-by-word translation of the entire text. The translation of Swami Prabhavananda is unparalleled for beauty and interpretation, so I recommend both translations

ON THE FIELD OF DHARMA

We begin with King Dhritarashtra, the blind father of the evil Duryodhana:

> **Dhritarashtra said: Assembled there on dharma's field–Kuruk-shetra–desiring war, what did my sons and the Pandavas, O Sanjaya? (1:1)**

The opening words of this verse are *dharmakshetre kurukshetre*: "the field of dharma, the field of the Kurus." Dharma means the right way of thought and action, but it can also mean the accurate expression of one's own dominant character, for dharma also means "quality." This entire world is a dharmakshetra, a field upon which we act out the character of our inner makeup–i.e., the quality of our emotions, mind, intellect, and will. We as individuals are each a dharmic field, expressing the actuality of our present level of evolution.

How is it, though, that the field of dharma is the field of the Kurus, the enemies of dharma? This is necessary for the portrayal of our present situation here in the world. Not only do negativity and ignorance–the enemies of dharma–dominate society in general, we find within ourselves a welter of negative impulses, conflicts, confusions, fears, and ignorance of all kinds. Yes; we are definitely in–and are–the field of the Kurus, whatever our intentions may be. We are going to have to fight through the whole field and wipe out all the Kurus and most of the Pandavas. Remember, we have lived millions of lives: mineral, plant, animal, and human, and we have brought all the impressions (samskaras) and habits (vasanas) of those lives along with us. Our past is our present. No wonder we are in trouble! But, as Swami Sri Yukteswar often said: "Forget the past. The vanished lives of all men are dark with many shames. Human conduct is ever unreliable until anchored in the Divine. Everything in future will improve if you are making a spiritual effort now." And the Gita will help us in this effort.

Desiring to fight

Yuyutsavah certainly means "desiring to fight," but it can also be translated "battle-hungry." There is deep within us an impulse to divinity, but it has been overlain and overruled by a multitude of impulses to delusion and delusion-produced desires. So they both fight with each other–often on the subconscious level. Both are "battle-hungry" for they are fighting for their very life.

The Mahabharata War is a historical fact, just as are the field of Kuruksheta, Krishna, and Arjuna. Yet Vyasa is using this setting and the conversation between Krishna and Arjuna to give us spiritual teachings, some of which are in symbol. In the real battle many families were represented on both sides, which depicts the inner conflicts of human beings, whether spiritually awakened or not.

The warriors of ignorance and delusion are children of the blind ego (Dhritarashtra), whereas the the inner soldiers of truth and higher consciousness are the children of the Spirit-Self, the divine Atman. The ego is the false self that reigns on the throne of our minds and hearts, blinding us to everything else, making us think that it is the reality of our being–that we are it. But it is a lie. Buried deep within is the real Self, awaiting its liberation and possession of its rightful kingdom. This is why the evil twin/good twin plot always appeals to people; it is symbolic of our dilemma of false self/real Self.

Son of Ego–more of the same

Sanjaya said: King Duryodhana, seeing the Pandava forces ranged ready for battle, approaching his teacher, Drona, spoke these words: (1:2).

5

Duryodhana is certainly his father in extension, but more dangerous because he can see–that is, he can consciously choose evil if he feels it suits his own ends. (By the way, Dhritarashtra literally means "He by whom the kingdom is held," and Duryodhana means "dirty fighter.")

The Bhagavad Gita occurs in the *Mahabharata* epic only after an immense amount of historical material is given, showing all that led up to the battle. There we see Duryodhana as one of the foulest, most evil figures in recorded history. Many times he attempted to kill the Pandava brothers, whose kingdom he had usurped. He also plotted the death of Krishna several times. He is evil, and Vyasa is going to show this to us by his conversation with Drona, a venerable man who was his teacher, the one who had given him all his education and training as a kshatriya (a member of the warrior-ruling caste). Actually, the whole Gita consists of two conversations: that between Duryodhana and Drona (though it was really a monologue in the style of all egotists) and that between Arjuna and Krishna. Arjuna pleads with Krishna to teach him, but Duryodhana only seeks to set Drona straight and accuse him for also being the teacher of Arjuna who is now facing him as an opponent in battle. So it begins…

> **Behold, O Teacher, this great army of Pandu's sons, assembled by Arjuna your brilliant pupil (1:3).**

See what I mean? "You got us into this mess" is the meaning. Next he rubs it in by enumerating the great warriors on the Pandava side:

> **Here are heroes, mighty archers, Bhima and Arjuna's equals, Yuyudhana and Virata, and Drupada the great car warrior (1:4).**

Bhima, one of Arjuna's brothers, was perhaps the strongest human being that has ever lived. He was all brawn and no brains, but beloved by those who could survive knowing him. He name means "tremendous," but in the sense of terrifying. All those listed by Duryodhana are maharathas–mighty chariot-warriors (car warriors) who could fight huge numbers of foot-soldiers singlehandedly.

Drishtaketu, Chekitana, and the valiant King of Kashi, Puru-
jit and Kuntibhoja, and Shaibya: the mightiest among men.
And courageous Yudhamanyu, and valorous Uttamaujas; the
son of Shubhadra and the sons of Draupadi: all great car warriors (1:5-6).

Well, that tells Drona! (Subhadra was Krishna's sister. "The sons of
Draupadi" are the children of the Pandava brothersGl.) Even though Drona
got Duryodhana into this tangle (egotists always take the credit for success,
even when it is not due them, but always manage to blame someone else
for failure), there is no need for worry.

Those of ours who are indeed distinguished, now know. O
highest of the twice-born, the leaders of my army I now recount unto you by name (1:7).

As if Drona would not know all of them very well! This is extremely
insulting–as is the way of all bullies. The fact that he speaks of "my army"
reveals his egotism. "Twiceborn" was a title referring to the three higher of
the four castes, referring to their having undergone a spiritual birth through
initiation into the Gayatri mantra and the spiritual rites of Vedic religion.

Your Lordship and Bhishma and Karna and Kripa, victorious
in war, Ashwattama and Vikarna, and the son of Somadatta
also. And many other heroes, whose lives are risked for my
sake, ready to discharge various weapons, all very skilled in
battle. (1:8-9).

Yes, all those who serve ego and work to ensure its preservation are
certainly risking their lives. It is amazing to see how the world and the ego
devour a person, sapping his life, turning him into an aimless husk, and all
the while he thinks he is really living the good life. This is the fatal illusion
in which humans dwell. Only those who have glimpsed the truth of their
inner divinity have a chance at escaping the realm of death.

Bravado, not bravery

> Sufficient is that force of ours guarded by Bhishma; insufficient, though, is that force guarded by Bhima. Stationed in your proper places, whatever be your positions, certainly all of you: protect Bhishma (1:10-11).

It is true that the Pandavas were greatly outnumbered by the Kauravas. So naturally, those that see only with the bodily eyes would think that their numbers were inadequate. But throughout history great victories have been won by a few—sometimes even by only one. In the Bible (the seventh chapter of Judges) we find that God kept telling Gideon that he had too many soldiers, and ordering that he pare down their numbers. He did so, and they routed a huge number of soldiers without even fighting! It is foolish to think that numbers make either strength or right. But that is the way of Duryodhana and his kind.

Empty noise

> To make Duryodhana happy, the aged Kuru grandsire, Bhishma, bellowing with a tremendous sound of a lion's roar, then blew his conch with great power, making a tremendous sound. Thereupon the Kurus' conches and kettledrums and cymbals and trumpets were sounded all at once, producing a tumultuous uproar (1:12-13).

This is nothing new. In many ways bullies and thugs make a lot of noise to intimidate others. And it often works. But not this time.

Divine sound

> Then Krishna and Arjuna, standing in the great chariot that was yoked with the white horses, sounded forth their divine conches (1:14).

This is something completely different, not just more of the same. The symbolism here is important. Horses are symbolic of life-force, of prana, of energy/power itself. White horses symbolize the powers of Divine Light. Furthermore, the conches of Krishna and Arjuna were not mere seashells like those of the Kurus, they were *divyau*–divine instruments of Light.

All that exists is vibration. The sound of the Kurus' conches represent the vibrations of Maya, of delusion and ignorance, of materiality and ego. But the sound of the Pandava conches represents the divine inner sound of the highest level of consciousness. The sound of the Kurus is intended to make the spirit faint, but the sound of the Pandavas, the vibration of Truth, enlivens, inspires, and strengthens the spirit. The names of the conches are titles of Divine Sound and indicate its powers when invoked by the yogi.

Krishna blew Panchajanya, Arjuna blew Devadatta, and Bhima of ferocious deeds, blew the great conch, Paundra. King Yudhishthira, Kunti's son, blew on Anantavijaya, Nakula and Sahadeva blew on Sughosha and Manipushpaka (1:15-16).

Panchajanya was the name of an evil enemy defeated by Krishna. Some say he owned the conch that later bore his name, some say that he was a shape-changing demon that lived in the conch (which was under the sea), and others that Krishna made a conch out of his bones. But a great yogi once told me during a conversation in Rishikesh that it is a contracted form of Panchavijaya, which means "Five Victories," meaning the spiritual victory over the five elements (bhutas) and mastery of the five bodies (koshas) and the five senses.

Devadatta means "God-given," the key to liberation given by God (Ishwara) himself to human beings.

Paundra, the yogi told me, means mighty sound, or "of a mighty sound."

Anantavijaya means "unending victory."

Sughosha also means "making a great noise," but the yogi said it also means "making a sweet, soothing sound."

Manipushpaka literally means "jeweled bracelet" or circlet. In verse seven of the seventh chapter we are told that "On me all this universe is strung like jewels on a thread." But the yogi told me its intended meaning is "mind like a flower," opened like a lotus at the shining of the light of the Self within. It can also mean "aerial chariot of the mind" opening and flying in the Sky of Consciousness, the Chidakasha.

Whether any of these meanings are correct or intended by Vyasa cannot be known for sure, since Sanskrit also has undergone mutations over time. Anyhow, these are very good speculations, I think.

The other Pandava leaders on the battlefield sounded their conches as well.

> And Kashi's king, the supreme bowman, and the great warrior Shikhandi, and Dhristadyumna and Virata, and the invincible Satyaki, and Drupada and the sons of Draupadi, O Lord of the Earth, and Shubhadra's son, the mighty-armed, each blew upon his conch(1:17-18).

This is a symbolic picture of the yogi engaged in the interior battle, who has marshalled all his faculties in meditation and united them, causing them to vibrate throughout his being. So the next verse says:

> Throughout the sky and the earth resounded the terrific noise which rent asunder the hearts of those in Dhritarashtra's ranks (1:19).

Divine Light and Divine Sound resound throughout the total being of the yogi, and burst apart the hearts of all the foes of the Self, first rendering them powerless, and then annihilating them.

TAKING STOCK

Then seeing Dhritarashtra's ranks drawn up in battle array for the forthcoming clash of weapons, Arjuna took up his bow, and said unto Krishna: O Lord of the earth, drive my chariot to stand in the midst between the two armies, until I can behold these battle-hungry men arrayed here with whom I must fight in this conflict. I would behold those who are about to give battle, having assembled here wishing to do service in warfare for the evil-minded son of Dhritarashtra. Thus addressed by Arjuna, Krishna brought the chief chariot to stand in the midst of the two armies. Thus facing Bhishma, Drona, and all the rulers of the earth, Krishna said: Behold, Arjuna, these Kurus assembled here. (1:20-25).

Authentic, traditional yoga is very serious and circumspect, and the intelligent yogi believes in the old adage: Look Before You Leap. Jesus put it this way: "Which of you, intending to build a tower, sitteth not down first, and counteth the cost, whether he have sufficient to finish it? Lest haply, after he hath laid the foundation, and is not able to finish it, all that behold it begin to mock him, saying, This man began to build, and was not able to finish. Or what king, going to make war against another king, sitteth not down first, and consulteth whether he be able with ten thousand to meet him that cometh against him with twenty thousand?" (Luke 14:28-31). Vyasa felt the same way.

There is an interesting detail here. Sanjaya, the narrator of the Gita, calls Dhritarashtra "Lord of the Earth," and Arjuna gives Krishna the same title—at least in the English translation. But in Sanskrit two different words are used. Sanjaya calls Dhritarashtra *Prithivipate*: Lord of the Earth, of prithvi, the earth element, the principle of non-sentient material existence. Krishna, though, is called *Mahipate*: Lord of the Earth (mahi) in the sense of the intelligent world of sentient beings. It is the difference between marble and a marble statue. One is mere matter, the other an expression of intelligence and artistry—even genius.

What Arjuna saw

Arjuna saw standing there fathers, grandfathers, teachers, maternal uncles, brothers, sons, grandsons as well as friends, fathers-in-law and companions in the two armies. In both of them he saw all who were relatives arrayed. Then filled with profound pity, desponding, he said:

O Krishna, seeing my own people standing near, desiring to fight, my limbs sink down, my mouth dries up, my body trembles, and my hair stands on end. My bow drops from my hand, my skin is burning, I am unable to stand; my mind is reeling.

Inauspicious omens I mark, and not good fortune do I foresee, if I should kill my own kinsmen in war. I do not desire victory, nor kingship and pleasures. What is kingship to us? What are enjoyments or even life? Those for whose sake we should desire kingship, enjoyments and pleasures, are arrayed in battle, abandoning their lives and riches: Teachers, fathers, sons, grandfathers, maternal uncles, fathers-in-law, grandsons, brothers-in-law, and other kinsmen, too. I do not desire to kill them who are about to kill—not even for the sovereignty of the three worlds; how then for the earth? What pleasure could the striking down of Dhritarashtra's sons be to us? Having killed these aggressors, evil would thus cling to us.

Therefore we are not justified to kill the sons of Dhri-tarashtra, our own kinsmen. Indeed, having killed our own people, how could we be happy? Even if those whose thoughts are overpowered by greed do not see the wrong caused by the destruction of the family, and the crime of treachery to friends, why should we not know to turn back from this evil through discernment of the evil caused by the destruction of the family?

In the destruction of the family, the long-established family dharmas perish. When dharma perishes, adharma predominates in the entire family. From overpowering by adharma the women of the family are corrupted. When the women are corrupted, the intermixture of caste is born. Intermixture brings to hell the family destroyers and the family, too. Indeed their ancestors fall from heaven back to earthly rebirth, deprived of offerings of rice and water. By these wrongs of the family's destroyers, producing intermixture of caste, caste dharmas and long-established family dharmas are obliterated. Those whose family dharmas have been obliterated dwell indefinitely in hell–thus have we heard repeatedly.

Ah! Alas! we are resolved to do great evil with our greed for royal pleasures, intent on killing our own people. If the armed sons of Dhritarashtra should kill me in battle, unresisting and unarmed, this would be a greater happiness for me.

Thus having spoken, Arjuna, in the battle which had already begun, sat down upon the chariot seat, throwing down both arrow and bow, with a heart overcome by sorrow (1:26-47).

This is long, but needs no comment. (We will be considering the subject of caste and caste-mixture later.) All we need understand is the great upset of Arjuna. It is the symbolism that matters. As already said, when we take stock of the inner conflict, we identify with both sides. Thinking that if they are dissolved or destroyed a part of us will cease to exist, we are appalled and feel that our very existence is threatened. Then, like all human beings who do not like the truth when they see or hear it, we become "confused" and try to avoid the unpleasant prospect. Bitter as death seems the inner battle, so we shrink from it and desperately try to find a way out.

So does Arjuna. In a lengthy and impassioned monologue he has presented to Krishna what is really a plea to inaction, to avoidance of conflict, thinking that such a negative condition is peace, whereas peace is a positive state, not the mere absence of unrest and conflict. It is also reached only through unrest and conflict, however little we like the fact.

Running away from spiritual obligation–and therefore spiritual life itself–the awakening soul on occasion brings all its ingenuity to bear on justification of such avoidance. Arjuna veils his aversion with words of compassion for others, when in actuality he is the sole object of his dishonest "compassion." He simply does not wish to see others suffer because that will make him suffer–and feel guilty for their suffering. Krishna makes this clear to him. The Stoic, Epictetus, was once visited by a man who told him that he loved his daughter so much he had run from the house rather than see her suffering from illness. Carefully, gently yet firmly, Epictetus led him to understand that it was his self-love that motivated him, not love for his child.

It is the same with us; ego-involvement–addiction, actually–grips us, and we are the only ones who can free ourselves from it. And battle is the only means.

Krishna's response

> Sanjaya said: To him who was thus overcome by pity, whose eyes were filled with tears, downcast and despairing, Krishna spoke these words
>
> The Holy Lord said: Whence has come this fainthearted-ness of yours in the time of danger–ignoble, not leading to heaven, but to disgrace? At no time should you entertain such cowardice–it is unsuitable in you. Abandon this base faint-heartedness and stand up.
>
> Arjuna said: But how can I in battle fight with arrows against Bhishma and Drona, who are worthy of reverence?

Better that I eat the food of beggary in this world instead of my slaying these great and noble gurus. If I should kill them, desirous for gain, in truth here on earth I would enjoy pleasures stained with blood. We know not which is preferable: whether we should conquer them, or they should conquer us. The sons of Dhritarashtra stand facing us after slaying whom we would not wish to live. Weakness and pity overcome my being; with mind in confusion as to my duty, I supplicate you: Beyond doubt tell me which is preferable. I am your disciple; do you direct me. Truly, I see nothing that can remove this sorrow that dries up my senses, though I should attain on earth unrivalled and prosperous dominion, or even the sovereignty of the gods.

Sanjaya said: Thus having addressed Krishna, Arjuna said, "I shall not fight," and became totally silent (2:1-9).

Hopefully we all sympathize with Arjuna and see his perspective which certainly seems to be that of dharma. Nevertheless, note that Arjuna at the end of his words asks Krishna to remove his error–if such it is. This shows his humility, in contrast to the arrogance and swaggering of Duryodhana. Therefore he merits the alleviation he pleads for. Even the wisest are conscious that they can be wrong.

THE SMILE OF KRISHNA

Arjuna, overcome with anguish at the prospect of killing in battle those he loved and was obligated to respect, presented to Krishna his reasons for refusing to fight. Hearing Arjuna's words:

> **To him who thus was despondent in the midst of the two armies, smiling, Krishna spoke these words: (2:10).**

The smile of Krishna

The smile of Krishna is extremely significant, and we must be grateful to the sage Vyasa for including this detail that carries a momentous message.

Why did Krishna smile, considering how grief-filled Arjuna was, and how impassioned he had been in his insistence that to fight would be the greatest of evils—in contradiction to the urging and advice of Krishna? Arjuna was both sad and rebellious. Yet Krishna smiled. The word in the Gita is *prahasann*, which means to smile before laughing. (Sargeant renders it: "beginning to laugh.") So it is not some weak smile, nor a condescending or sarcastic grimace, but a very positive sign of impending mirth. How is this? Krishna smiled for several reasons.

1. He was showing to Arjuna that he was not condemning him, that his words had in no way offended or angered him, that he could feel confident of Krishna's love and regard for him.

2. He was showing to Arjuna that he understood his feelings and his reasoning.

3. He was showing to Arjuna that all our little teapot tempests that we exaggerate and make into life-and-earth-shattering concerns and agonies are nothing to cause confusion, anxiety, anger, or grief, but rather are fever-dreams that will vanish the moment we rise to higher consciousness and behold them with the perspective of the divine spirit that is our true nature.

    This reminds me of an incident in the life of Sri Anandamayi Ma. A man came to see her, overwhelmed with grief at the recent death of his wife. "Ma will understand my suffering," he said to himself, "she will realize the extent of my sorrow." But the moment he entered the room, Ma began laughing merrily, looking at him all the while. "Ma!" he protested, "Seeing how unhappy I am, how can you laugh like that?" "Baba," Ma replied, "there is now one less obstacle between you and God!" I have witnessed similar incidents with Ma in which her laughter instantly healed the sorrow or anxiety of those who came to her for sympathy. Krishna is going to dispel the sadness and bewilderment of Arjuna in the same way.

4. He was showing Arjuna that his words meant nothing–that he was going to fight anyway, because Arjuna's kshatriya nature would impel him to do so, whatever he might think he thought. Further, in Krishna's perspective the battle was over and done; there was no question as to Arjuna's participation or the outcome: "These have already been struck down by me; be merely an instrument. [Only those] already killed by me, do you kill. Do not hesitate" (11:33-34).

5. He was showing Arjuna that nothing can change the state of divine consciousness, that the myth of a Pleased/Displeased God is a foolish fable. God is always God, and we are always ourselves. That is how God sees it–and so should we. Nothing we can say, think, or do can possibly change God in any way. If God could be angered or gladdened by us, he would be as ignorant, changeable, and subject to suffering as we are. In fact, we would have more control over him than he has over us, as we are continually ignoring him and being indifferent to him. Our changeability is

a myth, too, for all change takes place only in the delusive wrappings (prakriti, shakti) of our unchanging spirit (atma, purusha). Therefore, no matter what we think we do, God knows we have done nothing. Swami Prabhavananda's very interpretive translation says it very well: "You dream you are the doer, you dream that action is done, you dream that action bears fruit. It is your ignorance, it is the world's delusion that gives you these dreams" (Bhagavad Gita 5:14). Whatever our foolish antics, God smiles, knowing our eternal destiny within him.

RIGHT BUT WRONG

Smiling, Lord Krishna says an unexpected thing to Arjuna in response to his fervent disquisition on how he both should not and could not engage in battle on the field of Kurukshetra:

> The Holy Lord said: You have been mourning for those who should not be mourned for, though you speak words of wisdom. The wise mourn neither the living or the dead (2:11).

When I was a novice in a Greek Orthodox monastery which placed great emphasis on the mystical approach to Christianity and on meditation (Hesychia) particularly, one of the prime inspirations was Saint Gregory Palamas, a great mystic and author on the subject of interior prayer. When looking through the original Greek texts of the collection of spiritual writings known as the *Philokalia*, I came across a writing of Saint Gregory that had some diagrams. Not knowing any but the most elementary Greek (little more than the alphabet), I took the volume to a Greek-speaking monk and asked what the article as about. To my amazement he told me that it was an explanation of how the world was flat and how completely irrational and baseless it was to say the world was spherical! (Why such a subject would be treated in a collection of mystical writings was not explained to me.) Now, Saint Gregory possessed a brilliant intellect and his arguments were thoroughly logical–but he was wrong.

Later on I decided to read the complete writings of Saint Gregory of Nyssa, one of the greatest mystics of the early Christian Church. I was not disappointed, for his words are truly inspired and his insights invaluable. But then I came up against a real surprise. His brother, Saint Basil the Great, gave a series of discourses on the days of creation, but died before he could give the final sermon. So Saint Gregory decided to complete the work by writing an article on the final day of creation. In the article he discusses the human anatomy and for some reason presents a lengthy and complicated explanation of why and how human beings sneeze. The explanation is ingenious and equally erroneous, not to say genuinely funny. Again, the words were very logical, quite reasonable, but utterly mistaken to the point of silliness. And in both instances both the Gregories' sincerity and conviction counted for absolutely nothing. Wrong is wrong.

One of the funniest "wrongs" of a spiritual figure was the outlawing of hurdy-gurdies by one of the Popes in the Middle Ages. This was based on the fact that the hurdy-gurdy was the instrument played by wandering beggars, and wherever the beggars went the plague broke out. Not knowing about germs, the Pope concluded that hurdy-gurdy music caused the plague! Reason led to folly.

Millennia before the Gregories, Arjuna looked out at the battlefield, and seeing those he loved and even revered was overwhelmed with the enormity of killing them, and expressed his feelings to Krishna, as we have just seen in the previous article.

Krishna's reaction to this impassioned speech was to smile and say: "Your words are wise, Arjuna, but you are wrong." He then explained very fully just why Arjuna's conclusions were mistaken, and we will be looking at his explanations later, but for now it will be beneficial for us to pursue this matter of being wrong even when we seem to be right.

The fundamental problem is the character of the mind itself. It is intended as a link between the witness-consciousness that is our pure spirit and the outer world that is really only a dream in the mind of God and our minds, for we are co-dreamers with God, dreamers within the Great Dream of creation and evolution.

God and his creation are a bit like Moliere and his plays. Backstage he wrote out in large script the basics of the plot and the actors went onstage and improvised their lines and actions within Moliere's parameters. After many performances the words were written down and Moliere has received all the credit for their improvisation. In the same way God has set the boundaries and the basic scenario of evolution in consciousness. We then ad-lib our way through the whole thing until we develop the good sense to listen to those who have already trodden the way and given instructions on the right way to go about it. Part of this good sense is the awareness that we rarely know what we are doing or see anything correctly or fully–for that is the nature of the mind: distortion and incompleteness.

Yet the mind is part of our equipment for evolution, so what shall we do? Clarify and correct it: put Humpty Dumpty together. And that can be done by meditation. For Krishna is going to tell Arjuna: "The yoga-yoked sage quickly attains Brahman," and "He should practice yoga for the purpose of self-purification" (5:6; 6:12).

In the purity of mind produced by meditation, intuition comes to the fore, replacing discursive (and consequently tangled) thought, thus making the mind an instrument of perception rather than an interference in perception. For our thoughts are mostly static and distortion. In time through the effect of meditation we no longer think–we know. Therefore: "With mind made steadfast by yoga, which turns not to anything else, to the Divine Supreme Spirit he goes, meditating on him" (8:8).

BIRTH AND DEATH–
THE GREAT ILLUSIONS

No coward soul is mine,
No trembler in the world's storm-troubled sphere:
I see Heaven's glories shine,
And Faith shines equal, arming me from Fear.

O God within my breast,
Almighty, ever-present Deity!
Life, that in me has rest,
As I, undying Life, have power in Thee!

Vain are the thousand creeds
That move men's hearts: unutterably vain;
Worthless as withered weeds,
Or idlest froth amid the boundless main,

To waken doubt in one
Holding so fast by Thy infinity,
So surely anchored on
The steadfast rock of Immortality.

With wide-embracing love
Thy Spirit animates eternal years,

Pervades and broods above,
Changes, sustains, dissolves, creates, and rears.

Though earth and moon were gone,
And suns and universes ceased to be,
And Thou wert left alone,
Every existence would exist in Thee.

There is not room for Death,
Nor atom that his might could render void:
Thou—thou art Being and Breath,
And what thou art may never be destroyed.

Emily Bronte wrote the foregoing only a matter of weeks before her death, revealing a profundity of spiritual realization that belied her confined nineteenth-century rural Yorkshire background. Upanishadic as the above stanzas may be, the insights expressed therein seem to have arisen totally from within her own divine spirit. Years before she penned these lines, she wrote a poem in which the experience of samadhi is described as well as it can be. (There is a very slight chance that during her brief period of education in Brussels she might have come across a French translation of the Upanishads. This would not, however, account for the Advaitic content of her poetry written before that time.)

Emily Bronte has something in common with Arjuna: she was facing death, her own imminent death, and Arjuna was facing the surety of death for many he beheld on both sides assembled on the battlefield of Kurukshetra, as well as the likelihood of his own death. From the depths of her own immortal Self (Atma) the assurance of immortality arose in the mind and heart of Emily. From the front of his chariot, the voice of Krishna entered into the ears of Arjuna, awakening his innate under-standing, enabling him to see, as did Emily Bronte, the truth of his own immortal being.

One thing that marks out the various world religions from the vision of the Vedic rishis is the fact that they all claim to have a "new" message for a "new" age, a heretofore unheard-of annunciation of truth. The rishis, quite to the contrary, knew and said that they were speaking eternal facts that were like the principles of mathematics. Consequently, as Sri Ramakrishna stated: "The Hindu religion alone is the Sanatana Dharma. The various creeds you hear of nowadays have come into existence through the will of God and will disappear again through his will. They will not last forever.... The Hindu religion has always existed and will always exist" (*The Gospel of Sri Ramakrishna*, p. 642). The religion of the Vedas, Upanishads, and Bhagavad Gita alone are the Eternal Religion (Sanatana Dharma), for it is oriented toward eternity, not toward time, and takes into consideration only the Unchanging in the midst of the ever-changing.

Just as it was the spirit, the true Self, of Emily Bronte that was speaking in this poem, so it is our own true Self that is speaking to us through the mouth of Krishna in the Bhagavad Gita. When I first read the Gita, I did not have a sense of reading some ancient document or primeval wisdom spoken through the lips of a long-departed sage or avatar. Rather I felt that my own soul was speaking to me directly, that I was being taught by my own Self guiding me toward realization of my ultimate Self: God. I did not accept or adopt a religion–I awoke to the truth of myself and God. The Vedic sages did not have a religion in the commonly accepted sense: they had a Vision. And the Gita called me to that same vision, and pointed me toward meditation (yoga) as the only means of gaining it. The Gita gave me a pretty good idea of yoga, and Patanjali filled in the rest. Although she had no such books to guide and inspire her, the Yogi of Haworth, Emily Bronte, nonetheless attained the Vision by turning within and letting her inmost consciousness lead her to the Divine Center.

Now we are about to hear our own Self tell us the truth about ourselves and "all that we see or seem" which is indeed "but a dream within a dream," as Poe intuited.

The living and the dead

"The wise mourn neither the living or the dead," says Krishna to Arjuna. Why? Because there are no "living" or "dead" in the sense that those with bodies are alive and those divested of a body are dead. Nor is there such a duality as life and death. These are only the illusions produced by the distorting veils of ignorance.

"Lead me from death to immortality" is not a petition to gain a state where we will nevermore experience bodily death, but a plea to be led from the outward-turned consciousness that produces death to the in-turned consciousness that produces life. It is spirit itself that is immortality–nothing else. "Change and decay all around I see. O Thou Who changest not: abide with me." What we are praying for is consciousness itself.

The truth about us

Yes, the plain fact is this: There are no dead. For Krishna continues:

> **Truly there never was a time when I was not, nor you, nor these lords of men–nor in the future will there be a time when we shall cease to be (2:12).**

We are as eternal as God himself because we derive our very being from God. Just as there was never a time when God did not exist, nor can there be a time when he will not exist–especially since he is utterly outside of time–so there can never come a time when we shall not exist, for we, too, exist outside of time however enmeshed we are in the experience of time through the temporal instruments of the body and mind.

Krishna is also making it clear that our distinction as individuals–both from other finite beings and from God–is also eternal. There is absolutely no place in the Gita for the teaching that in time we melt into the infinite and exist no more as a distinct entity, only God remaining, our having never really existed at all. Yet Krishna does not say we exist separately from God and from one another at any time, for that is also impossible. There is absolute unity, yet within that unity is an eternal diversity. Advaita is the true view–Not Two, which is in no way the same as One, or Monism.

Although Krishna declares that he, Arjuna, and all those present on the battlefield exist eternally, he does not mean that their present conditioned personalities are eternal and unchangeable. Just as our spirits transcend time, so our personalities, which are nothing more than masks shaped by our past and present lives, exist only within time and are ever-changing until they are dissolved in the light of spiritual knowledge (jnana). Our personalities are indeed separate from God, and as long as we identify with them we will feel separated from him and engage in the delusional "search" and "reaching out" for God. I say delusional because our true selves (atmas) are never separate from God. "He is not far from every one of us: for in him we live, and move, and have our being; for we are also his offspring" (Acts 17:27-28). Our personalities can never find or touch God because they simply do not exist as actual–much less eternal–realities. It is those who identify with the personality and think it is their true Self that fall into the trap of either Dualism or Monism.

The result of immortality

Yet we are ignorant; without facing that fact we will never effectively aspire to the knowledge of Reality. And until we attain that knowledge what happens to us? Krishna supplies the answer:

> **As to the embodied person childhood, youth and old age arise in turn, so he gets another body–the wise are not deluded by this (2:13).**

Evolution is implied here, also continuity of consciousness/being and the utter naturalness and even painlessness of the process. It is all a matter of outer experience, not of inner reality. But we should look at the pieces of the puzzle as set forth in this verse.

The Number One Fact is the existence of "the embodied," the immortal Self. Here lies the core of the whole matter–literally. All experience which we undergo at any time is what motion picture theaters in the nineteen-sixties used to call "sense-surround." That is, our consciousness is surrounded by, enwrapped in, a series of sheaths (koshas) which convey all the experiences which it erroneously thinks are happening to it. Rather than understanding that it is merely watching screens on which are projected the various sensations–some seeming to be outer and some seeming to be inner–the spirit thinks that it is seeing, feeling, tasting, etc., that it is happy, sad, desolate, fulfilled, and so on (and on and on). In meditation we can think these "screen shots" are atmic experience if we are not careful.

Just how this all comes about is really in the field of Sankhya philosophy and Yoga which will be taken up later on by Krishna. For now the important point to realize is that we are ever separate from all that we see or seem. We are the tenant, not the dwelling; we are the worker of the machine, not the machine. This dweller in the body, our true Self or Atma, is the sole reality throughout our many incarnations. When we are centered in that we are free; when we are drawn out and into the surrounding show, we are bound. It is just that simple, though the process of involving and evolving is incalculably complex.

Evolution is also spoken of here. Through childhood, youth, and old age there is constant growth and development–at least for the awakening individual. That is the purpose of the cosmos itself: the evolution of the individual in order to develop the capacity for infinite consciousness. So this is the purpose of dwelling in the body–it is a tool for far more than mere learning, it is a means of evolving from finitude to infinity, from microcosmic to macrocosmic consciousness. And this evolution is as inevitable and natural as the aging of the body.

We have a great deal of fear about death and hear a lot about "hard deaths" and "death struggles," yet those who have recovered their memories of previous lives assure us that death is the easiest phase of life, that at the Great Moment the "dewdrop" really does "slip into the Shining Sea" with a great sense of peace and relief.

"He gets another body." This can literally be translated "he arrives at another body." That is, in time he will again pass into the material body and be reborn in the physical plane.

The wise know

However, "the wise are not deluded by this." Those who have gained some wisdom in previous births are able to understand, even in childhood, their actual separation from the inner and outer worlds. If their constant experience of those worlds does not overwhelm them, they are no longer deluded into thinking that their true Self has been born or shall ever die;

nor do they define themselves according to the movies shown to them on the screens of their acquired bodies. They do not identify with bodily conditions or even the states of mind that arise before their observing eye. In the ripest state of wisdom development they say with Shankaracharya:

I am not the mind, intellect, thought, or ego;
Not hearing, not tasting, not smelling, not seeing;
I am not the elements—ether, earth, fire, air:
I am the form of Conscious Bliss: I am Spirit!

I am neither Prana, nor the five vital airs;
Nor the seven components of the gross body;
Nor the subtle bodies; nor organs of action:
I am the form of Conscious Bliss: I am Spirit!

I have no aversion, clinging, greed, delusion;
No envy or pride, and no duty or purpose;
I have no desire, and I have no freedom:
I am the form of Conscious Bliss: I am Spirit!

I have no merit or sin, nor pleasure or pain;
No mantra, pilgrimage, Veda or sacrifice;
Not enjoying, enjoyable, or enjoyer:
I am the form of Conscious Bliss: I am Spirit!

I have no death or fear, no distinction of caste;
Neither father, nor mother, nor do I have birth;
No friend or relation, guru or disciple:
I am the form of Conscious Bliss: I am Spirit!

I am without attributes; I am without form;
I am all-pervading, I am omnipresent;
By senses untouched, neither free, nor knowable:
I am the form of Conscious Bliss: I am Spirit!

EXPERIENCING THE UNREAL

Krishna has just told Arjuna that birth and death are simple illusions–that the unborn and undying spirit (Atma) is the sole reality of our being. That is not so hard to accept if we have intuition or actual recall of the fact of our having previously dreamed the dream of birth and death many times. But the real trouble is our identification with the experiences that occur between the two poles of birth and death. It is like a joke I heard a very long time ago. In a small town where metaphysical speculation was completely absent, the postmaster was a Christian Scientist. One day he asked a little boy, "How are you?" And the boy replied: "I have an awful stomach ache!" "Oh, you just imagine that," chided the postmaster. "You only imagine you even have a stomach!" The next day the boy came in the post office and was asked the same question by the postmaster. He stood for a while, thinking, and then came out with: "I have an imaginary pain in my imaginary stomach that I don't really have. And it HURTS!"

It is just the same with us. Simply saying: "It is all an illusion," really does very little. Consider how we attend a play or a motion picture and become completely engrossed in the spectacle, responding with various emotions. All the time we know it is just pretend, but that does not keep us from responding as though it were real. How is this? It is the nature–yes, the purpose–of the mind!

I will never forget the first time I saw *Hamlet*. The next day I could not attend any of my classes at the university. I felt that I had seen an inexpressibly great person die right before my eyes. The words "Good night, sweet prince, and flights of angels sing thee to thy rest" had utterly overwhelmed me with chagrin. For a few days I went around in an aura of shock. I knew that I had only witnessed light and shadow patterns on a blank screen, that the people I had watched were actors playing a part—a part that my reading on the subject revealed was not even historically accurate. It made no difference. I was stunned by what I had seen. This is just the nature of the delusive mind. Unless that nature is transcended, we will experience that "the play's the thing" rather than an illusion. With this in mind, Swami Vivekananda subtitled his book *Raja Yoga*: "Conquering the Internal Nature." And part of its subjugation is the realization that the "inner" nature is also outside us.

Externals meet externals

Wherefore Sri Krishna next tells Arjuna:

> Truly, material sensations produce cold, heat, pleasure and pain. Impermanent, they come and go; you must endeavor to endure them (2:14).

Matrasparshas, "material sensations," literally means "sensations of matter" or "the touching of matter." Cold, heat, pleasure, and pain are brought about through contact with materiality, whether we think of it as contact of the sense organs with matter, or of contact of the mind with the internal senses that translate the contact of those sense organs into mental perceptions that we label as cold, heat, pleasure, and pain. Even the person who knows he is not the body, senses, or mind, yet does experience these things. He, however, understands what they really are and can, as Krishna urges, learn to endure them.

Both the senses and the objects are vibrating energy, merely differing waves in the vast ocean of power known as Prakriti or Pradhana. Prakriti is spoken of as illusion because it is constantly shifting like the sea with its ever-rising and ever-subsiding waves. Although Prakriti exists as Primordial Energy, the forms it takes are momentary modifications only with no lasting reality.

In the philosophical writings of India we often encounter the snake-in-the-rope simile. Even though the "snake" we see in a dim light is a projection of our mind, and when we perceive that it is only a rope the "snake" will disappear, the rope will remain. In the same way, Prakriti is the actually-existent substratum of which all things are its temporary mutations. They are mere appearances, yet their substance is real. It is this understanding that gave rise to the Buddhist concept of Emptiness–that there are no things in their own right, but only temporary appearances. When we see truly, things are seen to be no things at all. The truth is, Prakriti and the Great Void (Mahashunyata) are the same thing. It is only those who misunderstand them that think they are different.

In essence, we must come to realize that all our experiences, inner and outer, are really external to us and are simply shifting waves of differing vibrations. "Impermanent, they come and go," Krishna points out to Arjuna–and to us.

In the ancient world, including that of original Christianity, only that which remained perpetually constant was considered to be real. That which could change or cease to be was considered unreal. For this reason we find an exposition of the unreality of both the world and evil in the writings of Saint Athanasius the Great of Alexandria, even though that is in complete variance with contemporary Christian theology.

The thing is, *we* exist forever and unchanging. It is only our mistaken identity with our experiences–our identification of the screen with the temporary movie–that causes us to forget this truth and become immersed in the untruth of Unreality/Prakriti. It is no easy matter to genuinely see the truth of things in relation to our sense experiences. Consequently Krishna said: "This divine illusion of mine… is difficult to go beyond" (7:14). What shall we do about these illusions until we have broken through them? Krishna tells us: "You must endeavor to endure them." That does not mean that we must like them or want them. But we must accept them as inevitable until we truly do pass from the unreal to the Real. Later in this very chapter Krishna will describe how an illumined person functions in relation to sensory experience. For now we need only understand that the man of wisdom, the jnani, experiences them but accepts them and is unmoved by them.

Truly, the man whom these sensations do not afflict, the same in pain and pleasure, that wise one is fit for immortality (2:15).

What he does by nature we must do by will and reasoning until we, too, are enlightened.

THE UNREAL AND THE REAL

The miracle of the Gita

The Bhagavad Gita is a marvel of practical wisdom. In the Upanishads we find the truth about Brahman, Atman, and Creation, but it is mostly speculative, intended to awaken the hearer to the intuition of How Things Are—not to merely instruct or convince him. After reading the Upanishads the question of *realizing* the truths set forth therein becomes most crucial. Since we presently live two lives, the inner and the outer, we need guidance in how to lead both of them in such a manner that the Upanishadic Vision will in time be permanently established in our own consciousness. And that state will be liberation (moksha). To enable us to attain liberation, two books have been given us: the Bhagavad Gita for our outer, active life, and the Yoga Darshan (Yoga Sutras) for our inner, meditative life. Both contain counsel about the inner and outer way to realization, but each focuses mainly on one sphere. The Bhagavad Gita is the ultimate statement on How To Live. Yet it perfectly embodies and presents the philosophical principles of the Upanishads—so much so that it has been said that Vyasa, the author of the Gita, "milked" the "cows" of the Upanishads and presented to us the life-sustaining milk of Pure Wisdom. The Gita is a digest of the Upanishads, but also much more: it points the way to embody their teachings, to gain practical experience of their eternal truth, of Sanatana Dharma.

The right perspective

The basic ingredient of any endeavor is right perspective, so Krishna right away delineates two universal principles that must be kept in mind at all times, whether engaged in outer activity or inner meditation.

> **1. It is known that the unreal never comes to be, and the real never ceases to be. The certainty of both of these principles is seen by those who see the truth (2:16).**

Swami Prabhavananda's interpretive translation is: "That which is non-existent can never come into being, and that which is can never cease to be. Those who have known the inmost Reality know also the nature of *is* and *is not*."

> **2. Know indeed that That by which all this universe is pervaded is indestructible. There is no one whatsoever capable of the destruction of the Eternal (2:17).**

Prabhavananda: "That Reality which pervades the universe is indestructible. No one has power to change the Changeless."

Unless we are constantly aware of these two truths, any kind of endeavor on our part will result in the perpetuation of ignorance and its result: bondage. Nor are these abstractions to be merely accepted intellectually. They must be lived; and until they can be fully demonstrated in our life we must at least keep striving to bring our conscious thoughts and deeds into conformity with them. Jesus spoke of a man who wanted to build a house where there was sandy soil. Wisely he dug down until he found solid rock, and then only did he build the house so it would stand secure (Matthew 7:24-25). These two principles are the bedrock on which the structure of our entire life should be based.

What is not can never come to be

"The unreal never comes to be." A simple statement, but a profound realization about every aspect of existence–most particularly our own existence and status. We could restate the principle this way: "That which has not always been can never come into being." If we analyze things we will come to realize that only two things have ever been: God and us. Everything else is literally incidental. That is why the greatest monk of the Christian Church, Saint Arsenios the Great, when asked for spiritual counsel replied: "Unless you say, 'God and I alone exist,' you will not find God." So when we really bear down on the issue we come to realize that Spirit alone exists: Spirit as the individual consciousness and Spirit as the Infinite Consciousness. All other things are passing appearances only.

"The fashion of this world passeth away," said Saint Paul (I Corinthians 7:31). The word translated "fashion" in the sense of exterior appearance is *schema*, which means a figure or outline of something, either visual or ideational, a mere thought or "scheme" rather than a thing of actual substance. From this we see that Saint Paul considered the world to be a mere appearance, a temporary thought in the mind of God and man. And so did Krishna.

Seeing the Real in the unreal

Since the world and all that surrounds us, including the many layers of our present mode of existence as human beings, come from God, it would be foolish to consider them valueless and to simplistically try to disengage ourselves from them as though that would be the solution to everything. No. Krishna is telling Arjuna to fight–to act as though the world were real. Why? Because all our experience is a training film in the school of consciousness. By watching it and interacting with it we come to experience its substantial reality, but we also come to understand its meaning. For every particle of matter has a purpose and is a message from the Eternal to us.

Krishna is instructing Arjuna in the attitude, the perspective, needed to live life meaningfully. Arjuna wants to turn away from the battlefield, to avoid doing what he considers to be a terrible wrong, but Krishna restrains him and warns him against such a mistaken course of action, because to do so is to fail in learning the purpose of the situation. To leave the battle would be to deny the unreality of external appearance and to deny the reality of the inner spirit.

This verse carries great and freeing insight. We need not brood over our faults or be elated over our virtues since they have never really come into being. Neither should we be displeased at misfortune or pleased at good fortune, for they have never happened. Rather, the pictures of these things are being shown to us for our development and education leading to our mastery of them. It is not without basis that one of the first steps in occult development is dream control; for this whole world is a dream, and although there is a great deal of talk about awakening from the dream, we cannot do so until we can control it at will. This is what Yoga is all about—awakening through mastery.

Our eternal Self

But looking back at the subject of our own conscious development.... A lot of time is wasted "cultivating virtues" and pursuing yogic attainments. As Sri Ma Anandamayi often pointed out, getting implies losing. So any artificial progress we may make will evaporate in time. To bewail our sins or rejoice in our virtues is utter madness. *For neither exists.* What is necessary is that we learn to bring forth, to reveal, our eternal nature. When the qualities we exhibit are those of the ever-free and ever-perfect spirit, then alone will we have "done" something. Merely talking about our eternity and perfection, using such ideas as excuses for avoiding any spiritual pursuit or discipline, is thoroughgoing folly. The true Self, the Atman, must be *realized*—not just believed in or talked about.

And the world? We should look and learn. For everything has meaning. To say the world is unreal and dismiss it is worse than idiotic. A sign saying Danger is not danger, but it indicates danger. Words, figures, and lines on paper are not anything "real," but their import is very real. The word "fire" is not fire, yet when someone yells it we should get moving. In the same way, the world around us may not be ultimately real, but its message can lead us to the perception of the Reality behind it all, which is its Source.

Much of what I have written deals with the value of "unreality," but we must not forget the wonder and freeing nature of knowing what is real. For: "Those who have known the inmost Reality know also the nature of *is* and *is not*."

The Unchanging

Krishna further tells Arjuna: "That by which all this [universe] is pervaded is indestructible. There is no one whatsoever capable of the destruction of the Eternal." Once more we can invoke the insight of Emily Bronte to expound this truth in a direct and simple way that is equally profound.

> O God within my breast,
> Almighty, ever-present Deity!
> Life, that in me has rest,
> As I, undying Life, have power in Thee!
>
> Though earth and moon were gone,
> And suns and universes ceased to be,
> And Thou wert left alone,
> Every existence would exist in Thee.
>
> There is not room for Death,
> Nor atom that his might could render void:
> Thou–thou art Being and Breath,
> And what thou art may never be destroyed.

This is the fruit of following the thread of the unreal to its origin in the Real and discovering that our own Self, being part of that Reality which pervades the universe, also is indestructible. All fear, regret, and sorrow vanish like the unrealities they are once we realize that "there is no one whatsoever capable of the destruction of the Eternal" that is the Self of our Self.

THE BODY AND THE SPIRIT

Self-knowledge

Who am I? This is the Primeval Question, the sign that true consciousness is at last dawning in the evolving entity. Until this arises, the side queries such as: Where did I come from?… Where am I?… Where am I going?… and such like will result in very little. For it is the knowledge of Who I Am that alone illuminates them. Without this self-knowledge nothing else can really be known. Because of this Krishna opens his instructions to Arjuna with an exposition of the nature of the Self and the effect of self-knowledge on the individual, even though the subject at hand is why Arjuna should fight rather than abandon the battlefield.

This bears out the veracity of what I just said about self-knowledge being necessary for the right understanding of anything. It also demonstrates that those who promote study of scriptures, development of devotion to God or engagement in good works as the paramount factor in human life are far from being disciples of Krishna however much they may cite the Gita and profess an emotional devotion to him. "Why call ye me, Lord, Lord, and do not the things which I say?" (Luke 6:46) is still a relevant question.

Having spoken of cosmic reality and relative unreality, Krishna returns to a more personal aspect, continuing:

> These bodies inhabited by the eternal, indestructible, immeasurable, embodied Self are said to come to an end. Therefore, fight! (2:18).

Bodies are said to die

Since Krishna has assured Arjuna that the unreal cannot come into being and that the real cannot go out of existence, he obviously cannot state that death really occurs. Therefore he says: "These bodies are *said* to come to an end"—to die. They do not die for two reasons. The obvious one is that birth and death are mere appearances. Having never been born in reality how could the body die? However, the appearances of birth and death are part of the cosmic drama, part of the Divine Dream known as Pradhana or Prakriti. And interestingly, physics has demonstrated that absolutely not even a particle of an atom is ever destroyed; that every bit that existed/appeared in the beginning exists right now—only the arrangements of the particles have changed. This would have to be so. Since the Dreamer is eternal and outside of time, so also must the Dream be in its ultimate reality—for can anything of the Divine be unreal?

The dream occurs in the Eternal Now which is the abode of the Dreamer. This is why Sankhya philosophy, the philosophy espoused and expounded by Krishna, postulates that Prakriti is eternal. When we understand its nature as a mere dream, a thought, this is the only possible conclusion. It is when we think of it as an actual substance that can come into being and go out of being that we become entangled in error. And it is this error which the Vedantists deny, the seeming conflict between Sankhya and Vedanta on this point only occurring in the minds of those who have not experienced the vision behind both philosophies, themselves known as *darshanas* (viewings).

It is necessary for the serious student of Indian philosophy, Sanatana Dharma, to understand that the six orthodox systems (*darshanas*) of Hinduism are all equally true—otherwise they would not be orthodox. Rather, they represent different viewpoints or attitudes toward the same Reality, differing in emphasis, but never in substance. The preference for one over the others should be understood as a manifestation of personal nature (guna and karma—just as with caste) only and not evidence of one being true (or more true) and the others false (or less true).

But That which possesses the body is eternal

The famous baby doctor, Dr. Spock, opened his book on caring for infants with a statement that astounded everyone. Addressing the mothers reading the book he said: "You know more than you know you do." And urged them to rely on that knowledge. What he was saying, actually, was that they possessed "mother's intuition" and should learn to tap it and act on it. Even the most esoterically and philosophically unsophisticated people continually use expressions that show a subliminal knowledge far beyond their conscious awareness. One thing is the universal habit of referring to our bodies as "mine." "I broke my leg," we say, not: "I broke myself." We all know instinctively that we possess our body, that it is separate from us and is being used only as an instrument. Yes, we identify with it and say things like: "He hit me" when the body was struck, but usually we speak of the body as "mine" rather than "me." Or we even speak of it in a strange combination such as: "He hit *me* on *the* arm." However mixed these signals may be, the underlying consciousness is that of our being the owner of the body and not the body itself. Yet when we consciously identify ourselves and others with the temporary and the perishable, like Arjuna, we cannot help but be fearful and confused. But the truth is quite different: we are eternal, not just long-lasting. Moreover, what overwhelms us is really meant to be ruled by us.

It cannot be limited, or destroyed

We are tossed about and drowned in the ocean that we are meant to sail over unruffled and unaffected by wind or wave. See what Krishna says: We cannot be either limited or destroyed. This is incredible to us who are entrenched in the hypnosis called Maya. But the challenge is inescapable: this truth must be consciously experienced and permanently established in us. How to accomplish this is the message of the whole Gita.

Let us look at the implications of this. If we are in any way limited it is a result of our blindness. Remove the blindness and the limitations vanish. They need not be overcome but seen through as the mirages they really are.

If we think that we can die or be annihilated, we are deluded to the point of spiritual psychosis. For what can we do, then, but live in continual fear and despair? Just look at the death and burial customs of the world's religions, except for Hinduism. They affirm the immortality of the individual and assure those who remain behind that "they are in a better place." It is only natural to feel grief at losing the presence of those who are loved, but see how the bereaved act. Not only is there a sense of hopelessness at the inevitability of death, the bodies are treated as though they are the departed person. In the West we dress them up, put makeup on them, style their hair, and put them in metal boxes with innerspring mattresses. ("So they will rest easy," explained one mortician to a friend of mine.) Grave sites are often chosen with a view the departed (?) will be sure to like. And after burial they are "visited," given flowers, and often spoken to. In some cultures the families put food on the graves and even have a picnic there to share a meal with the dead. In Cairo, when you go to the pyramids you pass through a vast section of the city that is the City of the Dead, composed of small houses set along a labyrinth of streets. Each house is a tomb. On Fridays and holidays the families visit these houses and have lunch with the dead, who their religion says are not there at all but in another plane of existence altogether. This is craziness.

On the other hand, in India the body is wrapped in bright-colored cloth and borne through the streets as the bearers chant over and over: *Rama Nama satya hai*–the Name of God is real–or a similar affirmation that spirit is real and death is an illusion. Reaching the crematory ground, scriptural passages affirming the immortality of the spirit are recited as the fire is kindled. When the ceremony is finished the bearers walk away without a backward look. A television documentary entitled *Forest of Bliss*, showing a day at the burning ground of Varanasi (Benares) is worth viewing as it shows belief in immortality being lived out.

The key thing in all this is actual *realization* of our immortality, not just a hope or belief. And this is a matter of spiritual practice, as Krishna will inform Arjuna.

Therefore fight

Something must be done. We must enter the dharma-field of our inner awareness and do the needful. "For protection of the righteous and destruction of evildoers, for the establishing of dharma, I manifest myself from age to age" (4:8). Like Krishna we must release the holiness of our spirit and annihilate the delusion of sin. Then we will be righteous. Like Arjuna we may shrink back, get confused, and try to abandon our duty. But if, also like Arjuna, we make spirit-consciousness our charioteer we will come out all right, victorious and wise.

KNOW THE ATMAN!

He who thinks the Self is the slayer and he who thinks the Self is slain: neither of the two understands; the Self slays not, nor is it slain (2:19).

Except for the most unfortunately wounded in spirit, everyone is more than willing to accept the truth of their immortality. Because the authority of the Supreme Spirit is behind each word of Krishna's exhortation to Arjuna, something deep within us responds with recognition to each statement, and that includes his insistence on the eternal nature of every spirit. Consequently there is no need for me to keep going over and over that principle.

The body may appear to be killed, but never is the Self (Atman) slain. This does not mean that those who (seemingly) kill others are not culpable, for it is their murderous intention that is the root evil. Having learned this in India, Jesus insisted on its truth in his teachings. "Ye have heard that it was said by them of old time, Thou shalt not kill; and whosoever shall kill shall be in danger of the judgment: but I say unto you, that whosoever is angry with his brother without a cause shall be in danger of the judgment… Ye have heard that it was said by them of old time, Thou shalt not commit adultery: but I say unto you, that whosoever looketh on a woman to lust after her hath committed adultery with her already in his heart" (Matthew 5:21-22, 27-28).

He who thinks he can be killed is mistaken. This is not very hard to grasp, but the second part—the statement that the Atman can no more slay than be slain—is not so commonly accepted. So it needs due consideration.

What is going on here?

Krishna has already told Arjuna that all sensory phenomena are temporary. Later he will be explaining that they are nothing more than ever-shifting movements of energy that the individual consciousness is merely observing—not undergoing, as it thinks. Consequently the wise one watches the sense-movie and learns from it. As already cited, the Mundaka Upanishad expresses it thusly: "Like two birds of golden plumage, inseparable companions, the individual self and the immortal Self are perched on the branches of the selfsame tree. The former tastes of the sweet and bitter fruits of the tree; the latter, tasting of neither, calmly observes." In Western metaphysics the expressions "lower self" and "higher Self" are often employed for these two "birds."

The situation is this: The immortal part of us, the Atman, the pure spirit (consciousness) ever looks on at the experiences of the lower self—the mind, ego, subtle and gross bodies—all that go to make up our relative "self." But so convincing is the drama, so compelling and literally engrossing, that it loses itself in the spectacle and thinks it is born, lives, and dies over and over, feeling the pain and pleasure that are nothing more than impulses in the field of energy that is the mind. These are the vrittis in the chitta spoken of by Patanjali at the beginning of the Yoga Sutras, the *permanent* cessation or prevention of which is Yoga. Through meditation we come to separate ourselves from the movie screen of illusion. *Learning* is the purpose of the movie, so we do not just throw the switch and leave the theater. Rather, we watch and figure out the meaning of everything. When we have learned the lessons, the movie will stop of itself. Yoga is the means of learning.

So we are points of consciousness tied to the seats of our bodies, helplessly watching and identifying with the 360-degree surrounding screen, overwhelmed by the sensory avalanche. When we cease to identify and come to see with the clarity of objectivity (that is the reality of the situation), then we begin to really see and learn. Then, just as the ear is trained by listening to music, so the consciousness is developed by witnessing the drama of many lives. Yet it is not *changed*–it is freed. For change is illusion.

When we have experienced this–and therefore truly known–for ourselves, then we know that nothing has ever "happened" to us–only to the vibrating substance which we have mistakenly thought was us. Vairagya, detachment from all things, then arises, for that is the only realistic response or view of our life. Then perfection in true knowledge (jnana) becomes our only goal, for that perfection alone is freedom.

The lessons to be learned

Being either killer or killed is impossible; so Krishna assures Arjuna, and us. The Gita is being spoken on a battlefield, so martial action is the subject, but the principles presented by Krishna can be applied to anything in life. The fundamental lesson is twofold: 1) everything has a meaning for us, and 2) no happening or change is real. But *we* are real, and that should be the basis of our entire perspective on our present entanglement in the birth-death drama.

If we are not careful we will fall into the trap of considering only the negative as unreal and think of the positive as real and therefore to be accepted as such. This is not so. Sin and virtue, hellishness and holiness, are equally unreal. However, sin and evil render us incapable of seeing the truth of things, whereas virtue and holiness wean us from the illusions around us and purify our mind so we can come to learn the real Facts of Life from life itself.

Yet, no change is ultimately real. Not even the decision: "I want to know God." Insight and aspiration mean nothing of themselves. Only when they result in involvement in spiritual practice (sadhana, tapasya) do they mean anything. Yes, even the process of sadhana (meditation, yoga) is unreal, but its *result* is real in that it reveals the Real. In Indian thought spiritual practice is often spoken of as a thorn used to remove a thorn in the foot. Both are then discarded. Yoga is also just a movie, but it is a movie that leads to self-knowledge in which yoga ceases to be a practice and becomes a *state*–the state of consciousness that is our eternal being.

So all the holy and spiritual thoughts and feelings or philosophy we may come up with are just more of the same light and shadows that have been fooling us for countless creation cycles. They will eventually degenerate and reveal themselves as valueless as all our other fantasies. Only when they inspire us to take up meditation and authentic spiritual life are they of any worth, assisting us in drawing nearer and nearer to The Real.

The effects of self-knowledge

But knowing the Atman-Self is a different matter altogether. The attainment of self-knowledge is not the same as working out a puzzle or figuring out a riddle. It has a practical effect: eternal peace and freedom. Therefore Krishna continues:

> **Neither is the Self slain, nor yet does it die at any time, nor having been will it ever come not to be. Birthless, eternal, perpetual, primeval, it is not slain whenever the body is slain (2:20).**

This is the perspective that gives abiding peace to the seer. And further:

> **In what way can he who knows this Self to be indestructible, eternal, birthless and imperishable, slay or cause to be slain? (2:21).**

Do not dream: *know*. Then you will be free from the compulsions and anxieties of the world-dream.

When we cling to these compulsions and anxieties, birth, life, and death are agonies raking us like hooks and whips. But what are they in actuality? Krishna says:

> **Even as a man casts off his worn-out clothes and then clothes himself in others which are new, so the embodied casts off worn-out bodies and then enters into others which are new (2:22).**

How simple. And how effortless. It is our clinging, our grasping, that torments us. For though we do not realize it, aversion and distaste are also graspings. To push a thing away we have to touch it, to come into contact with it. And once touched it works its effect on us.

Although Krishna is speaking of the experiences of physical birth and death, the same is true of any kind of "becoming" or dissolving of both external and internal experiences. The same is true of the various states of consciousness that we pass through on the way to the goal of perfected awareness. We should pass into and out of them as easily as changing our clothing, neither clinging to them nor tearing them away from us.

Easefulness is the keynote of genuine spiritual development. There are no traumas, no cataclysms or sweeping shake-ups in the path to God. Such things only take place in the prisons of illusions. If they do occur we may know that we are either on the wrong path or are walking it in a wrong manner. Spiritual hypochondriacs revel in these things, regaling their hearers with lurid accounts of how traumatic and cataclysmic every step of "the path" has been for them. Their dramatic bombastic revelations are symptoms of mental illness, not of progress in spiritual life.

Finally, Krishna's statement that "the embodied casts off worn-out bodies and then enters into others which are new" is an indication of the truth that it is we and we alone that are always in control. But, like those afflicted with short-term memory loss, we put ourselves into a situation and then forget we did so, attributing it to God, fate, accident, or just about anything but ourselves. Therefore, praying to God, engaging in superstitious "good luck" practices (including much of religion), trying to "cheat fate" and suchlike are doomed to failure and frustration. WE are the key.

The immutable Self

Krishna's next statement is to be looked into beyond the surface appearance:

> **This Self by weapons is cut not; this Self by fire is burnt not; this Self by water is wet not; and this Self is by wind dried not (2:23).**

First of all, the four factors: weapons, fire, wind, and water, represent the four gross elements, earth, fire, air and water (ether being the fifth, most subtle element). By the "elements" we do not mean material earth, water, fire, etc., but the four types of creative energies that combine to make up all that is material. The names given to the elements are merely symbolic of their behavior and effects. We are encased in five bodies: annamaya, pranamaya, manomaya, jnanamaya, and anandamaya *koshas* (coverings). These are the "bodies" corresponding to the material, biomagnetic, mental, intellectual and will levels of our makeup. These, in turn, correspond to the elements of earth, water, fire, air, and ether. The idea is that no matter what our consciousness is encased in or what kind of external force is working on us, our true Self, our true nature, cannot be altered in any manner whatsoever.

Secondly: cut, burnt, wet, and dried are symbols of being changed, taken from or added to (increased or decreased). Since we cannot be altered in any way, anything that can be is not our Self. This is the very important teaching known in Sanskrit as *anatma*–the teaching regarding what is not the Self. Buddha emphasized this greatly, and was being completely traditional in doing so. Sadly, those outside India who encountered his teachings thought that the term (*anatta* in Pali) meant there is no Self. But the term means not-Self, not no-Self, which would be *niratma* or *niratta*. So wherever we see change…that is not the Self. "Change and decay all around I see. O Thou Who changest not, abide with me." Unfortunately, these words are addressed to God, Who is not the problem. What should be sought is the abiding experience of our own unalterable Self. For Krishna sums it up in this way:

This Self cannot be cut, burnt, wetted, nor dried. This primeval Self is eternal, all-pervading, and immovable (2:24).

The Self is the inmost reality and can only be known at the core of our being–which is the Self. Yet it pervades all that we call "us," enlivening all our body-levels in the same way the proximity of fire creates warmth in inert substances and the light of the sun stimulates the growth of living things. This is a basic concept of Sankhya philosophy. Primordial energy has no motive power of its own, but the proximity of Spirit causes it to "live" and move. It is with us as it is with God. The presence of God causes the primal matter to manifest as all creation; and it is the presence of our spirit that causes our own private prakriti to manifest as a chain of ever-evolving births and deaths. Self-knowledge is the apex of our evolution, after which our prakriti becomes a mirror, silent and motionless, no longer moving, but reflecting only consciousness itself.

PRACTICAL
SELF-KNOWLEDGE

Krishna has been telling Arjuna a great deal about the Self, and will continue to do so for several more verses. Yet he now explains that:

Unmanifest, unthinkable, this Self is called unchangeable. Therefore, knowing this to be such, you should not mourn (2:25).

"I only believe in what I can see" is one of the silliest things anyone can say. The "I" spoken about in this statement is never seen–not even by the speaker! Some years back I read in an Eastern Christian magazine about an incident that took place in Yugoslavia. A Communist indoctrinator was mocking the ideas of God and the soul, saying that they could not be seen or touched and so did not exist. When he stopped speaking a man stood up and said: "I have a question for everyone who has been listening to you." Then he turned to the assembly and asked: "Can you see this man's mind?" "No," they responded. "Then it does not exist, and to think so is superstition. So forget everything he just said–it was only a combination of physical forces without any meaning at all." Somehow the "wisdom" of materialism evaporated before good sense.

The truth is this: the more easily seen and dealt with by the body and the senses, the less real a thing is. And the less it is seen and dealt with by the body and the senses, the more real it is. The absolute realities of God and the spirit are, then, completely beyond the reach of the senses or the mind. Although many attempts are made in religion to infer or deduce their existence, they are vain and in time lead to annihilation of themselves. Every "proof" set forth by limited reason to establish the existence of God and the spirit can be turned right back around and used to disprove them–that is the nature of any intellectual proposition. This is why the most effective atheist-materialists usually have a strong religious background. Both Stalin and Lenin studied for the Eastern Orthodox priesthood. Intuition alone can give us a shadowy hint of the presence of the Divine Spirit. And we must progress beyond intuition to direct experience of these fundamental realities. That is what Yoga is all about. Without a viable sadhana, these things cannot be known, and in time the intuition of their existence will be eroded and even lost–either in this life or in a future birth.

God, the Paramatman, and the individual spirit, the jivatman, are beyond this world, beyond all experience or appearance. Yet they are "behind" the veil of external existence, immanent within it. It is their presence that causes all the forms of evolutionary change. It is true that we can see the effects of spirit, but there is no way reason can prove they really emanate from spirit and are not self-caused. Only those who are clear at the center–the core of their being which is spirit–can see God, as Jesus said: "Blessed are the pure in heart: for they shall see God" (Matthew 5:8). The word translated "pure" is *katharos*, which means to be absolutely clear, free of all obstruction or extraneous matter or elements. *Kardia*, translated "heart," means the core or center of something, and in Greek was a symbolic term for the spirit which is, of course, the absolute center of our being–*is* our being, actually.

We cannot see or think about our true Self, but we can enter into it and live in it–live *as* it. Then all change and uncertainty will cease. As Krishna says a little later on: "In tranquility the cessation of all sorrows is produced." Knowing this, we should not grieve over present troubles but look forward in hope to their cessation forever.

PERSPECTIVE ON BIRTH
AND DEATH

Inconsistency in outlook

Just because something is the truth does not mean that we can easily grasp or accept it, however sincere we may be in our truth-seeking. How many years can go by without our fully grasping that someone we dearly love has left their body–they are so living to us. Sometimes we experience intense grief at their departure and absence, and at the same time really cannot feel that they are no longer with us. After all, we are in this earth plane because we are completely irrational–especially on the subconscious and emotional levels. When my miracle-working grandmother died, I grieved and shed tears over the loss every single day for one year, and yet only on the anniversary day of her departure did I fully come to realize that she was gone! In my heart I could not believe that I would not find her in her house if I would just go there. So an intellectual understanding about birth and death does not help a great deal. If the facts will not take root in our minds, then we at least need a better perspective on things. So Krishna is now explaining to Arjuna how he should consider these matters even if he cannot take in the truth that birth and death are mere appearances only. He continues:

> **And moreover, if you think this Self to have constant birth and death, even then you should not mourn (2:26).**

Even if we consider birth and death to be real (which they are, as impressions in the mind), even then we should have no sorrow because:

Of the born, death is certain; of the dead, birth is certain. Therefore, over the inevitable you should not grieve (2:27).

In the West, the brilliant Stoic philosopher Epictetus counseled his students to study their lives and environment and determine what lay within the scope of their power to influence, produce, or eliminate. Having done this, they should put everything else out of their minds as things they should not even worry about. Birth and death are certainly major elements to cultivate indifference to.

The truth of things can be postponed or avoided for a while. But truth is our very nature, and must eventually be faced and undergone. So how long will we continue to violate it with more illusions?

The wisdom of Buddha

How rare are those who never concede to making demands for more fantasies to make them "happy"! Buddha was one such, and even after these thousands of years there are still many (including some who call themselves Buddhists) who consider that his utter realism was pessimism or indifference to people's feelings.

One incident that is not popular is his dealing with this subject of death and grief. A young woman whose infant had died came to Buddha and begged him to bring her child back to life. Buddha told her to go into a nearby town and bring him some rice from a family in which no one had ever died. She hastened into the town and spent the day going from house to house with her request. Everywhere she was told the same thing: death continually came to members of the family. In the evening she returned to Buddha and, bowing, thanked him for showing her the folly of her request. Having understood the universality of physical death, she saw that her grief and her request were based on ignorance–ignorance which was now dispelled. John Hay, in his poem "The Law of Death" told it this way:

And then from door to door she fared,
To ask what house by Death was spared.
Her heart grew cold to see the eyes
Of all dilate with slow surprise:

"Kilvani, thou hast lost thy head;
Nothing can help a child that's dead.
There stands not by the Ganges' side
A house where none hath ever died."

Thus, through the long and weary day,
From every door she bore away
Within her heart, and on her arm,
A heavier load, a deeper harm.

By gates of gold and ivory,
By wattled huts of poverty,
The same refrain heard poor Kilvani,
The living are few, the dead are many.

The evening came–so still and fleet–
And overtook her hurrying feet.
And, heartsick, by the sacred lane
She fell, and prayed the god again.

She sobbed and beat her bursting breast:
"Ah, thou hast mocked me, Mightiest!
Lo I have wandered far and wide;
There stands no house where none hath died."

And Buddha answered, in a tone
Soft as a flute at twilight blown,
But grand as heaven and strong as death
To him who hears with ears of faith:

"Child, thou art answered. Murmur not!
Bow, and accept the common lot."
Kilvani heard with reverence meet,
And laid her child at Buddha's feet.

Swami Kaivalyananda, a disciple of Yogiraj Shyama Charan Lahiri, once told Mukunda Lal Ghosh, later to be Paramhansa Yogananda, about miraculous healings done by his guru. But in conclusion he stated: "The numerous bodies which were spectacularly healed through Lahiri Mahasaya eventually had to feed the flames of cremation." So in the end it was all the same: death had its way.

We only torment ourselves with the desire and attempt to postpone or cancel the inevitable. Years ago I heard about a hillbilly who spent the entire day in a theater, watching the same film over and over. When asked why he did this, he answered that he did not like the way it came out and so was waiting for it to end differently. It was his incomprehension of the nature of motion pictures that gave him such a foolish hope. And so it is with us.

Earthly life

Beings are unmanifest in their beginning, manifest in their middle state and again unmanifest in their end. What lamentation can be made over this? (2:28).

Like the hillbilly we either do not know the truth about this evanescent life of earthly incarnation or we refuse to face it. Our appearances on this earth are but a part of our life history. For aeons beyond number we never came into material manifestation at all. Then we began doing so, like actors entering a theater and moving over the stage in a brief play and then leaving to return home until the next performance. Not only are our "appearances" but a fraction of our relative existence, they are fundamentally unreal. As Krishna implies, life on this earth is completely unnatural for us. It is natural to be out of the body, not in it. Yet we irrationally cling to it and to our memories of it, even trying to make each life duplicate the one before it, not even wanting the drama to develop or evolve. And we insanely identify with the ever-changing temporary states, totally forgetting the unchanging eternal state that is the only thing real about us. Many metaphysically-minded people begin heaping up even more folly through striving to remember their past lives and attributing full reality to them. Rare are those who utilize the memory of past lives to illuminate the problems of the present life so that they all can be let go of in order to pass on to higher life beyond any births.

All our "lives" are really deaths–descent into the worlds of change and decay, dreams caused by the fever of samsara, a disease whose cure we must vigorously seek and even more vigorously apply. Only when we come to know that we have never been born and have never died will we have peace and the cessation of sorrow.

THE WONDER OF THE ATMAN

The Seven Wonders of the World

Earlier generations grew up in awe of Richard Haliburton, the archeologist-explorer whose books read better than most novels, and whose every word was true. The most favored book was that in which he told of both the Seven Wonders of the modern world and the Seven Wonders of the ancient world. Many readers felt a real pang at the thought that they would never see the Colossus of Rhodes, the Great Lighthouse of Alexandria, or the Mausoleum. I was one of them for a long time. But when I read the Bhagavad Gita my regret was transmuted into optimistic awe, for I came to understand that my own Atman was a wonder beyond all earth or any other world could offer, and that I was destined to be established in permanent and perfect knowledge-experience of that Self.

The One Wonder of India

For thousands of years both readers and hearers in India (and in the West for a couple of centuries) have taken inspiration from the story in the Chandogya Upanishad about the sage Uddalaka teaching his son Svetaketu about the Self. In many ways he demonstrates the existence of the Absolute Self, concluding each time with the thrilling words: "All beings have their Self in him alone. He is the truth. He is the subtle essence of all. He is the Self. And that, Svetaketu, THAT ART THOU." As Sri Aurobindo has observed, even those that do not have direct knowledge of the truth of these words yet are inexplicably moved upon hearing them, knowing subliminally of their truth. Stirred to their real depths, the wise of many ages have been set on the path of Self-discovery by Uddalaka's assurance that they, too, are THAT.

Knowledge and ignorance

The fact is that there is only one real problem for us as human beings: ignorance of the Self. And the solution is obvious: knowledge of the Self. For this reason Arjuna could not be swayed by Krishna's exhortations to fight that were based on egocentric factors such as personal disgrace, hope of heavenly reward, social order, and such like. This much Arjuna understood. Having revealed this to Arjuna (for Krishna had no need to find it out for himself), Krishna went directly to the core issue of the Self and stayed there for the remainder of that miracle of wisdom we know as the Gita. Like Uddalaka he used many means to convey the single message: Know the Self.

The four states of understanding

After his initial exposition of the Self, already considered in previous essays, Krishna speaks of the responses human beings have to the teaching about the Self:

> **Some perceive this Self as wondrous, another speaks of it as wondrous, another hears of it as wondrous, but even having heard of this Self, no one knows it (2:29).**

Prabhavananda translates this: "There are some who have actually looked upon the Atman, and understood it, in all its wonder. Others can only speak of it as wonderful beyond their understanding. Others know of its wonder by hearsay. And there are others who are told about it and do not understand a word."

It is intriguing to see how the number four has significance in many ways in the scriptures of India. We usually think of seven as the mystic number (and it is), but four also comes into the picture many times, especially in considerations of the development of consciousness. For example, there are four castes based on the level of the individual's consciousness. (The present-day "caste system" is an unfortunate degeneration based on just about everything but the individual's state of evolution.) The solar system is said to pass through four ages (yugas) in which the general consciousness of humanity ranges from only one-fourth to four-fourths of its potential. This numbering is the most important of all considerations, because it deals with the unfoldment of consciousness, consciousness being the nature of the Self.

Even in the life of Jesus we find this fourfold categorizing of spiritual consciousness. Toward the end of his public ministry, in response to his prayer God spoke in a great voice from the heavens. In the Gospel of John (12:27-29) we are told that those present reacted in four ways: 1) some knew it was the voice of God, 2) some thought it was the voice of an angel, 3) some did not hear it as words or a voice, but thought it was thunder, and 4) some did not hear a thing. If we analyze these responses we will find exactly the psychology of the four castes being expressed. But let us return to Krishna.

According to Krishna there are four states of awareness in relation to the Self: 1) direct knowledge, 2) deep faith and conviction—an intuition of the Self's reality, 3) intellectual comprehension of the "theory" of the Self, and 4) complete non-comprehension.

Divine knowledge

"Some perceive this [Self] as wondrous." In the ultimate sense, to know something is to *be* something. Although we are always our Selfs and incapable of being anything else, because we have fallen into the pit of delusion we are aware of and "know" just about everything but our Selfs. This is an awesomely horrible plight. But Krishna tells us that there are those who have actually regained their self-awareness, "seen" themselves in atmic vision and comprehended what they saw, coming to know the Self in the fullest sense.

Divine intuition

"Another speaks of it as wondrous." Since we *are* the Self, we obviously know all about it on the real level of our being. Evolution consists mainly of development/elaboration of our body vehicles, including the mind, but it also entails a refining of those vehicles, a transparency in which intuition comes more and more into play. It is this which is the real transcendence of the mind (intellect) and entry into true knowing. As a prelude to the direct knowing of the Self, the intuition of the Self arises and increases, leading the sadhaka onward to that knowing.

Divine understanding

"Another hears of it as wondrous." Before intuition arises, the intellect is developed through evolution and becomes capable of grasping the concept of the Self–insofar as it can be intellectually grasped. No small degree of evolution is required before genuinely intelligent (buddhic) apprehension of the Self is possible. Therefore to simply have an intellectual comprehension of the incomprehension of the Self–to wonder at the truth of the Self–is itself a mark of significant spiritual development.

Uncomprehending ignorance

"But even having heard of this [Self], no one knows it." Simply hearing or reading about the Self is not knowing the Self, and never can be. This is not a matter of intelligence only, but also a matter of evolution of consciousness. I have met highly intelligent people who just could not comprehend even the simplest of the principles set forth in the Upanishads or the Gita. No matter how I tried to make their meaning clear by restating them in different ways, they remained incapable of even a glimmer of understanding.

For example, one very mentally active and intelligent man was thoroughly flummoxed by my statement that as long as we see life with the two eyes of duality we will wander in confusion and delusion, but as soon as we begin to see with the one eye of spiritual intuition we begin to understand our life and our selves. Again and again he asked me to explain, but he never got it in the least. He was very frustrated, at least realizing that I was making sense and the lack was on his part, but he never managed.

On another occasion one of the monks of our monastery was speaking to a Fundamentalist Protestant minister. The monk told him that we believed everyone could become exactly what Jesus was. Over and over he asked the monk to explain—he was not rejecting the idea: he just could not grasp it. And he never did.

As I have said, it is a matter of evolution, for non-comprehension is even lower than a mistaken understanding.

Sometimes, however, incomprehension is a matter of negativity. The Tibetan Buddhists say that stupidity is a "daughter of hell." Evolution of intelligence is a requisite, but it is certainly true that without purification of the intellect, however evolved, no understanding of higher spiritual realities is possible.

The four castes

Returning to the subject of caste, we can now realize in the light of Krishna's exposition that Shudras are those who are servants to materiality and ignorance, Vaishyas are those who have an intellectual understanding of the possibility of their betterment, Kshatriyas are those who, being close to apprehension of the Self, are able to intuit the truth of the Self while aware of their limitation, and Brahmins are those who see and know the Self. This is the sum of the entire matter.

THE INDESTRUCTIBLE SELF

In the first chapter of the Bhagavad Gita, which sets the stage for its other seventeen chapters, we are told that: "Krishna brought the chief chariot to stand in the midst of the two armies. Thus facing Bhishma, Drona, and all the rulers of the earth, Krishna said: Behold, Arjuna, these Kurus assembled here. Arjuna saw standing there fathers, grandfathers, teachers, maternal uncles, brothers, sons, grandsons as well as friends, fathers-in-law and companions in the two armies. In both of them he saw all relatives arrayed. Then filled with profound pity, desponding" (1:24-28), he spoke, filled with grief at the thought of the impending death of those he respected so highly and loved so dearly.

At first Krishna attempts to incite Arjuna to battle by speaking of duty and honor. This does not succeed, so he quickly passes on to the subject of the Self from which perspective alone could Arjuna truly engage in a righteous war. At one point he assures Arjuna:

This embodied Self is eternally indestructible in the body of all. Therefore you should not mourn for any being (2:30).

The Self is absolutely immutable. In a sense nothing ever even happens to it. Rather, it remains the silent, unchanging witness of all that goes on around it–but never within it or even with it or near it. In the fifth chapter Krishna describes the enlightened individual as being like a lotus leaf resting, unwetted, on water. This is not an ideal for Arjuna to strive for, but is the actual state of all sentient beings–they are never touched by anything, not even by God since God is the essence of their being. To understand that nothing ever really affects us is an essential insight, but the experiencing of it is much better.

The main point of Krishna's statement is that it is unreasonable to mourn or grieve for anyone, since nothing has happened to them, however horrendous the appearance might be. Nor has anything really happened to us who have witnessed it. Not even their death has altered us in any degree.

When we lived in the Anza-Borrego desert we encountered an eccentric man who was caretaker of a friend's property there. In speaking to us about him she commented that he had starred in his own movie for too long a time. That remark was both insightful and humorous, but it happens to be the truth about all of us. We are sitting in the "sense-surround" theater completely absorbed in the movies of our many lives and completely identifying with the spectacle. None of it is ultimately real, yet we suffer terribly. How is this? Unhappily, rather than "losing" our minds we have "found" them, become immersed in them, and now identify with them totally. All that happens to our body and mind we think is happening to us. And so we pass through a panorama of mistaken responses to the passing show.

Both birth and death are illusions, but that makes them no less painful if we identify with that which undergoes those changes. We must not just intellectually understand this, we must actually separate ourselves from the illusory contact and be what we already are: the indestructible Self. Then all suffering ceases–suffering that never really existed except as a mirage caused by non-existent phenomena. For Krishna assures us: "You dream you are the doer, you dream that action is done, you dream that action bears fruit. It is your ignorance, it is the world's delusion that gives you these dreams" (5:14. Prabhavananda translation).

"Happy The Warrior"

Happy?

Seeing and hearing the agony of Arjuna, Krishna smiled as he began the discourse we are analyzing. He smiled because he knew the truth of things, including the fact that Arjuna was about to come to the same understanding.

Literal and symbolic

Symbolism is an essential part of any viable spiritual tradition, and Indian spiritual lore is heavily symbolic, so much so that many begin to treat everything about it as a symbol. Christianity inherited this both from India and from Jewish philosophers such as Philo, to whom just about everything was symbolic. Origen refused to consider the Gospels as literal historical accounts and at one place in his writings mentions what a great difficulty the Christian encounters if he believes that Jesus rode into Jerusalem seated on a donkey. He does not explain what the difficulty would be and I have never known anyone who could even guess at his meaning.

For us who are sitting with Arjuna listening to Krishna's revelation, the Gita must be seen as simultaneously literal and symbolic. If we arbitrarily decide when the Gita is literal and when it is symbolic we will not only cut our understanding of its message by half, we will also confuse ourselves. It is also very necessary that we apply the Gita's statements to the physical, mental (higher mental, actually), and spiritual levels of our life. Otherwise we will miss many applications of its wisdom.

Why not you?

I would like to pause here for a serious statement. It is gratifying to me that you are reading my ideas on the meaning of the Bhagavad Gita. However it is my hope that you will read many commentaries on the Gita–those of past generations as well as the contemporary ones. This is because the Gita is as infinite as the Consciousness that speaks through it. Therefore a single human being cannot possibly encompass all the meanings of the Gita. Nor can the commentaries of several do so, either. So keep on reading!

You, too, need to study the Gita directly and gain your own insights. Jesus said that "every scribe which is instructed unto the kingdom of heaven is like unto a man that is an householder, which bringeth forth out of his treasure things new and old" (Matthew 13:52). The wisdom of the past is still wisdom, and the wisdom of the present is equally wise. Both are needed. The word *kainos* here translated "new" also has the connotation of freshness, the idea being that new insights can continue to be brought forth–and why not by you?

Mental viewpoint

Now having said all this about literal and symbolic I would like to analyze the next few verses from the psychological angle since it is the mind-intellect which influences both the physical and the spiritual life. As Sri Ramakrishna often observed, "The mind is everything."

The war

Anyone who wishes to better himself in any way faces the necessity of effort–even struggle. The war of the Bhagavad Gita takes place internally, is a spiritual struggle to the death of ignorance and the ascendance of illumination. Many never engage in the war, frightened away by the prospect of the sacrifice and strife. Those engaged in the spiritual war often would like to avoid it or mitigate it or somehow work out a cease-fire. They commit themselves to sure defeat by such a wish if they follow it through.

We, however, wish to succeed, to win the war. So let us listen to what Krishna tells us as we, too, quail before the prospects of battle.

It is our duty and our nature

> And just considering your swadharma, you should not waver,
> for truly to a kshatriya there is nothing greater to find than a
> righteous battle (2:31).

I plan to wait until the fourth chapter, where Krishna tells us that God is the originator of the four castes, to go into the subject of caste in any depth, so here I want only to point out that although translators may use the expression "caste duty" in translating this verse, the actual Sanskrit says *swadharma*, which is something far different. That, too, is best saved for an in-depth essay later on, but right now it must be made clear that swadharma means "self-dharma," the action which is in perfect accordance with our present state of evolution, which may be spoken about in terms of caste. Yet, the higher meaning is the dharma of the Self, the action that will best lead to the knowledge of our eternal being. So the purpose of this verse is to show that the inner struggle for enlightenment is twofold: a duty and an expression/manifestation of our true nature.

Since people are usually out of touch with who they really are, another kind of appeal is needed, and duty/responsibility is the most frequently and reasonably invoked. On the other hand, the spiritual struggle is our duty because it is our nature to ascend, to evolve. So they really are the same thing in the context of the Gita.

A problematic word

Now we need to go back a bit to a word whose analysis at that time might have distracted us from the main thrust of the Gita's message in that part.

"The Holy Lord said: Whence has come this faintheartedness of yours in the time of danger; ignoble [unaryan], not leading to heaven, but to disgrace?" (2:2). We must look at that word, *unarya*: unaryan: "not aryan."

Because the monsters who marched under the Nazi banner (which bore the sacred symbol of the swastika that was thereby dishonored and made to bear an odious connotation in the West) plagiarized the Sanskrit word *arya(n)*, it has become usual for us outside India to use the expressions "Vedic religion" or "Sanatana [Eternal] Dharma" in reference to the spiritual tradition of primeval India. These are accurate and bona fide expressions, of course, but Arya Dharma is the oldest expression and has a unique value. So important was arya in the vocabulary of the ancient Indian sages that India itself was known as Aryavarta, the Land of the Aryas, for the people living there were commonly known as Aryas. Buddha used the term a great deal. Although his teachings are referred to as "The Noble Eightfold Path" or "The Four Noble Truths," what he really said was "The *Aryan* Eightfold Path" and "The Four *Aryan* Truths." This is not without real significance, so we cannot avoid looking at the word, no matter how distasteful its use in twentieth-century racial bigotry and genocide has made it for contemporary sensitivities. Hitler liked to toss around "holy" and "God" in his rants–as well as "justice" and "freedom"–but that in no way invalidates them. Evil as he was, he did not have the power to corrupt or degrade such an ancient term of honor–only to condition our response to it. And we should not let his madness prevail in our personal reactions.

Arya comes from the root word *ri*, which means "to rise upward." A legitimate translation is "one who strives upward." This gives us the whole idea about wherever it is used. An aryan is one who puts forth real effort to improve himself in any area of life. Naturally arya was most fittingly applied by the philosophers of India to spiritual and personal life. The word "noble" is too inactive and can be interpreted passively, such as in thinking that a person is born noble or made noble by the declaration of another. An arya is one who labors to rise, exemplifying the saying that a diamond is a piece of coal that never gave up. Truly a saint is a sinner that never gave up, as Yogananda often said. In other words, an arya is one on the path to sainthood as well as one who has attained it.

In very ancient Indian texts humanity is divided into two classes: the aryas and the vritras, or dasyus. Vritra means "one who covers up" in the sense of burrowing into the darkness of the earth, of material consciousness and involvement. Dasyus are slaves–slaves of materiality living in willing servitude to lower life and consciousness. Aryas, on the other hand, strive upward into the light, into freedom.

No hesitation

Arya Dharma, then, is the course of action an arya follows to become a perfected being. Specifically, it is the mode of life and thought outlined in the Upanishads and the Bhagavad Gita. An arya is one who responds to the inner and upward call without hesitation. For there is nothing nobler than the struggle for higher degrees of life and awareness.

> **Happy are the kshatriyas to whom heaven's gate opens when by good fortune they encounter such a battle (2:32).**

Truly happy are those who engage in such a battle, for it opens the door to Infinite Consciousness, the true "heaven."

> **Now if you shall not undertake this dharmic engagement, then having avoided your swadharma and glory, you shall incur evil (2:33).**

Sanskrit words have many meanings, and it is good to consider all of them, since the sages packed their words with many relevant aspects. *Dharmyam sanghraman* also means "dharmic assembly." In the spiritual texts of India great emphasis is put on *satsanga* which, though literally meaning "the company of truth," is always considered to mean "company with the wise." Sri Ramana Maharshi said that for success in yoga, satsanga was an absolute essential, and Sri Ramakrishna said that spiritual life is simply impossible without continual association with other seekers for truth—and, hopefully, with those that have found it.

It is interesting that Krishna says avoiding the struggle for righteousness is an abandoning of both swadharma and glory (*kirtim*). Now we are able to easily consider that we have a higher duty, but usually forget that we are also glorious spiritual beings, however much ignorance may have covered up our glory. Human beings do not need to be told that they are miserable, awful, sinners, but the truth: they are glorious beings who are tragically caught in the net of "sin," but freedom is not only possible, it is inevitable, for it is their true nature. We do not need God to forgive us our sins. We need to awaken, stand up, and shake them off like the barnacles they are, and walk onward in strength and freedom.

The word translated "evil" is *papam*, which is often translated as "sin," but it means demerit–as opposed to merit (*punyam*). We can think of it as dirt or dust that obscures a pane of glass or a mirror. It in no ways means something that God has forbidden or which he "hates." Rather, it is a self-injury that inhibits and limits us. It is a bond that takes away our freedom. Consequently, we are free to choose which we want, otherwise we will be only servants and slaves. Only those who are free to be foolish have the freedom to be wise. This is the basis of the "live and let live" attitude of the East that so frustrates the missionary from the West.

Self-disgrace

If we turn away from this holy conflict we will be denying our nature and betraying and disgracing no one but ourselves.

> **And people will forever tell of your undying infamy. For the renowned, such disgrace is worse than dying (2:34).**

The word translated "disgrace" is *akirtim*–absence of our glory, loss of contact with what and who we really are. This is a death of consciousness much worse than physical death, for it can persist throughout countless incarnations.

> **The great car-warriors will believe you abstain from delight in battle through fear. And among those who have thought much of you, you shall come to be lightly esteemed. Your enemies shall speak of you many things that should not be said, deriding your adequacy. What, indeed, could be a greater suffering than that? (2:35-36).**

Yes, it is a painful thing to have others speak ill of us and despise us, but how much more painful it is to despise ourselves and consider ourselves to be degraded and unworthy. There are many sad forms of humanity, but none is sadder than those who have turned away from higher life and spent a lifetime in shame and regret, condemned by none other than themselves.

A great secret

In material life we are often promised great benefits if we will only do what the promisers want us to do, the implication being that if we do not obey we will lose or be denied the benefits. But Krishna has a very different thing to say. Happiness in both this world and the next are guaranteed to the yogi.

> **If you are slain you shall attain heaven; if you conquer you shall enjoy the earth. Therefore, stand up resolved to fight (2:37).**

In the sixth chapter Arjuna is going to present to Krishna the usual manipulative and resentful view of religionists: is not one who fails in or abandons spiritual life lost and hopeless? Krishna replies: "Truly there is no loss for him either here on earth or in heaven. No one who does good goes to misfortune" (6:40). And this is true in the inner struggle. If we literally die before winning the battle or are overcome in the battle and "slain" by the enemy, we shall still reap profound benefit. The intensely positive karma generated by meditation will result in our rising to high spiritual realms after death and enjoying its fruits there. Then, when we are reborn we will reap the good karma in the form of coming into the orbit of meditational knowledge and resume our practice. If on the other hand we persevere and win the ultimate victory we shall find life here on earth totally transfigured to a glory presently unimagined by us. In his book *Practice of Karma Yoga* the great Master Sivananda of Rishikesh expressed it this way:

> When I surveyed from Ananda Kutir, Rishikesh,
> By the side of the Tehri Hills, only God I saw.
> In the Ganges and the Kailash peak,
> In the famous Chakra Tirtha of Naimisar also, only God I saw.

In tribulation and in grief, in joy and in glee,
In sickness and in sorrow, only God I saw.
In birds and dogs, in stones and trees,
In flowers and fruits, in the sun, moon and stars, only God I saw.

Like camphor I was melting in his fire of knowledge,
Amidst the flames outflashing, only God I saw.
My Prana entered the Brahmarandhra at the Moordha,
Then I looked with God's eyes, only God I saw.

I passed away into nothingness, I vanished,
And lo, I was the all-living, only God I saw.
I enjoyed the Divine Aisvarya, all God's Vibhutis,
I had Visvaroopa Darshan, the Cosmic Consciousness, only God
I saw.

Sri Ramakrishna said that to the enlightened yogi the whole world that now is a sea of suffering becomes "a mart of joy." A Buddhist mystic wrote: "I walk through this world and no one guesses that Paradise is within [me]." Is it any wonder then that Krishna concludes: "Stand up, resolved to fight"?

Even more...
Krishna continues with even more astonishing facts, underlining the truth that the Gita is not only unique among the scriptures of India, it is *supreme*. For next he says:

> **Considering pleasure and pain, gain and loss, victory and defeat the same, then engage in battle. Thus you shall not incur evil (2:38).**

Talk about Blessed Assurance!
Meditation deals only with the ever-changing, ever-mutating levels of our being. As Patanjali says (Yoga Sutras 1:2), yoga is the entering into the state where these levels no longer change or even move, but become

transformed into a perfect mirror of spirit. This and this alone is Self-realization. But until then what a bumpy ride! This being so, we must adopt the perspective Krishna presents: "pleasure and pain, gain and loss, victory and defeat, are all one and the same." That is, they are all merely shifting sands, having no stable reality whatsoever. They are but fever dreams, delirium from which yoga is intended to awaken us.

Yogis must take their true Self very seriously–even reverently. But they must never take the antics of their Self's "wrappings" seriously at all, except to determine to tame and transmute them. For the yogi does not shed them and swim away into the ocean of Infinity. He changes them into that ocean and abides in them in freedom.

Wherefore let us go into battle and end even the capacity for wrong. Being sinners is not at all our nature, and once we become established in our true Self it will be as Saint John wrote: "Whosoever is born of God doth not commit sin; for his seed remaineth in him: and he cannot sin, because he is born of God" (I John 3:9). The Gita clearly shows the way to such an attainment.

BUDDHI YOGA

This buddhi yoga taught by Sankhya is now declared to you, so heed. Yoked to this buddhi yoga, you shall avoid the bonds of karma (2:39).

Sankhya

Since Sankhya is the philosophical basis of the Bhagavad Gita, we will be talking about it quite a bit. For now, here is *A Brief Sanskrit Glossary*'s definition of Sankhya: "One of the six orthodox systems of Hindu philosophy whose originator was the sage Kapila, Sankhya is the original Vedic philosophy, endorsed by Krishna in the Bhagavad Gita (2:39; 3:3, 5; 18:13, 19). Also, the second chapter of the Gita is entitled *Sankhya Yoga*. The *Ramakrishna-Vedanta Wordbook* says: 'Sankhya postulates two ultimate realities, Purusha and Prakriti, declaring that the cause of suffering is man's identification of Purusha with Prakriti and its products. Sankhya teaches that liberation and true knowledge are attained in the supreme consciousness, where such identification ceases and Purusha is realized as existing independently in its transcendental nature.'"

Not surprisingly, then, Yoga is based on the Sankhya philosophy.

Buddhi yoga

Buddhi is the intellect, understanding, and reason. It is not just the thinking mind, it is the understanding mind, the seat of intelligence and wisdom. Buddhi Yoga, then, is the Yoga of Intelligence which later came to be called Jnana Yoga, the Yoga of Knowledge. We have four levels of being, and the buddhi (also called the jnanamaya kosha) is one of the highest. So a buddhi yogi has his consciousness centered in the higher levels of his being. And he uses his buddhi to extend that yoga even higher into that level which is virtually indistinguishable from spirit. From then on Self-realization is assured. Yoga and Sankhya are inseparable, so buddhi yoga involves meditation as its paramount aspect. A Buddha is a successful buddhi yogi. Unprejudiced reading of the Pali Sutras of Buddhism will reveal that Buddha was not only an Aryan, he was a classical Sankhya philosopher, a buddhi yogi. Anyone who wishes to follow Buddha must be the same, just as anyone who wishes to follow Christ must follow Sanatana Dharma as found in the Gita. Then they, too, will be followers of Sankhya and practicers of Yoga.

"Yoga" comes from the Sanskrit root *yuj*, which means to join or connect or even to unite in the sense of making many into one. It can also mean to bring together. But in the scriptures of India it always is applied in a spiritual sense, meaning both union with God and the way by which that union is effected. Yoga, then is both spiritual life and the culmination of spiritual life. Yoga is union with the Supreme Being, or any practice that makes for such union.

According to Krishna, the direct effect of buddhi yoga is the dissolving of karmic bonds created by past actions (karmas) and the freeing of the yogi from the compulsion to future karma. So we should look at karma itself.

Karma

"Karma" comes from the Sanskrit root *kri*, which means to act, do, or make. It is exactly the same as the Latin verb *ago* from whose form, *actus*, we get our English words act and action. Both verbs are all-purpose words—that is, they can be applied in many situations to express the idea of many forms of action both mental and physical. This is important to know so we can realize that karma covers the entire range of human action, whatever its character.

Karma, then, means any kind of action, including thought and feeling, but it also means the effects of actions. For karma is both action and reaction. Being a fundamental principle of existence it may be thought of as the law of causation governing action and its effects in the physical and psychological plane. It extends back to the moment of our entry into relative existence and extends forward to the moment of our exit from relative existence—even if that exit is a matter of transmutation of consciousness rather than external cessation of manifestation in a relative form or body.

Psychological yoga

Buddhi yoga is performed for the revelation of divinity, all other benefits, individual and communal, being secondary. For it is purely psychological, even if sometimes expressed outwardly.

First we must be able to intellectually understand the principle and the practice. Then if we follow it the result will not be the benefit of others or satisfaction with ourselves for having done what is right. Instead it will be the breaking of the bonds of egoic desire which bind us to the wheel of birth and death and force us to act and to reap the results of our actions.

To even conceive of erasing the capacity for desire from our minds is audacious to the maximum degree. To strive for it is courageous beyond calculation. No wonder a battlefield and imminent war is the setting for Krishna's teaching.

We must understand that desirelessness is not a mere absence of desire or indifference or detachment. It is an absolute *incapacity* for desire. That is, desire cannot arise in the mind (buddhi), conscious or subconscious, of the perfect buddhi yogi.

People usually make the same mistake about buddhi yoga that they do about Patanjali's Yoga. They think that just not thinking is the state of yoga and just not caring is the state of karma yoga. But they are much, much more. Yoga is the state in which the mind substance (chitta) has evolved to the point where no modifications (vrittis or waves) can arise. Buddhi yoga is the state in which desire can no longer arise, being eclipsed by awareness of the spirit-Self. These are high ideals virtually beyond our present comprehension, but not beyond our attainment.

The safe path

Krishna continues to amaze us. Next he states:

> **In this no effort is lost, nor are adverse results produced. Even a little of this dharma protects from great fear (2:40).**

All effort is effectual, and there is no regression from progress attained in this yoga. It also protects the yogi from *mahato bhayat*–great danger or great fear.

Even to try the path of yoga for a while and then abandon it, or to try it and fail, or to follow it and die before making any significant progress–all these will result in tremendous benefit. Not one calorie of expended energy will slip away from us. This is incredible, and reveals the profound nature of authentic yoga. Yoga (the real thing, that is) inaugurates such a profound change in our entire mode of existence, such a deep-reaching extension of our higher will, that it cannot help but come to full effect in time. So powerful is the psychic restructuring accomplished by even a little yoga practice that we are permanently changed, as Krishna will expound later.

Even more: no negative effect can accrue from such yoga. In other endeavors failure or abandonment often produce psychic damage, weakening, or loss in some form. Not so with this yoga. So mighty is its effect that even walking away from it cannot cancel its positive and inevitable results. Only good can come of our attempts. For even a little practice of this yoga will save us from the terrible wheel of rebirth and death by at least to some degree breaking the chains of desire–or rather, the weakness and ignorance that render us capable of desire.

The secret of its effectiveness

> **In this matter there is a single, resolute understanding. The thoughts of the irresolute are many-branched, truly endless (2:41).**

In the practice of yoga there is only one ideal: liberation of the spirit (moksha). Nothing else can be a motive. It is like threading a needle. The thread cannot have fibers sticking out, otherwise it cannot be put through the needle's eye. In the same way the mind must be focused on the single purpose: freedom in union with the Divine. Many types of actions may be engaged in and many goals may be aimed for or achieved. Yet, to the yogi they are nothing in themselves. The final result alone matters and is ever before his inner eye.

It is much like the rays of the sun. They can be very hot in the summer, but if even in the winter they are focused by means of a magnifying or burning glass they will cause any flammable object to catch fire.

The narrower the point of a weight, the more pressure is produced. A brick weighing a pound or two will cause no discomfort if held in the hand. But if the corner of the brick is brought to bear on the palm it will be painful.

The idea of both these examples is that the more united or one-pointed the mind is made through yoga, the more powerful–and therefore effective–it is.

Single purpose

To lack this single-mindedness in relation to moksha is disastrous to the yogi. This cannot be overemphasized, because yoga is nothing less than the intense form of liberating sadhana Krishna envisions and which impels him to say: "The thoughts of the irresolute are many-branched, truly endless." Lost in the labyrinth of many goals and focusing on a multitude of objects, the aspiring yogi becomes lost in confusion and frustration. Krishna's picture of such a person was presented by the Canadian humorist Stephen Leacock when he wrote about a man who leapt on his horse "and rode madly off in all directions." In the Bible several times people are urged to walk straight forward without turning to right or left. (Proverbs 4:27; Deuteronomy 5:32, 28:14; Joshua 1:7) The meaning is the same as Krishna's.

Our slogan should ever be: Go Forward!

RELIGIOSITY VERSUS RELIGION

Seeing should not always be believing

"All that glitters is not gold" is especially true in the realm of religion. I can never hear that adage without remembering a walk I once took with the Russian Orthodox (OCA) Archbishop of Chicago. I was spending the weekend with him as I usually did at that time, and we were just wandering around aimlessly in the pre-spring weather, getting rather far from his small apartment next door to the renowned Holy Trinity Cathedral.

As we walked along, suddenly to our right loomed a huge church. It was painted a dark blue in the tradition of the Ukraine and topped with immense sparkling gold onion domes. At the peak of the roof in front was a gigantic Russian-style triple-bar cross, also covered in gold leaf.

"Oh, look!" I exclaimed while pointing. "An Orthodox church."

The archbishop looked at me reproachfully. "All that glitters is not gold," he said. "Go see." And he waved his hand toward the structure. So over I went and found by reading the sign by the door that it indeed was not an Orthodox church—not at all. "You must be careful," was the laconic admonition I received upon returning to the bishop. "Do not believe your eyes all the time."

This is very much true in the world of religion. All that looks godly is not necessarily godly. Often the opposite. Speaking of the religionists of his day, Saint Paul simply said: "They have a zeal of God, but not according to knowledge" (Romans 10:2).

Just because we believe in God (or at least in our concept of God) and are sincere and motivated means little in the sphere of the spirit. Rather, it is imperative that our religion be "according to knowledge." Regarding this Krishna now says:

Real religion

> **The ignorant, delighting in the word of the Veda, proclaim this flowery speech: "There is nothing else" (2:42).**

This verse may surprise us, especially since the Vedas are usually spoken of with highest reverence. But the truth is that there has been a great deal of progress in Indian philosophy over the past centuries since Krishna spoke these words.

The supreme teacher of wisdom, Shankara, was born at a time when Vedic religion was at its lowest ebb—so much so, that only a small minority even professed to follow it, the majority having abandoned its empty and superstitious ritualism for the superior spiritual perspective of Buddhism, which rejected the Vedas. Shankara's mission was to show that the ritualistic obsession of those who followed the karma-kanda—the ritual portion of the Veda—and who taught that Vedic ritual is the only path to perfection, were utterly wrong. By his masterly commentaries on the Brahma (Vedanta) Sutras, the Upanishads, the Gita, and the Yoga Sutras, he restored the original teachings of the ancient rishis and saved the very existence of Sanatana Dharma.

Today adherents of that Dharma study the Vedas to discover the wisdom hidden therein, not to simply recite them in a superstitious manner. Credit must especially be given to the nineteenth-century reformer, Swami Dayananda Saraswati, for first expounding the Vedas as purely spiritual texts that only appear to deal with externalities. Yet Krishna's words are still relevant, for throughout the world (including India) religious people are following only the external appearances of holy scriptures, and are intent only in getting "the good things of life" while in this world and going to a "heaven" after death that is nothing more than a version of the earth without the flaws. Gaining heaven and avoiding hell, getting reward and avoiding punishment—in other words, greed and fear—are their motives. The life of the spirit simply does not come into it. In fact, "there is nothing else" to their religion but their selfish purposes.

A profile of ignorance

Krishna has already told us that the sole purpose of yoga is the realization of the Self and the liberation that produces. It is not hard to conceive that this should also be the intent of religion, but it rarely is. For, lacking true knowledge and wisdom, the various religions set forth ways and means that are oriented toward just about everything material and egoic, not toward knowledge of the Self or the means to attain it. Just the opposite, they push their followers further into the mire of material consciousness, even promising them eternal physical embodiment after a mythical resurrection from the dead: a resurrection into matter instead of resurrection into spirit!

I do not mean to be pointing the finger only at Western religion. The popular religion of the East is even more adept at turning words of wisdom into nonsense—and very cleverly and plausibly, too. To gauge the truth of this assertion, read the Upanishads and the Bhagavad Gita and then take a broad look at contemporary Indian religion, and even yoga, in their popular forms. Are they the same? Almost never, no matter how much the Upanishads and Gita may be invoked by those whose entire religious practices are contrary or extraneous (irrelevant) to the philosophy of the ancient sages. This is a very serious and unfortunate situation.

Very often those who want to follow the way of the Gita and the Upanishads are deflected from that path by the very ones who claim to teach it and whom they trust as viable authorities. As Swami Prabhavananda's translation puts it: "Those who lack discrimination may quote the letter of the scripture, but they are really denying its inner truth." Krishna outlines the character and methods of such misleaders.

> Those of desire-filled natures, intent on heaven, offering re-birth as actions' fruit, performing many and various rites, are aimed at the goal of enjoyment and power (2:43).

Desire-filled. I must confess that these words of Krishna take me back to the religion of my childhood. I was fortunate enough to be raised in a spiritually serious church. The theology was full of holes and absurd in many (most) aspects, but the attitude was right on the beam: "Know ye not that the friendship of the world is enmity with God? Whosoever therefore will be a friend of the world is the enemy of God" (James 4:4). We understood that the world spoken of here was not the world of divine manifestation but the artificial structure of human society based on the egoic ignorance of human beings. To be a friend of the world means to be trapped in the realm of time and space, as well as the delusions perpetuated by humanity through the ages.

Not only Jesus, but we, too, can say with confidence: "I am not of the world" (John 17:14). For "the world" is everything that denies and covers up who we really are. It is only rational, then, to heed the admonition: "Love not the world, neither the things that are in the world. If any man love the world, the love of the Father is not in him. For all that is in the world, the lust of the flesh, and the lust of the eyes, and the pride of life, is not of the Father, but is of the world" (I John 2:15-16). We must note that the evils here listed are not said to come from "the devil," but from the world.

Most religion is sociopathic, and a fundamental trait of a sociopath is denial of any responsibility. Everything and everyone is responsible for the sociopath's problems except himself. Such religion teaches people that some invisible evil forces or visible instruments of those forces are what makes them do wrong. But Saint John tells us that it is the distortion produced by our association and identity with the material and the relative world that impels us to folly.

Speaking of the desire-filled teachers of religion, the Apostle says: "They are of the world: therefore speak they of the world, and the world heareth them" (I John 4:5). As Krishna states, these religionists are full of desires. Their minds are so warped by the fever of these desires, they see themselves and others in a completely twisted perspective. Their fundamental impulses are corrupted and lead to increasing corruption and ultimate destruction. Their whole way of looking at life is hopelessly distorted. And being sociopathic their major intent is to force everyone into their world view.

These people are the enemies of both the wise and the foolish. The wise they wish to subvert, silence, or destroy lest truth free their dupes from their grasp. On the other hand they are determined to keep the ignorant in the dark and in servitude to them and their ideas. So vast is the number of the ways in which they accomplish this, it is difficult to delineate them. Just take a look around, and everything you see will be–or at least reflect– their wiles and ways. If they were not a real danger to the sadhaka, Krishna would not bother to speak about them to Arjuna.

Intent on heaven. They obsessively grasp at every wisp of the world they see and proudly proclaim that their possession is a sign of divine favor, fulfillment of God's will for them, and proof that they are pleasing to God and right in their views. Yet they know that earthly gain inevitably ends in loss, and that even before the loss many defects are encountered and many failures to please or satisfy. This should turn any sensible person away from externality to seek the true satisfaction that is only found within. But they are not sensible, these dwellers in their own mirage, so they do not look within themselves but beyond this world to a heavenly world of blessed reward where no defect can mar their enjoyment of astral materiality. Consequently their scriptures and their propaganda is filled with descriptions of bright, beautiful, and happy worlds which will be the reward of those who subscribe to their religion and follow their demands.

Although they seem to have their sights on heaven, they are really hankering after the things of earth without their innate deficiencies. So even when they supposedly yearn for heaven they are really desiring earth. Some of them are so caught in this obsession that they assure their adherents that some time in the future they will all rise from the dead in immortal physical bodies and live forever on this earth that has been somehow cleansed and perfected.

Of course these delights are not just for the picking up. They are the rewards of a pleased and placated divinity. They are the carrots held out to the eager donkeys that follow them.

Offering rebirth. Yet, as Krishna points out, all they really offer is "rebirth as actions' fruit." How true this is of most religionists, whether clerical or lay. Desire for external material things or situations must come to fulfillment—this is the fundamental law. For karma is thought as well as act. Those who desire aught of the world shall inherit the world over and over through continued rebirth. Even desire for a heaven that is really only the earth without fault or loss brings us back to the earth itself. What to say, then, of the doctrine of the eventual resurrection of the body and eternal dwelling in that body? Such an aspiration can only lead to more and more births in a physical body, since the heaven of such people is only really the earth—just as their "God" is only themselves.

The great teachers come and proclaim that freedom from karma and rebirth is possible. And they show us the way to freedom. But their supposed followers instantly degrade the message and build up a religion that only perpetuates the old bondage. They promise life and deliver death. "A wonderful and horrible thing is committed in the land; the prophets prophesy falsely, and the priests bear rule by their means; and my people love to have it so" (Jeremiah 5:30-31). This is evidence that no one religion has a franchise on ignorance and bondage.

Performing many and various rites, are aimed at the goal of enjoyment and power. Lord Krishna is not speaking only of the people outside India. Throughout the Indian subcontinent right now millions are streaming in and out of temples, paying money for rituals and blessings that are intended to give them whatever they might want, and the three deities of ritualism—Pleasure, Power, and Prosperity—are diligently served by a greedy and materialistic priesthood. Those of us in the West whose contact with India has been in the form of visiting Indian spiritual teachers and yogis look at all this with a spiritual perspective completely incongruous with the truth. "Look at those vast and beautiful temples!" we enthuse, "all monuments to the spiritual aspiration and devotion of the people." Not at all. And almost never. Those temples are monuments to greed and superstition as well as

83

fear–both fear of lacking material things and of incurring the wrath of the skittish deities whose scriptural "biographies" are welterings of lust, anger, jealousy, vengefulness, and ego–just like their devotees.

Our situation is very much like that of some friends of mine who often went to India to visit the ashram of a renowned spiritual figure. Since they could not understand the saint's language, every word spoken in the ashram by the saint and the visitors seemed embodiments of spirituality, and the Western devotees felt edified every moment. But when my friends began picking up some knowledge of the language they found that most of the conversation was mundane and inane–in keeping with the consciousness of the local people who came to the ashram for the same motives they went to temples: "Give Me!" Most devotees in India are devoted only to themselves and to the saints as fulfillers of their desires. As one very famous Indian saint said to a crowd of such people: "When I give you what you want you love me, but when I do not give you what you want you hate me." This saint, like Jesus, certainly "knew what was in man" (John 2:24-25).

But back to the ritualists. They do indeed prescribe labyrinthine rites whose complexity demand a trained and well-paid priesthood. Sometimes the rituals are very obvious pullings of the Divine Vending Machine's handle, and sometimes they are masked with sentimentality passed off as devotion. One such, for example, is the extremely popular Satyanarayan Puja. This takes hours of ritual offerings, singing, and recitation of the glories of Vishnu (Narayana). But the glories recited are really accounts of all the amazing worldly advantages that have supposedly been gained through the ritual itself. In other words, God is not glorified at all–the ritual is glorified. It is just a Hindu religious version of the old patent remedy shows so popular in nineteenth and early twentieth century America, sort of a holy infomercial for the puja. To sponsor or attend such an event is considered a mark of devotion, but of devotion to what? Or whom? Do they worship the *gods* or the *goods*?

Such purveyors of worldly goods through worldly gods also teach elaborate modes of behavior as well to gain the goods. These range from long and arduous pilgrimages culminating in more rituals and generous gifts to temples and priests, to avoiding things the gods supposedly do not like and always having at hand what they do like, to the wearing of emblems honoring the chosen deity, to long recitations of the deity's praises, to elaborate personal worship of the deity in a home shrine, to fasting or abstaining from work on days specially devoted to or favored by the deity. Millions of poor Indians fast and worship annually on a day whose observance is guaranteed by the popular scriptures to bring lifelong prosperity by a single observance. No one seems to notice they stay poor year after year. They even assure others that the observance is sure to gain wealth to all who engage in it. The same is true of another day whose observance guarantees the conception and birth of a son (sorry, girls). So barren and sonless couples devoutly observe it year after year with no result—not even a resulting skepticism regarding its efficacy. The money just keeps rolling in—or out, depending on which side you find yourself. And that is the whole idea, really. For notice that Krishna does not say the rituals convey power and pleasure; only that they are supposed to.

The unhappy result

To those attached to enjoyment and power, their minds drawn away by this speech, is not granted steady insight in meditation (2:44).

Prabhavananda: "Those whose discrimination is stolen away by such talk grow deeply attached to pleasure and power. And so they are unable to develop that concentration of the will which leads a man to absorption in God."

The above is a remarkable statement. The word *chetasam* means both "thought" and "mind." In other words, the extravagant promises of ignorant religion, and the scrambling and scratching after the things of this world erode the mind and heart, the higher intelligence of human beings, and the power of the Self that is to be set forth to reveal itself. That is why he has already urged Arjuna to "rid yourself of the bondage of karma" which leads only to rebirth. "The yogi should fix his awareness constantly on the Self,... without desires or possessions" (6:10).

Krishna outlines to us the hierarchy of control in our own makeup, saying: "They say that the senses [indriyas] are superior [to the body], the mind [manasa] is superior to the senses, the intellect [buddhi] is superior to the mind, and much superior to the intellect is the supreme intelligence [param buddhi]" (3:42-43).

Putting forth our mind power to obtain the objects of desire destroys the true intelligence of the Self and substitutes the delusions of the ego, and so "steady insight in meditation is not granted." The Sanskrit literally says, rather awkwardly (in English): "And so the resolute-natured intelligence [buddhi] is not granted in meditation [actually: samadhi]." That is, the highest state of meditation–samadhi–cannot be attained, and the illumined will-power of the buddhi cannot come into force. How terrible! Yet there is a hopeful truth here, as well. If we constantly cut off our desires and addiction to their objects, we will develop the will that enables us to unite ourselves to Brahman.

"Thus constantly engaging himself in the practice of yoga, that yogi, freed from evil, easily contacting [touching] Brahman, attains boundless happiness" (6:28).

PERSPECTIVE ON
SCRIPTURES

Krishna has more to say about materially oriented scriptures and religion, though he just mentions the Vedas:

> The three gunas are the domains of the Vedas. Be free from the triad of the gunas, indifferent to the pairs of opposites, eternally established in reality, free from thoughts of getting and keeping, and established in the Self (2:45).

Again, by "the Vedas" Krishna means the ritualistic portion of the Vedas, the karma-kanda in contrast to the Upanishads, the jnana-kanda, which embody the highest spiritual wisdom and vision ever set down by human beings. They are really two opposing poles, one external and material, the other internal and spiritual. The karma-kanda insists that ritual is the only way to spiritual attainment; the Upanishads affirm exactly the opposite.

Krishna, continuing the theme of the previous verses, insists that however sacred the karma-kanda may claim its rituals to be, they really deal with nothing more than Prakriti, material nature, total involvement with which produces only ignorance and bondage culminating in rebirth.

The gunas

According to Sankhya philosophy, material energy behaves in three modes, or gunas (qualities). We will be considering them at length in

Chapter Fourteen, which is entitled "The Yoga of the Division of the Three Gunas." For now we need only think of them as three forms of material consciousness. Whereas the karma-kanda does nothing more than entangle its adherents in the three gunas, Krishna tells Arjuna that he must overcome the three gunas, that materiality must be transcended by entry into consciousness of the Self (Atman). But it is no easy matter to be free from the bonds of matter. Rather, the gunas must be overcome. This entails a struggle, and not an easy one, either, for Krishna later says to him: "Truly, this maya of mine made of the gunas is difficult to go beyond" (7:14).

The pairs of opposites

The dwandwas, the pairs of opposites, are also material phenomena, such as pleasure and pain, hot and cold, light and darkness, gain and loss, victory and defeat, love and hatred. Usually people think that the ideal is to eliminate one half of a pair and cultivate the other. This is the common attitude of religion throughout the world: seek the "good" and avoid the "bad." But the sages of India discerned that real wisdom is to be established in the state in which the pairs of opposites cannot affect us. We neither seek one nor shun the other, but see them for the momentary appearances they really are, only mirages cast by our own mind.

The word *nirdwandwas* means "untouched by–indifferent to–the pairs of opposites," and also "without the pairs of opposites." At first we are to be indifferent to them when they insinuate themselves into our experience. But in time we are simply without them–they will have ceased to even exist for us. Then we will not need to endure them: they will have vanished like the dreams they are.

Tranquility

"Eternally established in truth [reality]." A simple phrase, but a profound concept. Later in this chapter it is elucidated by Krishna saying: "With attraction and aversion eliminated, even though moving amongst objects of sense, by self-restraint, the self-controlled attains tranquility. In tranquility the cessation of all sorrows is produced for him. Truly, for the tranquil-minded the buddhi immediately becomes steady" (2:64, 65). This truth is illustrated by an incident from the life of Yogiraj Shyama Charan Lahiri Mahasaya. He continually expounded the idea that the goal of yoga is to be established in *sthirattwa*, in perfect tranquility.

A group of spiritual leaders in Calcutta once conspired against Lahiri Mahasaya. They invited him to join an evening discussion on spiritual matters. Lahiri Mahasays accepted the invitation and accordingly attended the meeting.

The conspirators had well prepared themselves to trap Lahiri Mahasaya. For example, if Lahiri Mahasaya were to express his preference for a particular deity, or *ishta devata*, then a particular leader would find exception to that choice.

In fact, each member of the group selected a particular *devata* (deity) such as Lord Vishnu, Lord Krishna, Lord Siva and the Goddess Kali, and prepared to debate and challenge Lahiri Mahasaya's choice.

As soon as Lahiri Mahasaya arrived, he was received in the traditional manner and shown proper courtesy. After a while one of the members of the group asked Lahiri Mahasaya, "Upon which deity do you meditate?" Lahiri Mahasaya looked at him but did not reply.

Then another gentleman asked him, "Who is your *ishta devata*?" Lahiri Mahasaya turned his head towards him and looked at him in the same way, while keeping his peace.

Finally, a third gentleman asked him, "Can you tell us upon which deity you usually meditate?"

Lahiri Mahasaya faced him and said very gently, "I meditate on *sthirattva* (tranquility)."

The gentleman replied that he did not understand what was meant by this. Lahiri Mahasaya continued to observe silence.

After some time, another gentleman asked him, "Could you please explain this? I do not understand exactly what you are saying."

Lahiri Mahasaya, as before, continued to maintain silence.

Another gentleman asked, "Can you enlighten me as to what you mean by that? I do not understand at all!" Lahiri Baba told him, "You will not be able to understand, and also I will not be able to make you understand (realize) through words."

The group was at a loss. All of their preparation and conniving had come to naught. Only silence prevailed. All kept silent.

After a long time Lahiri Mahasaya got up and silently prepared to leave the meeting. All showed him the traditional courtesy as he left.

Here we see how to fulfill Krishna's counsel: "Be… eternally established in reality."

Material detachment

Next Krishna utters another simple phrase: "Free from thoughts of getting and keeping." Frankly, this is such a high ideal there is little to say about it, except that it refers to intangibles as well as tangibles. To transcend the impulse to acquire or keep is itself liberation, for only a liberated consciousness is capable of such a condition (or non-condition). Practically speaking, the best policy is to immerse ourselves in sadhana that leads to liberation. Then we will attain the state Krishna has set forth to us.

Scriptures

> **For the wise Brahmin with true knowledge, a great deal in all the Vedas are of as much value as a well when there is a flood all around (2:46).**

As already said, the Vedas consist of both the karma-kanda, ritualistic expositions, and the jnana-kanda, expositions of the knowledge of the Self–just as other scriptures contain teachings regarding purely external life and also inner, spiritual wisdom. The enlightened need neither of them, both being irrelevant, but for different reasons.

The karma-kanda has been seen to be a force for bondage and therefore rejected by the liberated. The jnana-kanda, the Upanishads, on the other hand, has not been rejected by them. Rather the liberated embody and prove the truth of the Upanishads. For them the Upanishads are like a user's manual for a machine. Once the operation and maintenance of the machine is learned, the manual is no longer consulted. As long as they were learning, the Upanishads were essential, but once they attained true Knowing, they had no more use.

So the "uselessness" of the karma-kanda and jnana-kanda are of a vastly differing character. I point this out because the two should never be equated. For the jnani the karma-kanda is an obstacle, but the jnana-kanda is a valued though outgrown teacher, a door that is unnecessary only because it has now been passed through.

Yet I must add that I truly believe that no one ever goes beyond the Gita; that it should be our constant companion as long as we exist on this earth plane.

HOW NOT TO ACT

The next (third) chapter of the Bhagavad Gita is devoted to the subject of Karma Yoga–the yoga of selfless action, including the performance of one's own duty and the service of humanity. In my opinion, the final and complete word on the subject is Swami Vivekananda's small book *Karma Yoga*, and I recommend that you obtain and study it. But for now let us consider Krishna's anticipation of the subject.

> **Your authority is for action alone, never to its fruits at any time. Never should the fruits of action be your motive; and never should there be attachment to inaction in you (2:47).**

Karma/work and its fruit

Ordinarily when we speak of karma we mean the law of cause and effect, but it also means action or work. This is the usual meaning in the Bhagavad Gita. Karma includes both physical and mental activity, including both thought and feeling, which is why Jesus said that the mere desire to do evil was a form of committing the act (Matthew 5:21-22, 28). As Krishna says: "The path of action is difficult to understand.... He who perceives inaction in action and action in inaction–such a man is wise among men" (4:17-18). The fruit of action, *karmaphala*, is the result or effect of activity, both actual and intended.

Authorization to work

In some translations the expression "right to act" is used, but that is a very poor translation of *adhikara*, although just about everyone uses it.

Adhikara means authority, qualification, jurisdiction, or prerogative; only peripherally does it mean privilege—and never a "right."

Basically, by taking human birth we have been authorized or enabled to engage in action. In truth, we cannot escape such an engagement. Therefore we must learn from Krishna how to do it correctly. And even before that we have to learn how to view our action and its authorization. Krishna is teaching us the correct perspective we must have on our entire life, which consists of nothing but action and reaction to that action.

The way in and the way out

Presently we are caught in the net of constant activity, and consequently enmeshed in bondage. Action has put us in this mess and action can free us from it. As Swami Sivananda translates an upcoming verse (2:50): "Endowed with wisdom (evenness of mind), one casts off in this life both good and evil deeds; therefore, devote yourself to Yoga; Yoga is skill in action." We must walk the tightrope of right action, as Buddha has counseled us. Krishna has given us several principles we must understand and assimilate.

Your authority is for action alone...

The sole purpose of the universe—and our involvement in it—is evolution. And all growth is movement, either automatic or intentional. For us who have come to the level of conscious self-awareness, action is the answer. Until now we have been carried along by the wave of mechanical, involuntary movement—which was necessary, since we did not have the requisite level of development to take charge of our own movement forward. But now we do. During the period in which we were being impelled along by the currents of cosmic life (that are indicated by the movement of the planets), alternately emerging from and being submerged in the ocean of samsara, we set many forces in motion by our response to those ups and downs. These forces took the form of both karma and samskara (mental impressions from past action). So now that we are on our own to a significant degree, we have to deal with them, mostly by neutralizing them or using them as ascending steps in our inner growth. Because of all this we are authorized to engage in actions.

It is our desire for objects and our engaging in work meant to result in the fulfillment of those desires that has entangled us and put us in our present state of confusion and bondage. To engage in further action with desire as the moving force would only compound our dilemma. So we act for the sake of action alone–not random action, but action which will free us from the compulsion to act. In other words, we begin to act as free, conscious beings, not as semi-conscious wanderers or compulsives. By acting we bring about freedom from action.

...never to its fruits at any time

Right action is not supposed in and of itself to "bear fruit," but to free us from all "harvesting." Usually, when we act we put ourselves under the necessity of reaping the effects of the action, "for whatsoever a man soweth, that shall he also reap" (Galatians 6:7). But there is a way to act in which there is no result except the freedom from further action. Some actions forge chains and other actions break them. The latter is needful for our progress.

Never should the fruits of actions be your motive

Results in the form of external effects are not at all what ultimately matters. What does matter is the effect of action on our state of consciousness. To free our consciousness we must be totally free of desire for results. When we can act in this way all bonds drop away and we are free–not Self-realized as some erroneously think, but free to move on to higher degrees of evolution without any more entanglements. Then Self-realization is possible.

And never should there be attachment to inaction in you

It has to be admitted that a great deal of "detachment," "indifference," "uninvolvement," and "renunciation" is nothing more than classical laziness on the mental and physical levels. In India especially we find a lot of "renouncers" and "non-attachers"–both monastic and non-monastic–that are simply bundles of tamasic ignorance and indolence.

Years ago I heard a minister tell of a man in his home town who was "called by God," and consequently refused to engage in any "worldly" activity. All day long (in good weather) he sat on the front porch so he would be seen and read the Bible—or at least turned the pages in a leisurely manner. The pages were gilt-edged, so they flashed and gleamed in the sunlight. Occasionally his wife would ask him to do a simple task or give her a little help. He would smile, lift his voice so the neighbors could hear, and reply: "Why, wife, do you not know 'that I must be about my Father's business'?" And that was that. Much later I saw a television program in which some people announced: "We just want to do our own thing." When asked: "What *is* your 'own thing'?" They answered: "*Nothing*." Krishna warns us against this vacuousness of mind and heart.

By the way, Krishna urges us to *desireless* action, but not to *motiveless* action. There is a difference. We are to act with a motive: liberation.

HOW TO ACT

Krishna has told us how not to act, and now will tell us how to act.

> Steadfast in yoga, perform actions abandoning attachment, being indifferent to success or failure. It is said that such evenness of mind is yoga (2:48).

Steadfast in yoga, perform actions

The first factor of right action is the all-encompassing factor of fixing the mind and heart in yoga–that is, being constantly engaged in the interior process of yoga whatever the external situation or action. Ultimately it means to do all things with our consciousness united with divine consciousness: God. That is easy to say, but what does it really mean? Krishna is being eminently practical: the only way to act united to divine consciousness is to hold on to that Consciousness through continual immersion in yoga sadhana. "Established in yoga concentration,… he who thinks of me constantly, whose mind never goes elsewhere, for him, the constantly-joined [yoked] yogi, I am easy to attain" (8:12-14). There we have it as easy to see as the oft-cited amalaka fruit in the hand.

Having abandoned attachment

One of the major obstacles in our life is attachment to the fruits of our actions. This, too, will disappear as through interior cultivation our consciousness will turn inward, the inner divine eye will open, and seeing all things in their true nature, the fruits of our actions will no longer seem relevant to us.

Once we have tasted good food, bad food loses all attraction for us. Once we have tasted the Supreme, have touched "the hem of his garment," external attainments will mean very little–and in time will seem nothing. But this holy indifference can only come from touching the Divine. Mental gymnastics in the form of analyzing objects of desire and recounting their defects is ultimately without worth and is even harmful, for thinking so much about them (even though disparagingly) will attach us to them and draw them to us. "For a man dwelling on the objects of the senses, attachment to them is born," Krishna will tell us in the sixty-second verse of this chapter.

We detach ourselves from objects by attaching ourselves to God. It is the only way–not just the best or the easiest.

Become indifferent to success or failure

Even-mindedness in success and failure is impossible to achieve by mind-gaming and is in the final analysis worthless. Here, too, it is the fixing of the consciousness on/in God that does the needful. "Keep your mind on me alone, causing your intellect to enter into me. Thenceforward, without doubt, you shall dwell in me" (12:8). When a person dwells in God, what outside success or failure can mean anything to him? What desire or attachment can arise in someone who is united in consciousness to the Source of all?

So often in spiritual life we think of what we should not do, rather than be intent on what we should do. For example, in the consciousness of spirit greed cannot arise. So there is no need to go around telling ourselves: "I must not let greed enter my mind." Instead we should be intent on remembering God, fixing our mind on Divinity. Then greed will become impossible to us.

It is said that evenness of mind is yoga

Evenness of mind is possible only when the awareness is centered in that which is perfectly stable and still. And that is only a single thing:

Spirit. Everything else is changing and therefore unstable and subject to anxiety and compulsion. "Change and decay all around I see. O Thou Who changest not, abide with me," says the song. But God always abides with and within us. The problem is that *we do not abide* in the consciousness of God. And *this* is what is yoga: the uniting (joining–yoga) of our mind with God.

"Lose thyself in him, even as the arrow is lost in the target" (Mundaka Upanishad 2.2.4).

RIGHT PERSPECTIVE

Action is inferior by far to buddhi yoga. Seek refuge in enlightenment; pitiable are those who are motivated by action's fruit (2:49).

It is a fact that many aspiring yogis of East and West believe that mere good or right action is karma yoga. This is not so, as our study of the Gita will reveal later on. Karma yoga is acting with the mind fixed on God–not on the action. This is the real purpose of all action: the perfection of awareness. That is, by outer action we affect our internal state of consciousness. When we understand this and live out our life with this perspective, contentment is assured. Activity with desire is egocentric, whereas desireless action is spirit-oriented and results in freedom. An advanced disciple of Swami Sivananda once told a gathering of American yogis that Swami Sivananda was the only true karma yogi she had met in her life.

Action is inferior by far to buddhi yoga

Karma yoga is done by yoking our consciousness with the buddhi, the principle of enlightenment, our highest "mind" in the form of enlightened intuition. When the awareness is centered in–not just pointed toward–the divine consciousness that is common to both the individual Self (jivatman) and the Supreme Self (Paramatman), then we have peace, both because the Self is transcendental and beyond all possibility of agitation and because in the enlightened state we understand all that is going on as well as the roots of what is taking place. Having perfect peace and perfect understanding, we abide in perfect tranquility. In just a few verses from now Krishna will begin describing exactly what that state is and how it manifests in the illumined individual.

Buddhi Yoga is the Yoga of Intelligence which later came to be called Jnana Yoga, the Yoga of Knowledge.

Seek refuge in buddhi!

Krishna does not bother with short-sighted strategies, but tells us to literally shoot for the top, saying: "Seek refuge in enlightenment [buddhau]!" Buddhau means the state of consciousness that is attained through–and is–the buddhi. The buddhi is the source of both thought and intuition. If we center our awareness in that we will become ready for the ultimate intuition that is Brahmajnana, the knowledge of Brahman.

What other refuge can there be? Any conditioned state of mind must by its very nature be temporary. However beneficial any external condition, place, or object may be, still it, too, cannot last forever. But Brahman does. Most importantly, the Upanishads tell us the paramount truth: "He who knows Brahman becomes Brahman. He passes beyond all sorrow. He overcomes evil. Freed from the fetters of ignorance he becomes immortal" (Mundaka Upanishad 3.2.9). "He who knows Brahman attains the supreme goal. Brahman is the abiding reality, he is pure knowledge, and he is infinity. He who knows that Brahman dwells within the lotus of the heart becomes one with him and enjoys all blessings" (Taittiriya Upanishad 2:1:3).

It is true: "Pitiable are those who are motivated by action's fruit."

How to be free

> He who abides in the buddhi casts off here in this world both good and evil deeds. Therefore, yoke yourself to yoga. [This is a play on words since "yoke" and "yoga" have the same root: *yuj*.] Yoga is skill in action (2:50). The buddhi yogi "casts off, here in the world, both good and evil actions." It is

not a matter of "pie in the sky" after death. The buddhi yogi attains right here in this world.

The concept of casting off both good and evil actions is often misunderstood, so we should give it a careful scrutiny. Right away we must comprehend that Krishna does not mean that enlightened people are beyond the rules and can do any stupid or evil thing that crosses their minds, that somehow it is all right for them but not for us. This idiocy has produced the contemporary situation in both the West and the East in which we do not expect from the abounding gurus, masters and avatars the basic decency and good sense that we demand from ourselves and everyone else. Simple civility is not even expected of these miscreants, much less the conduct that Krishna will be telling us is the infallible mark of the illumined individual. There is no need for me to outline their iniquitous and preposterous minds and conduct. Krishna will unmask them by informing us as how the really enlightened act. Then if we do not get the idea it is because we do not want to.

But now let us return to the concept of freedom from virtue and vice. Liberation (moksha) includes freedom from all conditioning. Unhappily, most religion is nothing but conditioning, based on fear and greed: do what is wrong and you will be punished, and do what is right and you will be rewarded. Since fear and greed are instincts formed and rooted in our past incarnations in the subhuman levels, they are unworthy of human beings, much less those that aspire to divinity. Right conduct must be a free choice. A compulsion to do good and a compulsion to avoid evil is instinctual, not intelligent, and therefore not a matter of buddhi yoga. No matter how well-intentioned the formation of such compulsion might be, the aspiring yogi must eliminate all such instinctual reactions. Buddhi yoga arises from deep within the individual. Any external influence or coercion militates again this.

A few verses previously we were told: "Be indifferent to the pairs of opposites." Why? Because they are inherent in one another, they are inseparable. Anyone with experience or observation knows that love and hate easily morph back and forth, for they possess the same root—the ego. The same, then, is true of virtue and vice, good and evil, when based on the ego-personality of the conditioned individual. We often accuse people of being hypocrites, when actually they are under the sway of the dualities. We cannot cling to one and hope to be free of the other, for they are one and the same—only the polarity is different. True goodness, true virtue, has no opposite. Krishna is not speaking of this higher level, but rather of that on which Arjuna, in the grip of egoic emotion, is functioning.

Unity on all levels is the goal of the yogi, and that transcends the classifications of good or evil. The "good" of the enlightened, on the other hand, is not just relative good—it is the embodiment of divine good.

Back to the heart of things

Krishna, like any worthy teacher, again points us to the very core of the matter, saying: "Therefore, yoke yourself to yoga." There is really no other way to achieve anything true or real in spiritual life. "Seek ye first the kingdom of God, and his righteousness; and all these things shall be added unto you" (Matthew 6:33), said Jesus. We need not concern ourselves with a multitude of spiritual goals, but fix our intention on the single purpose of all relative existence: union with Brahman. This is why Jesus also said: "Martha, Martha, thou art careful and troubled about many things: but one thing is needful: and Mary hath chosen that good part, which shall not be taken away from her" (Luke 10:41, 42).

Skill in action

Krishna is not speaking of efficient work when he says: "Yoga is skill in action." The skill in action which Krishna declares to be yoga is action performed with ourselves yoked to yoga, united with Unity. It is work in which remembrance of God and centering in the Self goes on uninterruptedly. If we are distracted by our work and forget to maintain our sadhana throughout, then it is not skill in action. Only an adept yogi can engage in real karma yoga, for only those skilled in meditation are capable of karma yoga.

The way of the sages

> Those who are truly established in the buddhi, the wise ones,
> having abandoned the fruits of action, freed from the bondage
> of rebirth, go to the place that is free from pain (2:51).

That place or abode is our very Self, for That alone is free from pain
or the possibility of pain.

Now Krishna sums it all up for us:

> **When your buddhi crosses beyond the mire of delusion, then
> you shall be disgusted with the to-be-heard and what has
> been heard. When your buddhi stands, fixed in deep medita-
> tion, unmoving, disregarding the Vedic ritual-centered per-
> spective, then you will attain yoga (union) (2:52-53).**

WISDOM ABOUT THE WISE

Arjuna said: What is the description of him who is steady of insight, of him who is steadfast in deep meditation, of him who is steady in thought? How does he speak? How does he sit? How does he move about? (2:54).

Earlier, I spoke of how some supposed spiritual figures in both East and West are given a free hand to devastate the minds and lives of others just because they bear the title of "guru" or "avatar." This is because of a complete miscomprehension of the nature of enlightenment and how it manifests in the consciousness and behavior of the enlightened. In response to Arjuna's question, Krishna tells us everything we need to know–and which we should ever keep in mind when encountering supposedly enlightened people. Krishna will take eighteen verses to give Arjuna and us the total picture. Here are the first eight of them.

Without "wants"

The Holy Lord said: When he leaves behind all the desires of the mind, contented in the Self by the Self, then he is said to be steady in wisdom (2:55).

Nothing could be easier to understand: *an enlightened person wants nothing*, finding total fulfillment in the Self–both individual and universal.

Therefore when we see people with spiritual goals such as serving God in others or exhibiting a veritable passion about a world mission or saving or enlightening others, we can know they are not illumined, and therefore incapable of doing any of those things in a real manner, however fine the exterior machinery might appear.

A true spiritual teacher has no expectation of others whatsoever, never foists demands on them. Knowing that all growth comes from within, never from an outer factor–including him–the worthy teacher knows that it is his duty to teach, and that is the absolute end of the matter. From then on it is up to the student to either follow the teaching or not. If he asks for help or advice from the teacher, it is the teacher's duty to give the requested assistance *and then leave the matter alone.* In spiritual life as well as material life there is a division of labor that should be adhered to. Under the guise of love or devotion there should be no violation of spiritual law. And no authentic teacher will ever break any law.

In contrast

It is virtually impossible to find any popular "spiritual" teacher that does not live like the jewel in the lotus–both materially and socially. Although there is a pretense that their disciples are insistent upon it, it is really the guru that demands continual adulation and material accouterments that would have been considered extreme even for a Di Medici monarch. One guru in India has himself and his wife weighed every year and given their combined weights in gold. And the palatial living quarters of the gurus are like overdone satires of the houses of the most vulgar *nouveau riche.*

At the bottom of this outrageous aggrandizement on the psychological and material levels is a profound sense of insecurity, discontentment and often self-loathing on the part of the super-guru. I have had experience of this firsthand when visiting their ashrams and conversing with them. The pathology is very evident. Let me give a single example.

Once I was the guest of a super-guru after having spent several days at a yoga retreat sponsored by his organization. I had spoken to the retreatants several times during those days, and was being rewarded by being invited into the August Presence. (I had previously been asked to sign a legal document stating that I would never ask the institution for money in the future as payment for my speaking. I had refused to sign–and never asked them for money.)

As we sat at the table, being served by anxious, hushed, and devoted "gopis," Super-G began to tell me about the well-known rock groups that had asked him to come speak during their concerts both inside and outside the United States. Since I disliked all popular music (especially rock music), and being aware of the negative character of the groups he was naming, I was listening with a mixture of amazement and disgust. And then I got the idea: *he was trying to make me jealous!* Did he really think that, having lived with great masters in India and having received the grace of so many other great saints, I would be impressed by a listing of these aberrant drug-addicted pandemonium peddlers?

More was to come. Since I did not swoon at the listing of the rock groups, he passed on to speaking tours. He had been invited to speak in the Soviet Union! And also in a host of other gruesome places where there could not possibly be genuine spiritual interest. This list was peppered with the names of celebrities who would either be sponsoring or accompanying him.

That left me unaffected, so he moved on to the subject of living accommodations. First I got a recounting of what centers of his organization were engaged in providing luxurious apartments and houses for him, even stocking a complete set of his tailor-made silk clothes so he would never need to travel around the country with luggage. I dislike travel and being away from our ashram, so that moved me not.

Finally he resorted to real estate. First of all, a road for his exclusive use was being cleared in a local forest where some disciples had managed to purchase a large tract of land so he could be totally isolated.

(No matter how "loving" and "giving" the super gurus are, they like to have inaccessible retreats away from their disciples, some of them–usually the Americans–even doing some kind of "early retirement" so they will not have to have contact with their adoring devotees. Some of them claim to need solitude so they can "write," though little or nothing is ever published. However one super-guru emerged every week from his state of retreat to travel some hours to a major vacation-playground to take saxophone lessons from a well-known jazz musician.)

After the road was put in, a renowned architect was going to come and study the land and design a house specifically to fit in with the landscape and (of course) the ecology of the forest. Then the house would be built by the devotees–or at least by their money.

He had come to the end of the line. I was not impressed. I was appalled. He was miffed. I was glad to get out of there never to return. Fortunately I had many memories of simple, even barren, rooms in which I had sat with great saints in India, rooms where they stayed in joyful contentment, living the simplest of lives. Before going to India I had seen the two tiny rooms in which Paramhansa Yogananda, head of a world-wide spiritual organization, had lived for over a quarter of a century, as well as the simple little kitchen across the hall where he had so often cooked for his beloved students.

"Contented in the Self by the Self, then he is said to be steady in wisdom." I had seen Krishna's words verified in the lives of the true yogis.

Free!

> He whose mind is not agitated in misfortunes, freed from desire for pleasures, from whom passion, fear and anger have departed, steady in thought–such a man is said to be a sage (2:56).

"The kingdom of God is peace and joy in the Holy Ghost" (Romans 14:17). Living in the inner kingdom of infinite peace and joy, the enlightened are not affected by fortune or misfortune, for nothing can change their spiritual status. "The same in pain or in pleasure... [he] is fit for absorption in Brahman" (14:24, 26). Even for us, "He whose happiness is within, whose delight is within, whose illumination is within: that yogi, identical in being with Brahman, attains Brahmanirvana" (5:24).

Desire, fear and anger are manifestations of what we may justifiably call "raw ego." Other emotions are further removed from the source and their character not so easy to detect. This unholy trinity is thoroughly intertwined. They are ego-based responses to stimuli of differing character.

Desire arises when we think something external can change our inner or outer status for the better (or at least more enjoyable), fear arises when we feel endangered, and anger arises when we are mistreated or our desire thwarted. All other responses are permutations of these three, their offspring. The enlightened is free of them.

Please be wary of those who pretend that when they manifest these passions they are "just lilas," "mere appearances," "writings on water," etc. How can they benefit you by deceiving you or causing you pain and confusion by their seeming negative behavior? Lesser teachers may do so, erroneously thinking it is the only way to help you–as a kind of psychological shock treatment. But a truly illumined person will do no such thing. Their very presence can work in you the necessary changes. I have both experienced it and witnessed it.

Broken bonds

> **He who is without desire in all situations, encountering this or that, pleasant or unpleasant, not rejoicing or disliking–his wisdom stands firm (2:57).**

There are some key words here we need to look at.

Sarvatra means "on all sides," "everywhere," and "in all things."

Anabhisnehas means "without affection" "unimpassioned," and "nondesirous." So Krishna is saying that at all times, in all places, and on every level of existence, the wise one has no attraction toward something, no emotional reaction toward anything, and absolutely no desire for anything. Further, he is neither elated nor disturbed when *prapya*–encountering, obtaining, attaining or incurring–that which is *shubhashubham*–pleasant or unpleasant or a mixture of both.

Shubhashubham can also mean lucky or unlucky, fortunate or unfortunate. In other words, nothing moves him, for *tasya prajna pratishthita*–his consciousness, his awareness, and the wisdom that arises therefrom is established, standing firm at all times. For nothing can be added to him or taken away. For him pleasure and pain, gain and loss, victory and defeat, are all one and the same (see 2:38). "Content with what comes unbidden, beyond the dualities [pairs of opposites] and free from envy, the same in success or failure, even though acting, he is not bound" (4:22). "He has no purpose at all in action or in non-action; and he has no need of any being for any purpose whatsoever" (3:18). He is free indeed.

Living within

> And when he withdraws completely the senses from the objects of the senses, as the tortoise draws in its limbs, his wisdom is established firmly (2:58).

This is not referring to just control of the senses in a mechanical way, but to the fact that the enlightened person lives thoroughly within himself. Although we usually think of the senses as the material organs of perception, in reality the senses are astral and causal, and their main purpose is to see in the spirit. So the liberated person truly lives according to nature on all levels. Seeing with the inner eye, hearing with the inner ear, etc., he sees and hears true. Also, it means that when he withdraws the senses he does not become inert and unconscious in what the yogis jokingly call jada samadhi–a state of mental inertia which is neither meditation or samadhi. Rather, he is more conscious than otherwise. And it also means that when an accomplished yogi withdraws his senses he does not fall asleep as a consequence–something I expect we have all done to our embarrassment.

Desires

> Sense-objects turn away from the abstinent, yet the taste for them remains. But the taste also turns away from him who has seen the Supreme (2:59).

Prabhavananda: "The abstinent run away from what they desire but carry their desires with them: when a man enters Reality, he leaves his desires behind him."

How much is said in this simple sentence! The truly enlightened are not simply free from desire, they have become *incapable* of desire. This is extremely important to know. We must apply this to ourselves, and not foolishly think that just because we avoid the objects of desire and thereby experience no desire, that we are truly desireless. For just being without desire is not the same as having passed into the realm of consciousness where desire cannot exist.

The senses

> The troubling senses forcibly carry away the mind of even the striving man of wisdom. Restraining all these senses, he should sit in yoga, intent on me. Surely, he whose senses are controlled–his consciousness stands steadfast and firm (2:60-61).

People get fooled in relation to the senses, too. I think somewhere I have told about a little girl I knew whose parents tried for years to keep her from sucking her thumb. Even in the primary grades she sat around with her thumb in her mouth. One day, when she was visiting our house, she was watching television with thumb in mouth. At one point she pulled out her thumb, called to my stepmother who was in the kitchen: "Guess what! I don't suck my thumb anymore!" and put it right back in. Business as usual.

It is amazing to see the difference between the ascetic approaches of Western and Eastern religions. Western spiritual writers blame everything on demons, claiming that every evil thought and impulse comes from evil spirits. The yogis (Hindu, Taoist, and Buddhist), on the other hand, understand that these negative thoughts and impulses come from within us–that we are totally responsible for the folly that foams up in our minds. Western ascetics wear themselves out battling and driving away demons. What can they achieve by living out this fantasy? Certainly negative spirits exist, but what can they do to us in the final analysis? It is the enemy within–our own ego and its ignorance–that really harms us and none other.

A religion that does not teach its adherents to recognize and deal with their own culpability is right to be obsessed with sin, for what else can it produce? No wonder that Jews, Christians, and Moslems welter in fixation on sin and evil in contrast with the Hindus, Taoists and Buddhists who focus on innate holiness and perfection.

There was a great saint in the West–a Pope, actually–who tried to bring some light into the of darkness of Christian sin-consciousness and sin-obsession, but instead was condemned for heresy. Poor Pope Pelagius is immortalized only in Christian fulminations against the "Pelagian heresy" that man is essentially good and capable of holiness. Unintentionally, Roget's 21st Century Thesaurus gives an insight on this. Under the heading of "obsession," the first entry is "attraction." There you have it. Obsession with sin is attraction to sin; preoccupation with holiness is attraction to holiness. You get what you fix your mind on.

"Therefore at all times remember me, and fight with your mind [manas] and intellect [buddhi] fixed on me. Thus without doubt you shall come to me. With mind made steadfast by yoga, which turns not to anything else, to the Divine Supreme Spirit he goes, meditating on him" (8:7-8).

"Keep your mind on me alone, causing your intellect to enter into me. Thenceforward, without doubt, you shall dwell in me" (12:8).

WISDOM ABOUT BOTH THE
FOOLISH AND THE WISE

The next ten verses of the Gita are mixed in character. They tell us about both the foolish and the wise.

Forty-five years ago I read the Gita in Swami Prabhavananda's translation, which I still recommend as the best for getting an overview of the Gita's message. The Gita was so wonderful, so enlivening, that I read it while walking to school (university) and while walking back home. Home! It was not the building where I was residing that was home. Sanatana Dharma, the truth embodied in the Gita, was my true home. And I had at last found it.

Everything about the Gita astonished and delighted me, but one moment stands out vividly. I read the verses quoted in the next section, and paused in genuine awe. This book told me the exact stages of the mind as it becomes enmeshed in delusion and as it frees itself from delusion. What a find! What a contrast to the puerile religion I had heretofore struggled and agonized to make sense of–because it had no sense. Such simple and yet profound wisdom to be found in the Gita was surely the path to freedom. I have never changed my mind.

Human beings are rational creatures, at least potentially. It is our mind, our intellect, that is our distinctive mark. Animals certainly show both intelligence and even intuition, but the gap between them and us is virtually infinite. How terrible, then, to be trapped in behaviorist, dogmatic religions that have no psychology whatsoever, that comprehend nothing of the human status and composition, yet fume at us that we are sinners and worthy of divine punishment. Such religions are nothing more than versions of Animal Trainer (God) and Animals (us). The Trainer is motivated by an irrational and insane drive to be adored and obeyed while employing means that can only make him hated and feared. The animals are living on instinct alone (called "faith"), dominated by fear and greed. When the animals do their tricks right they get rewarded; when they do not, they get the whip. And when they get "retired" from earthly life, if they have performed well they will get yummies forever, and if they have not performed well they will be shunted into a dungeon and live in torture and misery forever. The more personal religions which endeavor to bring in emotion in the guise of love and devotion are equally ugly and irrational. With them it is all a matter of Abusive Parent and Abused Children.

To find the truth of the Eternal Self, the inner Tao, the Buddha Nature, is the only alternative to mind-numbness, atheism, or madness. The Bhagavad Gita is the revealer of truth, of reality. It awakens, inspires, and enables us in the unfoldment of our true nature.

How not to do it

> For a man dwelling on the objects of the senses, attachment to them is born. From attachment desire is born. And from [thwarted] desire anger is born. From anger arises delusion; from delusion, loss of memory; from loss of memory, destruction of intelligence. From destruction of intelligence one is lost (2:62-63).

It is true that the journey of a thousand miles begins with the first step. In these two verses Krishna has described the entire journey, beginning with thinking of sensory objects and experience and ending in total loss, in destruction. Each step should be considered well.

Thinking (dwelling on)

Thought is power—magnetic power, particularly. That is, thought can draw or repel whatever is thought about, depending upon the polarity of the individual mind. Many times we see that people bring to themselves the things they continually think about, but we also see that thinking about something can repel it from a person. For example, the Franciscan Order is almost obsessed with the idea of poverty, yet it is one of the wealthiest institutions in the world. Thinking about poverty brought them wealth! This is not said in jest. I have seen people draw to themselves the things they detested, and seen others drive out of their lives the things they yearned for. It is a matter of the polarity of the thought force, of magnetic energy.

As a rule, though, thought brings to us what we think about. Even if we begin by disliking or opposing the object of thought, in time we become attached to it, either by coming to like it (whether or not we admit the liking) or becoming unable to dispel it from our minds. We see this in the lives of many crusaders. They become what they oppose. In fact, they often oppose something to cover up their secret attraction to it.

It has long been known that the opposite of love is not hate, but indifference. Krishna is aware of this, and is counseling us to simply ignore that which we do not wish to become involved with. That is why in meditation we ignore any distractions and just keep relaxed in the awareness of the process of meditation–and nothing else. If we do this, in time the distractions will dissolve, and in the meantime, being ignored, they will not be distractions, practically speaking. So if we will not obsess on a subject, it will not touch or capture us. This is a major principle of spiritual life.

The stages of destruction

Dwelling on the objects of the senses, attachment to them is born. Attachment means having an affinity for something, or having some feeling of desire to be aware of it or have it present. It has a definite emotional connotation. It also means to feel some kind of kinship with an object, or to feel a need for it–even a dependency. Attachment also means to be linked to something, to become externally associated with it. This has already been discussed as a consequence of thinking continually of an object.

Obviously there is a positive side to this. If we think of that which is beneficial and elevating we will better ourselves. Sri Ramakrishna once met a young man who was psychically very sensitive, and who was being employed as a medium by some spiritualists in Calcutta. He spoke to him a truth that we should never forget or neglect to embody in our lives: "My son, if you think about ghosts you will become a ghost. If you think about God, you will become God. Which do you prefer?"

From attachment, desire is born. The word used here is *kamas* which means any degree of desire for something–from mild wish to intense craving. The implication is that the nature of objects is one of escalating absorption. We cannot stop at simple attachment. If we permit attachment, it will in time grow into something much worse: controlling addiction. This is the path to loss of freedom, to enslavement.

From [thwarted] desire anger is born. If we do not get what we want, or if we get it and then lose it, or if we get it and find it is not what we wanted–or less than what we desired–anger (krodha) arises in varying degrees and forms.

From anger arises delusion [moha]. We not only lose our freedom through addiction to objects, we also lose our rational faculty. For when our addictions are thwarted we respond with the ultimate irrationality: anger, which accomplishes nothing but misery and completely annihilates our good sense and reason. *Sammohas* also means confusion, not in the sense of simple disorientation, but in the sense of breakdown of mental coherence arising from delusion. It is a form of moral insanity.

From delusion, loss of the memory. Smritivibhramah literally means to wander away from what is known (remembered)–from what has been learned through experience. For it is what we know, and remember, from our own experience, inner and outer, that is fundamental to our evolution. That alone is living wisdom, everything else is merely theory, however true it may be objectively. The whole purpose of the chain of births we have undergone is our gaining of practical knowledge, knowledge that is fully ours because it has arisen from our own experience and our insight into that experience. Just as no one can eat for us, so no one, however evolved they may be, can gain knowledge for us, or even impart it to us. Until we know something for ourselves it is nothing more than speculation or theory.

From loss of the memory, destruction of intelligence [buddhi]. Our very faculty of intelligence, the seat of evolution, is destroyed by this amnesia.

This is terrible, for expanding intelligence is the fundamental characteristic of evolution. That is why Krishna speaks so often of buddhi yoga as the path to perfection.

From destruction of intelligence one is lost [destroyed]. When buddhi is destroyed, *we ourselves* are destroyed. (*Pranashyati* means both destroyed or lost.) This is no exaggeration, as the foregoing sections demonstrate. The purpose of our entry into relativity was the development of higher intelligence so we might be fitted to participate in the infinite consciousness of God. If we impair and erode that intelligence we frustrate the very purpose of our (relative) existence.

On the other hand, if we comprehend Krishna's words in this matter, we can see that the conscious deepening of our buddhi is the path to liberation. But most of all we can learn how to never take even the first step on the path to personal destruction. By refusing to allow our minds to mull over that which is delusive, we protect ourselves from future entanglement in the nets of delusion. If we are already somewhere along the path to destruction we can also use this list to see how to reverse the process. For the message of the Gita is always and at all times the message of hope and betterment.

THE WAY OF PEACE

Walking safely

> However, with attraction and aversion eliminated, even
> though moving amongst objects of sense, by self-restraint, the
> self-controlled attains tranquility (2:64).

The words translated "attraction" and "aversion" are *raga* and *dwesha*.
Raga is both emotional (instinctual) and intellectual desire. It may range
from simple liking or preference to intense desire and attraction. Dwesha
is the opposite. It is aversion/avoidance in relation to an object, implying
dislike. This, too, can be emotional (instinctual) or intellectual, ranging
from simple non-preference to intense repulsion, antipathy and even hatred.

We must keep in mind that anything can grow and change. Therefore
simple liking can develop into intense craving, and mild dislike can turn
into intense aversion or hatred. And since opposites are intrinsically linked
to one another and can even turn into one another, the philosophical and
yogic texts frequently speak of raga-dwesha, the continual cycling back
and forth between desire/aversion and like/dislike. Obviously, this makes
for a confused and fragmented life and mind, something from which any
sensible person would wish to extricate himself.

There are a multitude of supposed cures for what ails us. The vast majority do not work because they are not really aimed at what truly ails us. The
rest usually do not work because they are based on a miscomprehension

of the nature of the problem, or because they are simply nonsensical and time-wasters. This is true of most religion and of a great deal that is called yoga.

If we look at this verse we discover that Krishna is speaking of a very real inner state in which the individual is utterly free–and incapable–of raga and dwesha, and not just a psychological alteration coming from insight into or analysis of the defects of addicting objects. In fact, just the opposite will happen, for "thinking about sense-objects will attach you to sense-objects," as we considered previously. This is a law, and we will be wise to keep it in mind. There is no use in trying to talk ourselves out of delusion. We must dispel delusion–not by concentrating on delusion or resisting it, but by attaining jnana: spiritual knowledge coming from our own direct experience. This will dissolve delusion automatically.

Therefore, when we are no longer subject to attraction and aversion for objects, we can move among them without being influenced or moved in any way. But we must be very sure that we truly are no longer susceptible to them, and not just going through a temporary period in which we find ourselves indifferent to them. Such periods are sure to end in re-emergence of passions that in the meantime have grown even stronger within us. Many ascetics have been deluded in this way, so we must be careful.

I have left the most important for last. The Sanskrit has *atmavyashyair vidheyatma*: "having controlled himself by Self-restraint." That is, he has controlled his lower self by moving his consciousness into the higher Self. Until he does so, the lower self drags the higher Self along from birth to birth. But when the higher Self comes into control of the lower self the situation is different indeed.

Atmic consciousness alone is the antidote to all our ills. When the sadhaka no longer acts according to intellectual or instinctual motives, but rather is living out in the objective world the inner life of his Self, then and only then is true peace gained by him. Acting out of intellectual belief, faith, devotion, or even spiritual aspiration, can certainly elevate us, but ultimate peace cannot be found until, centered in the Self, we live our life as a manifestation of Spirit. It was the Self speaking through Jesus that gave the invitation: "Come unto me, all ye that labour and are heavy laden, and I will give you rest. Take my yoke upon you, and learn of me; for I am meek and lowly in heart: and ye shall find rest unto your souls. For my yoke is easy, and my burden is light" (Matthew 11:28-30). When the buddhi rests in the Atman, peace is inevitable. That is what a Master really is: one who lives ever in his Self. Everything else needful follows as a matter of course. And how can this come about? Krishna tells us clearly in the next verse.

> In tranquility the cessation of all sorrows is produced for him. Truly, for the tranquil-minded the buddhi immediately becomes steady (2:65).

Note that the cessation of sorrows is not bestowed on the buddhi yogi, nor does he acquire it. Rather, it is *produced*, it evolves, it grows like an embryo. First is conception, then growth and then birth. It is a process that goes in stages. It does not come like a lightning strike, but slowly and in an orderly manner, *for it is a natural consequence of the yogi's unfoldment through sadhana of his essential nature.* It is evolution, not revolution. This is why the idea of instant enlightenment, of instant liberation, springs from ignorance of the way things are. For the state of liberation through Self-realization is a revelation of the way things have always been. This is the real non-dual teaching of the Gita. The steadiness of the buddhi comes immediately upon the birth, but the birth takes time. That is what buddhi yoga is all about—coming to birth, truly being born again, really becoming a twice-born (dwija).

The uncontrolled

> For the undisciplined there is no wisdom, no meditation. For him who does not meditate there is no peace or happiness (2:66).

Prabhavananda: "The uncontrolled mind does not guess that the Atman is present: how can it meditate? Without meditation, where is peace? Without peace, where is happiness?"

It is a fact: the man who is undisciplined simply has no buddhi–has no intelligence or reason. And since the buddhi is so close to the Atman, without its being clear and operative there is no possibility of awareness of the Atman's existence. Just as there are many levels of intelligence, there are many levels of stupidity. Those who neither believe in nor perceive the reality of the Self are stupid in the higher levels of their being. And you cannot argue or reason with stupidity. Either you are spiritually aware or you are not. It comes from deep within, and no external factor can produce or affect it in any way. Argumentation and debate are positively meaningless in this area. We should realize this and avoid them.

So Krishna is telling us very forthrightly that the undisciplined and uncontrolled mind is no mind at all, spiritually speaking. This is especially significant at the present time when "go with the flow" and "do what you will" are the slogans of the unthinking (i.e. the undisciplined and the uncontrolled). How many times do we have to hear about how terrible censorship is, when in actuality civilized and lawful behavior is nothing but censorship. Nor is this censorship merely a private matter. Otherwise there could be no kind of society or culture at all. So the enemies of civilization and culture screech nonstop about the evils of censorship and control. They express the philosophy of the guilty and the anarchic: the subhuman. They truly do wish to live as animals and not as humans. For discipline, control, and–yes–even self-censorship of behavior are signs of intelligence, of genuine humanity. It is also called conscience. A collection of humans form a society and develop a culture based on the same principles. Of course, wisdom must be the guide, but in a society of true human beings that is always present.

Meditation

What is the paramount purpose of spiritual awareness? Krishna assures us that: "For him who does not meditate there is no peace or happiness." By implication this statement tells us that a person who develops spiritual consciousness will naturally turn to meditation.

This was certainly true in my case. At the age of twenty I did not even have a concept of meditation except just pondering some subject. That is manana–fiddling with the mind. Of dhyanam (true meditation) I had no idea whatsoever. All I knew about yoga was what I gleaned from seeing Clifton Webb standing on his head in the 1948 movie *Sitting Pretty* and saying: "When I do my yogi [sic] I am just out of this world." Also I had seen drawings in *Ripley's Believe It Or Not* of three yogis–one lying on a bed of nails, one with his arm "frozen" upright, and one who had gone blind from staring at the sun. Meditation did not come into any of these encounters. But one day like the proverbial "bolt from the blue" things changed. Here is how I have told about it in an autobiographical sketch:

"A door swung open within my conscious mind within a true 'split second in eternity' and revealed like a vast panorama the full knowledge regarding human birth and evolution–especially its necessary consequence: reincarnation.

"I also perceived the inevitable passage of the human being into higher dimensions of existence for the purpose of evolution far beyond the human status. The soul would continue to incarnate in countless forms of ever-increasing perfection until the final Great Passage could be made. Then it would return back into the Infinite from which it had originally come forth into the great drama of Life. This did not unwind before me or arise within my mind in a continual stream. Rather, it was fully impressed into my consciousness at one lightning flash of insight.

"I walked over to the sofa and sat down without missing a step. There I sat and took several hours to assimilate all I had seen in that moment of illumination. If I had begun to write what I at last *knew*, I could have written an entire book without stopping.

"The longer I sat, the greater grew the wonder and the delight. This was not theological theory from an external force–this was direct knowledge from within. My soul knew it, and now my poor brain was trying to grasp it all so no precious fragment would be lost. What I had forgotten upon coming into this incarnation was once again mine. Delivered from the hell of ignorance regarding the fundamental nature of myself and my life, I feasted on the paradisiacal fruit of eternal remembrance.

"At the same time awareness of the need to cultivate my innate inner wisdom also arose within me. My revelation had demonstrated incontrovertibly to me that real knowledge came from within, that ideas gathered from outside sources needed to be tested in the laboratory of interior life. External concepts, I realized, should only be the stimuli to evoke the spirit's eternal wisdom. Therefore I resolved to devote at least one hour a day in meditation."

The necessity for meditation and the resolve to do so were the immediate effects of my spiritual insight, of the illumination of my buddhi. I certainly did not have Self-realization, but I knew the way to it. And none of this was based on anything other than my awakening to the truth of the Self and its evolution toward freedom in perfection.

Krishna has presented us with a very simple principle: Meditation is the response of the awakening spirit.

Peace and happiness

"For him who does not meditate there is no peace or happiness." Peace and happiness are sought by all except the profoundly evil or the profoundly insane. The pursuit of happiness was a motivating factor in our American Declaration of Independence, and understood as a divine impulse manifesting within the individual.

Meditation brings peace and happiness, but meditation is not just one of many ways to peace and happiness. Krishna reveals to us that it is the only way.

Shanti is peace, calmness, tranquility, and contentment. *Sukham* is happiness and joy. They are the attributes of the Self, which is why Saint Paul wrote: "The fruit of the Spirit is…joy [and] peace" (Galatians 5:22). And: "The kingdom of God is…peace and joy" (Romans 14:17).

CALMING THE STORM

When the mind is led about by the wandering senses, it carries away the understanding like the wind carries away a ship on the waters. The intelligent, buddhic awareness of him whose senses are withdrawn from the objects of the senses on all sides will be found firmly established (2:67-68).

The theme of peace is being continued in these two verses, and its imagery brings to mind the following: "When the even was come, he [Jesus] saith unto them, Let us pass over unto the other side. And when they had sent away the multitude, they took him even as he was in the ship. And there were also with him other little ships. And there arose a great storm of wind, and the waves beat into the ship, so that it was now full. And he was in the hinder part of the ship, asleep on a pillow: and they awake him, and say unto him, Master, carest thou not that we perish? And he arose, and rebuked the wind, and said unto the sea, Peace, be still. And the wind ceased, and there was a great calm.... And they said one to another, What manner of man is this, that even the wind and the sea obey him?" (Mark 4:35-41) Rather than being some special, unique person that we can only admire, Jesus was exactly what each one of must become. We, too, must bring peace into our stormy minds.

The storm

It is the wind and rain of the senses that "carries away one's understanding, as the wind carries away a ship on the waters." However much the "captain" of the buddhi grasps the wheel and tries to hold the ship steady on its course, the struggle is hopeless. This is because, as the verse literally says, the mind wanders after the senses and becomes guided by them, losing its intelligent awareness (*prajnam*). Caught then in the heaving waters of samsara, of constant birth and death, with their attendant anguish, each of us is carried away by the waves, lost and disoriented completely.

Swami Prabhavananda renders this verse: "The wind turns a ship from its course upon the waters: the wandering winds of the senses cast man's mind adrift and turn his better judgment from its course." "Better judgment" is the translation Swami Prabhavananda uses for prajnam. Prajnam means both consciousness and awareness, and includes the knowledge gained by the evolving bodies of the Atman. Just as Krishna has described before that we lose "memory," the lesson of experience, it is prajnam that we lose.

The statement that we are turned from our course points out a basic truth: by nature we are all "on course," and our drifting is unnatural. Therefore when we set our wills to recover our course, there is no doubt that we will succeed. It is inevitable. In the Gita Arjuna says to Krishna: "The mind is truly unstable, troubling, strong and unyielding. I believe it is hard to control–as hard to control as the wind" (6:34). And Krishna will agree. But the mind must be subdued, nevertheless. That is easy to say, but *how?* "The awareness of him whose senses are withdrawn from the objects of the senses on all sides will be found firmly established." And how do we effectively say, "Peace, be still" to the senses?

The mind

We must understand that the senses are simply instruments (indriyas) of the mind, that although they "cast man's mind adrift" this is the reversal of the natural order, that it is the mind that is meant to "drive" the senses, the way a charioteer drives the horses that pull the chariot. Krishna surely had in mind this passage from the Upanishads:

"Know that the Self is the rider, and the body the chariot; that the intellect is the charioteer, and the mind the reins. The senses, say the wise, are the horses; the roads they travel are the mazes of desire. The wise call the Self the enjoyer when he is united with the body, the senses, and the mind. When a man lacks discrimination and his mind is uncontrolled, his senses are unmanageable, like the restive horses of a charioteer. But when a man has discrimination and his mind is controlled, his senses, like the well-broken horses of a charioteer, lightly obey the rein. He who lacks discrimination, whose mind is unsteady and whose heart is impure, never reaches the goal, but is born again and again. But he who has discrimination, whose mind is steady and whose heart is pure, reaches the goal, and having reached it is born no more. The man who has a sound understanding for charioteer, a controlled mind for reins—he it is that reaches the end of the journey, the supreme abode of Vishnu, the all pervading" (Katha Upanishad 1:3:3-9).

The awakened mind

Krishna expresses it to Arjuna this way:

> **The man of restraint is awake in what is night for all beings. That in which all beings are awake is night for the sage who truly sees (2:69).**

By "awake" Krishna means having the awareness centered in an area of existence. There are, then, two kinds of minds: those that are awake in the Atman and those that are awake in the senses, consciousnesses centered in the spirit and consciousnesses centered in matter. And of course, to be centered in something will cause us to be identified with it. Some identify with the immutable, imperishable Self, and some identify with the ever-changing, perishable world and the body which links us to that world. The Self, on the other hand, links us to the Supreme Self, Brahman. Both types are awake, having reached the evolutionary level of humanity, but the difference is vast, even abysmal.

How Jesus saw it

Jesus speaks of the awake mind in this way: "The light of the body is the eye: if therefore thine eye be single, thy whole body shall be full of light. But if thine eye be evil, thy whole body shall be full of darkness. If therefore the light that is in thee be darkness, how great is that darkness!" (Matthew 6:22-23) Two words in these verses are translated "light." The first is *luchnos*, which means a lamp or something that gives light. The other is *foteinos*, which means to be radiant or full of light. "Body" is *soma*, which not only means "bodily" as well, but also interestingly enough means *slave*! For the body is a slave to the world and the senses. *Ophthalmos* means both the eye and the faculty of vision.

Now things get really interesting. The word translated "single" (*aplous*) does not mean one in a numerical sense, but in the sense of unified, of having come into oneness with something. Its root is *pleko* which means to be twined together with something. The opposite of aplous is *poneros*, which though translated "evil," does not mean what it does in our time. "Evil" was used at the time of the King James' translators in the sense of misfortune and harm, as well as negative moral condition. It also means to be degenerated from essential character or virtue.

Putting this all together we see the meaning of Jesus. When the consciousness, the mind, is united to the Self, even our body is filled with the light of spirit. If, however, the mind is drawn away from atmic awareness and turned toward its antithesis, the world of the senses and mortality, then both body and mind are plunged into darkness. Consciousness is not extinguished, but is subverted, evoking the words of Jesus: "If therefore the light that is in thee be darkness, how great is that darkness!" In other words, we become conscious of unconsciousness, we "see" blindness. How great, then, is that darkness. For it is utter annihilation of the purpose of our existence.

Two darknesses

There are two forms of darkness. To the person awake in the awareness of the Self the world and life of the senses is rightly perceived to be darkness and death. But to the dead-alive person who is absorbed in the false life of the senses, the knowledge and knowing of the Self is absolute nothingness. Either he does not believe in the spirit, or he considers it thoroughly irrelevant, even disruptive to his desires and goals. Both of these individuals consider themselves wise, but only the one with atmic vision is really a knower of the truth. It is completely worthless for these two to dialogue or discuss. Each must pursue what he "sees" until it reveals its true nature to him. Both need the freedom to do this. They should leave each other alone, free to follow the way they have chosen.

Beyond disturbance

> Like the ocean, which becomes filled yet remains unmoved and stands still as the waters enter it, he whom all desires enter and who remains unmoved attains peace–not so the man who is full of desire (2:70).

As the ocean is unaffected by the flowing of rivers into it, so the restrained and awakened mind, the mind that has been returned to its true center, the Self, receives a multitude of desire-impulses, yet makes no response. This is the real meaning of Patanjali's definition of yoga: the non-responsiveness of the mind (chitta–the mind substance) to outer stimuli. The illumined individual does not become inert or unconscious, but becomes unmoved by that which perpetually agitates and conditions the mind of the ignorant, especially those who are *kamakami*–desiring not just the objects of desire, but desiring the state of desire. For:

> He who abandons all desires attains peace, acts free from long-ing, indifferent to possessions and free from egotism (2:71).

Ego and egotism are the twin roots of desire. If they are eliminated, desire becomes impossible.

The final word

> This is the divine state. Having attained this, he is not delud-ed. Fixed in it even at the time of death, he attains Brahman-irvana (2:72).

Prabhavananda: "This is the state of enlightenment in Brahman: a man does not fall back from it into delusion. Even at the moment of death he is alive in that enlightenment: Brahman and he are one."

These words are too sublime to need comment.

FIRST STEPS IN KARMA YOGA

I n the latter part of the second chapter of the Bhagavad Gita Krishna has
given us a perfect portrait of a man possessed of the true Brahmajnana,
the knowledge of Brahman. It is far from that of a devoted warrior in the
heat of battle. Wherefore Arjuna asks, protesting:

> Arjuna said: If it is your conviction that knowledge is better
> than action, then why do you urge me to engage in this terri-
> ble action? With speech that seems equivocal you confuse my
> mind. Tell me surely this one thing: How should I attain the
> highest good? (3:1-2).

Buddhi means both intellect and intelligence. So Krishna is saying
that intelligent insight, or jnana, is far superior to mere external action,
or karma. But Arjuna protests that this emphasis on buddhi is confusing
his buddhi! Emphasis on intelligence confuses his intellect! But he is not
so confused that he does not understand that he needs to know the way
to the highest good.

The two paths
In response Krishna begins:

The Holy Lord said: In this world there is a two-fold path taught by me long ago: knowledge, the yoga of the Sankhyas, and action, the yoga of the yogis (3:3).

Sri Ramakrishna often said that basically there were two yogas: karma yoga, the yoga of action, and mano yoga, the yoga of the mind–buddhi yoga, or jnana yoga.

For some reason through the intervening centuries people who are not correctly following either path insist that there is only one right or best way of the two, but Krishna is not really setting an either/or situation before Arjuna. Instead, he is speaking of two forms of emphasis–some develop better by focussing on knowledge (jnana yoga), and some develop better by focussing on action (karma yoga). But both engage in jnana and karma simultaneously–it is only in the degree of one or the other that the difference is to be found.

It is sadly true that through misunderstanding we find people who think that one should be cultivated to the complete exclusion of the other. This is not the intention of Krishna, as we shall see. After all, if each one leads to enlightenment, how can there be a "best"? In fact, how can they be exclusionary if they lead to the same goal?

Temperament is the deciding factor as to which of the paths to emphasize. It is really quite simple: we should take up the path that seems natural to us. And if further on down the path it seems natural to switch over to the other emphasis, that, too, is all right, for in some lives we have to take up more than one unfinished strand and complete them. It is natural for us to move in many directions throughout our life. Since there is only one God and therefore only one Goal, whatever we do will move us forward along the path. "In whatever way men resort to me do I thus reward them. It is my path which men follow everywhere" (4:11). "I am the Goal" (9:18).

In our evolution through many lives we take up many approaches that we do not complete for some reason. These remain unfulfilled, and it is necessary that we complete them or in some way combine and resolve them. So it is natural to be drawn to different attitudes and approaches at different phases of our spiritual development. A test of infants found that they instinctively knew exactly what they needed to eat at the time and would go right for those foods, including things with unpleasant taste. The same is true of our own heart. We know the way we should go, and to deny it is to deny our inner divinity.

How not to go about it

> Not by abstaining from actions does a man attain the state beyond action, and not by mental renunciation alone does he approach to perfection. Truly, no one for even a moment exists without doing action. Each person is compelled to perform action, even against his will, by the gunas born of prakriti (3:4-5).

Here "activity" includes mental action, conscious and subconscious. The law of karma consists of two forces: the impulse to act and the certainty of reaping the consequences of all acts. It is both cause and effect. And it is underlain by a more profound law, the law of evolution. Evolution is effected by action–action that informs and improves, but action nonetheless. So action is an absolute necessity for all beings.

Krishna assures us that inaction is impossible–even for God, so why not for the godlike? When we are in a moving vehicle we may not want to move or see the need for it, but move we shall. In the same way, the moment we enter into relative existence, into prakriti, we begin moving and we never stop until we transcend relativity and attain the Absolute. Therefore the gunas of prakriti, sattwa, rajas, and tamas, combine to force us to act. In this matter there is no free will–we cannot choose to act or not. The only freedom we have is to decide how we will act. This is why all religions place such importance on virtuous or right action. Act we must, so we must act rightly.

Only those who erroneously suppose the inner and outer, the spiritual and the material, to be not only different but in opposition to one another, think that abstention from action is the way to perfection or that escape is liberation. This is why the Gita is so incredibly important. It shows that right activity is as necessary for inner enlightenment as the more obvious means such as japa and meditation.

In the next chapter Krishna will speak of "the royal seers (rajarishis)." The holy kings who administered kingdoms and yet attained the knowledge of Brahman are the ideal he puts before us. He does this for two reasons: 1) so we will not think that avoiding activity and involvement is the way to enlightenment, and 2) so we will not use our earthly responsibilities and ties as excuses for not exerting ourselves to the utmost in the pursuit of liberation. How many times have spiritual layabouts talked to me about how God had given them "all these responsibilities" and consequently they were dispensed from seeking God. It is just the opposite. God intends for us to seek and find him in the midst of those responsibilities–that is their purpose. They are not barriers or obstacles, but doors to pass through into higher life. One man actually told me that he could not look after his spiritual life because God had given him children whose spiritual lives he was to cultivate! Having nothing himself, he was going to supply them. He also overlooked the fact that God had done no such thing as "give" them to him–he had traveled all the way to Asia and adopted them. Sad that he would use them as pretexts for neglecting his own evolution. As Yogananda said: "Human beings are so skillful in their ignorance!"

The essence is this: since we are forced to act, we should act in a freeing manner, not in a binding manner.

What we are really thinking and wanting

Whatever we do, it is our inner intention and desire that determines the ultimate result. Krishna explains this:

He who restrains action's organs while yet revolving in his mind thoughts of objects of the senses, is deluded, a hypocrite (3:6).

And we will see that what he really wants will eventually come to him. Then he will no longer be a hypocrite, unless he hides his involvement with them. Sometimes a "fall" is really a matter of honesty.

Sanatana Dharma is markedly different from other philosophies. They all threaten, cajole, and persuade people to join their ranks and "be good." True Dharma, in contrast, says: "Study yourself carefully, and if you do not want what we have to offer, then do not bother–you will not get anywhere anyway. But when the time comes that you really want the higher life, come see us." Sri Ramakrishna said that by always being truthful a person ascends to higher life, even liberation. There must be honesty in all things, including religion. Of course, there does come a pivotal moment, a midway point, where the individual must say: "I really want what is bad for me, but even more I want to rid myself of such a foolish 'want.' Henceforth I will cut it off and cultivate the right kind of 'want.'" That is not hypocrisy, but liberating discipline, because he openly admits his inner desire. But it must be self-initiated, not an effect of any external factor, including another person.

We are the savior

The only savior we will ever have is ourself–our own creative will. Later Krishna will say: "The self can truly be a friend of the self" (6:5). This is because it is our will alone that creates our entire life in all its aspects. As a Buddhist text says: "I have nothing but my actions; I shall have nothing but my actions." This is why Krishna also said: "Brahman is to be attained by him who always sees Brahman in action" (4:24). What you will is what you (really) want; what you want is what you (really) will. Hence, Krishna says:

> He who by the mind controls the senses, and yet is unattached while engaging action's organs in action, is superior (3:7).

When we really understand that every action has union with God as its core purpose and carry out each action with that perspective, then everything we do is genuine yoga, uniting us with God.

> Perform your duty, for action is far better than non-action. Even maintaining your body cannot be done without action (3:8).

Liberating action

The world is bound by the actions not done for sake of sacrifice. Hence for sacrifice you should act without attachment (3:9).

Up and Doing should be our motto. But up and doing for God, for our Higher Self and the Supreme Self.

From the Beginning to the End

In the beginning along with mankind Prajapati created sacrifice and said: "By this shall you increase: this shall be the granter of desires" (3:10).

Life is to be lived according to its purpose: the ultimate evolution/liberation of the individual. When life is lived in this way, every act is an offering to Spirit, both individual and Absolute. To live for the short-term goals of the ego, conditioned completely by our present status in just this one limited incarnation, is folly to the point of insanity. But we do just that, binding ourselves tighter and closer to the wheel of birth and death. Like Scrooge's partner, Jacob Marley, we forge chains which we bear with us for untold ages.

"It is my life and I will do what I want" is one of the stupidest things a human being can say, except, perhaps, for: "I don't see the need for a God." Both are expressions of an insular ignorance almost cosmic in scope. Every act must be begun and carried out within the perspective of our personal evolution. For our life is really an extension of the Divine Life–nothing else.

It was only logical, then, for Saint Paul to write: "I beseech you therefore, brethren, by the mercies of God, that ye present your bodies a living sacrifice, holy, acceptable unto God, which is your reasonable service. And be not conformed to this world: but be ye transformed by the renewing of your mind, that ye may prove what is that good, and acceptable, and perfect, will of God" (Romans 11:1-2). That is, we must not live according to the illusions of the world, but rather transform ourselves by living in the context of sacrifice, of giving our life to the search for the Highest. For to do so will accomplish the divine plan (will). As Saint Paul also wrote: "This is the will of God, even your sanctification" (Thessalonians 4:3).

Much earlier Patanjali taught in the Yoga Sutras that Ishwarapranidhana–offering of the life to God–was the path to the superconscious experience of samadhi.

Why?

Why, then, did Brahma the Creator (Prajapati is one of his titles) tell the first humans that living in sacrifice (offering) would result in prosperity and fullfil desire? Because when we live in harmony with the divine plan the entire cosmos works in concert to accomplish our perfection–which includes the supplying of all we need to live both the earthly and the spiritual life. Those who live in this manner only desire that which furthers their enlightenment. Krishna implies this elsewhere in the Bhagavad Gita also.

> It is noteworthy that this verse implies that we do not gain by grabbing but by giving, not by taking, but by offering–giving and offering to God, that is, and ultimately thereby to our true Self. It is not God that fulfills our desires, but our sacrifice-offering. No wonder Jesus said: "It is more blessed to give than to receive" (Acts 20:35). It is really a matter of karma. "Cast thy bread upon the waters: for thou shalt find it after many days" (Ecclesiastes 11:1). "Whatsoever a man soweth, that shall he also reap" (Galatians 6:7).

The "gods"

> "May you foster the gods by this, and may the gods then foster you. Then, each the others fostering, you shall attain highest welfare" (3:11).

Who are "the gods" (devas)? They are not to be confused with those of lesser (though powerful) evolution that, in the grip of ego, reward and punish those who please or displease them. Such deluded beings have been worshipped in various forms throughout the history of the world.

The devas spoken of by Krishna are highly evolved beings that have control over physical and astral forces, and who supervise the operations of the universe. When human beings live in accordance with material laws they aid in the processes of creation and are blessed by the devas, for their help in their work. Conversely, they hinder the devas when they break natural laws and despoil the world around them. Krishna is advocating both a material and a spiritual ecology.

But there is another, more personal aspect of the devas. The higher faculties of the human being are also devas, "shining ones," for they enable the person to understand outer and inner phenomena and give him the capacity to direct or alter such phenomena. When we live in accordance with our true nature and do those things that support and further our evolutionary impulse we are "fostering the gods." Our material nature becomes an assist to higher consciousness. It is only those who are violating nature, inner and outer, that complain of the human condition and this world as obstacles or injurious.

Actually, the words "nourish" and "foster" are both very inadequate and unsatisfactory. The word *bhavyata* really cannot be translated by a single English term. Bhavyata means: "may you cherish," "may you foster," "may you produce," and "may you increase the well-being of." Literally, it means "may you cause to be." The implication is that for the unaware and ignorant neither the devas in the universe nor the inner faculties exist. A long time ago I heard the challenge: "If God is God, then let him BE God!" The idea is that even God is only potentially God in our lives until we actively "make" him God, the way a king is not really king until he is officially crowned. So if the gods are to exist outside and inside us in a meaningful way, we have to make them gods by the practice of yoga. A part of the making is the cultivation of the capacity to perceive them. For this, meditation is essential.

The highest aspect of this is making our own selves into devas, into shining ones, by invoking the light of our eternal Self. Until then we do not exist in the fullest sense. We need to bring ourselves into being.

Fostering the gods

> "The gods, fostered by sacrifice, will give you desired enjoyments. But he who enjoys the gods' gifts without offering to them is a thief" (3:12).

This, too, is a matter of cosmic and individual import. Those who live according to the Eternal Dharma find that they receive the fulfillment of all needs. Those who exploit both the world and their own bodies and minds are thieves that shall find themselves imprisoned and impoverished by this world and by their own corrupted nature.

> The good who eat the sacrificial remains are freed from all evils. The wicked eat their own evil who cook food only for themselves (3:13).

In India there is the concept of prasad (literally: grace), that which has been first offered to God and then partaken of by the devotee. It is believed that the essence of the offering has been received by God and replaced with divine energy which greatly purifies and uplifts whoever partakes of the prasad. Miracles, such as healing, have taken place at the consumption of prasad, and many notice a definite increase in spiritual awareness after eating prasad.

That there is a basis to this was demonstrated in an ashram in the Himalayan foothills. A resident rat, known as "Mother's Bhakta," would only eat prasad. This was tested many times by putting identical items where he could find them. Some would be prasad and others would be ordinary food. He never touched the regular items but ate only the prasad. This occurred for many years.

Our whole life should be prasad. First it should be offered sincerely to God and ordered accordingly. Then what we enjoy as "leftovers" will accrue to our spiritual benefit. Although the cooking of food is the example used in this verse, the principle applies to every aspect of life. Everything we do should have the prime motive of our spiritual perfection, our liberation.

If we can live in the attitude of our life being an offering it will profoundly affect us. For one thing, it will keep us from that which is unfit to offer God: unworthy or selfish deeds or the injury of others. Taking this idea seriously can transform our lives and deliver us from mishaps and follies.

To realize that we are not living *our* life but the Divine Life which has been bestowed on us is a foundation stone of intelligent living.

"Food"

Food is much more than mere comestibles. The Upanishads speak a great deal about food (annam) as a metaphysical concept. The Taittiriya Upanishad says: "From food are born all creatures, which live upon food and after death return to food. Food is the chief of all things. It is therefore said to be medicine for all diseases of the body. Those who worship food as Brahman gain all material objects. From food are born all beings which, being born, grow by food. All beings feed upon food, and, when they die, food feeds upon them" (Taittiriya Upanishad 2:1:3). Here we see that "food" represents the cosmic life principle: Brahman itself. This really could not be otherwise, since Brahman is all that exists.

In the Gita, "food" is the life that is lived as prasad. So Krishna continues:

> **From food all beings are produced, and from rain all food is produced. From sacrifice there comes down rain. From action is born sacrifice. Understand that action arises from Brahma, Brahma arises from the Imperishable. Hence the all-pervading Brahma is eternally established in sacrifice (3:14-15).**

This second part (verse fifteen) rightly seems a bit confusing. Brahman is the Absolute, the Self-Existent, yet we are told that Brahman arises from the Imperishable. Aren't they the same thing? Yes, in the ultimate sense. But Krishna is speaking of the distinction between Divinity that is present (immanent) in creation and guiding creation and our evolution within it, and Divinity that is transcendent, completely outside or beyond relativity. It is the same Divinity, but two aspects of that One. In the other spiritual writings of India they are called Brahman and the Mahat Tattwa. But when Vyasa wrote the Gita a single word, Brahman, was used for both.

The teaching of this verse is that the consciousness, the seed of divine realization, is inherent in a life lived as an offering to the Supreme.

The foolish

Before Krishna tells us about the life-path of the wise, he disposes of the foolish in a single short verse:

> He who here on the earth turns not the wheel thus set in motion, lives full of sense delights, maliciously and uselessly (3:16).

Basically, the idea is that those who live for their personal gratification, with no wider interest or perspective, and who are oriented toward the body and its addictions (falsely called "needs" by the body-involved), injure both themselves and others, and really live to no real purpose, for death in a moment sweeps away everything they value, leaving them only with their addictions to dominate them in future lives. A horrible prospect, indeed. They are truly the living dead.

As Krishna said in the last chapter: "When the mind is led about by the wandering senses, it carries away the understanding like the wind carries away a ship on the waters. The [intelligent–buddhic] awareness of him whose senses are withdrawn from the objects of the senses on all sides will be found firmly established. The man of restraint is awake in what is night for all beings; that in which all beings are awake is night for the sage who [truly] sees" (2:67-69).

Freedom

> He who is content only in the Self, who is satisfied in the Self, who is pleased only in the Self: for him there is no need to act. He has no purpose at all in action or in non-action, and he has no need of anyone for any purpose whatsoever (3:17-18).

When our consciousness is centered in the Self we are out of the game and home free. As Sri Ramakrishna frequently said, using the game of hide-and-seek as a metaphor: "If you play hide and seek there is no fear once you touch the 'granny.'" And: "If you can but touch the 'granny,' you can live anywhere after you have turned into gold."

In atmic consciousness we become free from all compulsion to act–and equally free from any compulsion to inaction. We are truly free, able to act or not act, having transcended that duality by becoming its masters, not by becoming incapacitated in relation to them. Further, we are absolutely free and independent of all others, living in unity with our Self within Brahman.

Nevertheless…

Lest we fall into inertia, considering it a virtue, Krishna continues:

> **Therefore, constantly unattached perform that which is your duty. Indeed by unattached action man attains the Supreme. Indeed, perfection was attained through action alone by King Janaka and others. For the maintenance of the world, as an example you should act (3:19-20).**

Janaka was a royal saint mentioned in the Upanishads. He lived unattached, acting solely for the welfare of others, as must we. This lofty motivation is now expounded by Krishna.

> **Whatever the best of men does–this and that–thus other men do. Whatever the standard that he sets, that is what the world shall follow. I have no duty whatsoever in the three worlds, nor anything that must be attained, nevertheless I engage in action. Indeed, if I did not tirelessly engage at all in action, then mankind everywhere would follow my example. If I did not perform action these worlds would perish, and I would be the cause of confusion. I would destroy these people. As the unwise act, attached to action, so the wise should act,**

unattached, intending to maintain the welfare of the world (3:21-25).

Here Krishna speaks from the perspective of God, not just as an enlightened person, though he was a major leader of society at that time.

Showing the way

Now we come to a supreme counsel:

One should not unsettle the minds of the ignorant attached to action. The wise should cause them to enjoy all actions, himself engaged in their performance (3:26).

Movement (action) is life, whereas cessation of all movement is death. So it is natural for human beings to engage in action. The trouble is in the motive. So Krishna tells us that the wise must also work—often even more than others—to show how action should be carried on. Here, too, we see that the inner disposition is the secret. To engage in action intent only on the action itself or on the desired result is ignorance. Action done with the consciousness directed toward God as the ultimate "result" is wisdom. Action is then the path to freedom rather than the way of bondage.

THE REAL "DOERS"

Every action is really performed by the gunas

> In all situations actions are performed by the gunas of Prakriti.
> Those with ego-deluded mind think: "I am the doer" (3:27).

The Atman, the Spirit-self, is pure consciousness, and as such has only one function: witnessing the movements of prakriti, the creative life energies. The mechanics of this situation are virtually as incomprehensible as the Atman itself. In the Bhagavad Gita the energies are spoken of as surrounding or encompassing the Atman which experiences being at the center of them. But they are also declared to be utterly apart from the Atman, which witnesses them as totally outside it.

However that may be, Krishna is saying that all action is merely the movement–the combining, separation, and recombining in ever-changing patterns–of the three modes of energy behavior, the three gunas. Just as there are three primary colors from which all colors originate, in the same way the three gunas are the origin of all activity.

Man, deluded by his egoism, thinks: "I am the doer"

The witnesses of a motion picture, knowing full well that it is only a play of light on the screen, yet respond to it as being real. Each of us is even more enthralled within the motion picture of our daily experience, actually believing that we are acting and producing its changing movements.

Sankhya philosophy, the philosophy expounded by Krishna in the Gita, tells us that although we do not literally act within prakriti, the appearance of action caused by the movements of the gunas is produced by us–by our mere proximity to prakriti. We can understand this by the simile of modern gadgetry. There are devices which are activated just by someone approaching them–all the way from talking and moving figures to doors that open at our approach. In the same way prakriti is stimulated into motion by our approaching it in our awareness. It literally is the way we look at it that matters. Those who can look upon prakriti as detached witnesses will find themselves no longer part of the whirling movement that comprises the drama of life. This is really beyond the comprehension of the ordinary intellect, but the yogi who has clarified and stabilized his mind will understand to a great degree, for his outer life is seen to be an extension of his inner life. Meditation is the most viable School of Life.

Understanding the gunas

The gunas are not only three modes of material energy behavior, they are also three forms of material (matter-oriented) consciousness. So Krishna continues:

> But he who knows the truth about the gunas and action thinks: "The gunas act in the gunas." Thinking thus, he is not attached (3:28).

Krishna is not just giving us interesting facts about phenomenal existence; his intention is to bring us to detachment from that to which we never have been nor ever can be really attached. All attachment is only an illusion of the ignorant heart. He calls us to simple reality, not to some high-flown mystical state.

Guna guneshu vartanta means: "The gunas act in the gunas." Swami Prabhavananda renders it: "Gunas are merely attaching themselves to gunas." Swami Swarupananda: "Gunas as senses merely rest on gunas as objects." Swami Sivananda: "The Gunas as senses move amidst the gunas as the sense-objects."

A serious responsibility

> Those deluded by the gunas of prakriti are attached to the actions of the gunas. The knower of the whole truth should not disturb the foolish of partial knowledge (3:29).

This is almost universally disregarded in India, where the monastics have glorified inaction as wisdom (jnana) and action as ignorance. The result has been a shameful stagnation and idle-mindedness in themselves and those they influence. No one can count the number of wandering idlers falsely called sannyasis. The only thing they have renounced is responsibility.

"Those deluded by the gunas of prakriti are attached to the actions of the gunas." Why, then, would you not wean them from external involvements, from constant action? Because it is a matter of maturity. Just as the fruit should ripen before being taken from the tree, in the same way each individual must evolve to the point where he sees for himself the truth of things–not blindly believing in what others tell him about reality. Until then, just as with a child or mentally impaired adult, we have to speak to him on his level in his terms.

The wise must engage in right action so as to teach by example and incite even the ignorant to emulation. At such a stage actions certainly do speak louder than words. The infant must grow and learn to walk, talk, feed himself, and think objectively before we educate him and speak philosophically to him. It is the same way in practical life. Only those who learn the right way to act can learn the right way to withdraw from action.

OUR SPIRITUAL MARCHING ORDERS

There are many reasons why a battlefield was the appropriate place for the teachings of the Bhagavad Gita to be spoken. Life itself is a battle, and the world is the battlefield. Those who are developed enough in consciousness to take upon themselves the responsibility for their evolution and ultimate liberation are certainly warriors. Krishna is the voice of the Supreme Commander–our own divine Self and Brahman the Absolute, the Self of our Self. He issues to us our marching orders in a single verse:

Renouncing all actions in me, intent on the Supreme Spirit, free from desire and "mine," free from fever: fight! (3:30)

It is important to realize that good intentions, dedication, and enthusiasm are not sufficient in the spiritual battle. That is why Krishna leaves the order to fight for the last. Here they are.

Renouncing all actions in me. The Sanskrit term *sannyasya* means relinquishing, entrusting, and renouncing. All apply here. First, we give up or give over to God all that we do, saying: "This is all done by your power, by your instruments, by me who also am yours. So may this all be your doing." This is a very important attitude. We entrust our actions to God when we offer them and rely on God to make everything come out all right. When I was little we used to sing in church: "When you have done your best, let Jesus do the rest, *and keep your eyes upon the goal.*" I did not understand what I was singing, but many years later after reading the Gita I did. Reliance on God is often the secret of detached action. Renouncing all action has pretty much been covered, but it is very much an attitude of indifference–not being numb in the mind or alienated from our surroundings, but being so intent on God that our actions are no longer ours but God's. And if God is not interested, neither are we. So no problem. This gives profound peace of mind.

Everything we do must be seen as serving a single purpose: the revelation of the Divine Self within our own Self. Obviously Infinity needs nothing, and the idea of giving It anything is absurd. But since the intention of the Absolute in manifesting the relative is our ascension to complete freedom in spirit, whatever we do to further that can be considered dedicated to God. Here, too, Krishna is speaking of Ishwarapranidhana, the offering of the life to God.

Intent on the Supreme Spirit. Adhyatma chetasa means consciousness absorbed in the Self within (adhyatman), both the individual Self and the Cosmic Self. No need to look for fire in water or dampness in fire. The Self and the world mutually exclude one another. So we need not flee the world or even reject it; we need only turn within and enter the realm of the spirit. Then like the chick's shell the world will fall away, no longer able to confine or hold on to us. "This I say then, Walk in the Spirit, and ye shall not fulfill the lust of the flesh" (Galatians 5:16).

Free from desire and selfishness. There is no use in facing west to see the rising sun. In the same way there is no point in looking to material existence for fulfillment of that deep longing which impels us into so many frantic and fruitless searches from life to life. We do not expect a stone to fly or sing to us. In the same way we must not expect from the world the very thing it prevents us from attaining.

The ego only exists in the world–or rather in the mind that is absorbed in the world and identifies with the world, thinking the Self is a part of it, capable of affecting it and of being affected by it. That is a sure gateway to frustration and false assurances. The only way to be free from the sense of ego is to become identified with the Self.

Free from fever. Ignorance is the root of all our problems and their attendant sufferings. Unfortunately, it is not a passive condition like blindness or

147

deafness, but actively produces the fever of a myriad delusions and desires which impel us into a myriad of thoughts and acts that proliferate into more delusions and pains. It is horrible to contemplate, engendering in us a sense of utter helplessness and hopelessness. But that mistaken view is the ultimate delusion which, if we accept it, will ensure our perpetual confusion and misery.

The truth is that all our delusions and suffering are illusions, having no substance other than our own mind or any power other than our own intellect and will. They are dreams from which we can awaken. No external force can produce this awakening–we must do it ourself. Teachers can instruct us in the means and ways of awakening but the cure must be totally accomplished by us.

Ignorance is only a shell, a veneer. Beneath it lies the eternal truth of our Self. The shell need only be cracked open and shaken off. Just as the chick cracks its shell from within and pushes its way outward, breaking and casting aside the shell, so are we to do, becoming, like Buddha, Self-awakened.

Fight! When ignorance and delusion are vanquished, dependence on the world ended, consciousness of the Self established, the sense of ego dissolved, and all our life seen as an offering unto God, we have not attained the goal–we have only then become capable of fighting and conquering the cosmic evil that has dominated and enslaved us from the moment we became an atom of hydrogen.

One of the greatest errors of spiritual life is mistaking mere spiritual fitness for spiritual perfection. Saint Clement of Alexandria lamented that already in the beginning of the third century the Christian Church mistook for perfection and the end of the struggle that which at the time of Jesus was looked upon as just the beginning, only the readiness to begin the path to perfection. The same is true in all religions today. Those who are hardly qualified novices are acclaimed masters and even avatars. This is a tragedy beyond calculation.

But we need not fall into the illusion. We can and will move onward to the real battle; and we will win.

Fighting is going forward, but many people get stuck on their successes in spiritual life rather than pushing onward to better things. There are people who sit and rhapsodize about an extraordinary meditation instead of keeping on and having even more remarkable meditations. Or they go on and on about some incredible incident in their spiritual search, not realizing that they are no longer searching but mired in self-congratulation. It is good to be pleased with our spiritual life and progress, but that must be a stimulus to keep on moving into new territory. Alexander the Great, whose kingdom was but a fraction of the earth, sat and wept, lamenting that he had no more lands to conquer. We must avoid his small-mindedness and press on.

No matter how good things are at the moment, they can become better—even to the extent that what we are impressed with now will in time seem very elementary, and even negligible.

FREEDOM FROM KARMA

Do you remember the television ad that asked: "Why trade a headache for an upset stomach?"? Many people trade fear of sin and hell for fear of bad karma and bad karmic consequences. That is a perfect example of Jesus' statement that "no man putteth new wine into old bottles; else the new wine will burst the bottles, and be spilled, and the bottles shall perish. But new wine must be put into new bottles; and both are preserved" (Luke 5:37, 38).

It is pointless to adopt new ideas while retaining the old attitudes that were consistent with or shaped by the old rejected ideas. The resulting inconsistency will have a negative, even a disruptive, effect. As Jesus said before the passage just cited: "No man putteth a piece of a new garment upon an old; if otherwise, then both the new maketh a rent, and the piece that was taken out of the new agreeth not with the old" (Luke 5:36). Putting a new top layer over the old leads to the ruin of both.

This is why the majority of Westerners who think they have adopted Hinduism or Buddhism have really only created their personal simulations of those religions. For they have only changed or rearranged their intellectual furniture; everything else remains the same. In fact, under pressure the old ideas emerge as entrenched as ever. For example, those who for years have professed belief in karma immediately wail: "Why did this happen to me?" when something unpleasant occurs. After 9/11 a multitude of American book-Hindus began demanding why it took place, many of them suggesting far-fetched reasons; but not one of them said the k-word.

As Sri Ramakrishna observed, you can teach a parrot to call out: "Radha-Krishna! Radha-Krishna!" but when you pull its tail it only squawks. It is a simple matter to jump from Western religion to Eastern religion, but to really become a Hindu or a Buddhist is a matter of profound transformation, having little to do with mere ideas.

Once in a conversation with Swami Maheshananda Giri, one of the leading sadhus and yogis of Northern India, I asked him: "Have you ever met a Westerner who really understood Sanatana Dharma?" "No," he answered, "and neither have I met an Indian who understood Western religion and philosophy. For to do so, both would have to completely tear down their present ideas and build anew from the ground up." Since Swamiji had held the chair of Sanskrit and Indology for many years at Harvard, I knew he had a basis for his opinion. There must be a complete sweeping away before a new structure can be erected in the mind (buddhi) of the prospective seeker. This had been my own experience when like a thunderclap all I thought I "knew" was wiped out in a moment, and real life and understanding began for me.

That is what *I* have to say: now we should listen to what Krishna tells us about freedom from karma, not forgetting that good karma is as binding as bad karma.

Right action

> Those who constantly follow this teaching of mine, full of faith, not opposing it, they are released from the bondage of their actions (3:31).

Karma need not be worked out or worked through. As Krishna says later on: "He has consumed his karma in the fire of knowledge" (4:19).

This is one of the most important verses in the Gita, for it tells us how to attain moksha (liberation) in the simplest possible way. (I said, simple; not easy.) There are some words that deserve contemplation. *Shraddhavanto* means "believing" and "full of faith." *Anasuyantas* means quite a few things: "not sneering," "not spiteful [in the sense of being annoyed at having been told the truth]," "not caviling," "not grumbling [complaining]," and "not speaking ill of [what has been taught]." In short: "whiners never win."

If the Gita is diligently studied daily by the serious sadhaka and followed with faith and without any reservation or compromise whatsoever, he will be "released from the bondage of actions." A knowledge of the Gita and a living out of its precepts are a guarantee of liberation. Nothing more is needed. It may seem too simple, but why not try it out?

On the other hand...

> But those opposing and not practicing my teaching, confusing
> all knowledge, know them to be lost and mindless (3:32).

There is not much need to comment on this verse. Those who in their ignorance disregard or even despise the principles set forth in the Gita are hopeless. Everything they think they know is an illusion. Life itself proves the truth of this. When I hear someone say: "I have never been impressed with or interested in Indian philosophy or religion," there is no need for me to mentally cross them off the list: they are not even there.

"Nature"

Two "natures"

There are two Sanskrit words that can be translated as "nature," though both have primary meanings beyond that.

The first is prakriti. Prakriti usually means causal matter or the fundamental power (shakti) of God from which the entire cosmos is formed. Prakriti is undifferentiated matter, the root base of all elements, the material cause of the world. It is also known as Pradhana.

Prakriti can be translated "nature" when the fundamental energy (shakti) of an object is being spoken of. It is not a perfect simile, but a stone sculpture can give us some idea. If it is a sculpture of a horse it can be referred to as either horse or stone. If we had many sculptures of varying subjects, "stone" would be applied to all of them when speaking of their fundamental nature.

The other word sometimes translated "nature" is bhava. Bhava is the subjective state of being–attitude of mind, or mental feeling. Although rendered "nature," bhava is a state of prakriti, the way "carved" would be applied to our theoretical stone horse. This is in contrast to prakriti being used for nature; for in that instance it is the character, the quality of something that is being indicated–stone, for example.

Let us stay with our horse sculpture simile to clinch the idea. Suppose we have identical horse sculptures, but some are wood, some are clay, and some are stone. Sculpted, soft, hard, smooth, or rough would be the "bhava." Wood, clay, and stone would be the "prakriti." One is the shape of something and the other is its substance.

The Gita speaks

There are many impossible things in this world. One is that it is impossible to find an irrelevant statement in the teachings of the Bhagavad Gita. In this small book Vyasa has said virtually everything we need to know regarding spiritual philosophy and spiritual practice. It would be pointless to attempt rating the level of importance of each verse, but surely one of the most informative is this:

> **One acts according to one's own prakriti–even the wise man does so. Beings follow their own prakriti; what will restraint accomplish? (3:33)**

Prakriti is vibratory energy. Krishna tells us that all living beings act according to their prakriti. For example, under intense pressure a wheel made of rubber will bend, one made of wood or plastic will break, and one made of iron or steel will hold its shape and endure. The shape may be the same, but the substance makes the difference.

The prakriti of each one of us–especially the energy of our minds–determines how we act, think, and speak. It is possible to temporarily suppress the natural movements of our prakriti, but in time we will revert to our fundamental modes of behavior. Sri Ramakrishna illustrated this fact, saying: "At Kamarpukur mongooses live in holes up in the wall. When a mongoose stays up there, it is very comfortable. Some people tie a brick to its tail, so it is forced out of the hole by its pull. It is forced out of its hole by the pull of the brick as many times as it tries to go inside to stay in comfort there."

The mongoose is the individual and the brick is the prakriti. The brick has been tied to the mongoose's tail, and our prakriti has been attached to our Atma-Self. It is inescapable. We must deal with it–not by merely controlling or repressing it (though sometimes this must be done), but by transmuting it into a higher form.

Krishna's statement is not fatalistic, but optimistic, for we can change the present state of our prakriti, especially through continual japa and meditation. We can–and must–change the prakriti-lead into prakriti-gold. This is possible through yoga. Ethics and religious orientation can certainly assist the process, as can external purification and right behavior, but they can only produce a favorable condition for the necessary transmutation.

Restraint

When Krishna asks: "What will restraint accomplish?" he is not subscribing to the prevalent Western attitude that suppression or repression are harmful to the individual. Rather, he is telling us that mere behavior modification is valueless because in time reversion to negative or foolish activity will occur. If the prakriti is not changed the behavior will not be permanently changed.

More than behavior

Prakriti determines our psychological state, and that is the source of our thought and action. The way a person thinks and speaks is a matter of prakriti, as is his view of himself, others, and life itself. This is why we cannot reason or cajole a person into thinking differently than he presently does. Externally-produced conversion is actually impossible, though a person may discover ideas that vibrate in consonance with his prakriti and intellectually adopt them. This is particularly true in religion. Religion shapes no one's mind—it is the other way around. Religion does not make people bigoted or hateful. Instead, bigoted and hateful people create or gravitate to bigoted and hateful religion. Cultish people join cults. Idiots join idiotic movements and ideologies. As the prophet said: "Ephraim is joined to idols: let him alone" (Hosea 4:17). And Jesus: "Let them alone: they be blind leaders of the blind. And if the blind lead the blind, both shall fall into the ditch" (Matthew 15:14). There is nothing *we* can do; *they* must do it.

Our part

All right, what should we do with ourselves? Krishna is not counseling doing nothing until our yoga sadhana transforms us. Instead, he says:

> **Attraction and aversion are inherent in the contact of the senses with sense-objects. One should not come under the power of these two—they are indeed his enemies (3:34).**

This verse is about bhava, and it tells us what to do: resist it when it is negative or foolish. Realize that it prevents our ascent in consciousness. The word translated "enemies" can also legitimately be translated as "hindrances," or "opponents."

The shifting movements of body, emotion, and intellect are natural, because they are manifestations of the present character (quality) of our prakriti. Krishna prescribes none of the positive-prettythink strategies so beloved in the West. He has only one counsel: Hold on! Do not give way. Resist. And in the meantime fill every waking moment with higher consciousness. This is why he says: "Make a habit of practicing meditation, and do not let your mind be distracted. In this way you will come finally to the Lord, who is the light-giver, the highest of the high" (8:8. Prabhavananda).

Krishna speaks of the "attraction and aversion [which] are inherent in the contact of the senses with sense-objects" to let us understand that the attraction and aversion is purely material—prakriti based—and has nothing to do with us in the truest, the atmic, sense. Feelings do not come from the intelligence or the inner consciousness. They are a mayic delusion. Here again we see why we must change our prakriti.

The spiritual alchemy of yoga is the answer. It always is.

SWADHARMA

Better is one's swadharma, though deficient, than the swadharma of another well performed. Better is death in one's own swadharma. The swadharma of another brings danger (3:35).

Relative existence—and we who find ourselves evolving within it—is dual in nature, comprised of Consciousness and Energy. Krishna has just explained to us that our actions must match our energy-nature, our prakriti. When they do, that is our swadharma, our self-dharma. Now he says that our actions, including our livelihood, must be consistent with our state of consciousness, our swabhava, our self-nature. Our swabhava is our inherent psychic disposition, our psychological nature. It is not just the ebb and flow of our mental and emotional tides on the surface of the mind, but its bedrock condition that prevails throughout any momentary fluctuations.

That mode of external life which is consistent with our swabhava is our swadharma, the mode of life and duty that is natural to us, being based on our karma and samskara. Our swadharma is consistent with our natural current of evolution. Swabhava and swadharma are the natural consequences of our present evolutionary status. They both match our prakriti. Just as external restraint is worthless, so action not according to swadharma is wasted action and hinders our progress, sometimes even harming us.

This is no small thing. How do we determine our swadharma? Not by letting others tell us what it is, or letting society impose it on us. (This is the great evil of the degenerate "caste system" of India which is far from Krishna's meaning when he speaks of caste.) The only way to intelligently perceive our swadharma is to engage in swadhyaya, self-analysis, as recommended by Patanjali in the Yoga Sutras, thus underlining the fact that yoga is inseparable from an ordered and meaningful life.

This self-analysis is both intellectual and intuitive, and our intellect and intuition must be developed through meditation if our endeavor is to succeed. We must discover and live out our swabhava through our swadharma. This is the only way to peace and harmony within ourself.

In the Grip of the Monster

Why?

I think that one of the saddest things I have seen in life is a little child who has done something wrong or silly being confronted by a parent. The dialogue is always this:

"Why did you do that?"

"I don't know."

It is sad when the child says "I don't know" in hope that the parental anger will be deflected or defused. But it is much sadder when the child is speaking the truth–he really has no idea why he did what he did. There was an impulse, and he followed it. And now look at the consequence.

We pride ourselves on being adults, but no matter how much we have learned about the world and life, what do we really know about ourselves? What, especially, do we know about the "why" of our actions? When something happens to us we glibly say it is karma, but why do we do the things that create our karma? Speaking for us, Arjuna puts the question to Krishna, the embodiment of Infinite Consciousness:

> **Arjuna said: Then by what is a man impelled to commit evil, against his own will, as if urged by some force? (3:36).**

The word translated "evil" is *papa*, which means any kind of negative action, one which accrues negative karma or demerit. A secondary meaning is misfortune or harm–the results of papa, just as karma is both action and reaction.

Arjuna was a great yogi. According to the Mahabharata he lived without needing to sleep–a condition far more psychological than physiological–and could easily pass at will from this world into any higher world he might wish to visit. The bonds of body and mind rested very lightly upon him. But in the Gita he is questioning Krishna on behalf of all humanity, so he sometimes asks things to which he already knows the answer. (And we must not forget that Vyasa wrote the Bhagavad Gita as a universal instructor for humanity and adjusted it accordingly. I hope nobody thinks that Arjuna and Krishna spoke to each other on the battlefield in blank verse.)

Arjuna's question here assumes that action can take place without our conscious will being involved, as though there is another kind of impulse that pushes us into evil deeds. Those who are self-aware to any significant degree know that such impulses come from inside us, not from outside. "The devil made me do it" is one of the most shameless evasions of responsibility of which the human being is capable. Too bad it happens to be ingrained in Western religion, and no wonder we have a sociopathic society. All such impulses come from us alone, and are our choices, our mental habits, on some deep subconscious level. The problem is, we have many "minds" and many "wills," as we are presently mostly a conglomeration of fragments. The phenomenon of multiple personality disorder demonstrates that. Buddha spoke of us as being a collection of skandhas–literally "heaps."

Know the enemy

Krishna goes directly to the root of the whole matter:

> **The Holy Lord said: This force is desire and anger born of the rajo-guna, the great consumer and of great evil. Know this to be the enemy (3:37).**

Rajas means activity, passion, or desire for an object or goal. The quality of rajas is the rajoguna, which impels us to those things. This raging fire has two major flames: kama and krodha, desire and anger. However, it is the rajoguna itself that is "the enemy." And what an enemy! Krishna calls it *mahashano*, "mighty eater" or "mighty consumer," and *mahapapma*, which means "great evil," "great misfortune," "great sin," "great harm(er)," and "great(ly) injurious." It must be reckoned with. But right now our attention has been drawn to desire and anger.

Although we know academically that desire includes lust, in both English and American usage it has such a strong sexual connotation that it overshadows the simple word "desire" when we encounter it in the Gita. Kama is desire in any degree or form. Fundamentally, kama is desire for any object, whether it is solely mental or produces an overt act or speech. Even simple wishes are pastel shades of kama. So simple "desire" is still the best translation. Krodha is anger in any degree, including wrath and fury. Hatred is essentially krodha.

It is necessary for us to understand that desire and anger in even the slightest degree is still a problem, an obstacle to real peace. Simple attraction (raga) and aversion (dwesha) are not passions, but they, too, must eventually be expunged from the yogi's heart. How much more, then, must kama and krodha be seen as the dangerous forces they actually are, "the great consumer and of great evil." They prey on us unmercifully, ravaging us on all levels of our being. That is why Socrates, later in life, spoke of the fading of lust as "freedom from a harsh and cruel master." Of all sins, desire and anger are the most lethal.

We must be vigilant and sensitive to the presence of these two assassins of the soul. Desire and anger take many forms. They arise in us wearing an array of masks–many of them seeming righteous and even holy–but we must ruthlessly strip them away and expose their real character. Otherwise these snipers of the heart will destroy us. There can be no truce with them. They are implacable enemies, and we should be as implacably inimical to them. No quarter should be given or any prisoners taken. As Krishna will soon tell us in verse forty-one, we must "kill this evil being, which destroys ordinary knowledge and supreme knowledge."

The "works of the devil"

It is not so hard to detect the evil of anger and hatred. Their destructive nature is readily seen. Anger and hatred, even when willfully indulged, are essentially painful to us. But desire (kama) promises us pleasure, a wheedling false friend that leads us into suffering, but which first drugs us and makes us think we are enjoying ourselves. It is a terrible trap which few escape. For anger can burn us out, but desire is an addiction augmented by its every indulgence. Krishna's exposition will cover it thoroughly.

> As fire is enveloped by smoke, as mirrors are covered by dust, as wombs cover embryos, in the same way knowledge is covered by this, the constant enemy of the wise, having the form of desire which is like insatiable fire (3:38-39).

As long as you feed it, the fire keeps burning. And it will burn anything it touches, as well. Desire cannot be fulfilled any more than a fire can be put out by adding fuel to it. It is true that if we dump a huge amount of solid fuel on a fire it may become invisible to us, but it is down there working, and will eventually blaze up even stronger. It must be extinguished fully.

Desire is a fundamental denial of our nature which is satchidananda: existence, consciousness and bliss. It makes us feel we need some pleasure or power, object or state, that such things will somehow make us more than we presently are and will make us happy. In this way desire is the prime force of the not-self. There is no way our true nature can be altered, diminished, or destroyed, but desire certainly alters, diminishes, and destroys our perception of reality, burying our Self beneath its insubstantial debris that is really nothing. It makes us like fools fishing in a pond for the moon. This is because:

> The senses, mind, and intellect are said to be its abode. With these it deludes the embodied one by veiling his innate wisdom (3:40).

Desire grips us in compulsions that end in terrible suffering. It is indeed "the constant enemy of the wise," for its enmity is without cessation or mitigation and is all-embracing.

The fire of desire is, according to this verse, inherent in the senses, mind, and intellect. And when it blazes up in them its smoke obscures and even conceals the Self. In ancient India it was considered that fire was inherent in whatever was flammable, that it was evoked by friction or external heat, but it was always there in potential form. And when fire "went out" it really just withdrew to some subtler, inner level of existence.

So when Buddha used the simile of fire for the Self of a person, he did not mean that it became "extinguished" or annihilated, but that it simply passed into another level of being, that objects and desires were the fuel that kept it trapped here for a while. Once they were gone, the fire-Self was liberated. And that was Nirvana.

The cure

Therefore, controlling the senses at the outset, kill this evil being, which destroys ordinary knowledge and supreme knowledge (3:41).

We can rid ourselves of this awful addiction, this horrible hallucination that is desire. It is not easy, but it must be done.

The first step is control of the senses. This is impossible without the observance of yama and niyama, the ten commandments of yoga:

1. Ahimsa: non-violence, non-injury, harmlessness
2. Satya: truthfulness, honesty
3. Asteya: non-stealing, honesty, non-misappropriativeness
4. Brahmacharya: sexual continence in thought, word and deed as well as control of all the senses
5. Aparigraha: non-possessiveness, non-greed, non-selfishness, non-acquisitiveness
6. Shaucha: purity, cleanliness
7. Santosha: contentment, peacefulness

8. Tapas: austerity, practical (i.e., result-producing) spiritual discipline
9. Swadhyaya: introspective self-study, spiritual study
10. Ishwarapranidhana: offering of one's life to God
    (For explanations of all these, see *The Foundations of Yoga*.)

The two absolutes for success in sense control are a vegetarian diet and meditation. But Krishna has more to tell us regarding this.

> They say that the senses are superior to the body, the mind is superior to the senses, the intellect is superior to the mind. And much superior to the intellect is the supreme intelligence. Having learned this, sustaining the lower Self by the higher Self, kill this difficult-to-encounter enemy which has the form of desire. (3:42-43)

This is why meditation is necessary. Only through the practice of yoga can we ascend the ladder of senses, mind, and will to reach the Self, the only source of mastery and freedom. At the same time we have to use our good sense, so Krishna tells us that we must "kill this evil being, which destroys ordinary knowledge and supreme knowledge." For it is really the ego who is masquerading in the form of desire so it can persuade us that it is really us who are the source of its impulses. It wants to blame us and even make us feel guilty—another delusion. Instead we must see it for what it is, cast off our non-existent weakness, and confront it with the truth of our almighty Self.

We are not to simply overpower desire, or banish it, or merely weaken it, or come to some kind of peace agreement with it. For it is "the constant enemy of the wise" and will eventually return to the attack with increased strength. It must be killed out by the very roots. And we must do it by the power revealed within us by yoga sadhana.

"Always disciplining himself thus, the yogi whose mind is subdued goes to the supreme peace of nirvana, and attains to union with me.... Therefore be a yogi" (6:15, 46).

"Devotee and Friend"

The "genealogy" of yoga

After outlining the basic way of yoga, Krishna then tells Arjuna:

> The Holy Lord said: This eternal yoga I taught to Vivaswat, Vivaswat taught it to Manu, and Manu taught it to Ikshwaku. Thus, handed down in succession, the royal seers knew it. After a long lapse of time, this yoga was lost here on earth (4:1-2).

Vivasvat, Manu, and Ikshvaku were ancient sages–primeval sages, actually, at the beginning of the human race. God himself directly taught yoga to those sages. That is why Patanjali says in the Yoga Sutras: "He is Guru even of the Ancients" (Yoga Sutras 1:26).

Just how the yoga was forgotten (lost) is not told to us, but it is important that we realize that this world, whose nature is bondage, is not a friendly environment for that which liberates. Whether the yoga was lost by carelessness or defects or omissions in teaching, or whether a time came when no one was even interested, the result was loss of the knowledge.

The same is true of our personal world. The mind is extremely gifted in forgetting or distorting the correct practice of yoga. Therefore we should be very vigilant and make sure that our practice is exactly correct, with not a single detail being neglected or left out. There are several contemporary spiritual organizations that over the course of years have so altered the yoga methods they teach that they have been rendered ineffectual–and in some cases, detrimental.

How do we protect ourself from this spiritual erosion? Study the Gita. It is all there. If we read the Gita, the eleven authentic Upanishads, and the Yoga Sutras of Patanjali without prejudice or preconception we will find they are unanimous in their teaching on meditation.

Who is Krishna in the Gita?

We have already finished three chapters of the Gita, and it is time for us to understand who the figure of Krishna really is–and what the Gita really is, as well.

First we must understand the context of the Gita. The Gita is seven hundred verses within an epic poem known as The Mahabharata, that chronicles the Mahabharata (Great Indian) War that took place about three thousand years ago (according to the calculations of Swami Sri Yukteswar Giri). The original poem was written by the great sage Vyasa, perhaps the single most important figure in Indian spiritual history.

The Bhagavad Gita is the supreme scripture of India, for it is the essence of all the basic texts that came before it. Further, it supplies a psychological side to spiritual practice that can be found in no other authoritative text. If someone desires, he can confine his study to the Gita alone and yet know everything that is in those texts. Although it contains some references to elements distinctly Indian, it is the only universal scripture, its teachings (including those about caste) being relevant to the entire human race.

Having said that, we must realize that although the Gita takes the form of a conversation between Krishna and Arjuna on the eve of the Great Indian War, it is not a historical document in the literal sense. Rather, Vyasa chose this critical juncture in Indian history as the setting for a complete exposition of spiritual life–itself a battle of sorts. It cannot reasonably be thought that Krishna and Arjuna sat in a chariot in the midst of a battlefield discussing all the topics presented in the Gita, and in metrical stanzas of four lines containing eight syllables each (sometimes eleven syllables when Vyasa needed the extra length to get in all his ideas). Rather, the Gita is Vyasa's presentation of the Eternal Dharma, though there is no reason to doubt that the wisdom of Krishna is embodied in it, or that much of it–at least in general–was spoken to Arjuna at Kurukshetra.

One of India's greatest yogis in the twentieth century was Paramhansa Nityananda of Ganeshpuri. One day someone cited a portion of the Gita, prefacing it with the statement: "Krishna said in the Gita...." Immediately Nityananda said: "No. Vyasa *said* Krishna said...." This is the correct perspective on the entire Gita. What we are reading is the enlightened understanding of Vyasa, who in the Gita is presenting us with a digest of the yoga philosophy of the Upanishads combined with both yoga psychology and instruction in yoga meditation. It is not amiss to say that Vyasa is the most important figure in Sanatana Dharma. If all other scriptures and commentaries disappeared and only the Gita remained, the Dharma would still be intact.

In general, then, Krishna is the voice of Vyasa, but within the Gita he is at times the voice of both the Atman and the Paramatman. So when we ponder the meaning of his words we should consider how they might be understood in this dual manner. For example, when Krishna tells us to fix our minds on him and worship him single-heartedly and steadfastly, he is not telling us to worship a God that is outside, but that which is the inmost dweller of the heart. He also means that the focus of our attention must be on our individual being as well as on the infinite. For they are one in essence.

The qualified student

During my first trip to India I met two Westerners who told me they had come to India to seek out a "qualified guru." I laughed and with my usual lack of tact asked: "Are you qualified disciples? Do you think a qualified guru would accept you?" They looked very taken aback and then admitted that it was not likely. But when I met them some months later they told me they had gotten initiation from every guru they met. "Just to make sure," was their explanation. They had not gotten the idea.

But who is a qualified disciple? Krishna tells Arjuna:

This ancient yoga is today declared by me to you because you are my devotee and friend. This secret is supreme indeed (4:3).

Devotee and friend. Here we have the marvelous, seeming contradiction that is the jewel of Eastern religion (including Eastern Christianity): the ability to be simultaneously absolutely reverent toward and yet absolutely familiar with and at home with God. The fear and trepidation, so beloved to Western religion past and present, simply do not come into it. Why? Because the orientals intuit their unity with God, while the occidentals feel utterly separated and alien from God. Consequently Western religion demands reconciliation and placation while Eastern religion simply calls us to unity, a unity that is essential and eternal. Westerners doubt their salvation, but Easterners know that they may have forgotten their unity with the Divine, but they have never lost it. They do not find salvation, they recover it. The infinity of God and their finitude does not daunt them in the least. They rejoice in both as devotees and friends of God. Because only such people can know this, Krishna says it is a secret–the Supreme Secret indeed.

THE ETERNAL BEING

Having been told that Krishna had taught Yoga to the most ancient of human beings:

> **Arjuna said: Your birth was later, and Vivaswat's birth was earlier. How then should I understand that you taught this in the beginning? (4:4)**

Krishna replies most directly and simply:

> **The Holy Lord said: Many of my births have passed away, and also yours. I know them all; you do not know them (4:5).**

Buddha taught that remembrance of all our past lives occurs at the time of enlightenment. However, some believe that recall of all previous lives can occur even before that. Whichever it might be, the idea is that every moment of our previous lives remains embedded in our subtle bodies and can influence and even determine our present lives.

Coming into "being"

Yet, we are something more than a story–we are Being itself, waves of the ocean of Infinite Being. Krishna, speaking as that Being, begins telling Arjuna of what he really is, and the truth of his relation to the world:

Although birthless and imperishable, although the Lord of all beings, controlling my own prakriti, I come into manifested being by my own power of maya (4:6).

Being completely outside of time, space, and all relativity, God (Brahman) is beyond birth and death, and any change whatsoever. The rest of us come and go, come and go, but Brahman abides forever; there is no coming or going for him. Never must we consider God as being conditioned in any way by relativity. This is not easy for us in the West who have lived from birth in an assumption that God perpetually reacts to us—that it is we who determine the state of God far more than he determines our state—and that we can control God's "moods." We have thought that our words, thoughts, and deeds will determine God's relation to us and how he thinks of us and cares or does not care about us. This is a tremendous error. However choppy the waves may be, the ocean remains stable and constant. It is the same with our tiny, tempestuous minds and lives in contrast to the utter Changelessness of God.

Yet, he has the most intimate connection/relation with us as our Lord (Ishwara), our inmost Self (Antaratman) and Ruler (Antaryamin). How can this seeming contradiction be? The illusive power known as Maya. Therefore Krishna continues:

Why

Whenever dharma decreases and there is the arising of adharma, then do I manifest myself. For protection of the righteous and destruction of evildoers, for the establishing of dharma, I manifest myself from age to age (4:7-8).

Whenever dharma decreases and anti-dharma rises up, Ishwara manifests himself through a liberated master, who is an avatar, an incarnation of divine consciousness. Why? *Paritranaya* means "for giving refuge," "for protecting," "for preservation," and "for the deliverance"—all that. And for whom? For the righteous—those that seek the Real, the True: Brahman.

Krishna means this in the sense of anyone who pursues Brahmajnana, such as the yogis who seek union with Brahman. There is an implication here, then, that dharma is essentially–even exclusively–the seeking for God, the living of the yoga life.

But others are involved here: *dushkritam*, the doers of evil. His plan for them is *vinashaya*, "for the destruction," of the evildoers. When this is done, dharma is reestablished on a solid basis and the righteous can pursue their aims in the right way in a harmonious and conducive environment. And this is done *yuge yuge*–from age to age. Whether Krishna is referring to the concept of ascending and descending ages (yugas) as is current now, or whether he just means eras of human history cannot be known for sure. The important idea here is that whenever there is a need there is a manifestation of the Divine.

Because of the present-day obsession with gods and avatars, it is assumed in India that Krishna is speaking of yugavatars–avatars of the age–that appear rather like the figures in mechanical clocks, every hour on the hour. However that may be, the idea is that God does something at times of spiritual crisis. It is commonly assumed that God is born on earth at those times, but *sambhavani* means "I come into being," or "I originate myself." Now there is no place in Sanatana Dharma for the idea that God comes into being at a point in time, or somehow creates himself. Consequently, "I manifest" is the safest translation. Although there can be no argument against births of perfected beings (siddhas) that are in a very real sense incarnations of God Consciousness, divine manifestations can take place in many ways to awaken straying humanity. I know of situations where the people of entire countries had profound spiritual awakening while the rest of the world snored away. Such an event was the Welsh Revival at the beginning of the twentieth century. At the end of the nineteenth century, the Ramakrishna Mission, inspired by Sri Ramakrishna and Swami Vivekananda, was the impetus for a powerful movement whose effect is felt throughout the world even now. Nearer our time, the arising of the Thai Forest Tradition in Thailand was a miraculous, spontaneous awakening that is still bearing fruit.

We must not forget that Krishna says this happens through his Maya, not through Shakti. So the creative power (prakriti) of God is not the deceiver it is always being claimed to be. Maya just means that the whole creation and what takes place therein is an illusion, like a motion picture. Only the consciousnesses, the spirits, that are witnessing the movie as though they were inside it and part of it, are real.

God is "born" in his creation, yet he is not born at all. Rather, through his power of Maya, he "dreams" creation and shows those dreams to us, enabling us to enter into his dream and dream along with him the dreams that will culminate in our awakening into his own Consciousness and Being, nevermore to forget ourselves in a dream body in a dream world. We, too, are ever unborn, though dreaming innumerable births and deaths.

Why? Because each life we dream is an exercise in consciousness, a means of developing (evolving) our scope of consciousness and understanding (jnana). We suffer because the dreams get out of our control, but once we master our dreaming all confusion, doubt, weakness, and ignorance will cease and we will be "born again" into perfect spiritual awareness, into the ultimate liberation for which we were destined before we first entered into relative existence–or appeared to enter, for it was all a series of educational dream-movies in the cosmic school of God Consciousness.

I manifest

From age to age, and in every age, we see the advent of divine consciousness in the world. Sometimes this takes place in the form of spiritual revelation to purified individuals who can perceive the divine revelation and convey it to others. But sometimes beings of such high consciousness and power come among us that they are truly manifestations of God himself. Whether these Great Ones are direct manifestations of God in human form, or are perfect, liberated beings who have long ago transcended the human condition and evolved upward unto total unity/identity with God, really has no relevance to us. What matters is the light they shed into our darkness and their teachings which, backed by infinite will, are truly "spirit and life" (John 6:63). Our obligation is not to define these holy messengers, but to carefully follow their teachings. "Whosoever shall do and teach them, the same shall be called great in the kingdom of heaven"

(Matthew 5:19. See Matthew 7:21; Luke 6:46). For they lead unerringly to the kingdom of infinite life.

We, too

We also, through our personal prakriti, our own maya, come back in each life to purify and evolve ourselves, to reveal that which is holy and innate in us, and to dispel the sin and ignorance into which we have strayed, finally establishing our consciousness in the Consciousness with which it has ever been one. Here, too, it is a sleeping and a forgetting until we awaken, remember, and say with the Psalmist: "When I awake, I am still with thee" (Psalms 139:18). The dream of separation and limitation is over forever. The purpose of life is liberation.

Self-knowing

> He who knows in truth my divine birth and action, leaving the body is not born again: he comes to me. Free from greed, fear and anger, absorbed in me, holding fast to me, purified by knowledge-based tapasya, many have attained my state of being (4:9-10).

Knowing that the advent or "birth" of Divine Light in the world–and in our own individual consciousness–has our enlightenment as its sole purpose, we can intelligently move toward freedom from rebirth. If we live accordingly we shall transcend the need for birth in any relative world and live in God fully. Rising above all passions rooted in the ego–and above the ego itself–we stand forth in the purity of being that is God.

THE PATH

In whatever way men resort to me do I thus reward them. It is my path which men follow everywhere (4:11).

For us raised in the "light that is darkness" of Western religion, every verse of the Gita is a revelation of stunning proportions. Certainly this is one of the most revelatory of them all–it opens vistas that free and expand the heart as we never dreamed possible. Let us continually look at them and rejoice in them. For Sanatana Dharma is not a dose of medicine or a contract of obligation, it is the key that unlocks our shackles, the light that dispels darkness and reveals the wonders of the way things are.

In whatever way men resort to me do I thus reward them. Bhajami basically means "I reward," but it can legitimately be translated "I share with" and "I love." In other words, however we may approach God, he will respond and fulfill our spiritual needs, loving us as his own being. It is all a matter of the disposition of our inmost mind and heart. Many people think they are seeking God, and many more tell others that they are seeking, but God truly knows, and responds–or not–accordingly. What is so heartening here is that however God is approached, he responds. Since we are incapable of meeting him on his own terms, he meets us on ours, and enables us to come up to his standards in time. For his motive is love. Those religionists whose motive is hate, greed, and ego, say otherwise, but that is their problem. While they are trying to beat others into conformity and submission to them, God's truth sets their victims free from such tyranny.

If we come seeking spiritual relief and healing, we will receive that. If we come seeking understanding, that will be given us. If we come yearning for living contact with God, that shall be ours. In other words, God will listen to the inmost movements of our hearts and grant any worth seeking. It is the character, the quality, of our taking refuge that will determine the outcome. No legitimate seeking is fruitless. It is not the form of the seeking, the externalities, that matter, but the interior intention and disposition of the heart that evokes the divine response and determines its character. Here, too, it is a matter of sowing and reaping.

It is my path which men follow everywhere. Of course! There is nothing other than God, and all relative existence is his manifestation/embodiment. So obviously there is no other path but his. Even Shakespeare knew this, saying: "There's a divinity that shapes our ends, rough-hew them how we will." However much we tangle things up and subvert our true nature, however horrific the mess of our life may be, yet we are walking on the One Path. The problem is, we walk the path in our manner, according to our arrogant (and errant) ignorance. Nevertheless, it is his path, and the moment we turn toward him, however blindly or uncomprehendingly, we will start to walk it in his way–a glorious way, for it ends in him. So we can say with Horatio, to whom Hamlet addressed the previous quote: "That is most certain."

This is wonderful to contemplate, so let us not leave it just yet. Every single human being is traveling a path that ultimately belongs to God. This is logical, since he is the source of all. They may be misusing that path, but it cannot change the fact that every thought and act of a human being has its roots in the Divine Being. Humans may subvert and trivialize the power of God, but they cannot wrest it from him. In time its true nature will be revealed. This is why we read so much of men and women who were spiritually awakened and redirected in the midst of their folly and wrongdoing. Some have stepped from darkness into light in the very act of evil–which they turned from in gladness. Many have found God present in the depths of degradation. That is why the Psalmist wrote: "Whither shall I go from thy spirit? or whither shall I flee from thy presence? If I ascend up into heaven, thou art there: if I make my bed in hell, behold, thou art there. If I take the wings of the morning, and dwell in the uttermost parts of the sea; even there shall thy hand lead me, and thy right hand shall hold me. If I say, Surely the darkness shall cover me; even the night shall be light about me" (Psalms 139:7-11). This we can know: whatever path anyone is now following, however foolish or negative it may seem, it is fundamentally God's path. It is the way we walk it that gets us in or out of trouble.

Thinking of this, I recalled a wonderfully peaceful evening when I was going down the holy Narmada river in a sailboat to an ashram located on its banks. As the boat glided along it came to the large bathing ghat of the town of Chandod. A hundred or more people were there, sitting looking over the river, visiting, or engaged in various tasks including bathing and laundry. As I watched this tranquil spectacle, for some reason the Christian missionaries in India popped into my mind. What a different reaction they would have! To my mind I was viewing blessed souls making their way toward the Divine Goal, souls whose ultimate destiny was assured. But the missionaries would see lost and darkened souls destined to be dragged off to eternal hell unless they (the missionaries) proclaimed the Gospel and persuaded them to "accept the Lord Jesus Christ"–someone they already believed in as a Son of God in a manner far more realistic than the erroneous theology of the missionaries. Because of this difference in viewpoints I was living in heaven; but they would be in hell–already.

Wherever a human being walks, however tangled the path or how dark the surroundings, eventually it will emerge in the light and they will know themselves as children of the Light. This is a marvelous truth. It also points out that all spiritual seeking, whatever its flaws may be, will lead in time to God. Yes, even the anxious and miserable missionaries will find in time that their sincere endeavors have produced positive karma for them that will enable them to move from ignorance to wisdom. Then they, too, will know the truth expressed here in the Gita.

A "footnote"

Of course, not all seeking is spiritual seeking. Therefore Krishna makes this comment:

Longing for success in action, in this world men sacrifice to the gods because success from such action is quickly attained in the human world (4:12).

Whether many gods, or the One God, are worshipped by people, their worship is usually not God-oriented, but centered in this world and their material aims. However, those aims are obtained by them, because no attention given to God is in vain. Moreover, faith is produced in them by their answered prayers so that when they do come to seek God for the right reasons their faith will strengthen and motivate them.

The sum and substance is this: Worship God, worship God, worship God... and find God. It is assured.

CASTE AND KARMA

Karma

Action–karma–is the basis of our continuing existence within the realm of relativity, even though our essential nature, the Self (Atman), transcends all relative modes of being. In other words, it is action that binds us. Fortunately, action can also free us, so Krishna is explaining to us all about action, its nature, purpose, and effects.

The word karma is derived from the Sanskrit root *kri*, which means to act, do, or make. Karma is any kind of action, including thought and feeling. It also means the effects of action. Karma is both action and reaction, the metaphysical equivalent of the principle: "For every action there is an equal and opposite reaction." Saint Paul expressed it perfectly when he wrote: "Whatsoever a man soweth, that shall he also reap" (Galatians 6:7). It is karma operating through the law of cause and effect that binds the jiva or the individual soul to the wheel of birth and death.

Karma is both the cause and the effect of our evolution and of our duty (swadharma), which includes caste in its metaphysical sense.

Caste "ism" and caste "system"

Before looking at the next verse which is about caste, we should consider what Krishna is not at all speaking about, even though for centuries–if not millennia–it is assumed in India that he is.

First, he is not at all speaking of a rigid, imposed system of social stratification where people are assigned a place in society simply because their parents occupied that place. In actuality, birth is not a determining factor in caste, although it can sometimes reflect it. Second, he is not speaking of valuing a person according to his imposed caste position or birth. Caste "ism" and the caste "system" have no place in Krishna's teaching, but are a corruption of caste based on ignorance, oppression, and egotism. The early scriptures of Hinduism bear this out, speaking of people's caste being determined by their character, and even telling of those who moved from one caste to another in a single life because of their personal development. For example, the philosopher-king Janaka, a kshatriya, in time was recognized as a brahmin.

Caste

Although he will be expounding the subject of caste and caste-duty in the final chapter of the Gita, Krishna briefly introduces it, saying:

The fourfold caste was created by me, based on guna and on karma (4:13a).

The word translated "caste" is *varna*–color. Krishna says: *Chaturvarnyam maya srishtam*–"The four castes [colors] were created [brought forth] by me." Krishna is saying that the Supreme Spirit has brought forth into manifestation human beings of a fourfold kind. And this Supreme Lord has not "created" human beings as four types, but has manifested them *guna karma vibhagashah*–"according to the sharing of their guna and karma." That is, all human beings fall into four very broad categories according to the evolutionary level of their development: according to the quality (guna) of the energies of which their subtle and gross bodies are formed, and according to the karmas which they have been born to fulfill. The "color" of each caste is either symbolic or a matter of the dominant color that can be clairvoyantly perceived in their aura. In either case, our caste is determined solely by the innate vibratory qualities present within us. No one assigns us a caste, though others may be able to perceive it, perhaps better than we do.

It is essential to grasp the fundamental fact that caste has absolutely nothing to do with a person's livelihood, though caste will certainly influence what we will gravitate to as our profession. Consequently, the general and natural situation was for shudras to be the servant class–those who assisted the three other castes in their respective functions; vaishyas to be the artisan/merchant class (which included agriculture); kshatriyas to be the warrior/ruling class (which included law enforcement); and brahmins to be the teaching/priestly class (this included the making of laws and magisterial duties).

All castes had their function that was essential to society. All were respected for their skills and for the benefits they provided for all in common. It is extremely necessary for us to see that the shudras were not half slaves at the bottom of society in mere servitude. Certainly some were in domestic service, but many–if not most–were found at the side of the other classes to help them in their work.

The idea of outcastes who would be relegated to the work everyone else was considered too superior to do, was absolutely unknown. The only "outcastes" practically speaking were criminals doing voluntary penance outside the context of normal society, and they would be reinstated once their penance had been completed. The outcastes of today are the descendants of incorrigibles who refused to observe the penances (not punishments) imposed on them by the brahmin judges and instead took to a wild and wandering life that often included crime.

In modern times certain very traditional institutions such as the Arya Samaj provide the means for these people to be reinstated into normal Hindu society if they desire. (Most do not–so it is their choice to remain in degradation.) In the last century Pandit Anandapriya of the Arya Samaj enabled over half a million of these and other estranged groups to return to traditional Hinduism. Vishwanath Brahmachari of Bombay (Galgoan) also returned many "no-castes" to Hinduism by giving them a caste status based on guna and karma. Like the Arya Samaj, he also enabled many non-Indians to also adopt Sanatana Dharma in the fullest traditional manner, assigning them a caste, as well.

Color (varna)

So what are the "colors" of the four castes? There may be more than one answer to this, however in the dharma (or grihya) sutras, ancient texts dealing with the gurukula, the place where Indians were originally educated, we find colors assigned to the clothing of the four castes. (Notice that all four castes were going to attend the school, not just some "higher" castes.) White was the color of shudras; yellow the color of vaishyas; red the color of kshatriyas, and orange the color of brahmins.

White is actually not a color, but all colors combined. This would be appropriate for shudras, since they were involved in the duties of all the castes. It also expresses their social fluidity, for originally the shudras were the most frequently transferred into other castes.

Yellow is the auric color of intelligence and initiative–an essential trait for agriculturalists, artisans, merchants, and those that comprise the vaishya caste.

Red is the color of dynamic power, discipline and assertiveness, so it naturally fits the kshatriyas.

Orange (gerua) is a combination of yellow and red, for brahmins must have the mental acumen and vigorous personal energies of the vaishyas and kshatriyas combined with a dominant spiritual consciousness. Fire is the essence of the original sacred rites of India, so its orange color represents spiritual consciousness and its transmuting powers.

It is interesting that all four colors are to be found in levels of the Indian monastic life. The standard color of full sannyas is appropriately orange, for it is the color of the crematory fire in which the earthly body is consumed, and the sannyasi's aim is to reduce to ashes all that is earthly within himself by means of the fire of spiritual realization.

The gurukula

In primeval Indian society, the male children were sent at an early age to live in a gurukula, the home of a teacher, until reaching adulthood. The vastly comprehensive education in a gurukula could last from fifteen to twenty years. At the end of his education, the young man returned to his parents, was married, and established his own household. By that time it was necessary that his caste be known so he could fulfill his caste duties. The gurukula was the place where his caste was determined by careful observation on the part of one or more teachers. Only after careful analysis of his personality was his caste determined.

Although there are many progressive educational institutions in India that are based on a spiritual viewpoint, it was only in the schools of Swami (later Paramhansa) Yogananda Giri that the ancient gurukula system was revived in its fullness. Yogananda drew up a Psychological Chart for the use of the teachers in his schools. Through the years each student was observed by those teachers and was finally classified according to his guna and karma, just as it had been done thousands of years before. This was something absolutely extraordinary and revolutionary, and even today is hardly recognized for what it is (was). If he had not come to America, who can say what modern Hinduism might have become through Yogananda's influence.

Personal meaning

For us living in the West in the twenty-first century, caste has meaning for us since knowing the character of our guna and karma is part of the knowledge that can lead to Self-knowledge. Although it may be a purely personal matter, it is good for us to know what our caste is, and live our lives accordingly.

In reality, each one of us is a kingdom, a "nation" to ourselves, and all four castes can be found within our psychological makeup. There are times when we must be shudras, others when we must be vaishyas, and so on. When there is "caste mixture"–that is, when in one aspect of our life we live according to a manner inappropriate to it–great harm can result. For example, in religion we must not be vaishyas, turning it into a business, nor must we be kshatriyas, trying to use it to coerce others to accept our spiritual ideas. Instead we must be brahmins–simple and self-contained, oriented only toward our spiritual development, making our religion truly a matter of consciousness, free from materiality. On the other hand, in practical (including economic) matters we must not be materially indifferent brahmins or aggressive kshatriyas, but worthy vaishyas. When considering principles of personal conduct or dealing with negativity, we must be valiant kshatriyas, giving no thought to economic gain or loss, or conciliatory compromises.

The subject of caste merits our attention and application as sadhakas. For caste duty is more than social, it is the way to hasten and facilitate our endeavors in personal evolution.

ACTION–DIVINE AND HUMAN

Krishna, having referred to caste as the basis of intelligent human action, now begins to speak of divine action–that of both the individual and the cosmic Self:

> **Though I am the creator thereof, know me to be the eternal non-doer (4:13b).**

The transcendent and the immanent

Both the Paramatman and the jivatman share the qualities of being simultaneously transcendent and immanent. This is a major insight, without which their seemingly contradictory manifestations and perceptions produce only confusion and contradiction. Religions throughout the ages have been torn by arguments about views considered contradictory that are in reality facets of a single truth. Even in India conflict is found regarding whether or not God has form or is formless, has qualities or is devoid of qualities, is personal or impersonal, is definable or indefinable, when God (Brahman) is all of these. But only those whose inner consciousness is opened can begin to comprehend this.

How is God beyond action? Since all things proceed from him, including their movement and change, can we really say he does not act? Even if his sole act is the emanation of the universe, that is no small deed. Evidently he is the non-doer in that no action can affect him in any degree or produce any kind of conditioning in him. Krishna now expounds on this.

Actions do not taint me

Actions do not taint me, nor is desire for action's fruit in me. He who thus comprehends me is not bound by actions (4:14).

Patanjali tells us in the Yoga Sutras: "Ishwara [God] is a particular Purusha [Spirit, Person] Who is untouched by the afflictions of life, actions, and the results and impressions produced by these actions" (Yoga Sutras 1:24). The key point here is that God is untouched–free from–any compulsion to act or the result of actions, both of which condition the finite individual. The laws of causation apply only to those intelligences who are moving within the plane of relative existence. It is necessary for them to be "touched" by action, otherwise they would not evolve beyond relativity. But this is never the case with the Transcendent who is in some incomprehensible way the untouched and inactive Source and Maintainer of all. When we think about this we can understand why philosophies such as Sankhya reject the idea of Brahman as a Cosmic Doer–Ishwara or Bhagavan. If, however, we realize that all relativity is but an appearance without actual substance, then, just as we momentarily appear to be humans but are not really so at any time, so Brahman is that Reality which appears to us as though it is Ishwara or Bhagavan. In the final analysis we realize that action does not affect God because action–in the way we understand or mistake it–is impossible for him. And also impossible for us!

Nor is desire for action's fruit in me

To desire something is to imply a lack, deficiency or a defect in one's self or one's life. Since there is no lack, deficiency or defect in God, it is impossible for him to even desire–much less desire either to act or to produce an effect of action. This, too, is our situation. It is only our lesser being that can desire, act, and experience the consequences of action. God has no motive that could produce an action, either. A question such as "Why did/does God do…?" is simply absurd, and any answer we come up with is doubly absurd. A classic example is the question: Why did God make the world? and the even sillier answer: Because he was lonely. The answer,

So he could share himself with others, is really inexcusable, because we are eternally a part of him and already partaking of his being. As I say, any answer is foolish. No wonder the wise are so often silent.

Krishna has already spoken of Prakriti, the creative energy by and through which all things are done. It is Prakriti that evolves, both in its cosmic and its individual states. So, then, is Prakriti a "thing" separate from God that somehow does his "will"? No; rather, Prakriti is the creative dreaming faculty of God. Just as we dream our many incarnations, so God dreams the many cycles of creation. God, however, controls his dreams, whereas we do not until we master our dream through the practice of yoga. Then we, too, will no longer have desire for the fruits of action, for we will know that there are no actions–only dreams.

Those who understand the foregoing facts can only be the master of their activity, never its slave. Because, after all, it is only a concept, a mirage–necessary, but not ultimately real.

The practical application

> **Knowing thus, the ancient seekers for liberation performed action. Do you, therefore, perform action as did the ancients in earlier times (4:15).**

In prehistory there were no such things as mirrors. To see themselves, people had to look into water. Some, leaning over to see themselves reflected on the water's surface, fell into the water and drowned. In the same way nearly all sentient beings fall into the mirage of relative existence by identifying with it and forgetting their transcendental reality. Thus they drown in their finite life, suffocating and floundering, yet without being released from it until after incalculable ages they find the way back onto the shore of their true Self. Until then any hope of peace and freedom from pain is tormenting and tantalizing, as delusive as the rest of their experience.

Action, then, is dangerous, a looking into the pool of samsara. In old Greek mythology the youth Hylas looked into a pool inhabited by water spirits who reached up and pulled him into the water and drowned him so they could keep him with them always. In keeping with the rationalizing and delusive nature of the human mind, it was reported that he had chosen to go into the water. Well, if he did, he was still just as drowned and dead as if he had not made that choice.

Since this is our situation, Krishna speaks of how "the ancient seekers for liberation performed action." For we, who also seek liberation, must know how to do the same, performing action "as did the ancients in earlier times."

THE MYSTERY OF ACTION AND INACTION

What is action? What is inaction? Even the poet-sages were bewildered regarding this matter. This action shall I explain to you, which having known you shall be freed from evil (4:16).

When we understand the nature of action (karma) and inaction (akarma) we will become free from all impurity in the form of the conditioning resulting from action/inaction which we commonly call karma. This verse implies that such knowing is purely a spiritual matter and must be approached accordingly. It also implies that all karma, positive and negative, are blockages to spiritual progress. We need to keep this in mind, as we tend to think of karma only as one or the other.

The foundation of understanding

Truly the nature of action, of wrong action and of non-action is to be known. The path of action is difficult to understand (4:17).

Prabhavananda's translation is interpretive, but all translators agree with his interpretation and his wording is beautifully clear, so I would like to use it as the basis for commentary. "You must learn what kind of work to do, what kind of work to avoid, and how to reach a state of calm detachment from your work. The real nature of action is hard to understand."

You must learn what kind of work to do, [and] what kind of work to avoid. There is no place here for the moral dilettante's beloved "situation ethics." Regarding the rules of right conduct, in the Yoga Sutras Patanjali assures us: "These, not conditioned by class, place, time or occasion, and extending to all stages, constitute the Great Vow" (Yoga Sutra 2:31. See *The Foundations of Yoga*). They can be neither mitigated nor abrogated. Many religionists attempt to do so, but their failure in spiritual life demonstrates their folly. In contrast, the yogi must carefully study the words of realized men and women—not the words of revealed "messengers of God," but of true saints, true masters, who proved in their lives that their consciousness was united with God. These great teachers tell us by their living examples and their words what is to done and what is to be avoided.

That is easy to say, but how can we know that a teacher really is genuine? Actually, it is not that hard to figure out: *The holy ones of all true religions say the same thing.* Those who deviate from the unanimous testimony of the saints are not to be fully trusted, even though they may be sincere and have good qualities. Only those who live in the same vision and inner state are completely trustworthy. That, too is easy to say. What are some traits we should look for in spiritual teachers? Here are a few. They teach:

    a) that religions other than theirs are also true.

    b) that all seekers of God are finders—no one is condemned because he does not believe in one particular religion, scripture, teacher or prophet.

    c) the necessity of personal and public morality, and are unanimous in affirming the moral teachings to be found in the Yama and Niyama of Patanjali, the Ten Commandments of Judaism, the Five Precepts of Buddhism, and the Eight Beatitudes of Christianity.

    d) that every human being is meant to know God in a direct and immediate manner.

    e) that an interior life is indispensable for knowing God.

You must learn... how to reach a state of calm detachment from your work.
Such a state of mind is not attained by reading a few pages of convincing
philosophy, but we must pursue a path of mental cultivation that will enable
us to be established in the witness consciousness that is our essential nature.
Our problem is that we identify with the many layers of energy through
which we experience relative existence. We not only mistakenly identify
with the means of perception, we go a step further and identify with what
is perceived. This is known as drowning in the ocean of samsara. The only
antidote to this condition is the practice of yoga, as Krishna points out to
Arjuna throughout the Gita.

The real nature of action is hard to understand. This is because of our
mistaken identities, as just pointed out. Mere intellectual acceptance of "the
message of the Gita" is of no value. We must strive for the transmutation
of consciousness that is itself liberation–liberation from both action and
inaction.

Two common delusions are to assume that action is the way and inaction must be avoided, or that inaction is the way and action is to be
avoided. These two delusions dominate just about everybody. In India
the action/inaction controversy continues, to absolutely no conclusion
or practical value. The Gita gives a completely coherent answer, but still
the confusion goes on. This is because it is not a matter of thinking about
it, but of experiencing the truth of it. Krishna now brings this fact out.

Seeing

> He who perceives inaction in action and action in inaction–
> such a man is wise among men, steadfast in yoga and doing
> all action (4:18).

Prabhavananda fills it out very well: "He who sees the inaction that is
in action, and the action that is in inaction, is wise indeed. Even when he
is engaged in action he remains poised in the tranquility of the Atman."

"I am ever the same," says the Self, for it never at any time acts or
undergoes any change. And yet, it is the presence of the Self that causes

the dance-drama of the entire chain of evolutionary births which the Self witnesses without ever really taking part. This is impossible for the ordinary intellect, however keen, to penetrate. But the yogi, daily experiencing himself as the eternal witness (the same experience which is intrinsic to God) comes to see that behind all action is the inaction of consciousness. Yet, it is the unmoving presence of consciousness that stimulates Prakriti, the Divine Creative Energy to act. The Actionless causes all Action to take place. Only the yogi can really know this. "Even when he is engaged in action he remains poised in the tranquility of the Atman."

THE WISE IN ACTION

The eleven major Upanishads present the supreme philosophy, the supreme ideal. The Gita, being a virtual digest of the Upanishads, does the same, but it goes into the practical application of those principles, and even further into a description of the effects of that application. The Gita describes perfectly the state of the enlightened human being–at least as perfectly as human speech is able to delineate. It is these descriptions which we should study carefully, leaving aside the absurd questions that contemporary mind-gamers have come up with such as: Does a jnani have a subconscious mind–and if not, does the jnani dream?

In the Gita we find the psychology of the jnani completely expounded, and it is something that cannot possibly be observed by any other than the jnani himself. As Yogananda wrote: "He who knows–he knows. None else knows." Our job is to become jnanis, not to figure out if someone else is a jnani–though that is a lot easier on the ego.

Krishna is now going to give us a picture of a sage in action, and yet beyond action.

Whose undertakings are devoid of plan and desire for results, whose actions are consumed in the fire of knowledge–him the wise call wise (4:19).

Devoid of plan and desire for results. To act rightly–to do the right thing in the right way at the right time in the right place–and nothing more: that is the way of the Gita. Therefore, to keep the fruit, the effect, of an act in mind as our purpose, is to deflect ourselves from the right motivation and to entangle ourselves in the net of egotism and the snare of binding deeds. Two forces impel us into this trap: desire (*kama*) and motive (*sankalpa*).

Kama is desire, passion, or lust. The first meaning, that of desire, is uppermost in this part of the Gita. Though people can pursue action with a blinding and binding passion, it is best for us to think mostly of simple desire, since the palest shade of desire can mar our action. Also, desire can be incredibly subtle and undetectable to any but the keenest intelligence. Passion and lust, on the other hand, are extremely obvious and impossible to disguise–though many in their grip pretend that they are being dedicated, noble, and fervent in a righteous cause. Human beings can talk themselves into anything. But sensible people can see the fiend beneath the fever. Desire, though, is capable of disguising itself or hiding itself completely from all but the most perceptive. This is why tapasya, not intellectual analysis, is the only sure way of uprooting this subtle enemy.

Sankalpa is wish, desire, volition, resolution, will, determination, and intention. Yes; all that. Any kind of intentions–including subconscious ones–mar action. Even the slightest wish or hope in relation to the result of an action turns it into a bond. No wonder Krishna says later on: "Truly this maya of mine made of the gunas is difficult to go beyond" (7:14).

But when a person becomes absolutely free of kama and sankalpa, his action slips away like a loosened bond. Even more: the binding power of the act is broken so it cannot arise in the future to be a hindrance. Someone in this state then ceases to create any more karma.

Whose actions are consumed in the fire of knowledge. There is a lot of talk about eliminating karma, as though it were something to throw away or wash down the drain. Not so. Karma must be burned in the fire of knowledge–*jnanagni*. As genuine camphor burns and leaves no residue whatsoever, but just vanishes, so it is with karma burned in the fire of knowledge. It is absurd to say that a liberated person still has to undergo his prarabdha karma–karma that has begun to manifest and bear fruit. This mythology is a rationalization put forth by whose who claim their guru is liberated while still very obviously bound by karma. A liberated person may decide to remain in this world, though having no karma to fulfill. God does not need karma to enable him to project the creation, and a liberated being does not need any karma to remain here on earth. If he cannot do so, then he is not a Master, and not liberated.

(However, some masters can selectively burn their karma, and retain miniscule karmic "threads" which they can use to more easily come into future incarnations. Nevertheless, they are not bound or obligated by prarabdha karma. They are masters even of karma.)

Complete in the Self

> Having abandoned attachment for action's fruit, always content, not dependent on anything even when acting, he truly does nothing at all (4:20).

Nevertheless, he does act. That is, he turns his face from the fruits of action, not even looking at them, lest like Eve (Genesis 3:6), he be drawn again to desire them and fall away from the state he has so laboriously attained.

The enlightened man is literally *Self*-sufficient. "When he leaves behind all the desires of the mind, contented in the Self by the Self, then he is said to be steady in wisdom" (2:55). "He who is content only in the Self, who is satisfied in the Self, who is pleased only in the Self: for him there is no need to act" (3:17).

Having gone beyond the realm of action, he truly "perceives inaction in action and action in inaction" (4:18).

Complete control

> Acting with the body alone, without wish, with thought and lower self restrained, abandoning all acquisitiveness, though acting he incurs no fault [guilt or evil] (4:21).

Here again we see that Krishna is not advocating some kind of self-effacing passivity. Rather he is showing us heroic endeavor. Certainly the wise man does not desire or will the fruits of action, but to ensure he never again falls into the old pattern of delusion he exercises absolute control over body and mind. Enlightenment is not an avoidance of body and mind and their influences, it is mastery in the fullest sense.

For ages in India a crippling passivity and indifference has been cultivated due to the degenerative influence, especially, of ignorant sannyasis who have held a completely wrong idea about their own way of life—a wrong idea which they hold up to non-monastics as an ideal to also follow. Shamefulness has become a virtue, cowardice touted as courage, and ineffectiveness as skill in action. Yet the Gita has all the time stood in virile contrast to this effete cowardice and cultivated incompetence.

Swami Vivekananda devoted his life to arousing his countrymen to abandon the horrible morass into which they were complacently sinking. Still the illusion prevails. No wonder many in India feel that they need to shake off religious influence to become self-respecting and worthy human beings. This is a sad misconception, for as Vivekananda remarked upon returning to India after his first trip abroad, India's problem is not its religion, but the fact that it has not been rightly practiced. The deadening effect of the false "brahmarishis" has blinded not only India but the world to the way of the "rajarishis" advocated by Krishna.

Controlling body and mind the wise realizes that he is the Self. Nothing is his own, for the Self transcends all things. Thus he acts and incurs no karma.

Symptoms of control

Now comes a verse that the foolish have used to bolster their advocacy of passivity and worthlessness—of spiritual and mental novocain.

> **Content with what comes unbidden, beyond the pairs of opposites and free from envy, the same in success or failure, even though acting, he is not bound (4:22).**

I will not waste your time pointing out what this does not mean. Others will do that gladly—and solely.

Content with what comes unbidden. That is, he is content with whatever occurs or comes to him as a result of his prarabdha karma, the karma that is presently manifesting as this particular life. This karma is spontaneous, occurring automatically.

The wise man accepts that which comes to him because it is his own action coming to fruition. He does not desire or anticipate the fruits of his present actions, but he thoroughly accepts the advent of the results of his past actions that have created this life and determined its quality and events. Does this mean he is merely passive, with a "What can I do?" attitude? Not at all. He understands that his prarabdha karma is not some kind of reactive payback for past deeds, but that its purpose is his learning, his evolution. Karma is a real lesson in living. We accept it, but we also study it and learn what it is saying to us. Otherwise we will fail the lesson and have to keep taking it over and over until we do learn. The adage that history repeats itself is true because we do not learn from it and apply it to our personal life as well.

The intelligent individual understands that all our life is a learning session, that pleasant karma is not to just be enjoyed or unpleasant karma endured or avoided. Rather, it is to be learned from. We must get involved with our karma and use it for our betterment. Karma is not fate; it is opportunity. Only when we live accordingly can we be considered worthy of human birth. Meeting karma head-on is the way to master it and profit from it. This requires our full acceptance of it, but with the right understanding of it.

Beyond the dualities [pairs of opposites]. Whatever comes or goes is a matter of his own previous choices—so the yogi views all phenomena, not preferring one or the other. This is because he sees value in both the pleasant and the unpleasant, seeing neither of them as undesirable. They are part of his life-script which he must read and comprehend. Everything is for his betterment. Consequently he looks to the wisdom to be gained and not the superficial external experience.

Free from envy. He is free from envy or greed because whatever comes to him is a matter of his own doing. Who will he envy? Can he be jealous of someone who had the good sense to order the right things from the store-house of life? He could have the same if he had been wiser, and he can get anything he wants in the future. He need only use life more competently.

No wonder Buddha kept emphasizing the need for skillful action. It is pointless to attempt transcending this life until we have lived it worthily. Many yogis come to naught because they think yoga is a means of escape from the lessons of life. Until we learn, we do not graduate to a higher grade. "Those who are too good for this world are adorning some other," as Swami Sri Yukteswar often pointed out. Until then, here we will stay.

The same in success or failure. This is not because he shrugs and says: "Oh, well, that is my karma," and bumbles on without a sense of responsibility. Yes, indeed, it is his karma, whether of the present or the past, and it reveals how well or how poorly he acted in the past. He may not desire certain results of his actions, but he definitely gets their message. Success and failure are only symptoms of wisdom or folly. He astutely evaluates the root of his consciousness, seeing his actions as the branches and leaves of that root. His work is with the root; the rest will follow suit when the right quality has been attained. Effects have value only as indicators of the nature of the cause. He knows this, and is intent only on the rectification of the cause: his state of awareness.

Even though acting, he is not bound. For he does not look at the results of action, but is the witness of the acts. The Self is never touched or bound by action. Centering his consciousness in the truth of his being through diligent practice of meditation, he is freed from karmic effects.

Once again we see the value of Vyasa presenting the teachings of the Gita in the context of the Mahabharata War. Krishna is urging Arjuna to engage in battle, assuring him that if he does so rightly he will incur no negative karma. Instead, he will be released from the karma that brought him to Kurukshetra, the Field of Dharma. If this is true of warfare, how can we hesitate to engage optimistically in our comparatively easy and insignificant karmic struggles?

The result

> The karma of one who is free from attachment, whose thought is established in knowledge, undertaking action for sacrifice, is wholly dissolved (4:23).

It is a matter of both knowledge and attitude.

Brahman is the offering, Brahman is the oblation poured out by Brahman into the fire of Brahman. Brahman is to be attained by him who always sees Brahman in action (4:24).

Knowers of Brahman know their entire life as sacrifice (yajna). Here, particularly, the fire sacrifice or havan is the symbol of the Brahmajnani's unbroken awareness of Brahman.

Brahman is the offering. All action whatsoever is a manifestation of the power of God. Everything that is done is God. This is because the entire realm of relative existence is not a thing at all; at no time does it have a material, objective existence. Rather, it is the thought of God, the divine Thinker, the dream of God, the divine Dreamer. It is a motionless movement within the Consciousness that is God. Thus everything is God in the most literal and most absolute sense. The "offering" of evolution within relative existence is Brahman itself. There is nothing else.

Brahman is the oblation. Everything that we deal with in our evolutionary journey, whatever we employ to further the expansion of our consciousness, whatever we offer to God in our attempt to ascend to the Absolute—all that is Brahman alone.

Poured out by Brahman. All the waves of the ocean are the ocean. Every sentient being, every spark of individualized consciousness, is Brahman. Those who seek Brahman *are* Brahman. That is, Brahman is their essential, inseparable nature. None but Brahman worships and seeks Brahman. None but Brahman finds Brahman.

Into the fire of Brahman. Again, the entire range of dynamic, seemingly ever-changing field of evolutionary life is Brahman alone. It is Brahman that is the transmuting fire of the cosmos. Brahman is itself the Eternal Phoenix that is perpetually consumed by itself and produced from itself in never-ending cycles that are themselves "the fire of Brahman."

Brahman is to be attained by him who always sees Brahman in action. "The yogi whose mind is truly tranquil, with emotions [passions] calmed, free of evil, having become one with Brahman, attains the supreme happiness. Thus constantly engaging himself in the practice of yoga, that yogi, freed from evil, easily contacting [touching] Brahman, attains boundless happiness. He who is steadfast in yoga [yoga-yukta] at all times sees the Self present in all beings and all beings present in the Self. He who sees me everywhere, and sees all things in me—I am not lost to him, and he is not lost to me. He, established in unity, worships me dwelling in all things; whatever be his mode of life, that yogi ever abides in me" (6:27-31).

Even if at the time it is mostly intellectual rather than purely intuitive, we must strive to "see through" all action to Brahman, the Ground of All Being.

SACRIFICIAL OFFERINGS

The ideal of sacrifice

In every religion we find the idea of sacrifice, of making offerings to God Who, being infinite and all-encompassing, and therefore all-possessing, cannot really be offered to. Yet, in the training film we call samsara, the act of will involved in offering to God is essential to the development of each of us. For we can make offerings to our own Self—and hence to Brahman—in the form of acts which purify and evolve the vehicles of the Self. Krishna is now going to enumerate the various forms of sacrificial elements and acts.

Before studying this and the next verses it is necessary for us to understand that all described here are yogis, that Krishna is not denigrating anyone, nor he is propounding a narrow vision of what is acceptable sacrifice to the Divine. He is, instead, showing us that there are many ways to offer unto God, and that all are legitimate and worthy of regard. Certainly, some are more sophisticated than others, yet every step in the stair, every rung on the ladder, is important for it leads us on to higher realities.

This is particularly seen in the following verse, where Krishna presents as viable two approaches that today are almost universally viewed as antithetical to one another, the first usually being considered useless and ignorant.

Gods and Brahman-Self

Some yogis offer sacrifice to the gods alone, while others offer the [individual] Self as sacrifice unto the [Supreme] Self into the fire that is Brahman (4:25).

Here we find two approaches to Divinity: that which sees it as object–gods or God–and that which sees it as Subject–Brahman or the Atman-Self. Both approaches are legitimately yogic. Certainly worship or meditation directed to God as a separate being is not as on target as meditation on the identity of the yogi's Self with Brahman. Nevertheless such meditation leads the consciousness of the yogi upward and will eventually bestow on him the wider vision of Divinity as one with him. To despise the lesser approach is as silly as to despise learning the alphabet because it is superseded by reading. The latter cannot occur without the former. The offering of the first type of yogis is devotion of the heart–no small gift. The second type of yogi offers his Self by merging it into the greater life of Brahman. Brahman is called fire because such a union purges the yogi of all extraneous matter, of all that is not eternal and divine. Yet, the first form of offering will culminate in the second form if persevered in.

Yajnam yajnena is an interesting expression: "sacrifice by sacrifice." The original sacrifice (yajna) was the projection of all levels of relative existence along with the entering into it of Brahman as the Witness of All. That is, Brahman dreamed the dream of creation and of incarnating within it as its all-experiencing Self. Brahman is dreaming the same dream we are, but without loss of control or consciousness. This is an important fact for us to know. In Sanskrit terminology formulated later than the Gita, the witnessing consciousness of Brahman within creation is called the Mahat Tattwa, the Supreme Principle, Ishwara.

The great Christian esotericist James Ingall Wedgwood, a leading figure in the Theosophical Society and founder of the Liberal Catholic Church, wrote the following prayer: "We lift our hearts in adoration to Thee,… Who, abiding unchangeable within Thyself, didst nevertheless in the mystery of Thy boundless love and Thine eternal sacrifice breathe forth Thine own divine life into Thy universe,.... Omnipotent, all-pervading, by that self-same sacrifice Thou dost continually uphold all creation," referring to it as "the enduring Sacrifice by which the world is nourished and sustained."

Just as we experience a series of incarnation in bodies, so Brahman, in Its extension as Ishwara, experiences a series of incarnation through an unending series of creation cycles—days and nights of Brahma. Seeking for union with Brahman in an intelligent and orderly manner—in other words, through the practice of dharma and yoga—is our way of engaging in "sacrifice by sacrifice."

The senses

> Others offer senses such as hearing into the fires of restraint; others, sound; and others objects of the senses into the fire of the senses (4:26).

It is significant that the sense of sound (shabda) which arises from the subtlest level of our being, the akasha (ether), is mentioned specifically here. Yogis employ subtle sound in and out of meditation in the form of japa: mantra repetition.

Once again we encounter a duality. See the eminent wisdom of Krishna. He does not disdain one and exalt the other just because one may be more disciplined and consistent with ultimate spiritual principles than the other. He affirms the value of both. There can be sectarianism of discipline as well as of doctrine, and Krishna is leading us away from that error.

Some yogis cut off and avoid all sense-experience beyond what is inevitable in the maintenance of a simple life. Many refuse to look around them but always look down so as not to be distracted by the sense of sight. Others contrive to avoid enjoyment of the taste of food in various ways, such as mixing ashes with their food (not a very healthy practice) or mixing all the types of food together in a kind of hodgepodge, combining even the sweet with the salty. (This latter is more common among Indian yogis, Yogananda even having done so in his youth.) To such yogis "senses are the offering, and self-discipline the sacrificial fire" (Prabhavananda).

A completely opposite course is allowing sense-impressions without avoidance, keeping vividly in mind that all things are manifestations of Brahman. We must not misunderstand this approach. It is not "living life to the full" by romping around greedily pursuing and delighting in mere sensory experience, wallowing in the mire of material consciousness while claiming that "all is God." This is the perversion of ignorance. Rather, Krishna is speaking of those who willingly experience natural beauty and the enjoyment of simple and beneficial things such as food, the warmth of shelter, the ease of good health, and suchlike. Even these yogis would be considered much too disciplined and ascetic for the hedonistic "spirituality" of the incurably worldly.

This second type of yogi freely employs the senses in spiritual devotion. They offer the fragrance and beauty of flowers, the perfume of incense, the light of lamps, and the taste of food (prasadam) in worship. They also enjoy the beauty and inspiration of divine imagery and of devotional music. In this way they consciously offer Brahman to Brahman.

There is a third way in relation to the senses:

Some offer all the actions of the senses and the functions of the life force (prana) into the fire of the yoga of self-restraint, which is enkindled by knowledge (4:27).

Whereas the two types of yogis mentioned before have some identity with the senses, this third type "renounces" them and their functions. The way they do this is described in the next chapter of the Gita in these two verses: "'I do not do anything;' thus thinks the steadfast knower of truth [while; when] seeing, hearing, touching, smelling, eating, walking, sleeping, breathing, speaking, releasing, and holding, opening and closing his eyes—convinced that it is the senses that move among the sense-objects" (5:8-9).

We will look into this more later in considering the next chapter. But we should seriously consider that Krishna tells us this form of offering is "kindled by knowledge," indicating that this discipline is established only in those who have begun to already experience or intuit the Self within themselves through buddhi yoga. He also is telling us that discipline is a result of wisdom. So when we encounter a "sage" who freely imparts his "knowledge" we should look at how disciplined he is, and thereby know whether his knowledge is real or mere words.

Renunciation, discipline, and knowledge

> Those whose sacrifices take the form of yoga offer material possessions and tapasya as sacrifices; while ascetics with stringent vows offer self-analysis [swadhyaya] and knowledge as sacrifice (4:28).

Dravyayajnas means those who sacrifice through material things by either using them for higher purpose, or by renouncing them. For example, a person might give away all or much of what he has in good causes, or he also might renounce by refusing to engage in a form of livelihood that will bring in much money but distract him from spiritual life by making too many demands on his time. Refusing to do something unethical that would have resulted in material gain is also a form of renunciation-sacrifice.

Spiritual discipline and practice, especially yoga, is a very high form of sacrifice. And those who are intensely serious will ruthlessly study and analyze their inner and outer actions as well as their mental states in order to detect any hidden negativity or ignorance and cut them off, objectively diagnosing their present spiritual status. The knowledge they offer is threefold: that gained from self-study, that attained through intuition developed by meditation, and that found in the study of sacred texts and the teachings of the wise. They also may extend or intensify their disciplines and spiritual practices.

The pranas (life forces)

> Some offer inhalation into exhalation, and exhalation into inhalation, restraining the paths of inhalation and exhalation, intent upon control of the breath (pranayama) (4:29).

The senses are merely instruments of perception powered by various forms of subtle life force known as the pranas. In Patanjali's Yoga

Sutras we are told that meditation consists of several ingredients. One is pranayama.

It is usually thought that pranayama is composed of the words *prana* and *yama*, which mean breath (or life-force) and restraint (or control). But it really comes from *prana* (breath) and *ayama*, which means lengthening, expansion, and extension. In meditation the breath becomes subtle, refined, and slow (lengthened, expanded, and extended). Yoga Sutra 2:50 says that pranayama "becomes measured or regulated [paridrishto], prolonged [dirgha], and subtle or attenuated [sukshmah]." "Prolonged and light [subtle]," says Vyasa. Sometimes it is long and slow and sometimes it is slow but short. Whichever it may be, it is always spontaneous and not controlled–or even deliberately intended–in any way. Pranayama, then, is an effect, not a practice. This can be accomplished through objective observation of the breath, or even by simply sitting in right posture (asana) in a relaxed manner and being inwardly aware in meditation. However it is accomplished, if it is offered to God pranayama becomes a factor for the yogi's upliftment. This verse is also about the pranayama called "circling" in which the inhaling and exhaling breaths are seamless, smooth and continuous. That is, there is no deliberate pause between them, but the moment the inhalation ends the exhalation begins, and vice versa. When the yogi is truly relaxed this is his natural way of breathing.

Others who have restricted their food offer the pranas into the pranas [since all the forms of prana are derived from food] **(4:30a).**

That is, they offer the prana of the food they eat into the present pranas of the body.

The food we eat nourishes and conditions the various streams of life-force, of prana, in the body, so diet is also a means of controlling prana. Regulation of food includes moderation in the amount of food eaten, and also discrimination in the type of food eaten. The yogi must adopt a diet that conduces to health of body and stability of mind. Consequently he must absolutely avoid all meat, fish, eggs, alcohol, nicotine, and mind-altering drugs. At the same time the food he eats must be beneficial to the body and not whimsical or faddish. Krishna will discuss this at length in the beginning of the seventeenth chapter.

The various sacrificers

> All these are knowers of sacrifice whose wrongdoings have been annihilated through sacrifice (4:30b).

Kalmasas means evils or wrongdoings–the negative karmas (including mental effects) accruing from negative actions. By the many sacrifices listed by Krishna, the negative karmas and conditionings produced by past negative action are dissolved and the yogis attain freedom.

> Eating the amrita of the sacrificial remains, they go to the Eternal Brahman. Even this world is not for the non-sacrificing–how then the other worlds? (4:31).

The entire life of the knowers of sacrifice is prasadam–that which has been first offered to God and is thus holy and purifying to the partaker. Such a life leads to participation in the life of Brahman.

But those whose lives are not sacrifice, are not worship of the Eternal, will find that there can be no lasting peace or meaning for them in any world, because all worlds are manifestations of God whose sole purpose is the life in God–nothing else. Those who live selfishly and godlessly alienate themselves from the entire cosmos. Where, then, can they find any rest? It is hopeless. But those who live sacrificially in the spirit of worship find themselves at home everywhere.

> Sacrifices of many kinds are spread out before the face of Brahman. Know them all to be born from action. Knowing thus, you shall be liberated (4:32).

Once more Krishna points out the necessity of action and the impossibility of inaction for the adept yogi.

THE WORSHIP OF
BRAHMAN

Better than the sacrifice of material things is knowledge-sacrifice. All action without exception is fully contained in knowledge (4:33).

To know God is the supreme sacrifice-worship, immeasurably beyond offering material objects in sacrifice. Yet, once more Krishna is warning us away from ignorant snobbery. For he assures us that all action–including ritualistic, material sacrifice and worship–leads to the attainment of knowledge. We must never disdain any endeavor in spiritual life, for such action creates positive spiritual karma that will eventually result in enlightenment. Enlightened people are aware that every attempt to attain higher life will in time uplift the seeker. Remembering their own past struggles, they know that no effort is ever wasted, that the intention will perfect the action. "In this no effort is lost, nor are adverse results produced" (2:40), Krishna has told Arjuna.

Teachers

Know that by prostrating yourself, by questioning and by serving them, the wise who have realized the truth will therefore instruct you in that knowledge (4:34).

Since this verse is continually misapplied to the cultish slavery of guru-dom, we should analyze it very carefully.

First we are told that illumined teachers will instruct us in knowledge (*upadekshyanti te jnanam*). They will teach us the principles of Brahma-jnana, which includes the practice of meditation by which the knowledge of Brahman is attained. This is a wonderful prospect, but it says nothing more than this. There is no word of empowerment or diksha (initiation) being given by the teacher, or his taking on the student's karma or the forging of some type of eternal bond in which the teacher is obligated to bestow enlightenment. In other words, the manipulative super-parent type of disempowerment and enslavement so current today in guruland is not in Krishna's mind.

He does tell Arjuna that the seeker must approach the teacher with humble salutation (*pranipatena*) and must actively question (*pariprashnena*) him. Moreover, the seeker must render service (*sevaya*). This is because at the time of Krishna teachers lived in forest ashrams and seekers were expected to live with them for some time to learn the practice of spiritual life as well as its philosophy. Therefore they helped in any kind of work that needed doing.

Krishna was quite familiar with a type of seeker found even today. Approaching the teacher as a virtual equal, they set themselves down in front of him and unload a barrage of metaphysical questions intended to determine whether or not the teacher is worthy of their attention. If they decide the teacher is worthy, they proceed to monopolize his time and attention, disregarding anyone else, expecting to be waited on and supplied with whatever they might want, assuming that everyone in the ashram is a servant whose existence is justified by serving them and the guru.

Krishna points out that the seeker is expected to help out in the ashram and be of benefit to his fellow seekers. Be assured that this has nothing to do with the "karma yoga" projects of ambitious gurus entailing grinding labor and "voluntary" deprivation. The service an authentic spiritual teacher desires is careful attention and the putting into practice of the teachings he imparts. Unlike the ancient Pharaohs, such a teacher has no desire to turn his students into slaves dragging over hot sands the stones with which he will build a monument to himself. Remember: Krishna has in mind the quiet forest ashrams where the teacher and students lived in utmost simplicity. The service expected was equally humble and simple.

Also, since the days when Vyasa wrote the Gita on palm leaves with a wooden stylus dipped in ink made of berries, a wonderful thing has appeared in the world: the printing press. Millions throughout the world can now learn the wisdom of great master-teachers of all ages and traditions. It is still good to find a worthy teacher who will share his accumulated knowledge with us and give us personal advice, but it is not absolutely necessary. "Spirituality cannot be gotten out of books!" some may hasten to say. True. But neither can you get spirituality from any external source, including the greatest of yogis. Spirituality arises from within as a result of spiritual maturation and the personal application of spiritual teachings–teachings that *can* be gotten from a book as well as a person. Even when reading the writings of a great master we must be respectful and alert, seeking to comprehend the slightest and most subtle of his teachings–and intend to apply them.

True masters never die. We can approach them prayerfully in the depth of our hearts and seek their spiritual assistance. There is no reason why we cannot become the disciple of any master, no matter how long ago he lived on the earth. Like Jesus, true masters can assure us: "Lo, I am with you alway, even unto the end of the world" (Matthew 28:20). Nor need we limit ourselves to inwardly approaching only one teacher.

True jnana

Know this, and you shall not again fall into delusion. By this you shall come to see all creation in your Self and then in me (4:35).

True enlightenment is a state in which delusion can no longer arise. The enlightened are absolutely incapable of falling back into ignorance. Until this state is reached, however, no matter how highly evolved a person may become he is still capable of being overcome by ignorance and of plunging back into the swamp of spiritual degradation. Therefore we must be wary at all times and aware of our potential for a fall. (It is not a bad idea to keep in mind that this is true of most teachers, as well.)

The sure sign of a coming fall is a yogi's boasting that he has transcended all evil and is incapable of wrongdoing. No enlightened person speaks in such a manner. Those who have confidence in their attainment are still in the grip of ego, and therefore capable of any evil. This is why genuine humility is a characteristic of the truly enlightened. No boasting or claims are made by the truly wise, nor do the liberated crow about their freedom.

The fundamental trait of enlightenment is stated by Krishna: "By this you shall come to see all creation in your Self and then in me." Infinity will become the constant interior state. Nothing as petty as psychic powers or fascinating personality traits constitute the profile of the enlightened. Infinite consciousness is the trait of the illumined being. If you had met the great Swami Sivananda you would know what I mean. His infinity and his humility were equally evident.

The enlightened person perceives both his Self and the Supreme Self. He sees them as two and knows them as One. Regarding this he can say, speaking of his Self and the Absolute Self:

That is the Full, this is the Full.

The Full has come out of the Full.

If we take the Full from the Full

It is the Full that yet remains.

This is the authentic advaita vision, not the simplistic monism so common today, especially in the West. Those who study and apply the wisdom of the Gita will avoid much error and outright nonsense.

Made pure

Even if you should be the most sinful among all the sinful, yet you would cross over all sin by the raft of knowledge alone. As the kindled fire reduces wood to ashes, in the same way the fire of knowledge reduces all karmas to ashes. No purifier equal to knowledge is found here in the world. He who is himself perfected in yoga in time finds knowledge in the Self (4:36-38).

It is frequently stated that Shankara in his commentaries and other writings seems to overemphasize jnana (knowledge), but when we look at portions of the Gita such as this one we see why he considered jnana the prime necessity. For here Krishna is telling us that jnana is the absolute power of liberation–specifically liberation from the effects of evil action.

Knowledge–the divine knowledge inherent in the Self–frees us from evil in two aspects. It frees us from the psychological conditionings–especially the addictions–resulting from wrongdoing, and it burns to ashes the karmas we have accumulated by past wrong action. In every way, jnana destroys sin (papa) to the uttermost degree. And Krishna assures us that jnana itself can do this–nothing else is needed. Further, he tells us that when we are perfect in yoga we find this knowledge in our own hearts, for it is eternal, inseparable from the Self. So can we fault Shankara for putting such a high valuation on jnana?

Faith leads to knowledge

> He who possesses faith attains knowledge. Devoted to that pursuit, restraining the senses, having attained knowledge he quickly attains supreme peace (4:39).

Since knowledge is the last step in enlightenment, there must be many prior steps. The one next to knowledge is faith–shraddha. Now, shraddha is not the weak "faith" of the English language, based on intellectual belief or blind acceptance of another's words, but is a dynamic force, a spontaneous uprising from within of an intuitive knowledge or conviction. It is a kind of precognition, and is itself an embryonic form of knowledge. So it is knowledge, a foreshadowing of the fully developed vision that culminates in enlightenment, that *is* enlightenment, the Supreme Peace (*param shantim*).

Doubt

> The man who is ignorant and without faith, of a doubting nature, is ruined. Neither this world, nor the next, nor happiness is for the man of doubt (4:40).

The way in which Krishna puts this first sentence, we can see that to him a doubter is ignorant and faithless, that the three qualities of ignorance, infidelity, and doubt are united in such a one and that destruction is the natural consequence for him. Not that the Self is ever destroyed, but certainly the intelligence that is the distinctive characteristic of the evolving human being can be so distorted and fragmented that it can be said to be destroyed—useless and even destructive. It is not impossible for the subtle bodies to become so damaged that they do dissolve and the individual spirit has to begin its evolutionary journey over again—sometimes from the very beginning. But though such a thing may be rare, for all doubters there is no happiness or peace in this or any other world.

Is Krishna agreeing with all the religions that sharply condemn those that doubt their teachings and predict dire consequences for their doubt? No. Krishna is not speaking of someone who honestly questions or wonders if the doctrines of religion are true. Those who have honest doubts or questions need not feel censured by Krishna. Without doubt of the right kind there is no resolution of doubt and the gaining of right conviction. Rather, Krishna is speaking of those in whom doubt is a symptom of willful ignorance, of refusal to accept what they inwardly know is truth. We all know people who reject the truth when it inconveniences, embarrasses, or condemns them. It is this deliberate and conscious denial, this hypocrisy, that later manifests as the kind of doubt Krishna is referring to. Many people actively war against what they know to be right and true. It is these that shall in time find there is no place for them in any world. Having sinned against truth, what is left for them? In contrast:

Action does not bind him whose actions are renounced in yoga, whose doubt is severed by knowledge, and who is self-possessed (4:41).

The core problem

Krishna is not a mere speaker of words, but a knower of the hearts of those to whom he speaks. Going directly to the root of Arjuna's hesitation in the face of battle, he says to him:

> Therefore, having severed with the sword of your own knowledge this doubt that proceeds from ignorance abiding in your heart, arise! Take refuge in yoga (4:42).

Doubting the Self

There are doubts that are rational and doubts that are irrational. Relative experience has dominated us for creation cycles, so it is understandable that we might doubt the glorious truth of the Self–not the fact that it exists, but the fullness of its wonder and its transforming, creative, transcendent power, what to speak of its accessibility through yoga. It is, of course, delusion that hides the reality of the Self from us and makes us doubt the words of Krishna and the sages of the Upanishads upon whose teachings the Gita is based. Yoga, however, directly reveals to us the truth of the Atman-Self and removes doubt as the rising sun dispels even the densest darkness.

The sword

Before we experience the Self, however, we must set our will to practice yoga for its revelation. This requires some intellectual conviction. We need to analyze our entire life, and especially our consciousness of it, for that consciousness is our Self. We need to distinguish (discriminate) between that which is experiencing our life and that which is being experienced. One is unchanging and the other is ever changing. We must look to the unchanging and know that as real, and understand the shifting patterns of light and shadow around us as a dream–necessary and instructive, but for all that only a dream. With the sword of our discrimination, then, we can pierce through the veils that hide the truth from us and cast them aside forever.

It is no small thing that Krishna refers to "the sword of your own knowledge," for nothing but our own realization will erase ignorance and doubt. If we have no knowledge of our own, then any "faith" we may think we have is a fantasy, a delusion. People who believe something merely because some person or book–including the Gita–says so have no faith at all, only superstition. Until they rid themselves of such non-faith they will never know the truth which Krishna speaks. This is why atheism can be a positive thing: we often have to rid ourselves of silly and baseless religion before we can clear our minds enough to come to true faith and knowledge. Once a man told Sri Ramakrishna he was an atheist. Sri Ramakrishna said: "That, too, is a stage" on the way to realization.

We cannot live on the food other people eat, and we cannot live on the knowledge of others—who, if they were real knowers (jnanis) would tell us that themselves.

Arise!

Positive action is required of us—not a running about and making noise as is the way of so much religion, but an interior activity: meditation. We must express in our outer life the insight meditation has given us. Then we can fight the battle of life from within the fortress of Right Action, of Karma Yoga.

At all times we are Arjuna, needing to heed the life-evoking words of Krishna, words that are the doors to freedom in the Self—in God.

ACTION: RENOUNCED AND PERFORMED

Duality and differentiation are the bedrock of relativity and delusion, and human beings desperately cling to them to preserve their beloved illusions and maintain their false independence from Spirit–a condition that produces nothing but suffering, yet is desperately held on to. Why is this? Because the Self has been pushed out of the way by the ego which has taken control. By keeping our consciousness in duality and differentiation the ego perpetuates its power–even its very existence, for the consciousness of Oneness that is the truth will dissolve the ego. So although I have said that "we" cling to delusion, it is the ego that is holding on "for dear life"–not us. Only when we break that hold will we truly begin to live.

Even as we progress in consciousness we find the habit of duality persisting, and we often drag it into our attempts at spiritual reasoning. More than once in the Gita Arjuna presents Krishna with an either/or question that mirrors this illusion. Krishna explains the truth of the matter, and in doing so reveals the error of the question itself. We have come to one of those points. Not without a hint of complaint and accusation:

> Arjuna said: You praise renunciation of actions and again you praise karma yoga. Which one is the better of these two? Tell me definitely (5:1).

In other words: "Which one of these can I throw away?" In our intellectual laziness we demand a simplistic, streamlined outlook so we can avoid the effort of combining two seeming contradictions in order to find out the truth that lies between them—and includes them. We demand a false unity so we can perpetuate our false duality. Fortunately for Arjuna and us Krishna never concedes to this intellectual indolence (and cowardice), but reveals the whole picture, refusing to serve up to us the Truth Lite we crave. So:

Both

> The Holy Lord said: Renunciation of action and karma yoga both lead to the highest happiness; of the two, however, karma yoga is superior to renunciation of action (5:2).

Action is rightly renounced when we refrain from an action because it is negative, useless, or foolish. Action is also rightly renounced when we act, but in a calm and detached manner, wishing only to do the right and not demanding any particular result. This, of course, is the yoga of action, karma yoga. Both bring us freedom and are superior to merely not acting because we are unsure or afraid and merely want to avoid shame and pain, not taking into account the right or wrong of the situation. Such a motivation is centered fully in the ego, not the buddhi (intelligence).

The inner state

> He is a constant renouncer of action who neither dislikes nor desires, who is indifferent to the pairs of opposites—truly he is easily freed from bondage (5:3).

He who neither hates nor desires is free from *raga* and *dwesha*—attraction and repulsion, both rooted in ego instead of understanding. When we see with the eye of the spirit rather than feel with the compulsions of egoism, we neither like nor dislike an action, though we do value the doing of our duty. In that perspective our detachment will not waver and we will not hesitate to do that which is right to do. This is the path to freedom.

In what follows in this chapter we must keep in mind that the simple term "yoga" always means karma yoga.

The way of the wise

> "Sankhya and karma yoga are different," the childish declare—not the wise. If one is practiced correctly, that person finds the fruit of both. The realization that is attained by the followers of Sankhya is also attained by the followers of karma yoga. Sankhya and karma yoga are one. He who perceives this truly perceives (5:4-5).

There is an amazing phenomenon that has existed in the world for ages beyond calculation. In all religions the teachings of great Masters and scriptures are praised and adulated—yet hardly ever really followed. These two verses are truly "honored only in the breach" in India where the vast majority insist that the way of knowledge is incompatible with the yoga of action. The Gita is chanted there daily by tens—if not hundreds—of thousands, yet its clear message is assiduously disregarded. As I have pointed out before, Adore the Messenger but Ignore the Message seems to be the motto of all religion.

Only the ignorant say that jnana is incompatible with karma. What about Shankara then? His many works seem to affirm this incompatibility. When Shankara speaks of karma he is referring to the karma khanda, the ritualistic part of the Vedic tradition, as well as of busyness with ego-inspired action. Krishna is speaking of the doing of right action in the right manner, right action being the duty, the swadharma of the individual. "Better is one's swadharma, though deficient, than the swadharma of another well performed. Better is death in one's own swadharma; the swadharma of another brings danger" (3:35). Without fulfilling that duty through right action, there can be no spiritual release for anyone.

Knowledge and action are one when action is the manifestation of knowledge. An individual may choose to view life more in the aspect of intellectual knowledge or in the aspect of duty and right action. The viewpoint may differ, but the actual living will be the same whichever view is chosen. That, too, is a matter of the natural condition of the aspirant's mental energies, and is of no great consequence, for moksha (liberation) is the inevitable culmination.

The necessity of both

Indeed, renunciation is difficult to attain without karma yoga. The yoga-yoked sage quickly attains Brahman (5:6).

Sri Ramakrishna often said: "The mind is everything." This is especially seen to be true in this part of the Gita. It is not action that is either the problem or the solution–it is the state of mind, including the attitude and the perspective, that determines whether an act is a hindrance or a help toward liberation. It is important for us to realize that Krishna is not advocating simple good behavior as a means to self-upliftment, but is intent on the psychological condition of the seeker as he engages in action. At all times the aspirant must strive to "see true" throughout daily life; then he can "live true."

It is a great error to suppose that Krishna is presenting his teaching as a kind of "live right" lesson. Rather, he is speaking to "the yoga-yoked sage," and to no one else, for the state of mind (bhava) he is advocating is impossible to attain by the non-yogi.

The prerequisites

Yoga-yoked, with the lower self purified, with the lower self subdued, whose senses are conquered, whose Self has become the Self of all beings–he is not tainted even when acting (5:7).

When I was reading through the catalog of university courses before my first semester, I was continually frustrated because all the courses that really interested me had a list of prerequisite courses that had to be taken first. And many of the prerequisites did not interest me! Now I am a bit more adult and realize the frequent need for prerequisites in all aspects of life, also. Childish people get an idea and think they need only jump in, thrash about, and they will achieve what they want. This almost never works. Krishna knows this, so he lists to Arjuna the things needed to really be a karma yogi. Mere aspiration accomplishes nothing of itself.

Yoga-yoked. The expression in the Sanskrit text is really *yogayuk-ta*–"united with yoga," one who is irrevocably, inseparably, engaged in the practice of karma yoga.

With the lower self purified. Good intentions are not enough. There has to be a change of heart and mind in the form of purification. The ordinary Sanskrit word for "pure" is *shuddha,* but the word used in this verse is *vishuddha*–supremely pure, totally pure. The intriguing thing is that karma yoga is the way to produce these prerequisites, and yet can only be practiced when they have already been developed. This is the mystery of karma yoga which is obviously itself supernatural.

With the lower self subdued. Not only the mind, but the body must be purified and mastered. Morality is of the essence, for karma yoga is not really a physical process, but a mental-spiritual procedure. Physical purity is also essential, especially in the matter of diet.

Whose senses are conquered. The senses must not just be controlled occasionally, they must be permanently mastered. This mastery will be relatively easy when the heart and body are made pure. Yet, mastery of the senses must not be assumed, for they have their own petty treacheries. The mind, body, and senses have long been in the complete control of the ego and thereby become oriented to its war against the Self and its revelation. To conquer them and enlist them on the side of right in the form of karma yoga is no easy or simple matter.

Whose self has become the Self of all beings. Brahman is the Self of all, including the individual Self. Therefore when we begin to experience the infinite and finite Selves, we begin to intuit the unity of all things in Spirit–and therefore our unity with all sentient beings.

Not tainted even when acting. When all these components are in place, karma yoga can take place, ensuring that the karma yogi shall not ever be touched by karmic reactions on any level.

The karma yogi's perspective

How can we be capable of action that produces no effects on us? It seems impossible. But Krishna explains:

> "I do not do anything;" thus thinks the steadfast knower of truth while seeing, hearing, touching, smelling, eating, walking, sleeping, breathing, speaking, releasing, and holding, opening and closing his eyes–convinced that it is the senses that move among the sense-objects (5:8-9).

Again and again we encounter the profound uniqueness of the Bhagavad Gita as a scripture, even when compared to the Upanishads which it greatly reflects. Here, too, we find wisdom that can be found nowhere outside the Gita. We are given a description of the continual experience-insight of the illumined individual.

The enlightened knows that any "happening" occurs only to the body, the senses, mind or intellect–that he is ever, and only, the unacting witness, the consciousness that perceives without acting in any manner whatsoever. In the Gita we find a clearly-drawn distinction between purusha and prakriti, between the conscious witness and the moving energies that are witnessed. Always the perfect karma yogi is in this state of *experiential* distinction–it is not a matter of intellectual conception, but of the living fact.

In the third chapter we have already found this summation: "In all situations actions are performed by the gunas of Prakriti; those with ego-deluded mind think: "I am the doer." (3:27)

But he who knows the truth about the gunas and action thinks: "The gunas act in the gunas. Thinking thus, he is not attached" (3:28).

Offering

Next Krishna tells us that the enlightened live their life devotionally, saying:

> Offering actions to Brahman, having abandoned attachment, he acts untainted by evil as a lotus leaf is not wetted by water (5:10).

This is important, first for its practical application, but it also frees us from the common idea that the life of the wise, of the jnani, is somehow antiseptic in character and devoid of involvement with God in a personal manner. In the Yoga Sutras it is stated that samadhi, the entry into super-consciousness, is the result of Ishwarapranidhana–offering the life to God, to Ishwara, the personal aspect of God. This is underscored by Krishna saying later on: "Those who are ever steadfast, who worship me, fixing their minds on me, endowed with supreme faith, I consider them to be the best versed in yoga" (12:2).

Not I–but them

Krishna puts it all together by simply saying in conclusion:

> **Karma yogis perform action only with the body, mind, intellect, or the senses, forsaking attachment, performing action for self-purification (5:11).**

Self-knowledge is the key to karma yoga as well as its ultimate fruition.

FREEDOM (MOKSHA)

Those of us born in America were virtually baptized in the word Freedom. But freedom means many things, some of them specious in the case of dictatorial governments and individuals. Freedom has many levels. Some are satisfied with the freedom to buy whatever color or length of shoelace they want. Others with a freedom to do wrong that is not freedom at all but license. According to the development of the individual, so will be his concept of freedom and the kind of freedom he desires. Krishna speaks to those ready to graduate from earthly experience, saying:

> **He who is steadfast, having abandoned action's fruit, attains lasting peace. He who is not steadfast, attached to action based on desire, is bound (5:12).**

Those who have established themselves in yoga are immediately freed from the law of cause and effect, of action and reaction. Karma ceases to exist for them. They are not compelled to act by past karma, nor do their present actions produce any karma that would result in a future compulsion to action. This is true freedom. Acting in full awareness of Spirit, they have perfect peace. Although moving within this world, the center of their consciousness is in the transcendental realm of Inaction.

No matter how spiritually advanced someone may be, until the attainment of absolute liberation, until he is irrevocably established in the consciousness of Brahman and living ever in the state of Brahmanirvana, like everyone else caught in the net of Maya (Delusion), he is bound by actions prompted by desire, no matter how subtle or tenuous that bondage, action, or desire might be. But of the liberated-in-life, the jivanmukta, Krishna says:

> **Renouncing all actions with the mind, the embodied one sits happily as the ruler of the city of nine gates, not acting at all, nor causing action (5:13).**

Centered in the truth of his Self, abiding happily within the nine-gated body, such a one may to outward appearance seem to be the most active of men.

The saints

Often we see that the saints accomplish much more than ordinary people. One of the few books Yogananda read in the West and which he recommended to his students, was *The Saints That Moved the World*. Not only that, their influence on others may last through centuries, maintaining and ever-increasing the works they began in their lifetime. This is only natural for, being one with God, they possess his creative powers and abundance. Consider the present-day "kingdoms" of Krishna, of Buddha, and of Jesus within the hearts of human beings.

We admire, even revere, many great men and women of our human history, but the majority of them are only memories. In contrast, the saints and masters are living presences; the very thought of them brings us into subtle contact with them, awakening our inner consciousness, inwardly drawing us toward the higher levels of existence in which they dwell. The mere sight of their forms produces a positive change in our conscious-ness—at least in the consciousness of those who are willing to be changed. Moreover, any action we do in response to their influence on us will not create karma for us. If we act in conformity with their teachings and as a result of their inspiration, that action will liberate rather than bind us.

The source of delusion

Now Krishna introduces a major topic: the source of delusion. It is interesting how psychopathic people can become when confronted with their folly and evil. They blame anyone and anything for their error. Everybody is a factor in the situation but them. In Genesis we see how Eve blamed the serpent and Adam blamed not only Eve but hinted that God was responsible (Genesis 3:9-13). "Why does God do this?… Why does God allow this?" is a common protest. Few are those who understand that they, and they alone, bear the responsibility for their actions and their reactions. But now in this fifth chapter of the Gita the liberating truth is being given to us.

The Lord does not create either means of action or action itself in this world, nor the union of action with its fruit. On the other hand, the swabhava impels one to action (5:14).

Prabhavananda's interpretive translation says it quite well, even if not literally: "Do not say: 'God gave us this delusion.' You dream you are the doer, you dream that action is done, you dream that action bears fruit. It is your ignorance, it is the world's delusion that gives you these dreams." Saint James spoke of the same situation, saying: "Let no man say when he is tempted, I am tempted of God: for God cannot be tempted with evil, neither tempteth he any man: But every man is tempted, when he is drawn away of his own lust, and enticed. Then when lust hath conceived, it bringeth forth sin: and sin, when it is finished, bringeth forth death" (James 1:13-15).

The truly comforting part of Prabhavananda's version is the word "dream." All relative existence is a dream. We are co-dreamers with God. God dreams the cosmos, and we dream our involvement within it. No matter how horrendous or magnificent the dream may be, at the moment of awakening it will be revealed as nothing but ideas–creative ideas, but still just ideas. Only the two realities–God and the spirit–will remain. Blessed cessation, blessed peace and freedom. So when confronting the truth about delusion we need not be horrified or devastated by the fact that it comes from us. After all, even God dreams–why not us? God dreams rightly, but we dream wrongly. First we correct our dreaming, begin dreaming rightly along with God, and then we awaken. No more dream, no more delusion. Only Truth.

The primary focus of the Bhagavad Gita is Karma Yoga, the Yoga of Action. Yet Krishna tells us that the whole things is a dream, a product of ignorance. Even so, the dream is of importance, because through this dreaming we develop and expand our consciousness. The dream is not worthless and is certainly not evil or wrong. It is our loss of control and the resulting confusion and bondage that is wrong. The correct perspective on this is necessary for our controlling the dream and enabling ourselves to awaken from it.

If we ingest hallucinogenics we will have hallucinations. If we abstain, they will not occur. If we "ingest" the world and come to think we are part of it, we will only dream more and more, each dream becoming more distorted and misery-producing. When we draw back into our pure consciousness and begin to live in abstinence from the hallucinogenic of the world, we will begin to see through the veil into the Reality behind it. Eventually the veil melts away and we find ourselves face-to-face with the Real. Until then we are the source of the trouble.

Swabhava

This truth is expressed even more clearly by the inclusion of the word swabhava (self-nature), the real actor or mover in all this.

It is very comfortable for most translators to use the word "nature" with a capital N. They are children of Adam, throwing the blame on the creation, and therefore on the creator. The word swabhava does not mean prakriti, but the inherent disposition, nature, or potentiality of each one of us, our inherent state of mind, our state of inner being. An apple tree bears apples and a grapevine bears grapes. It is a matter of manifesting the inner nature, the swabhava of the plant.

Our entire life is a manifestation of our swabhava. This is unsettling if our life is unsatisfactory or overtly negative. We pity ourselves and enlist the sympathy of others, but it is our inner nature that is being revealed by the outer. You may not be able to judge a book by its cover, but you can certainly judge it by its contents. So it is with our life. That is its purpose: to reveal the character and quality of our inner condition through outward appearances. We should read the message and learn. Otherwise there is no alleviation from life to life. We are the problem and we are the solution.

Since our swabhava is the root of the dilemma, Patanjali says that a necessary practice for the yogi is swadhyaya–self-study, self-analysis. Only if we come to know the truth about our inner nature will we be able to intelligently work on it. We must first know the facts about our false self before we can uncover and know our true Self.

Divine indifference

It is embarrassing and painful to see and acknowledge our faults and wrongs, but Krishna helps us in that department, also.

> The Omnipresent takes note of neither demerit nor merit. Knowledge is enveloped by ignorance; as a result of that people are deluded (5:15).

Obviously a perfect being cannot be shaken from his perfect equilibrium. Just as a human being could hardly be upset or angered at the action of an ant many feet down in the earth, neither can God be affected by the deeds of anyone. After all, God has manifested this universe for the purpose of our acting therein and learning the way of right action and to freedom from action. Consequently, whatever we do is for our interest only. As Krishna will say later in the Gita: "I am the same to all beings. There is none disliked or dear to me" (9:29)

It is we who must become concerned over the question of sin and virtue–and for the right reason: liberation. What has God to do with it? What is our dream to him? We are dreaming because the Light that is our Self is covered by our ignorance in the form of a self-perpetuating dream. The wise know that human beings choose to be either self-deluded or self-illumined.

The end of darkness/ignorance

> But those in whom this ignorance of the Self has been destroyed by knowledge–that knowledge of theirs, like the sun, reveals the Supreme Brahman (5:16).

The Self and Brahman being one, when the Self is revealed so also is Brahman revealed—not outside us as an object, but from within us as the Source of our very existence. To find God, then, we must look within. As Saint Nectarios of Aegina, a twentieth-century Greek Orthodox saint, said: "If you cannot find God in your heart you will never find him." As Krishna continues:

> Those whose minds are absorbed in That, whose Selves are fixed on That, whose foundation is That, who hold That as the highest object, whose evils have been shaken off by knowledge, attain the ending of rebirth (5:17).

THE BRAHMAN-KNOWER

Seeing the One in all

Brahman is the origin of all, hence Krishna has this to say about the way the enlightened views all around him:

> The wise see the same Self in a wise and disciplined Brahmin, in a cow, in an elephant, in a dog, even in an eater of dogs (5:18).

Most of the dogs in India are wild animals related to jackals and hyenas, and many of them are terribly diseased. They often travel in packs, even in the cities, and have been known to pull down, kill and eat a child. I was threatened by a pack of about thirty dogs right in Varanasi. They were rushing at me, but knowing that bullies are cowards, I picked up a big brick and made a throwing motion with it, and they ran back. But I got out of there immediately!

There are ashrams in India where they pretend to embody this verse. They feed and fawn over the mangy street dogs (or the purebred dog of the guru) and say: "God is Dog. Dog is God." But an interesting thing can be observed: they show no such respect to Brahmins, and certainly not to poor and "common" Indians. Apparently they follow George Orwell: all may be equal, but some are more equal than others. Sometimes the cows get almost–but not quite–the same respect as the dogs. Such is life–and delusion.

The capacity to see the unity that is the truth behind all diversity, is unique to the enlightened. However much the unenlightened may verbally affirm unity, the pressure of life-experience dispels it like a mirage. Truth is only truth when it is *realized*.

The enlightened person is aware of diversity even though he perceives the underlying unity. And this is the crux of the matter: Unity is the underlying reality, but on the surface differentiation must be both seen and reacted to accordingly. For example, proper food and poison may be metaphysically the same, but the enlightened eat one and avoid the other. As long as we are in the world we must act to some extent as though it is real, just as in a dream we have to follow the rules even though we know we are dreaming. For example, we cannot walk through a dream wall, but must use a dream door. Sri Ramakrishna spoke of the unripe understanding of non-duality that can get us into difficulties. Here is the story he told regarding it:

"In a certain forest lived a holy man who had many disciples. Once he taught the disciples that they should bow down to all recognizing that God dwells in all beings. One day one of the disciples went to the forest to bring firewood for the sacrificial fire. All of a sudden there was an outcry, 'Run, run all, wherever you are! A mad elephant is passing!' Everybody ran, but the disciple did not flee. He knew that the elephant was also God. So he thought, 'Why should I run away?' So thinking he stood still and began to sing praises, bowing before the animal. The mahout on the elephant was, however, shouting, 'Run, run!' The disciple still did not move. Finally the elephant came and lifting him up with its trunk threw him on one side and left. The disciple was heavily bruised and lay unconscious on the ground.

"Hearing what had happened, his teacher and the other disciples came and carried him to the ashram. He was given medicine. Upon his regaining consciousness sometime later some one asked him, 'Why did you not run away after hearing that the elephant was coming?' He said, 'The teacher had told me that God himself had become all these men, animals and the rest. That is why I did not move away, seeing that it was only God who was coming as an elephant.' The teacher then said, 'Yes, my child, it is true that the elephant God was coming, but the mahout God did warn you.

Since all are God, why did you not pay heed to his words? One should also listen to the words of the mahout God.'"

A serial killer and a saint are fundamentally the same, but our conduct in relation to them had better be based on their difference.

Living in Brahman

> Even here on earth rebirth is conquered by those whose mind is established in evenness. Brahman is without fault and the same to all; therefore they are established in Brahman (5:19).

Compulsory rebirth is conquered by the sage whose mind abides ever in the perfection of the Self and Brahman. Having gained the highest knowledge, he has no more need for rebirth. If he returns it will be to help others as he has been helped.

> One should not exult when encountering what is liked, and one should not be repulsed when encountering the disliked. With firm intellect, undeluded, the knower of Brahman is established in Brahman (5:20).

This is because he knows that the pleasant and the unpleasant are both mere dreams, that the joy he experiences in his oneness with Brahman is the only real experience. Therefore:

> He whose Self is unattached to external contacts, who finds happiness in the Self, whose Self is united to Brahman by yoga, reaches imperishable happiness (5:21).

Beware

> Truly, pleasures born of contact with the senses are wombs of pain, since they have a beginning and an end. The wise man is not satisfied with them (5:22).

This is a very easy concept to grasp and a tremendously hard one to follow unwaveringly–such is our conditioning from millions (if not billions) of lives in which the senses have dominated our consciousness and blinded us to the Self. It would be wise to disregard the pleasures of the senses from the fact they are fleeting, and the truth that they will inevitably result in pain (dukha). That should seal our certainty that avoidance of such things is only good sense. Yet, as the camel chews the thorns, cutting and bloodying its lips, refusing to give up its pain-bearing enjoyment, so it is with us until we truly do "get a grip" and refuse any future folly. For this reason:

> He who is able to endure here on earth, before liberation from the body, the agitation that arises from desire and anger, is steadfast, a happy man (5:23).

Mastery is the needed factor, for control is necessary for the requisite development of our will. Although we like the idea that everything falls into place automatically, the truth is we will have to get our hands dirty–and blistered–by good old-fashioned effort. As a professor in a major British university once told his class on the first day of the term: "In this course you will have to acquaint and accustom yourself to a venerable old four-letter Anglo-Saxon word: *Work*." No glory without gore.

The inner orientation

> He whose happiness is within, whose delight is within, whose illumination is within: that yogi, identical in being with Brahman, attains Brahmanirvana (5:24).

Over and over we need to keep reminding ourselves of this principle, for no matter how spiritual we may consider ourselves to be, we are so habituated to externality–often in the form of dogmas and religious observances–that we easily fall into the trap of materiality masquerading as spirituality. Continually we must check to see that our entire thought and life is oriented toward the inner kingdom of Spirit. Especially our meditation must be inward, ever inward, and so must be the focus of our awareness outside meditation. Only inward joy, inward peace, and inward vision fits us for the liberation of Nirvana.

The traits of liberation

Krishna now enumerates the traits of those who have entered Nirvana.

> The seers whose evils have been annihilated, whose doubts have been dispelled, whose inner being is mastered, who rejoice in the welfare of all beings, attain Brahmanirvana (5:25).

Each thing listed here is easy to comprehend, but it is worth pointing out that the knowers of Brahman do not become abstracted or self-absorbed, unaware of the terrible suffering in the world. Just the opposite. They are filled with compassion and do what their inner guidance shows them to help those around them. In India the words saint and philanthropist are synonyms. My beloved friend Swami Sivananda of Rishikesh dedicated his entire life to the welfare of others. As his disciple Swami Chidananda has said, his every waking thought was how to benefit others. Daily I witnessed his abounding love toward everyone—not a theoretical love, but one which continually manifested in concrete ways. This is no exaggeration, as those who met him know. In Sivananda I saw every virtue lived to the maximum degree, but his loving mercy was the most evident. He was a perfect illustration of the next verse:

> Released from desire and anger, with thoughts controlled, those ascetics who know the Self find very near to them the bliss of Brahmanirvana (5:26).

How it is done

This is all very fine, but how will we manage to reach such an exalted state? Krishna tells us:

> Excluding outside contacts, turning up the eyes toward the two brows, equalizing the inhalation and exhalation moving within the nostrils, (5:27).

Earlier (4:29) I described the circling of the breath. That is what is meant here by equalizing the inhalation and exhalation of the breath. Krishna advises to do this with the eyes turned upward "toward the two brows." This is not focusing the gaze between the eyebrows as is often thought. That would strain the eyes. Once in the holy city of Naimasharanya I asked Sri Ma Anandamayi about certain aspects of meditation. She very forcefully told me that I must never focus the gaze between the eyebrows as that will strain and may even damage the eyes. Krishna wants us to simply look up as though looking toward a distant point. This is very helpful to cultivate awareness of the sahasrara chakra, the thousand petalled lotus in the head. But there must be no strain. (Sometimes the yogi will find his eyes naturally drawn upward, even with some intensity, but when it is spontaneous there is no detriment.)

The result

> With his senses, mind and intellect controlled, with liberation as his highest aim, free from desire, fear, and anger: such a one is forever free. Having known me, the enjoyer of the tapasyas offered as sacrifice, the mighty Lord of all the world and the friend of all creatures, he attains peace (5:28, 29).

Not only is God the goal, he is also "the enjoyer of the tapasyas offered as sacrifice" engaged in on the way. Whoever engages in spiritual practice is already in touch with God, for it is God who makes us able to pursue spiritual life. God is not waiting for us at the end of the road, he is within us, walking the road along with us. For he is "the friend of all creatures." *Suhridam sarvabhutanam* also means "the companion of all beings," for God is seated in the hearts of all beings, living their lives along with them as the eternal witness. "I am the Self abiding in the heart of all beings; I am the beginning, the middle, and the end of all beings as well" (10:20). "The Lord dwells in the hearts of all beings, causing them by his maya to revolve as if mounted on a machine" (18:61).

How could we help but enter the peace of his presence, since that presence is ever within us?

THE GOAL OF KARMA YOGA

For some inexplicable reason, throughout the ages in both East and West the idea has prevailed that spiritual people do not engage in practical matters, that to really be spiritual is to be incapable of skill or efficiency in any kind of material activity, or even in the maintenance of material objects. Some years ago we had a phonograph record of religious music whose cover was a hazy photograph of a monk holding a rosary and looking at it blankly (contemplatively?). One of our members pointed to it and said: "Before I came to the monastery I thought that was what monastic life was like." Both members and visitors have expressed to me how surprised they were that in the monastery we actually work instead of sitting around talking profound philosophy. But Sri Ramakrishna, speaking of this kind of misunderstanding, used to say: "If you can weigh salt, you can weigh sugar," meaning that a person competent in spiritual life will be competent in material life–and often the other way round, though not always.

The idea that spiritual people are fluff-headed drones sitting around wondering where their next mystical experience is coming from is absurd. Whether this silly image comes from lazy monastics and fake mystics or from those who hope spiritual people will be too stupid or impractical to see through them and their material ways, I have no idea, but it has been around much too long and accepted by people much too intelligent to believe such mythology. That nonsense was around in Krishna's time, so he addresses it in this sixth chapter of the Gita.

Yogi and monk (renouncer)

> **The Holy Lord said: He who performs that action which is his duty, not caring for the action's fruit, is a renouncer and a yogi, not he without sacrificial fire and sacred rites (6:1).**

First, a bit of Sanskrit. Sannyasa means renunciation, and in modern times is applied to monastic life. It literally means "total casting aside." A sannyasi(n) is a renunciate, a monk, who has totally cast aside all that which would bind him. It is not the negative rejection or giving up that characterizes monastic life or renunciation in the West. Rather it is a freeing of oneself from the ties that bind. The Hindu monk does not consider that he has sacrificed or denied himself anything. Rather, he considers that he has freed himself from that which would hinder his Self-realization. It is a joyful, liberating thing.

In his autobiography, Paramhansa Yogananda tells of a great saint, Nagendranath Bhaduri, and gives the following telling incident:

"'Master, you are wonderful!' A student, taking his leave, gazed ardently at the patriarchal sage. 'You have renounced riches and comforts to seek God and teach us wisdom!' It was well-known that Bhaduri Mahasaya had forsaken great family wealth in his early childhood, when single-mindedly he entered the yogic path.

"'You are reversing the case!' The saint's face held a mild rebuke. 'I have left a few paltry rupees, a few petty pleasures, for a cosmic empire of endless bliss. How then have I denied myself anything? I know the joy of sharing the treasure. Is that a sacrifice? The shortsighted worldly folk are verily the real renunciates! They relinquish an unparalleled divine possession for a poor handful of earthly toys!'

"I chuckled over this paradoxical view of renunciation—one which puts the cap of Croesus on any saintly beggar, whilst transforming all proud millionaires into unconscious martyrs."

Krishna is using sannyasa and sannyasi in the pure sense of a renouncer, whether monastic or non-monastic, pointing us to the interior disposition that is absolutely essential, whatever our external situation. Being a yogi, a sannyasi, is a matter of that disposition, of the right intention, in all moments of our life. Simply doing nothing is neither yoga nor sannyasa. This does not mean that the solitary or enclosed life is invalid, for the true hermit or world-renouncer is intensely active inwardly and necessarily active outwardly at least minimally for the simple subsistence of his life.

> That which they call renunciation, know that to be yoga. Without renouncing selfish purpose no one whatever becomes a yogi (6:2).

There we have it. The yogi must be a sannyasi and the sannyasi must be a yogi.

The yogi's path

> For the sage desirous of attaining yoga, action is said to be the means. For him who has already attained yoga, tranquility is said to be the means (6:3).

Karma yoga is necessary for the aspiring yogi, for the same positive kind of detachment and inner calm essential for karma yoga is also needed for proficiency in meditation. The fact is, karma yoga trains us for meditation and meditation trains us for karma yoga. In essence they are the same thing, for both are psychological in character.

> When he is truly attached neither to sense objects nor to actions, and has renounced all purpose (sarva sankalpa), then he is said to have attained yoga (6:4).

Sarva sankalpa sannyasi–"having cast aside all sankalpa." Sankalpa is a strong exercising, or resolution, of the will based on some desire. So here, too, we see that desire is the serpent beneath the rose, the root of the whole trouble, whatever form it takes.

GETTING THERE

While we exist in relativity there are two selves, the lower and the higher. The higher is the true Self, and the lower is the pretend self, which is nevertheless necessary at this moment for our evolution. Until the real Self masters the lower self they are in continual conflict with one another, often on a subconscious level. Krishna is now going to talk about this. He will use only a single word, Atman, but will mean it in these two virtually antithetical selves. By using small and large "s" we can convey the idea. However, translators do not agree as to which self is meant at the various times the word is used. So I am going to give the translation without capitalization and then analyze it in both ways.

One should uplift oneself by the lower self; one should not degrade oneself. The lower self can truly be a friend of the lower self, and the lower self alone can be an enemy of the lower self. For him who has conquered himself by the lower self, the lower self is a friend. But for him who has not conquered himself, the lower self remains hostile, like an enemy (6:5-6).

The lesser aspects of our being, our lower self, are not negative by their nature, but ignorance and misapplication of will have corrupted them and reversed their polarity. The first step, then, for the aspiring yogi is their purification, correction and repolarization. This is accomplished in the very first step of Patanjali's eightfold yoga: yama and niyama.

Prerequisites for yoga

"Yoga is for the purpose of knowledge of truth," says Shankara. Knowledge (jnana) does not come about from practice of yoga methods alone.

Perfection in knowledge is in fact only for those who practice virtue (dharma) as well as yoga.

All things rest upon something else–that is, all things are supported by another. This is because a foundation is needed for anything to exist. Being Himself the Ultimate Support of all things, God alone is free from this necessity. Yoga, then, also requires support. As Trevor Leggett says in his introduction to Shankara's commentary on the Yoga Sutras: "This is yoga presented for the man of the world, who must first clear, and then steady, his mind against the fury of illusory passions, and free his life from entanglements." Patanjali very carefully and fully outlines the elements of the support needed by the aspirant, giving invaluable information on how to guarantee success in yoga.

The first Yoga Sutra says: "*Now* the exposition of yoga," implying that there must be something leading up to yoga in the form of necessary developments of consciousness and personality. These prerequisites are known as Yama and Niyama. Shankara says quite forcefully that "following yama and niyama is the basic qualification to practice yoga."

Yama and Niyama

Yama and Niyama are often called the Ten Commandments of Yoga, but they have nothing to do with the ideas of sin and virtue or good and evil as dictated by some cosmic potentate. Rather they are determined by a thoroughly practical, pragmatic basis: that which strengthens and facilitates our yoga practice should be observed and that which weakens or hinders it should be avoided. It is not a matter of being good or bad, but of being wise or foolish. Each one of these Five Don'ts (Yama) and Five Do's (Niyama) is a supporting, liberating foundation of Yoga.

Yama means self-restraint in the sense of self-mastery, or abstention, and consists of five elements. Niyama means observances, of which there are also five. Here is the complete list of these ten elements of successful yoga as given in Yoga Sutras 2:30, 32:

1. Ahimsa: non-violence, non-injury, harmlessness
2. Satya: truthfulness, honesty
3. Asteya: non-stealing, honesty, non-misappropriativeness

4. Brahmacharya: sexual continence in thought, word and deed as well as control of all the senses
5. Aparigraha: non-possessiveness, non-greed, non-selfishness, non-acquisitiveness
6. Shaucha: purity, cleanliness
7. Santosha: contentment, peacefulness
8. Tapas: austerity, practical (i.e., result-producing) spiritual discipline
9. Swadhyaya: introspective self-study, spiritual study
10. Ishwarapranidhana: offering of one's life to God

All of these deal with the innate powers of the human being–or rather with the abstinence and observance that will develop and release those powers to be used toward our spiritual perfection, to our self-realization and liberation. Shankara says quite forcefully that "following yama and niyama is the basic qualification to practice yoga. The qualification is not simply that one wants to practice yoga. So yama and niyama are methods of yoga" in themselves and are not mere adjuncts or aids that can be optional.

But at the same time, the practice of yoga helps the aspiring yogi to follow the necessary ways of yama and niyama, so he should not be discouraged from taking up yoga right now. He should determinedly embark on yama, niyama, and yoga simultaneously. Success will be his.

Only through establishment in yama and niyama can anyone "uplift oneself by the lower self." If yama and niyama are not observed then there is no other result than that the person shall continue to degrade himself. By yama and niyama "the lower self can truly be a friend of the lower self," which before was its enemy. The diligent yogi makes the lower self his friend, but if he lapses in yama and niyama the lower self reverts to being his enemy.

Tranquility

> The highest self of him who has conquered himself and is peaceful, is thus steadfast in cold, heat, pleasure, pain, honor and dishonor (6:7).

Peace is a matter of the exercise of will. Never will our life be free from the pairs of opposites, from ups and downs and changes of all kinds, pleasant and unpleasant, if the will is not strong and operative. If the will is in peace, in the Self, then the sadhaka will be in peace. This is a very high and subtle state, and many think they have attained it merely because they have developed a kind of Stoic numbness in relation to their life. (This prevails in India.) But this is not so.

The serenity spoken of by Krishna comes from identification with the immutable Self. Two examples of this in modern times are Swami Sivananda of Rishikesh and Swami Ramdas of Anandashram. They were often seen to be happy and peaceful in adversity and good fortune, and especially in honor and dishonor. Swami Ramdas' autobiography, *In the Vision of God*, illustrates this many times.

Supreme peace

> **The yogi who is satisfied with knowledge and discrimination, unchanging, with senses conquered, to whom a lump of clay, a stone and gold are the same, steadfast–is said to be in union (yukta) (6:8).**

The human race is gripped in the delusion that if a thing looks like something, then it is that. Even worse: that if someone acts like they are in a certain state, they have that state. I vividly remember seeing Alan Watts pretending (very poorly) to be in the state of satori (enlightenment) as he rubbed away on an ink slab (!?). At that very moment he was an alcoholic–not a state or action produced by enlightenment. People think that if they act kindly then they are kind, if they act generously they are generous, and if they act like aristocracy they are aristocracy. Not so.

Swami Sivananda cleared up the whole question by four little words he formed into a motto that he even had printed on pencils: BE GOOD. DO GOOD. Throughout every morning at satsang with him in the Diamond Jubilee Hall, right behind him above the door which we had all entered, we saw those words in huge letters. First we must *be*; then we can *do*.

We do not have measles because we have red spots on our skin; rather, we have red spots on our skin because we have measles. This is incredibly simple, but few people, especially in the West, grasp the nature of cause and effect. They continually get cause and effect reversed, thinking an effect can become a cause. "If I act like it, then I will become it." This is philosophically translated into the absurdities of Positive Thinking. "If we just hold that good thought it will come about… We will just know that everything will be all right…." and other nonsensical platitudes. Thoughts may be things, but things are not inner states. "Satisfied with knowledge and discrimination,… steadfast in yoga," are absolute requisites.

When Brahman is experienced, then the fluctuations of the senses are no more than driftwood on the vast ocean of Spirit. All that which men prize and despise are both seen as the same: dreams. Sri Ramakrishna tested his mind by holding a lump of clay in one hand and a rupee in the other. Saying: "Rupee is clay and clay is rupee, clay is truly rupee and rupee is truly clay," he tossed them into the Ganges, affirming their sameness–for all things must in the end merge into Brahman.

> He is preeminent among men who is impartial to friend, associate and enemy, neutral among enemies and kinsmen, impartial also among the righteous and the unrighteous (6:9).

For he sees all *in* Brahman *as* Brahman.

THE YOGI'S RETREAT

The yogi in the world

Krishna has told Arjuna that a yogi can attain perfection here in this world, even while fulfilling his earthly responsibilities. In the third chapter he said:

"Therefore, constantly unattached perform that which is your duty. Indeed by unattached action man attains the Supreme. Indeed, perfection was attained through action alone by King Janaka and others. For the maintenance of the world, as an example you should act.

"Whatever the best of men does–this and that–thus other men do; whatever the standard that he sets–that is what the world shall follow. I have no duty whatsoever in the three worlds, nor anything that must be attained, nevertheless I engage in action. Indeed, if I did not tirelessly engage at all in action, then mankind everywhere would follow my example [*literally:* path or way]. If I did not perform action these worlds would perish, and I would be the cause of confusion: I would destroy these people.

"As the unwise act, attached to action, so the wise should act, unattached, intending to maintain the welfare of the world. One should not unsettle the minds of the ignorant attached to action; the wise should cause them to enjoy all actions–[himself] engaged in their performance" (3:19-26)

Those who pretend to the ideals of yoga while really loving the world and its toys, exuberantly put forth the image of the worldly-wise and debonair yogi, busily rushing around like a squirrel, gathering and storing the nuts of material success and enjoyment "while yet finding time to meditate." They picture a "balanced life of yoga and action" that shows an overwhelming involvement in action and very little in yoga. (After all, a day in a truly balanced life would consist of eight hours spent in sleep, eight hours spent in work, and eight hours spent in meditation.)

I know of many "balanced" yogis that can barely meditate for an hour even after decades of meditation practice. When they do "meditate" for longer periods of time, they spend a lot of it in chanting and listening (with closed eyes) to inspiration in the form of sermonettes. Many of them cannot sit for meditation in silence, but must have some kind of music or mantra recording going all the time. I do not say this to disparage them–it is not their fault that their yoga methods and their teachers are duds. But I do think that after some years they might figure those facts out and start looking for something better. For it is there. They can find it in the Gita and have no less a teacher than the avatar Krishna and the recorder of his teachings, Vyasa.

The yogi's retreat

There is no doubt that the yogi may have to work among the noise of urban business, that telephone and computer may be ringing, buzzing, and beeping, and people be talking, talking and talking throughout the day. But when the work time is over it should really be over and the guidelines given by Krishna should be adhered to as much as possible. Here they are:

> **The yogi should fix his awareness constantly on the Self, remaining in solitude, alone, with controlled mind and lower self, without desires or possessiveness (6:10).**

The yogi should fix his awareness constantly on the Self. Unless this is done, what value do the other observances have? No one can sit in meditation twenty-four hours a day, but through constant awareness produced by japa outside meditation he can unceasingly fix his mind on the Self every waking moment of his life. In the thirteenth chapter Krishna will speak of the ideal yogi as having "unswerving devotion to me with single-minded yoga, frequenting secluded places, [having] distaste for the society of men" (13:10).

Remaining in solitude. This can be done in two ways. You can live in a quiet place where after your daily work you can go and be by yourself, where the world can be shut out and forgotten about. If the place is in a solitary location away from town or neighbors, that is best, but any place where you can shut and lock the door and be alone is sufficient, if it is quiet and free from noises of the world and the worldly. Even if you have to move occasionally to ensure this, you will be glad you did.

In the thirteenth chapter of *Autobiography of a Yogi*, the master yogi, Ram Gopal Muzumdar, asked Yogananda: "Are you able to have a little room where you can close the door and be alone?" When he said that he did, the saint told him: "That is your cave. That is your sacred mountain. That is where you will find the kingdom of God." This is really important for the unmarried yogi unless he can find other yogis (of the same sex) who will live with him in a quiet place and keep to themselves, out of sight and sound.

Occasionally you should go away even from your home and live in solitude–not in some busy ashram where you will do "karma yoga" and take part in "spiritual" group activities. It is better to stay at home than waste your time in this way. Instead, you should find a place where you can really be all to yourself. If you can prepare your food and eat in solitude, this is good, but if you can go somewhere for (vegetarian) meals where you need speak to no one socially and can immediately go back to your place, that is also good, though not as good. A truly quiet hotel that has room service can be perfectly acceptable, but if you can be alone in some kind of house, cabin or room, it is better.

Sri Ramakrishna had this to say about such solitude:

"It is very necessary now and then to retire into solitude and think of him. In the beginning it is very difficult to keep the mind on God without retiring into solitude.

"When a plant is young it is necessary to put a fence round it. Without a fence it is eaten up by goats and cows. To meditate you should withdraw yourself within or retire to a secluded spot or into the forest and always discriminate between the real and the unreal. God alone is truth; namely, the reality, and all the rest is unreal and transitory. Discriminating in this manner renounce the transient things from the mind....

"Keshab Sen, Pratap and others told me, 'Sir, ours is the view of King Janaka.' I said, 'One doesn't become King Janaka by mere words of mouth. King Janaka first performed so many austerities in solitude. Do something first. Then only you may become King Janaka.'...

"And notice also that this very mind acquires knowledge, dispassion and devotion by dwelling on God in solitude.... The world is water and the mind is like milk. If you pour milk into water they get mixed and you cannot find pure milk anymore. If you churn butter after turning milk into curd and put it in water it will float. So first churn the butter of knowledge and devotion by following spiritual practices in solitude. That butter will never mix. Even if you put it in the water of the world it will float."

Sri Mahendranath Gupta, known as "M," was a disciple of Sri Ramakrishna and the recorder of these words in *The Gospel of Sri Ramakrishna*. In Yogananda's autobiography he is called "Master Maha-shaya, the blissful devotee." He followed these words of Sri Ramakrishna all his life. He had several isolated places right in Calcutta, known only to himself, where he would go for days at a time to practice meditation. On occasion he would come home for meals and then go back to his secret haven. At other times he left Calcutta for a solitary ashram owned by him.

Both forms of solitude—at home and away—are necessary for the yogi.

Alone. If the yogi is married, still it is important to spend time by oneself each day. This is not impossible. I have an Indian friend whose mother is a great tapaswin. Though living in a joint family, occasionally she retires to a quiet room in the back of the house and stays there for days, weeks, and even months, seeing no one and having her food put outside her door. During these periods, if for some reason she comes into another part of the house everyone knows she is coming because a strong fragrance of roses precedes her, and if she speaks it is as though she is spraying rose essence into the air. I know other yogis in India and America, both men and women, who have private areas in their home for their sadhana. One friend even has a secret room she alone knows how to get into. Another has a small temple behind his house.

The important thing is to be alone in your mind. When you are in your "holy place" let no one interrupt you or call out to you or communicate with you in any way. During my first trip to India, in the ashram of Anandamayi Ma I met an astonishing man, Doctor Pannalal. Someone told me that he had at one time been the governor of Benares and lived in a palace. Behind the palace he had a small hut (kutir) built for meditation. He gave strict orders to everyone that he was never to be disturbed when he was in there. But one day the palace caught fire, so someone ran and banged on the door, shouting that the palace was burning. "I don't care. Leave me alone!" he called back. This was repeated some more times–always with the same response. After some hours he came out of the hut and found the palace a heap of ash and rubble. Walking over to where his family, staff, and onlookers were standing, he calmly observed: "It looks like we need to build a new one." That was all.

And by the way, wherever you are, do not overdo "satsang." Occasional company with other yogis is beneficial if only spiritual subjects are spoken of, but let it be no more than once or twice a week, unless you are living with other yogis and want a daily satsang.

With controlled mind and [lower] self. I think you will find that solitude will help tremendously in mastering body and mind. However, yama, niyama, meditation and proper vegetarian diet are absolute essentials of such control. You will also find that spiritual reading has a very beneficial effect on your endeavors to purify mind and heart. By "spiritual reading" I mean holy scriptures, teachings of God-realized masters and the biographies of saints. Some philosophical or devotional books can also be good, but be sure the authors have spiritual experience so its vibration will be conveyed to you through their words.

Without desires or possessions. Now this is very important. The karma yogi is not just to work, he is to work well and carefully–not the sloppy and careless way that supposedly is a mark of a "spiritual" person who is indifferent to material things. At the same time, the yogi must not become caught in the trap of perfectionism, of "success," of the "bigger and more is better" attitude which would push him onward to increase his involvement in the world.

A devotee once asked Sri Ramakrishna: "What about worldly activities, duties of life?" He replied: "Yes, do them too as much as is necessary for living in the world. But you should pray to him crying in solitude so that you may perform them selflessly. And you should say to him, 'O Lord! Please reduce my worldly duties because, O God! I find that if I get involved in too much work I forget you. I may think I am acting selflessly but it turns out to be selfish.'"

There we have it: the yogi should not avoid responsibility, but he should sincerely pray that his worldly duties and obligations will be reduced as much as possible—leaving it up to God to decide what "as much as possible" means. At the same time, the yogi should actively simplify his life in relation to the world, including the matter of personal possessions. (That does not mean getting rid of sacred and spiritual things, including books. I have known some deluded yogis who every time they "simplified" their life only got rid of holy imagery and spiritual books.)

So we are back at the home base of solitude. "Dwelling in a solitary place,... he is fit for union with Brahman" (Bhagavad Gita 18:52-53). I am not speaking of being anti-social, but of being a serious yogi.

THE YOGI'S INNER AND
OUTER LIFE

A significant word in Sanskrit writings on spiritual life is *adhikari*—the state of being qualified or worthy, implying both fitness and capability. This is especially meaningful in the subject of yoga, for how can an individual engage in that which is the highest endeavor possible for any sentient being unless he is capable of sustaining and succeeding in his practice? The yogi is a very special person, indeed. As Paramhansa Yogananda said: "Yoga is the beginning of the end." The yogi is one entering the last stages of ripening on the tree of life.

Krishna tells Arjuna the basic requirements for a yogi, since simply knowing the mechanics of yoga is not at all enough, any more than knowing the rules of a sport can make someone a proficient athlete. The yogi, too, must live perpetually in training if he is to win the gold of spiritual realization.

Krishna has explained to Arjuna the need for living in a quiet and retired environment, even though active in the world. No matter how spiritual we like to think ourselves, our immediate environment and the condition of our body is a major factor in how our mind behaves in meditation. The external often dictates the condition of the internal. Now he takes up the subject of what the yogi should be doing in his retreat—whether at home or on retreat elsewhere. He has already mentioned the major activity, saying: "The yogi should fix his awareness constantly on the Self." So he proceeds:

The yogi's seat (asana)

Establishing for himself a firm seat in a clean place, not too high and not too low, covered with kusha grass, an antelope skin and a cloth, (6:11).

Krishna assumes that the yogi will be sitting on the ground, as was usual in India at that time and even today in many instances. We will look at that first and then consider other options. The ground should be firm, neither soft nor shifting as sand or gravel or on a heap of things that could slide. Sand is pulverized stone and after sitting awhile literally becomes stone-hard. Not being soft indicates also that the ground should be dry. The place should be clean, without dirt or debris. The yogi should not perch himself in a tree, on the edge of a precipice, or in/on any place where he might fall off if he fell over, either in sleep or samadhi.

Dampness and cold are often properties of earth where the yogi might sit, so he is directed to first put down some kusha grass. Kusha grass is considered purifying, and rings woven of it are sometimes worn in worship to keep the hands ritually pure. It is also a remarkable insulator against cold and damp. In India I have used kusha mats with a blanket on top for sleeping on damp ground in bitterly cold weather, and was never bothered with either damp or cold underneath me. Such mats also make very good meditation seats, covered with a cloth. However, only dried kusha grass is used in matting, and the edges are very sharp and liable to cut the one handling it carelessly.

To compensate for this, and to increase the insulating effect, a deer skin may be placed over the kusha grass. A deer skin is the only animal skin considered appropriate for the yogi's meditation seat (asana) because the vibration of the deerskin is neutral and therefore conducive to peace and tranquility. However, the deer must have died a natural death. To use the skin of a deer killed for its skin is to violate the precept of ahimsa. One of my vivid memories of the Hardwar bazaar is seeing deer skins for sale that had bullet holes in them. When I once expressed disapproval of this to a shop owner, he was quite sympathetic and said: "I understand how you feel about the deer being shot by a gun. Quite a few yogis object to that. If you give me some time I will find you one that was killed with a bow and arrow. And I will provide you with certification to that effect." When I explained that I was objecting to the killing of the deer, no matter what form it took, I could see that he thought I was being quite eccentric. Nevertheless, leading yogis have told me themselves that the deer must have died naturally. This makes such a skin hard to come by, since decay will begin right away. But it is possible, for I have seen them.

To keep the deer skin from becoming worn (I knew one yogi that wore out a skin every four years because he traveled almost constantly), Krishna instructs that a cloth should be placed over that (my yogi friend did not do this). He does not specify what kind, but it is a good idea to use cloth made of natural fibers. (Not silk, which is the congealed saliva of worms who are killed to obtain it.)

The yogi's chair

In the West many yogis prefer to use a cushion on the floor or sit on a chair. Both are perfectly fine, for the posture that will soon be described by Krishna is possible in a chair. It is important that our meditation posture be comfortable and easy to maintain. If you can sit in a cross-legged position without your legs going to sleep and making you have to shift them frequently, that is very good. But meditation done in a chair is equally as good. Better to sit at ease in a chair and be inwardly aware than to sit cross-legged and be mostly aware of your poor, aching legs.

The chair should be comfortable–not hard, yet not so soft that you bob around when you sit upright. It should also be of a design that will prevent your falling over in deep relaxation. A padded armchair can be very good for this, or one which has a curved back that will keep you upright.

The chair should not be so high that your feet cannot be resting flat on the floor, or so low that your knees are markedly above the base of your spine and can cause backache.

The insulation provided by kusha grass and deer skin are unnecessary when meditating in a chair so you need not bother with them. It is good if the chair can be used only for meditation. (The same applies to a pad or mat used for cross-legged meditation on the floor.). This will pick up the beneficial vibrations of your meditation, and when you sit on it your mind will become calm and your meditation easier. If you cannot devote a chair to your meditation, find some kind of cloth or throw that you can put over a chair when you meditate and remove when you are done.

The inner seat

Shankara wrote a short essay in which he analyzed the symbolism of the eight limbs of Patanjali's Yoga. He says that the yogi's asana (seat) must be a steady mind which remains focused on its object of meditation. With this in mind, Krishna adds:

> **There, having directed his mind to a single object, controlling thought and activity of the senses, sitting on the seat he should practice yoga for the purpose of self-purification (6:12).**

The senses, their functions, and the inner memory of their past sensations in various forms are to be held at bay by the meditator. As he does so, absorbed in his meditation on the Divine, his heart becomes increasingly pure.

The yogi's posture

> **Holding the body, head and neck erect, motionless and steady, looking toward the origin of his nose [nasikagram] and not looking around, (6:13).**

Holding the body, head and neck erect. The Kaivalya Upanishad (5) says: "Keeping the head, the neck and the body in a straight line." The purpose of this is to ensure that the upright body will be balanced and not move. The head should be held so the chin is parallel to the ground. You need not be painfully exact about this. The idea is to hold your head at such an angle that it will not fall forward when you relax. Otherwise you will be afflicted with what meditators call "the bobs"–the upper body continually falling forward during meditation.

Motionless and steady. As the yogi meditates his body should not move back and forth or side to side, but be completely still. This is ideal, but please do not think that Krishna is advocating some kind of self-torturing coercion of the body. He does not say we should sit as stiff as a petrified mummy, for that is just self-torment. The great yogic adepts also say that the posture must be comfortable–easeful and relaxed. The Yoga Sutras say: "Posture should be steady and comfortable" (Yoga Sutras 2:46). The *Yoga Vashishtha* simply says: "He should sit in a comfortable posture conducive to equilibrium" (*Yoga Vashishtha* 6:1:128). Shankara comments: "Let him practice a posture in which, when established, his mind and limbs will become steady, and which does not cause pain." Relaxation is the key, for the Yoga Sutras further say: "Posture is mastered by relaxation" (Yoga Sutras 2:47).

Looking toward the origin of his nose [nasikagram]. It is equally reasonable to consider that the nose originates at the nosetip or at the point between the eyebrows. But since Krishna says later on (5:27), "turning up the eyes toward the two brows [bhruvoh]," we can be sure he means the eyes should be turned gently upward as though looking at a distant point. He should not focus them on the point between the eyebrows as that will pull the eyes slightly inward and cause strain.

Not looking around. This is not so hard to manage–keep your eyes turned up and closed!

Common sense must always be used. For example, those with back difficulties should make compensation for them, and not mind if they cannot sit fully upright.

Krishna makes no mention of the hands, because it does not really matter. Just rest them in your lap or on your thighs and forget about them.

The yogi's inner work

> **With mind quieted, banishing fear, firm in the brahmachari's vow, controlling the mind, with thoughts fixed on me, steadfast, he should sit, devoted to me (6:14).**

Just as there are several points for the yogi's outer practice, so it is with his inner practice, and we should consider them.

With mind quieted. Many people become impatient with themselves or their practice if right away their mind does not calm down, but that is why yoga is a practice and not a matter of instantaneous effect. After all, each day we spend hours and hours stirring up our mind and forcing it into reactions of all kinds. Moreover, it is a living entity, not a machine that can be switched off with the flick of a finger. Right meditation practice will certainly still the mind after a while. But we must be helping it by arranging our life in such a way that distractions will be minimal. Diet is also crucial here. A rajasic or tamasic diet (to be discussed in the seventeenth chapter) hinders the efficiency of yoga meditation. And most of all, our thoughts and emotions condition the mind substance, making it either easier or more difficult to still.

Banishing fear. This is not often discussed in writings or talks on yoga, but it should be given attention. It is no surprise that when we sit for meditation we will find that our mind is restless and trivial. We also realize that long-buried impulses from the past (including past lives) may surface, such as anger, lust, greed, and so forth. But in so many lives, as well as this one, we have been in situations that produced a great range of fear in us, from simple apprehension to absolute terror. When such things surface we are not aware of the cause, only the fear itself, and this actually compounds the fear. The fear of death also can arise, because in meditation, as in sleep, there is an approximation of the withdrawal of the life force that occurs in death. I have known a few people who were bothered by the fear of death in the beginning of their meditation practice. How did they overcome it? By the determined practice of meditation itself—nothing special was needed. So when unreasoning fear rushes over us, we need only keep on as usual and it will be banished. At times we may feel anxiety at the onset of peculiar sensations in the body as well as the mind, and fear that we may be harmed by whatever is producing them. There is also fear in the form of doubt to be contended with: fear that our meditation may be of no effect, or fear that we will not attain as much as we should, and even fear that we will not live long enough to make any significant progress. All these are just vagaries of the ego-mind and should be ignored.

Firm in the brahmachari's vow. Certainly, part of the brahmacharin vow is celibacy, for even non-monastics must live a disciplined and non-sensual life. The idea that God created or ordained marriage so men and women could have all the sex they wanted in an approved setting is outrageous. All who aspire to true humanity—much less divinity—must be chaste in body and mind. Those who do not wish to so live should do as they please, but leave yoga alone. This is why Patanjali says that the first step in yoga is moral observance (yama-niyama) which includes brahmacharya.

The Dharma Shastras which describe the correct life of non-monastics are quite explicit about the need for husband and wife to lead lives of continence. See how the yogi parents of Paramhansa Yogananda lived it as presented in *Autobiography of a Yogi.* In the very first chapter we find: "Mother made a remarkable admission to my eldest sister Roma: 'Your father and myself live together as man and wife only once a year, for the purpose of having children.'" The fact that Yogananda, a devoted son and a pure-hearted yogi, would reveal this to the world in the pages of a book show how necessary he felt it was for both Eastern and Western readers to be shown the standard of chastity that yogis should observe in their life, not using their non-monastic status as excuse for lesser behavior. He underlined this later in the forty-fourth chapter, giving these words written to Mahatma Gandhi by his wife Kasturbai: "I thank you for the most perfect marriage in the world, based on *brahmacharya* and not on sex." Please note that these are examples of married yogis, not monks imposing their ideas on others. Also remember that the guru of Yogananda's parents was himself a married yogi, so there is no monastic influence in their case.

Having said all this, I must point out that the brahmacharin vow (vrata) involves the discipline, purification, control, and non-indulgence of all the senses. Furthermore, it is a vow—a voluntary resolution. Those who do not wish to make such a resolution need not do so. But they should not lie to themselves and others by claiming to be yogis.

Controlling the mind. When the mind is quieted, rendered fearless, and strengthened by the power (virya) accumulated through continence and discipline of the senses (for the word "virtue" is derived from the Latin word for power), then—and only then—it can be controlled.

With thoughts fixed on me. The mind must not be made empty and static, for that would be stagnation and conscious coma. Rather, mantra japa that impels the consciousness toward God must be generated in a constant, though calm, stream.

Steadfast. The mind must be gathered up and made unitary. This is the meaning of the word "yukta" in this verse. The mind must be joined or "yoked" first to itself and then to God in the state of yoga, of union.

He should sit. Both body and mind need to be steady. Shankara says that asana means steadiness of mind as well as of body. It has been said that Buddha became enlightened because he knew how to "sit" through firm resolution, holding body and mind under his control.

Devoted to me. Such union is not abstract, it is a filling of the consciousness with God as the eternal Object-Subject. The first step, the precursor to God-awareness, is Self-awareness. In that awareness we find our true Self and then the Self of our Self, God. That is why Jesus spoke of "losing" our life to "find" it in the greater, primal Life that is God (Matthew 16:25).

The yogi's Goal

> Always disciplining himself thus, the yogi whose mind is subdued goes to the supreme peace of nirvana, and attains to union with me (6:15).

Ever keeping this in mind and following what Krishna has just told us, the yogi will come to the Goal unerringly and, comparatively speaking, easily.

A general principle

Now Krishna gives us a general principle for our way of life:

> Yoga is not eating too much, nor is it virtually not eating at all; not the habit of sleeping too much, and not keeping awake too much, either. For him who is moderate in food and diversion, disciplined in action, moderate in sleep and waking, yoga destroys all suffering (6:16-17).

Prabhavananda puts it very smoothly: "Yoga is not for the man who overeats, or for him who fasts excessively. It is not for him who sleeps too much, or for the keeper of exaggerated vigils. Let a man be moderate in his eating and his recreation, moderately active, moderate in sleep and in wakefulness. He will find that yoga takes away all his unhappiness."

Except in the matters of yama and niyama, which are absolutes, moderation is the yogi's motto. Cool-headedness is essential for him. As Sri Ramakrishna often remarked, crazes and extremes are detrimental to spiritual life. This is especially true because crazes and extremes often mask or express mental and spiritual pathologies. We should be enthusiastic about the spiritual life, but we must be equally sensible and moderate. Then yoga will be for us.

Union With Brahman

Krishna tells us the facts

How can we tell who is an enlightened person? The answer is to be found in the Gita. There the internal state of the perfected yogi is outlined–a state that can only be known to the yogi himself, that cannot be observed externally and subjected to a checklist, for it is purely internal in character. As Yogananda used to sing: "He who knows… he knows. None else knows!" The Kaivalya Upanishad describes the enlightened person as saying: "I know all that is, but no one knows me" (Kaivalya Upanishad 21).

A truly enlightened person will say what is found in the Kena Upanishad: "I cannot say that I know Brahman fully. Nor can I say that I know him not. He among us knows him best who understands the spirit of the words: 'Nor do I know that I know him not.' He truly knows Brahman who knows him as beyond knowledge; he who thinks that he knows, knows not. The ignorant think that Brahman is known, but the wise know him to be beyond knowledge" (Kena Upanishad 2:2, 3). Nevertheless, Krishna is able to give us a working idea of enlightenment, one which can be useful to the individual yogi so he will not mistake the goal or mistakenly assume he has attained it before he really has.

It is all in the mind

> When he is absorbed in the Self alone, with mind controlled, free from longing, from all desires, then he is known to be steadfast (6:18).

Here we find three traits of mind necessary for enlightenment: 1) total absorption in the Self, 2) perfect control of the mind, and 3) complete freedom from desire. This is a great deal for us to work on, and without diligent yoga practice it is impossible. Some or all of these may be managed occasionally in meditation, but that is not enlightenment. For Krishna continues:

> As a lamp in a windless place flickers not: to such is compared the yogi of controlled mind, performing the yoga of the Self (6:19).

Flashes of enlightenment can come to the yogi, but he must not be satisfied with fleeting experiences of the Self, but must strive to become permanently established in consciousness of the Self. This state cannot be attained by talk and wishful thinking. Rather:

> When the mind comes to rest, restrained by the practice of yoga, beholding the Self by the Self, he is content in the Self (6:20).

There is no way to enter into the state of enlightenment except through yoga. Certainly we sometimes hear of rare individuals who entered into perfect knowledge of the Self with minimal effort or even upon merely hearing of the Self. But such persons have attained illumination in previous lives. There are no shortcuts to enlightenment.

When the mind ceases its movements and becomes permanently stilled, the Self is known. As long as the surface of water is moving to any degree there is distortion in the reflected image, but once it comes to absolute stillness, the image is perfect (complete) and undistorted. It is the same with the mind. The mind can be likened to a double-sided mirror which reflects both the outer world and the inner Self. Both sides must be stilled through yoga. Then the yogi finds profound peace and rests contented in the Self. Only in the illumined Self does he behold (know) the Self. For it is *swayamprakasha*, self-illuminated and self-illuminating.

He knows that endless joy which is apprehended by the bud-dhi beyond the senses; and established in that he does not deviate from the truth [*tattwatah*: thatness] (6:21).

That the infinite happiness of the Self can be experienced by the buddhi is an extremely important point. Infinite consciousness transcends the senses and therefore the sensory mind, the manas, but it is not beyond the experience of the buddhi, the higher mind, the intellect. For the word buddhi is derived from the root verb *budh*, which means "to enlighten, to know."

The buddhi can be illumined by the Self. This is most significant, for it is usually assumed that all levels of the mind are dissolved at the advent of enlightenment, that the liberated yogi has no mind. But this is a misunderstanding. As Sri Ramana Maharshi continually pointed out, at the onset of enlightenment the buddhi is not destroyed, but rather is transmuted into the Self–for nothing ever really exists but the Self. As I say, this is important, for those who have no actual experience or realization make all kinds of statements, such as that since the enlightened have no mind they have no subconscious mind, and therefore cannot dream. And they love to challenge a yogi with the question: "Do you dream?" If the answer is Yes, they declare the yogi unenlightened. But when Ramana Maharshi was confronted with this silly question he simply said: "Yes. But not like your dreams." When asked what his dreams were like, he answered that when asleep (yes, he did sleep) he saw the forms of deities and temples–two nemeses of contemporary "advaitins."

Unshaken by sorrow or suffering

Standing firm in his realization, the yogi never loses or moves away from his perceptions of Reality.

Having attained this, he regards no other gain better than that, and established therein he is not moved by heaviest sorrow (6:22).

No suffering can overshadow or cloud the yogi's inner vision, no matter how terrible or prolonged it may be. Two events come to mind that illustrate this.

Sri Ramakrishna was in the final stages of throat cancer. Its ravages were terrible. One day he began pathetically describing the horrible pain to a disciple. After listening a while, the disciple interrupted him, vehemently saying: "No matter what you say, I see you as an ocean of bliss!" Sri Ramakrishna smiled, turned to a disciple standing nearby, and said: "This rascal has found me out!" And that was the end of the subject.

Toward the end of his earthly life, Paramhansa Yogananda had severe trouble with his legs, at times being unable to walk. Sometimes when the pains were so bad that he could not sleep, close disciples would sit with him in his bedroom. Often he asked them to play recordings of Indian devotional music to take his mind to higher levels. Once, though, he fell asleep as his first American disciple, Dr. M. W. Lewis, and his wife kept sad vigil in his room. After some time, Yogananda began to softly moan, and then his groans became increasingly louder and more expressive of the awful pain. Both devoted disciples began to weep in sympathy for his sufferings. Instantly Yogananda stopped groaning and began laughing. Then they understood: the great Master was always immersed in divine bliss, however much the body might suffer.

The real yoga

> Let this dissolution of union with pain be known as yoga. This yoga is to be practiced with determination, with an assured mind (6:23).

The most important part of this is to realize that cessation of suffering is not a side effect, but can be pursued directly. The Gita uses the tongue-twister *dukhasamyogaviyogam*—the yoga of the dissolving of union with pain.

How shall we succeed in this yoga?

Abandoning those desires whose origins lie in one's intention—all of them without exception—also completely restraining the many senses by the mind, (6:24).

Desires may persist, but we must steadfastly turn from them, restraining the senses by the mind. We need not even cut them off. Instead we should fix our minds on God. For since all desires are merely aberrations of the primal desire to find God that is in each one of us, the false desires will melt away. Yet it is not enough to just want to cut off desires, for desires are not self-existent entities. Rather, they arise from the senses as a result of contact with sense-objects. So the senses must be thoroughly controlled and restrained, placed under the directorship of our intelligent will.

It will not be an overnight matter or instant success. So Krishna says:

With the buddhi firmly controlled, with the mind fixed on the Self, he should gain quietude by degrees: let him not think of any extraneous thing whatever (6:25).

That is quite clear, but it should be pointed out that the constant practice of yoga in the form of japa and meditation is the only way to fix our mind on the Self and keep it steadily there so that in all the experiences of life we will remain in unbroken awareness of Spirit. It is through japa and meditation that we can also follow Krishna's next directive:

Whenever the unsteady mind, moving here and there, wanders off, he should subdue and hold it back and direct it to the Self's control (6:26).

This is immeasurably important. We restrain and control the intellect by immersing it in the Self. The Sanskrit text literally means "he leads it into the Self." In other words he establishes, he centers, the buddhi in the Self (Atman). The fact that the buddhi can experience the Self must never be forgotten by us. This revolutionizes our entire approach to attaining realization of the Self. The means is right at hand. We need only know the way and do it. It may not be fast, but *it will be sure.*

Success

Shankara says at the beginning of his commentary on the Yoga Sutras that unless the aspiring yogi knows the benefits which the practice of yoga will bring it is impractical to think that he will persevere. After all, who would work to gain something he does not really know about? "Some kind of reward" would not be enough of an incentive. Krishna then speaks of the results of the yoga he has been recommending to us:

> The yogi whose mind is truly tranquil, with emotions calmed, free of evil, having become one with Brahman, attains the supreme happiness (6:27).

Peaceful, passionless, pure, and blissful–who would not earnestly strive for such a prize? Even more:

> Thus constantly engaging himself in the practice of yoga, that yogi, freed from evil, easily touching Brahman, attains boundless happiness (6:28).

He still walks the way, and does so until he attains the highest realm and merges with the Absolute, but it is now easy (sukhena) and ananda-mayi–filled with bliss.

The eye of the yogi

> He who is steadfast in yoga (yoga-yukta) at all times sees the Self present in all beings and all beings present in the Self (6:29).

What a glorious vision! Since the Self and Brahman are one, the Self being the microcosm and Brahman the macrocosm, everything that exists can be found in either one, though in the individual Self it is only a kind of seed-reflection.

It is essential for us to comprehend the fact that the illumined yogi never confuses himself with Brahman the Absolute. Even if he says: "I am Brahman," he means that Brahman is his essential nature. For example, we can say of a gold statue that it is gold, but we will not mean that it is all the gold in the world–only that it is made from gold. In the same way our Self is of the substance of Brahman, but it is not the totality of Brahman.

So the yogi does not experience that he, personally, is in all things and all things within him in the same way that Brahman experiences unity with all. The yogi does experience a unity with all things, and as I say he experiences all things within himself as seed-reflections. I once described this kind of experience in an autobiographical writing in this way:

"While meditating one day all ordinary physical sensation vanished. Spatial relation ceased to exist and I found myself keenly aware of being beyond dimension, neither large nor small, but infinite (for infinity is beyond size). Although the terminology is inappropriate to such a state, to make it somewhat understandable I have to say that I perceived an infinity of worlds 'within' me. Suns–some solo and others surrounded by planets–glimmered inside my spaceless space. Not that I *saw* the light, but I *felt* or intuited it. Actually, I did not 'see' anything–and yet I did. It is not expressible in terms of ordinary sense experience, yet I must use those terms.

"I experienced myself as everything that existed within the relative material universe. Or so it seemed, for the human body is a miniature universe, a microcosmic model of the macrocosm. The physical human body is a reflection of the universal womb that conceived it. I had experienced the subtle level of the physical body that is its ideational (i.e., causal) blueprint. On that level it can be experienced as a map of the material creation."

Later, Dr. Judith Tyberg, director of the East-West Cultural Center in Los Angeles, told me that she had attended a lecture at Benares Hindu University in which a map of the universe and charts from *Gray's Anatomy* were compared and seen to be strikingly alike.

Such an experience as mine is not what is meant by Cosmic Consciousness, but rather is consciousness of the inner reflected cosmos.

Nevertheless, it has value. However, the perfected yogi has the same experience in a much more profound and practical manner, and actually knows and perceives all things in an incomprehensible manner. I have told my experience so those who have similar events will not assume they are the Infinite.

Now here is the really important part of the matter. Ignorant people experiencing momentarily what the yoga adept sees always, will be keenly aware of the What of their seeing. But the enlightened yogi sees the Who, as Krishna points out, saying:

He who sees me everywhere, and sees all things in me–I am not lost to him, and he is not lost to me (6:30).

Prabhavananda: "That yogi sees me in all things, and all things within me. He never loses sight of me, nor I of him." The yogi sees Brahman at all times, understanding that all things are but waves in the ocean of Brahmic Consciousness, including himself. This is depicted in Swami Sivananda's thrilling poem, *Only God I Saw*:

When I surveyed from Ananda Kutir, Rishikesh,
By the side of the Tehri Hills, only God I saw.
In the Ganges and the Kailas peak,
In the famous Chakra Tirtha of Naimisar also, only God I saw.
In the Dedhichi Kand of Misrik,
In the sacred Triveni of Prayag Raj too, only God I saw.
In the Maya Kund of Rishikesh and
In the springs of Badri, Yamunotri and Gauri-Kund to boot, only
  God I saw.

In tribulation and in grief, in joy and in glee,
In sickness and in sorrow, only God I saw.
In birds and dogs, in stones and trees,
In flowers and fruits, in the sun, moon and stars, only God I saw.

In the rosy cheeks of Kashmiri ladies,
In the dark faces of African negroes, only God I saw.
In filth and scents, in poison and dainties,
In the market and in society, only God I saw.

In trains and cars, in aeroplanes and steamers,
In Jutkas and dandies, in tumtums and landan, only God I saw.
I talked to the flowers, they smiled and nodded,
I conversed with the running brooks, they verily responded, only
    God I saw.

In prayer and fasting, in praise and meditation,
In Japa and Asana, in Tratak and concentration, only God I saw.
In Pranayama and Nauli, in Bhasti and Neti,
In Dhouti and Vajroli, in Bhastrika and Kundalini, only God I saw.

In Brahmakara Vritti and Vedantic Nididhyasana,
In Atmic Vichara and Atmic Chintana, only God I saw.
In Kirtan and Nama Smaran, in Sravana and Vandana,
In Archana and Padasevana, in Dasya and Atmanivedana, only God
    I saw.

Like camphor I was melting in his fire of knowledge,
Amidst the flames outflashing, only God I saw.
My Prana entered the Brahmarandhra at the Moordha,
Then I looked with God's eyes, only God I saw.

I passed away into nothingness, I vanished,
And lo, I was the all-living, only God I saw.
I enjoyed the Divine Aisvarya, all God's Vibhutis,
I had Visvaroopa Darshan, the Cosmic Consciousness, only God
    I saw.

Om, Om, Om, only God I saw.

What better comment could there be on Sivananda's attainment expressed in this poem than Krishna's next words:

> **He, established in unity, worships me dwelling in all things. Whatever be his mode of life, that yogi ever abides in me (6:31).**

The main characteristic of Sivananda was his love of all humanity and indeed of all sentient beings. Daily I saw his compassion for all he encountered. So Krishna's next words describe his state of mind and heart as well as that of all who truly know Brahman:

> **He who judges pleasure or pain by the same standard everywhere that he applies unto himself, that yogi is deemed the highest (6:32).**

Krishna has in these verses given the real facts about the interior state of those who know Brahman. It is wisdom to ever keep these in mind when encountering those who are thought to be enlightened, and even more wisdom to keep applying them to ourselves so we will press onward to the fruition of yoga: Brahman, and Brahman alone.

THE YOGI'S FUTURE

The dilemma

Krishna has told Arjuna of the disciplines necessary for the yogi and has told him of the exalted states which he can attain. To all this Arjuna puts the following question-statement:

> Arjuna said: This yoga which is taught by you characterized by evenness of mind, I do not see how it endures, owing to the mind's restlessness. The mind is truly unstable, troubling, strong and unyielding. I believe it is hard to control—as hard to control as the wind (6:33-34).

A common simile of the mind used in India is that of a kite which can fly very high into the sky, so high it can barely be seen, yet a tug on the line and down it falls to earth! Sri Ramakrishna was very fond of two songs on this theme:

> In the market place of the world, O Mother, you are flying kites.
> They fly high lifted by the wind of hope and held fast by the string
>   of maya....

and:

> The kite of my mind was flying in the sky of the Mother's feet.
> Jolted by the evil wind of sin it turned over and fell down.

It became heavy and tilted on one side by maya.
I cannot raise it up again....
Its crest of knowledge has been torn.
It falls down no sooner I lift it up....
It was tied to the string of devotion,
But it became confused as it got into play....

Sri Ramakrishna often compared the unpurified mind to a vulture that flies so high it is hardly even a dot in the sky, yet its entire attention is centered on the earth below, looking for dead bodies to eat. The idea of both similes is that the sensory mind–the manas, not the buddhi–is capable of rising very high, but yet it is tightly bound to earth and will after a while descend. Anyone who seeks higher awareness knows this to be all too true.

There is hope, nevertheless:

What can be done

> The Holy Lord said: Without doubt the mind is hard to control and restless; but through practice (abhyasa) and dispassion (vairagya) it is governed (6:35).

Abhyasa and vairagya will tame the wandering mind. Abhyasa is not just spiritual practice, but *sustained* spiritual practice–perseverance. Although spiritual practice is a fundamental need for the yogi, it must be done with a proper attitude toward that which agitates the mind and sends it sinking toward the very things the yogi wishes to escape. Therefore vairagya is also necessary. Vairagya is non-attachment or indifference to those disturbing elements–even a distaste for them. This is not an easy outlook to gain, but steadiness in the practice of meditation will make it possible. For Krishna continues:

> I agree that yoga is difficult to attain by him whose lower self is uncontrolled; but by him whose lower self is controlled by striving by right means, it is possible to attain it (6:36).

It is a fact: yoga is not for the weak or the lazy.

Fear–or hope?

Arjuna has already protested that he thinks it is impossible to control the mind. Such an attitude springs from inner negativity and troubles many yogis, especially in the beginning. Now another face of the ego emerges: pessimism.

> Arjuna said: One who has faith but is uncontrolled, whose mind has fallen away from yoga without reaching perfection in yoga–which way does he go? Is he not lost like a dissolving cloud, fallen from both worlds–here and hereafter, having no solid ground, confused on the path of Brahman? You are able to completely remove this my doubt. Other than you there is no one who can dispel this doubt (6:37-39).

If I had the proverbial nickel for every time some spiritual loafer asked me if there are not people who just are not ready for yoga, and would it not be better to not try than to try and fail, I would not have the proverbial fortune, but I would have a hefty sack to carry around. Arjuna is following the same line, which I expect was old and tired even then, thousands of years ago.

Krishna, worthy teacher, now tells Arjuna–and us–the real facts of the matter.

The yogi's future

> The Holy Lord said: Truly there is no loss for him either here on earth or in heaven. No one who does good goes to misfortune (6:40).

We must fix this truth firmly in our minds. First, in relation to ourselves: seeking Brahman assures us of a good end, especially if we persevere. Second, in relation to others: even if they turn away from the search for

God, the force of the spiritual karma created by their spiritual searching at least for a while will guarantee a positive future for them, even if only in the next or a future life.

There is a technical term in Sanskrit for one who has fallen away from the practice of Yoga: *yogabhrashta*. Krishna now discusses the good fate of the yogabhrashta:

> **Attaining the worlds of the meritorious, having dwelt there for countless years, he who has fallen from yoga is reborn in a happy and illustrious family (6:41).**

After death the former yogi will go into the higher astral regions, impelled by the tremendously positive karma that is always produced by yoga practice. In those realms of great peace, happiness, and clarity of mind he will remain for a long time, continuing to refine his understanding and preparing for a spiritually fortunate rebirth. After that, he will be reborn in a happy and illustrious (*shuchinam shrimatam*) family. For the yogi's parents will be of admirable character and recognized for it by those around them. This is why in India it is assumed that a saint will have been born of spiritually illustrious parents, perhaps even having saints in his ancestry.

> **Or else he may be born into a family of wise yogis. Truly, a birth such as that is more difficult to obtain in this world (6:42).**

It is difficult because there are so few families of accomplished yogis, and because such persons, habitually observing brahmacharya, will have very few children, if any.

> **There he regains the knowledge he acquired in his former incarnation, and strives from thence once more toward perfection. Truly without his willing it his previous practice impels him on the yogic path. He who just desires to know about yoga goes beyond the Vedas (6:43-44).**

How wondrous is yoga. Although it is sad to see someone fall away from the yoga life, the spiritual force generated will manifest in the next birth. We can be totally optimistic about anyone who takes up yoga, for those who just want to know about yoga enter into a stream of life that will carry them onward and upward.

I know this is true because I met a yogi in India who told me that he remembered his previous life as a Franciscan monk in Italy. He had heard that in India there were people called yogis who knew the way to God. From that moment onward he yearned to go to India to meet those who could tell him how to find and know God. He even tried to find some way to get to India. He died with this unfulfilled desire and in his next life was born in India and became a yogi.

Another man I met in India was a European who had entered a Roman Catholic seminary with the specific purpose of becoming a missionary to India. "After a few years," he told me, "I realized that I did not want to be a missionary at all–I just wanted to go to India!" So he left the seminary and went to India, where I met him in the ashram of the great Swami Sivananda of Rishikesh.

By persevering effort and mastery, the totally purified yogi, perfected through many births, reaches the Supreme Goal (6:45).

Ultimate success in yoga is assured–in contrast to every other earthly endeavor. So the wise do not delay, but become yogis now and persevere.

Great is that yogi!

The concluding words of this sixth chapter of the Gita are intended to inspire us to seek out and follow the path of yoga. For as Shankara observed at the beginning of his commentary on the Yoga Sutras, if the prospective yogi has no idea of the value of yoga practice he cannot be expected to persevere. So Krishna says:

The yogi is superior to ascetics [tapaswins], and considered superior to jnanis and superior to those engaged in Vedic rituals [karmakanda]. Therefore be a yogi (6:46).

Being immersed in body-identification, people are very impressed with anything physical. Asceticism and unusual physical control are prized even by those who claim to identify with the spirit instead of the body. Those with a bit more evolution to their credit are more impressed with intellectual attainments, especially with the ability to write or speak in an arresting or inspirational manner. The majority, however, are mostly impressed by good deeds of many kinds: philanthropy, heroism, great success, and power. But Krishna tells us that those who seek union with Brahman are far greater than any of these. Then he gives the traits of a real yogi destined to attain Brahman:

Of all the yogis, he who has merged his inner Self in me and honors me, full of faith, I consider him the most devoted to me (6:47).

True worship of God is not ritual worship or good works but consciously uniting ourselves with God. This is real faith and devotion directed to God. So if we wish to be truly great men and women, all we need do is seek God. For those who find God find everything to an infinite degree.

SUCCESS IN YOGA

S uccess is one of the gods of the modern world–but only material success. Krishna, however, is interested in success of spirit, and we should be, too. So:

> **The Holy Lord said: With mind absorbed in me, practicing yoga, taking refuge in me, hear how without doubt you shall know me completely (7:1).**

Perhaps one of the reasons Vyasa chose a battlefield as the setting for the immortal dialogue of the Gita is the necessity for cutting straight to the facts without delays. Once the battlefield is entered, diplomacy is left behind–if it had not failed there would be no battle. Only the facts–the immediate facts–now matter. It is no surprise, then, that in all spiritual traditions we find military references and symbols to some degree. This verse certainly embodies the factuality and urgency of battle–traits that we require in our own personal battle for higher consciousness. Here then are the factors necessary for our success.

With mind absorbed in me, practicing yoga. It is only to be expected that an inquirer will not commit to such an intense involvement with yoga until first some experience of its value has been gained. But it is absolutely essential that once the aspirant comes to see the value of yoga he must consider the necessity of making yoga practice the core of his life–everything else must become secondary. Further, anything found to conflict with the practice of yoga must be eliminated from the yogi's inner and outer life. Without this complete dedication success in yoga is impossible.

I am not saying that everything in a person's life is to be displaced by yoga, that yoga is supposed to crowd out everything so that nothing else remains, but only that yoga must be central to the yogi's life and be given first priority. This is because every element in our life must be looked at from a yogic perspective and ordered accordingly. Since most people's lives are conglomerates of addictions rather than principles or rational choices, this can be a very difficult matter indeed. To reach the sweet we must first go through the bitter. It would not be honest to tell you otherwise.

When Mahendranath Gupta asked Sri Ramakrishna: "How ought we to live in the world?" Sri Ramakrishna told him: "Do all your duties, but keep your mind on God. Live with all–with wife and children, father and mother–and serve them. Treat them as if they were very dear to you, but know in your heart of hearts that they do not belong to you.

"A maidservant in the house of a rich man performs all the household duties, but her thoughts are fixed on her own home in her native village. She brings up her Master's children as if they were her own. She even speaks of them as 'my Rama' or 'my Hari.' But in her own mind she knows very well that they do not belong to her at all.

"The tortoise moves about in the water. But can you guess where her thoughts are? There on the bank, where her eggs are lying. Do all your duties in the world, but keep your mind on God.

"If you enter the world without first cultivating love for God, you will be entangled more and more. You will be overwhelmed with its danger, its grief, its sorrows. And the more you think of worldly things, the more you will be attached to them.

"First rub your hands with oil and then break open the jack-fruit; otherwise they will be smeared with its sticky milk. First secure the oil of divine love, and then set your hands to the duties of the world.

"But one must go into solitude to attain this divine love. To get butter from milk you must let it set into curd in a secluded spot; if it is too much disturbed, milk won't turn into curd. Next, you must put aside all other duties, sit in a quiet spot, and churn the curd. Only then do you get butter.

"Further, by meditating on God in solitude the mind acquires knowledge, dispassion, and devotion. But the very same mind goes downward if it dwells in the world. In the world there is only one thought: 'woman and gold.'

"The world is water and the mind milk. If you pour milk into water they become one; you cannot find the pure milk any more. But turn the milk into curd and churn it into butter. Then, when that butter is placed in water, it will float. So, practice spiritual discipline in solitude and obtain the butter of knowledge and love. Even if you keep that butter in the water of the world the two will not mix. The butter will float.

"Together with this, you must practice discrimination. 'Woman and gold' is impermanent. God is the only Eternal Substance. What does a man get with money? Food, clothes, and a dwelling-place–nothing more. You cannot realize God with its help. Therefore money can never be the goal of life. That is the process of discrimination. Do you understand?"

There should be no "hidden charges" in yoga. Right from the first we should know what will be required of us if we intend to persevere. And we must decide to meet the requirements. Otherwise it is all a waste of time for everyone. The mind must be totally dedicated to God as the Supreme Goal and the Supreme Means. This is because real yoga is nothing less than communion with God right from the start, however faint or tenuous it may be. For "the path of the just is as the shining light, that shineth more and more unto the perfect day" (Proverbs 4:18).

Taking refuge in me. That is, we must make God the only answer to our internal problems, and not resort to mental and emotional gimmicks, such as purely intellectual "jnana" and whimsical "bhakti," that will only hide the troubles. Even though we should sensibly do our best in a practical manner in relation to our external difficulties, even there God should have priority so our external tangles will not turn into mental turmoils.

If we will observe these two principles, Krishna assures us: "without doubt you shall know me completely." Then he continues:

> To you I shall explain in full this knowledge, along with real-ization, which, being known, nothing further remains to be known in this world (7:2).

275

Then we will be ready to get out of what a friend of mine used to call "this dumb kindergarten of earth" and move up to a higher level of evolution.

The few

The benefits of yoga are so marvelous, yet:

> **Of thousands of human beings scarcely anyone at all strives for perfection, and of those adept in that striving, scarcely anyone knows me in truth (7:3).**

"Then said one unto him, Lord, are there few that be saved? And he said unto them, Strive to enter in at the strait gate: for many, I say unto you, will seek to enter in, and shall not be able" (Luke 13:23, 24). Why so few? Because few will devote their whole mind to God, practice yoga, and take refuge in God alone, making God the Sole Reality in their life. Such persons are rare, but we must at some time or other in the round of rebirths become one of them. So why not now, rather than later?

THE NET AND ITS WEAVER

A few verses further on from where we are at the moment Krishna says: "Truly this divine illusion [maya] of mine made of the gunas is difficult to go beyond" (7:14).

Since time immemorial Maya has been referred to as a net such as is used for catching fish and birds. However hard it may be to break through this net, we must all do so in time, and the spiritually intelligent try to break through right now without delay. We need to understand the net very well. And so Krishna says:

Prakriti

Earth, water, fire, air, ether, mind, intellect and ego-principle: these are the eight divisions of my prakriti (7:4).

Before we look closer at this listing, we must keep in mind that there are two Prakritis, the lower and higher, or the lesser and the greater. Everything mentioned in this verse is energy, because the lower Prakriti itself is Primal Energy or Power (Shakti). Everything that exists is energy, part of the lower Prakriti. What we have here is a listing of the lower Prakriti. Since mastership is our goal as yogis, Krishna is enumerating that which must be directly controlled through our yogic development. The list is short, but the challenge is long.

First we have the five primal elements (panchabhuta): earth, water, fire, air, and ether. Everything else is a combination of these five forms of

THE BHAGAVAD GITA FOR AWAKENING

energy (more accurately: five forms of behavior or arrangement of energy). The three remaining are "mirrors" of intelligence: mind (manas), intellect (buddhi) and ego (ahankara).

The manas is the sensory mind, the perceiving faculty that receives the messages of the senses. Buddhi is the intellect, the faculty of understanding and reason–the thinking mind. Ahankara is the feeling of "I am." It is not the true Self–for the Self is pure wisdom and need not feel or think. Rather, it is the ego-sense, the intermediary between the Self and the bodies in which it is encased. Because it often takes over and blinds us to the Self, the ego is usually spoken of in a very negative sense. But without the ego the Self could not possibly operate through the energy-complex necessary for our evolution.

The manas sees a shape. The buddhi says: "That is a tree." The ahankara concludes: "I am seeing a tree." All experience, inner and outer, is processed by these three. In fact, most of us are confined to our experiences that proceed from them. However:

Behind it all

> This is my lower prakriti, yet know my higher prakriti as consisting of all jivas [individual spirits], by which this world is sustained (7:5).

Prabhavananda: "You must understand that behind this, and distinct from it, is That which is the principle of consciousness in all beings, and the source of life in all. It sustains the universe." This verse is not easy to translate, because the word *jivabhutam* can mean either "consisting of spirit-beings" or "the world of Spirit." One means many spirits and the other only one Spirit. In truth, both are correct, as the universe exists solely through the presence within it of the many eternal, individualized consciousnesses. And of course it exists because it is the dream of Brahman–but it is our dream, too. God and the spirits are existing in a sublime unity incomprehensible to any but the enlightened. The lower Prakriti is energy, but the higher Prakriti is consciousness.

Everything Krishna says is vastly important, including this point. It is rather common for people to think that if they know the enemy or the adversary well they are going to easily come out the victor or the master. But this is not true when considering Maya, for Maya of itself is nothing, though it has a source and an enlivener. True, it has cut itself off from that source and has taken on a kind of independent life of its own, but that is its own illusion catching up with itself. The bedrock truth of all things is that behind and separate from them is the Primal Purusha, the Supreme Consciousness that is inseparable from all beings and the very Principle of the existence of all things, including our own jivatman, our own individual Self.

"The immortal Self is the sun shining in the sky, he is the breeze blowing in space, he is the fire burning on the altar, he is the guest dwelling in the house; he is in all men, he is in the gods, he is in the ether, he is wherever there is truth; he is the fish that is born in water, he is the plant that grows in the soil, he is the river that gushes from the mountain–he, the changeless reality, the illimitable!" (Katha Upanishad 2:2:2)

"Him the sun does not illumine, nor the moon, nor the stars, nor the lightning–nor, verily, fires kindled upon the earth. He is the one light that gives light to all. He shining, everything shines" (Katha Upanishad 2:2:15, Mundaka Upanishad 2.2.10).

It is this twofold-yet-one Primal Being that must be known if we are to elude the snare of Maya and transcend its influence forever. We must always have in mind the fact that the Reality behind the deluding appearance is the Infinite Self from which we draw our very existence. And I do not mean this in a merely intellectual fashion. It must be a knowing, a perception arising from the experience that is gained from intense sadhana alone.

Realize that these two prakritis are the wombs of all beings. Of this entire world I am the origin and the dissolution (7:6).

To know Maya truly we must know the Lord of Maya, Ishwara, for they are inseparably united. We must shake ourselves awake from the dream of separation. Part of knowing ourselves consists in experiential awareness of our origin: Prakriti united with Purusha. This is why the concepts of

Heaven-Father and Heaven-Mother are central to any intuition-based spiritual view. One without the other is nonsense. Even in the Upanishads which so emphasize the transcendent aspect of reality that can be symbolized as Father, the necessity of the Mother is found. (See the third chapter of the Kena Upanishad.)

As Prakriti the Parampurusha is the womb which brings all things into being and dissolves them as well. Sri Ramakrishna told of having a vision in which he saw a woman in labor give birth to a child and then after a short while eat it completely. At first he was shocked, but then he realized that what he was seeing was a symbol of the ways of Prakriti. Expansion and contraction, manifestation and dissolution, beginning and ending–all are manifestations of divine consciousness and Divine Power. This is why in the book of Revelation we find: "I am Alpha and Omega, the beginning and the ending" (Revelation 1:8, 11; 21:6; 22:13).

The Original Cause

Than me there is nothing higher. All this creation is strung on me like pearls on a thread (7:7).

This means that there is no source or cause beyond Brahman, that all things proceed from It, that It is the substratum, the support, of all being, of all worlds. Brahman is the essential being of all. Therefore It is called the Sutratman, the "Thread-Self," with this verse in mind. Whatever its apparent character, everything we perceive or experience is ultimately Brahman alone. This is almost impossible to maintain as an intellectual concept throughout our daily life, but it can be experienced in meditation and carried over into our life. Without yoga the ideal of the Gita is unattainable. "Therefore be a yogi," as Krishna counseled Arjuna.

And the Caused

Krishna develops these ideas, saying:

I am the taste within water, the radiance of the moon and the sun; the Pranava [Om] in all the Vedas, the sound in the ether and the manhood in men (7:8).

The universe is often spoken of in Indian scriptures as an ocean of potential existence–the causal waters. Here its meaning is that God is the essence of the cosmos. Further, God is Light, of which the sun and moon are but hints. And he is also Sound (shabda) itself which arises from the element of ether (akasha). Therefore, as Vyasa concludes in the final verse of the Brahma Sutras: "By sound one becomes liberated [*anavrittih shabdai*]."

Also of importance is the factor *paurusham nrishu*: manliness, potency, virility, and courage in human beings. This is very significant, for these words, unlike some expressions of the Gita, carry no connotation of gender, but of humanity in general. All of us, whether male or female in body, must manifest the essential powers of humanity, including the courage that such a manifestation requires. In other words, God is manifesting as the power and determination that is so needful for perfection in yoga.

Lest I seem in this commentary to put too much emphasis on yoga, please do not forget that at the end of every one of its chapters the Gita is described as "The Science of the Eternal, the Scripture of Yoga."

I am the pure fragrance in the earth, and the brilliance within fire; the life in all beings, and the tapasya of ascetics (7:9).

Brahman is the very living earth and the yoga of yogis. God is present in tapas, so let us be perpetual tapaswins and be ever-present with God.

Know that I am the eternal seed of all beings, the intelligence of the intelligent, and the splendor of the splendid (7:10).

Since God is "the eternal seed of all beings," there can be no other view than that all things, all beings, are part of God.

Desirable desire

> I am the strength of the strong, free from desire and passion.
> I am the desire in beings that is according to dharma (7:11).

This final clause is extremely important. Desire (kama) is spoken of unfavorably throughout the Gita, but it is impossible to live without desire. When we eat we desire to gain strength, when we study we desire knowledge, when we are kind we desire to comfort and sustain–is this wrong? No. When Krishna speaks disapprovingly of desire he means an ego-centered force that clouds the intelligence and impels the will to unreason. In other words, he is speaking of desire that is not an act of intelligent will but a product of egoic passion, and therefore of delusion. But desire that does not abrogate or contravene our nature as the eternal Self is a manifestation of divinity in us and is to be honored and followed. This is important to know since ignoramuses in Asia (not just India) like to ask: "But isn't the desire for enlightenment and liberation a desire, too?" In this way they hope to silence the wise who are exposing their ignorance in the form of their desires.

The gunas–threads of the net

> Know that sattwic, rajasic and tamasic states of being proceed
> from me. But I am not in them–they are in me (7:12).

The major strands of the Mayic Net in its external constitution are the three gunas. And having said that I realize that nowhere in these essays have I really discussed the three gunas, waiting for the section where they are discussed by Krishna. But that will not be until the fourteenth chapter, so I had better outline them here.

In *A Brief Sanskrit Glossary* found on our website–which I recommend you download or purchase and use for reference–the following is the definition for Guna:

"Quality, attribute, or characteristic arising from nature (Prakriti) itself; a mode of energy behavior. As a rule, when 'guna' is used it is in reference to the three qualities of Prakriti, the three modes of energy behavior that are the basic qualities of nature, and which determine the inherent characteristics of all created things. They are: 1) sattwa–purity, light, harmony; 2) rajas–activity, passion; and 3) tamas–dullness, inertia, and ignorance."

That covers it quite well. Some of the implications we can leave for comment when we come to the fourteenth chapter. There is no form of energy manifestation that cannot be put into one of these three categories, though they may also be of mixed character so that an object is only predominantly in one of these classifications.

Nothing is random or "unto itself." Rather, everything proceeds from Brahman, for Prakriti itself is merely a "thought" of Brahman Who is one with all. All is contained in Brahman, but Brahman is not contained in them. This principle enables us to not fall into the error of thinking that God is nothing but the sum total of all things. Instead, all things are God, who yet remains separate from them. For Krishna next says:

> All this world is deluded by the three states produced by the gunas. It does not perceive me, who am higher than these and eternal (7:13).

We, too, through the practice of yoga meditation must regain the truth of our being. For we also stand apart from all that we experience. We, too, are supreme and deathless. This is the glory of the Eternal Dharma: it tells us the plain truth about ourselves.

Breaking free from the net

Now we come back to the verse cited at the beginning, but in its complete form:

> Truly this maya of mine made of the gunas is difficult to go beyond. Verily only those who attain me shall pass beyond this maya (7:14).

How do we attain God? Not by religious acts or other pious gymnastics or by ascribing to dogmas. Since God is Consciousness, we take refuge by elevating and merging our consciousness into the divine consciousness, henceforth to live in Divine Unity. This is the goal. This is salvation. But in the meantime, Maya is truly divine, for its purpose is our evolution beyond its bonds.

The bound

But, since duality is fundamental to existence on this earth, there are those who do not break through Maya, for they do not take refuge in the divine consciousness that is really their own consciousness. Rather than move upward into the light, they burrow down and down into the dark. Of them Krishna says:

> **Evil-doers, the lowest of men, bereft of knowledge by maya, do not seek me, being attached to (existing within) a demonic mode of existence (7:15).**

A ladder, a stairway, and even a mountain have one thing in common: they can be ascended or descended. So it is with the cosmos, with Maya, the shared dream of both God and sentient beings. Those who do wrong–especially those who knowingly do wrong–become ever more *willfully* deluded by Maya (we all know people who fool themselves). Since they are resisting the sole purpose of human incarnation–ascent in consciousness–they are the lowest of beings, since they seek the lowest rungs of the evolutionary ladder. Such persons will never seek God, though some will be avowed atheists, others agnostics, others middling religious and others (the worst of all) zealously religious but without any spiritual consciousness or conscience whatsoever. Such persons, though in human form, live the life of demons–asuras: those who dwell in darkness. Since God is Light they are the truest atheists: those without God (*a Theos*).

THOSE WHO SEEK GOD

Among the virtuous, four kinds seek me: the distressed, the seekers of knowledge, the seekers of wealth and the wise (7:16).

Now a great deal of people think they are religious, that they "seek the face of God," but Krishna is presenting us with four broad categories of seekers.

The distressed. The *Artas* means those who are intensely troubled–bereft, afflicted, distressed, or suffering. Wisely they seek for relief in God, rather than try to distract themselves or deny their problems. Nor do they fool themselves with the false answers and delusive things of the deluded world.

The seekers of knowledge. The *Jijnasus* are those who desire knowledge and understanding, who really want to find the answers to the why and wherefore of themselves and their life, past, present, and future. They both think and realize that there is more to themselves and to life than they presently know. Like Socrates, they know that they know virtually nothing. But they yearn to know, realizing that without spiritual knowledge they are adrift on the ocean of relative existence without any sure hope. They will be satisfied with nothing less.

The seekers of wealth. The *Artharthi* are those who seek attainment and welfare, but not the temporary and changeable things of the world. They want something that lasts and cannot be lost. Right now they may not know it, but inevitably they will come to realize that they are really looking for God alone.

The wise. A *jnani* is one in whom true wisdom has arisen in the form of spiritual intuition, and who now consciously and very actively seeks the knowledge of Brahman which is itself Brahmanirvana, the state of enlightenment in Brahman. In Krishna's listing the jnani is not a perfect knower of Brahman, otherwise he would not be a seeker, but he is a knower who is impelled by what he knows to seek Supreme Knowledge and the Supreme Knower. It is only natural that Krishna would continue, saying:

The highest seeker

> Of them, the wise man, ever united, devoted to the One, is pre-eminent. Exceedingly dear am I to the man of wisdom, and he is dear to me (7:17).

It is obvious from this verse that the jnani is a yogi, for he is devoted to God and to no other for two reasons. First, he values God above all else. Second he knows that God alone is real, that all else is unreal and therefore unworthy of his dedication. But his valuation is not an impersonal factoid. Rather, God is dear to him and he is dear to God. Priya means both "dear" and "beloved." Actually, Krishna uses two words: *atyartham priya:* "exceedingly dear"–even "extraordinarily dear." So God fills the heart and mind of the jnani, just as God is fully intent on him. As Solomon sang: "My beloved is mine, and I am his" (Song of Solomon 2:16. See also 6:3 and 7:10).

Then Krishna tells us:

> All these indeed are exalted, but I see the man of wisdom as my very Self. He, with mind steadfast, abides in me, the Supreme Goal (7:18).

The jnani does not love God because of what he can get from him. He loves God because he alone is worthy of his love. Our English word "worship" was originally "worthship"–accounting someone worthy. We do not love God for any trait or deed, but for what he is in his essence. He is the ultimate and only Goal of all sentient beings. And devoted hearts alone reach that Goal.

Just a bit more:

> **At the end of many births the wise man takes refuge in me. He knows: All is Vasudeva [He Who Dwells in All Things]. How very rare is that great soul (7:19).**

Vasudeva is the Universal, All-Pervading God. The jnanis have ripened throughout many dedicated lives in which God alone has been their goal and refuge. For they know that God is all, the beginning and end. Rare indeed are such great ones. Yet, all of us are destined to be rare like them. Happy destiny!

THOSE WHO WORSHIP
GOD AND THE GODS

Krishna has told us about the four kinds of God-seekers, extolling the man of wisdom, the jnani, and urging us to be the same. But he does not shunt aside those with lesser motivations, for they, too, embody the divine Self and from that perspective are of value, also. So he tells Arjuna:

> Those whose knowledge has been stolen away by various desires resort to other gods, following various religious practices, impelled thus by their own natures [prakriti] (7:20).

The sole real purpose of human life is the realization of the Self and God. The path to this realization is the only true religion. In the beginning this was known, and human beings sought for realization and nothing less. But as ages passed, this insight faded away to be replaced by earthly desires. Not being able to get all they wanted materially, humans—who still retained a goodly portion of their original psychic perception—began to resort to external powers to assist them in the desired gain. At first they no doubt simply used their psychic understanding to manipulate the subtle levels of existence to manifest what they wanted, but when their psychic powers declined they had to resort to other intelligent beings that were not human, such as those who control the forces of nature. These beings became "gods" to them. Also, humans formulated thought-forms, constructs of psychic energies that could respond to their wishes and provide them with what they wanted to gain or accomplish.

Both the natural and fantasy gods were fed by the wills of their votaries. In many places sacrifices or offerings were made to them from which they drew power. The more degraded humans even offered blood sacrifice to beings of low evolution. These, too, drew power from such vile offerings. The higher gods drew power from ritual worship, praisings, devotional acts, and such like. Images of the gods were made and sometimes energized as focal points by which the gods were contacted. The images themselves took on a kind of semi-life, even semi-consciousness.

In India, at the time of Krishna at least, the low spirits we may rightly call demons were not worshipped–only higher nature-guardians and thought-created entities that were of a benevolent and pure nature. It is those deities that Krishna is talking about when he says:

> **Whoever wishes to worship whatever form with faith, on him I bestow immovable faith. He who, endowed with this faith, desires to propitiate that form, receives from it his desires because their fulfillment has been decreed by me (7:21-22).**

The Sanskrit is a bit tricky to untangle, but Prabhavananda no doubt has put it best: "But it does not matter what deity a devotee chooses to worship. If he has faith, I make his faith unwavering. Endowed with the faith I give him, he worships that deity, and gets from it everything he prays for. In reality, I alone am the giver."

This is the expression of the great care and mercy of God. Unlike the false gods created by egoistic mankind, the true God wills only our welfare–even physically–and will foster our reaching out to something beyond ourselves even if that reaching is done ignorantly and short-sightedly. He is willing to do this, for in this chapter he has already told us: "I am the desire in beings that is according to dharma" (7:11). It is these things alone that he will give to those who worship mistakenly. The evil things gained from other worship comes from the corrupt will of man, whether alone or linked with a demonic intelligence or force.

Answered prayers...

We can understand from all this that answered prayers tell us nothing about the validity of a worshipper's worship. Prayers are answered in many cases by the released will-power of the worshippers–power they have no idea is really theirs. Some prayers are answered by natural spirits (even those of the dead), and some by God (Ishwara) or those he has designated to foster humanity in this way. So the fact that we get what we want is no proof at all that we are praying in either the right way or to the right deity. "The god that answers prayer is the true God," was a slogan in the propaganda a friend once sent me about her new-found false religion. She was wrong, as these verses from the Gita show.

"And Jesus answered and said unto her, Martha, Martha, thou art careful and troubled about many things: but one thing is needful: and Mary hath chosen that good part, which shall not be taken away from her" (Luke 10:41, 42). The validity of a religion is shown only when the "one thing needful" is sought, when the seeker seeks enlightenment through the realization of his Self and God–and does attain it. Miraculous powers in a person are as meaningless as the answered prayers of common religion. The real miracle a Master performs is the awakening of consciousness in those who come in contact with him. And that takes place only in those already evolved to the point where they can be awakened.

It is true that when it furthers the divine plan for humanity masters will work miracles, but they are only secondary, and the masters and their true disciples know that well. In speaking of the miracles of his guru, Swami Kaivalyananda (Kebalananda) told the future Paramhansa Yogananda: "The numerous bodies which were spectacularly healed through Lahiri Mahasaya eventually had to feed the flames of cremation. But the silent spiritual awakenings he effected, the Christlike disciples he fashioned, are his imperishable miracles" (*Autobiography of a Yogi*, Chapter Four).

An unexpected "payment"

But Krishna is not finished, for being the embodiment of Divinity, of Truth itself, his intention is to make full disclosure on this subject. His next words, then, are these:

But temporary is the fruit for those of small understanding. To the gods go the worshippers of the gods; those who worship me come unto me (7:23).

Swami Prabhavananda: "But these men of small understanding only pray for what is transient and perishable. The worshippers of the devas will go to the devas. So, also, my devotees will come to me."

There are two flaws in ignorant worship. One is that only the "transient and perishable" can be gained by such worshippers. Moreover, since they desire and identify with the transient and perishable, they themselves seem to become just as transient and perishable as well. The other flaw is even less desirable: After death the votaries go into the subtle worlds inhabited by their gods and serve them just as they had been served by having their prayers answered. In some astral regions they truly do become servants of their gods, trapped and enslaved. That is simply the manifestation of the law of karma. Having incurred debts by being given the objects of their desires, the unfortunates must now serve the gods and do what they will.

There are many worlds where various kinds and levels of "gods" abide. Some are pleasant, some merely boring, and others miserable and filled with pain and malice. According to the kind of god worshipped, so will be the fate of the devotees. But this one thing is common to all: they are imprisoned in those worlds and unable to escape until released through payment of their karmic debt. And then they fall back down to earth, helpless as before.

The fate of those who go into the worlds of even the positive gods is also seen as unfortunate, for of them Krishna says later in the ninth chapter: "These men pray for passage to heaven, thus attaining the realm of Indra, home of the happy; there they delight in celestial pleasures. Pleasures more spacious than any earthly they taste awhile, till the merit that won them is all exhausted: then they return to the world of mortals... hungry still for the food of the senses, drawn by desire to endless returning.... such men must return to life on earth, because they do not recognize me in my true nature. Those who sacrifice to the various deities, will go to those deities. The ancestor-worshippers will go to their ancestors. Those who worship elemental powers and spirits will go to them. So, also, my devotees will come to me" (9:20, 21, 24, 25.–Prabhavananda).

The good part

At the end of this section from chapter seven as well as that of chapter nine we are told a wonderful thing: "those who worship me come unto me." Those who worship the Absolute Being through striving to live a purified life, engaging in spiritual disciplines leading to liberation and enlightenment (most importantly, meditation), will surely go to God by becoming irrevocably united with Supreme Consciousness, free forever from all bonds, conditionings, and limitations. Ever abiding in the consciousness of I AM, they will have attained the infinite being of Satchidananda, infinite Existence-Consciousness-Bliss itself. When a yogi has that, "nothing further remains remains to be known here in the world" (7:2).

THE VEIL IN THE MIND

Krishna has spoken of the strong net of Maya that is difficult to break through. Now he speaks of Maya as a veil that darkens and blinds the minds of those over whom it lies. We must keep in mind that in this section—as in most others—he is speaking both as the Supreme Self and the individual Self. So not only is God speaking to us, so is our own divine spirit.

Mistaken views

> **Though I am unmanifest, the unintelligent think me entered into manifestation, not knowing my higher being which is imperishable and unsurpassed (7:24).**

This verse tells us about traits of Brahman and the jiva (individual spirit) that are not perceived by the ignorant.

Unmanifest. Spirit is never manifest in the sense of becoming touched by material existence, or any form of relative existence at all. It is also unperceivable to the senses, the mind, and the intellect. Only that part of us which is forever beyond those three faculties can come into contact with Spirit and know it.

Entered into manifestation. Vyaktim apannam actually means "fallen into manifestation" or "changed into manifestation," the meaning being that God has lessened and limited himself through manifestation. But that is not the reality. God does not become material or changeable by manifesting the cosmos. And we ourselves are not human beings although we are experiencing humanity in an objective manner in which illusion has become distorted into seemingly subjective experience. There is nothing but Brahman. To mistake ourselves for anything less is deadly to us.

Imperishable. Although God is the source of all things, manifesting as all things, seated in the heart of all and experiencing all things, He is not in any way changed or affected by that. Nor are we, mirroring the Divine Being on the limited and finite level.

Unsurpassed. Both we and God transcend all relative existence, including that of mortal bondage, which is the state of all humanity. It is our nature to be beyond all the dreams of illusion which we call Maya.

Those who mistakenly assume differently as to the nature of God and themselves are impelled into a multitude of delusions from which arise a myriad false and impossible hopes and fears. Misunderstanding both themselves and God, they stumble, and often crawl, through a wilderness of spiritual and material death. Only when they emerge from it, as they all shall in time, will they realize the enormity of their ignorance and suffering. Then they will rejoice at having emerged from unreality into reality, from darkness into light, from death into immortality. For they and God have ever been the Real, the Light, the Immortal.

The unseen seer

"If God exists, why can't I see him?" is a sensible question. Krishna tells us exactly why:

> **Veiled by Yogamaya, I am not manifest to all. This deluded world perceives me not who am unborn and imperishable (7:25).**

God is veiled by Maya; but Krishna uses the expression Yoga Maya. This is a key concept of Sankhya philosophy. Yoga Maya is, of course, the power of Maya, of divine illusion. Those who are deluded by it cannot perceive the Divine Presence within all. Some do perceive higher realities, at least in a kind of dim intuition, in contrast to the majority of people.

They have evolved to such a point that the inner eyes and ears have become at least partially opened on their inner, higher levels. But those blinded by Yoga Maya identify with the human body and condition and experience nothing but change within and without. They cannot possibly perceive or even guess the realities that lie within themselves–including the Divine Presence.

But why does Krishna say *Yoga* Maya? What is yogic about it? Nothing. But yoga means union, and Krishna means that the mayic creation results when God "touches" or unites himself with Prakriti, the Universal Energy. Actually Sankhya says that God only approaches or becomes very near to Prakriti and it immediately seems to come to life, moves and begins to appear in many manifestations, all of which are Maya, Illusion, and not really Prakriti in its true nature any more than they are Spirit in manifestation.

> **I know the departed beings and the living, and those who are yet to be, but none whatsoever knows me (7:26).**

Why is this? Because God is beyond relative being and can never be an object of intellectual knowledge. Since God is the Eternal Subject, he knows (perceives) all the waves that appear and disappear upon the ocean of being which he is. By his nature he knows all things, but "things" by their nature cannot know him. It is a matter of Who in contrast to What. We, being part of God, have the same capacity but in us the experience of "thingness" has swallowed up awareness of our true nature. This condition is not native to us, so in time it will melt away and we will once more know truly. Of course we have to work at that, which is what yoga is all about. We can once again be established in our Self, and from that center we can come to know God who is at that center. That is why Jesus said: "Blessed are the pure (*catharos*: clear) in heart (at the center: *kardia*): for they shall see God" (Matthew 5:8).

The problem

Misery may not always love company, but it certainly *has* company, for Krishna now says:

By desire and aversion rising up through duality's delusion, at birth all beings fall into delusion (7:27).

How could we not believe this world is real? Its pain and fear block out from our minds all other aspects of existence, draw our awareness totally outward into the material world, and imprison us there. Certainly that imprisonment is a delusion and not a reality, but we neither know that nor are capable of believing it when we first hear of it. But it is not the world that is at fault. Uncomfortable as it may be to face, the fault lies in us, in our continually veering back and forth between the two poles of desire and aversion. I Want and I Don't Want push us back and forth and even morph into one another. Our minds become like a tennis ball, batted in opposite directions until they lose all perspective and orientation. As long as we are subject to these warring forces we can never know either peace or clarity of mind and heart.

The solution

The sole answer lies in changing ourselves, in establishing our consciousness in the right place. For Krishna tells Arjuna:

But those whose wrongdoing has come to an end, whose actions are righteous, freed from the delusions of the pairs of opposites–they worship me with firm resolve (7:28).

Now this is most interesting. Mere philosophizing or theologizing will not clear up our dilemma. "The truth" as verbal or intellectual formulations will avail nothing, either. Rather, it is what we actually do that will neutralize the forces that work against our progress. By right action we expunge the force of past negative actions.

The word *vrata*, here translated "resolve," means a resolve in the sense of a resolution which manifests as a rule of conduct in right action. God-oriented thought and action is the only cure for the malady of bad karma and susceptibility to the forces of like and dislike, both of which spring from the ego alone. This is further underlined as Krishna continues:

> Those who strive toward freedom from old age and dying, tak-
> ing refuge in me, know Brahman totally, and know the Self
> and karma perfectly (7:29).

Old age (jara) and dying (marana) are inevitable processes of the material body, including the astral and causal bodies, but do not touch the
spirit. The wise therefore strive toward the realization of Brahman, the
Imperishable and Immortal Spirit of which they are a part.

Guru Nanak continually spoke of "the Godwards" in his hymns.
Krishna here tells us that those who are totally Godward, whose every
thought, word, and deed is directed toward God with the intention of
knowing and uniting with God, will indeed come to know God and their
Self and the true nature of this world and that which lies beyond it. The
relative and the absolute will all be known to them.

This will be no temporary high or psychic flash that comes and goes,
but:

> Those who know me as the Primal Being [Adhibhuta] and the
> Primal God [Adhidaiva], as well as the Primal Sacrifice [Adhi-
> yajna], they know me with steadfast thought also at the time
> of death (7:30).

These terms will be defined after the next verse. The idea here is that
Brahman is all this in relation to relative existence and the evolution going
on within it. Krishna is speaking here of the Ring of Return made perfect
and complete.

THE BIG PICTURE

A friend of mine used to tell people: "You will only get what you settle for." He meant that if you will settle for little, that is what you will get. But if you will settle only for much, that will come to you. Apparently Arjuna held this same philosophy, for now he is going to ask some very vast questions. But Krishna will easily answer all these things in terms that millions throughout the ages will understand.

The questions

> Arjuna said: O Supreme Spirit [Purushottama]: What is Brahman? What is the Primal Self [Adhyatma]? What is action? What is the Primal Being? What is the Primal God? What, and in what way, is the Primal Sacrifice here in this body? And how are you to be known at the time of death by the self-controlled ones? (8:1-2).

Krishna will answer these, but here are the definitions of all the technical terms in this verse as found in *A Brief Sanskrit Glossary*:

Brahman: The Absolute Reality; the Truth proclaimed in the Upanishads; the Supreme Reality that is one and indivisible, infinite, and eternal; all-pervading, changeless Existence; Existence-knowledge-bliss Absolute (Satchidananda); Absolute Consciousness; it is not only all-powerful but all-power itself; not only all-knowing and blissful but all-knowledge and all-bliss itself.

Adhyatma: The individual Self; the supreme Self; spirit.

Karma: Karma, derived from the Sanskrit root *kri*, which means to act, do, or make, means any kind of action, including thought and feeling. It also means the effects of action. Karma is both action and reaction, the metaphysical equivalent of the principle: "For every action there is an equal and opposite reaction." It is karma operating through the law of cause and effect that binds the jiva or the individual soul to the wheel of birth and death.

Purushottama: The Supreme Person; Supreme Purusha. *Purusha:* "Person" in the sense of a conscious spirit. Both God and the individual spirits are purushas, but God is the Adi (Original, Archetypal) Purusha, Parama (Highest) Purusha, and the Purushottama (Highest or Best of the Purushas).

Adhibhuta: Primal Being; Primal Element; Primordial Matter. Also: Supreme Being and Supreme Element.

Adhidaiva: Primal God; Supreme God.

Adhiyajna: Primal Sacrifice; Supreme Sacrifice.

Brahman, Adhyatma, and karma

> The Holy Lord said: The Imperishable is the Supreme Brahman. Its dwelling in each individual body is called the Primal Self; the offering in sacrifice which causes the genesis and support of beings is called Karma (8:3).

Brahman is the supreme, unchanging Being, the eternal Fact of existence itself, the First to which all else is second. Since nothing can really be said about the transcendent Brahman, Krishna quickly passes on to that which we can comprehend, at least to some degree.

Adhyatma firstly is the principle of the indwelling Brahman in all beings as their Eternal Witness. But it is also the principle of the individual spirit's eternal distinction from Brahman which enables it to manifest and dwell in many forms in succession. The power which brings this embodiment about is karma in its fundamental nature. So from this we see that karma is not only a reaction, but the action that originates our coming into relative existence. Karma both initiates and maintains the rebirth process.

World, man, and God

> Primal Being is perishable existence; the Primal God is the Supreme Divine Being; and I myself am the Primal Sacrifice (8:4).

I have pointed out previously that the Bhagavad Gita is an exposition of the Sankhya philosophy. Sankhya postulates the existence of three eternal entities: God, the individual spirit, and the Divine Creative Power within which the individual evolves. This verse is about them. The Primal Element, the Adhibhuta, is Parashakti, the Supreme Energy which manifests as the entire range of relative being, including all the forms assumed by sentient beings in their evolutionary pilgrimage within itself. The Primal Deity is the individual divine Self, the jivatman, the purusha which is moving up the ladder of Adhibhuta. The Adhiyajna, the Primal Sacrifice is Brahman itself, dwelling in the body [*dehe dehabhritam*] along with the individual Self.

The new idea presented in this verse is the concept that by entering into all beings as their Indweller God has become the Primal Sacrifice. Interestingly, the best elucidation of this idea is to be found in an esoteric Christian ritual–the Mass rite formulated by Bishop James I. Wedgwood, founder of the Liberal Catholic Church. As referred to previously, in one of the prayers God is addressed as him "Who, abiding unchangeable within Thyself, didst nevertheless in the mystery of Thy boundless love and Thine eternal Sacrifice breathe forth Thine own divine life into Thy universe…. Omnipotent, all-pervading, by that self-same Sacrifice Thou dost continually uphold all creation, resting not by night or day, working evermore through that… enduring Sacrifice by which the world is nourished and sustained."

God does not only sacrifice himself by entering into limited modes of being, he also does so by willingly experiencing all the attendant changes and states of mind and body inherent in those conditions. Many people ask how God can allow people to suffer, not realizing that he is experiencing every pain and sorrow that all sentient beings—not just humans—are enduring. A dying person only experiences the suffering and death of a single body, while God is experiencing the suffering and death of an almost infinite number of bodies, all at the same time. There is no nuance of struggle or suffering that God does not undergo right with us. Is this not a sacrifice beyond all conception? The sufferings we undergo are for our eventual benefit; they are necessary for us. Yet God, who certainly needs no such, agrees to live in us and experience all that we experience. There could be no greater sacrifice, no greater mercy, no greater love. So the next time we feel like complaining about our "fate" let us remember that God is enduring the same fate right along with us.

THE SURE WAY TO REALIZE GOD

The easy way out

The attainment of liberation (moksha) is very simple in principle, and in practice, as well. Perhaps it is its simplicity that keeps people from attaining it. However it may be, Krishna explains the whole matter in a very simple manner:

> **At the time of death he who remembers me while giving up the body attains my Being—of this there is no doubt (8:5).**

This is quite straightforward and easy to understand. The moment of death is perhaps the most important moment in our life, equalled only by the moment of birth. Dr. Morris Netherton, formulator of the Netherton Method of Past Life Recall, has found that the most significant factors in our life can be either birth or death trauma. The same would be true of positive experience during birth or death, which is why in India sacred mantras are recited during both times—at least by the spiritually intelligent. In this way the individual both comes into incarnation and leaves it accompanied by the remembrance of God.

The principle

Sanatana Dharma is never a matter of Shut Up And Accept What I Tell You. So Krishna explains to us how it is that if we are intent on the remembrance of God at the time of death we will go to God.

Moreover, whatever he fixes his mind on when he gives up the body at the end, to that he goes. Always he becomes that (8:6).

All translators I know of have translated this verse to mean that whatever we think of at death, we will go to that thing, to whatever world in which it exists. The conclusion is then that if we remember God in life we will go to God at the time of death. Sounds, simple, easy, and certainly noble. But it is not true, as no simplistic formula is ever true. Sargeant alone, as far as I know, translates this verse correctly.

It is not "who" or "what" we merely think of intellectually that determines our after-death state, but the state of mind and being, the bhava, that we are in at the time of death. *A Brief Sanskrit Glossary* defines bhava in this way: "Subjective state of being (existence); attitude of mind; mental attitude or feeling; state of realization in the heart or mind." In short, it is our state of consciousness, and that is a matter of evolution, of buddhi yoga. Religiosity and holy thinking fail utterly; it is the level of consciousness that alone means anything.

When we die, we gather up all the subtle energies that comprise our astral and causal bodies—energies that ultimately are seen to be intelligent thought-force. Then we leave the body through the gate (chakra) that corresponds to the dominant vibration of our life and thought. If our awareness has been on lower things we will depart through a lower gate and go to a low astral world. If we have been spiritually mediocre we will go to a middling world. But those who have made their minds and bodies vibrate to Divinity through authentic spiritual practice (tapasya) will leave through the higher centers. Those who have been united with God even in life will go forth to merge into Brahman forever.

Some people pay attention to the first part of this verse only, and think that they will cheat the law of karma which operates mentally as well as physically. They think that if at the moment of their death they will say a few mantras, then off they go to liberation (or at least heaven) no matter how they have lived their lives. Others, not quite so crass, decide that after having lived in a materialistic and spiritually heedless manner they will get religious during the last few years of their life and then be sure to be in the right state of mind and being as they die. But there is no cheating or cutting corners. What we sow that we reap–nothing else.

The outspoken Ajahn Chah, a meditation master of the Thai Buddhist forest tradition, said that many people pester their grandmother at the moment of death, calling out: "Say 'Buddho [Buddha],' grandma, say 'Buddho'!" "Let grandma alone and let her die in peace!" said Ajahn Chah. "She did not say 'Buddho' during life, so she will not say 'Buddho' during death." Sri Ramakrishna said that even at the moment of death a miser will say: "O! look how much oil you are wasting in the lamp! Turn it down." He also said that you can teach a parrot to constantly say "Radha-Krishna!," but if you pull its tail feathers it will only squawk. In the same way, when death pulls our "tail feathers" we revert to our swabhava, our real state of mind and consciousness.

Although not of the spiritual sophistication of the Gita, the American country singer, Roy Acuff, wrote about the same idea in his song "Wreck on the Highway."

> Who did you say it was, brother?
>> Who was it fell by the way?
> When whiskey and blood run together,
>> Did you hear anyone pray?
>
> I didn't hear nobody pray, dear brother,
>> I didn't hear nobody pray.
> I heard the crash on the highway,
>> But I didn't hear nobody pray.
>
> When I heard the crash on the highway
>> I knew what it was from the start.
> I went to the scene of destruction
>> And a picture was stamped on my heart.
>
> There was whiskey and blood all together
>> Mixed with glass where they lay

Death played her hand in destruction,
    But I didn't hear nobody pray.

I wish I could change this sad story
    That I am now telling you,
But there is no way I can change it,
    For somebody's life is now through.

Their soul has been called by the Master.
    They died in a crash on the way.
And I heard the groans of the dying,
    But I didn't hear nobody pray.

I didn't hear nobody pray, dear brother,
    I didn't hear nobody pray.
I heard the crash on the highway,
    But I didn't hear nobody pray.

Yogiraj Shyama Charan Lahiri often said: "If you don't invite God to be your summer Guest, he won't come in the winter of your life."

In the area where I was born there was intense, virulent prejudice against the Roman Catholic Church and its members. One of my aunts confided to another aunt: "I go to a Protestant church, but I believe the Catholic religion is the right one. And when I realize that I am dying I will call for a priest and become a Catholic." After many years, without any warning she passed into a coma, remained in that condition for six months and died without ever regaining consciousness. Her deathbed conversion plan never had a chance.

What we do not sow, we do not reap.

The lesson we must learn

There is a lesson here for all of us. As Jesus said: "Lay up for yourselves treasures in heaven," in the realms of higher consciousness, "for where your treasure is, there will your heart be also" (Matthew 6:20, 21), even at the time of death.

Therefore at all times remember me, and fight with your mind and intellect fixed on me. Thus without doubt you shall come to me. With mind made steadfast by yoga, which turns not to anything else, to the Divine Supreme Spirit he goes, meditating on him (8:7-8).

This is the necessary bhava we must cultivate at all times, fighting the battle of life in the conditions and situations dictated by our karma.

The Lord

We are not going to heaven–we are going to God! And we do not just believe in God, we intend to unite with God. So Krishna further says:

He who meditates on the Seer, the Ancient, the Ruler, subtler than the atom, Support of all, whose form is inconceivable and radiant like the sun and beyond darkness, at the time of death with mind unmoving, endowed with devotion and yoga power, having made the prana enter between the eyebrows, he goes to the Divine Supreme Spirit (8:9-10).

One of the gates to higher worlds is the "third eye" between the eyebrows. During meditation the yogi sometimes finds his awareness drawn spontaneously to that point. It is the same at the time of death. The purified and divinely-oriented life force (prana) automatically exits through that gate and goes to God, bearing us upward, even as the Egyptians pictured the freed soul flying in a spirit-boat to the sun.

There is more:

That which the knowers of the Veda call the Eternal, which the ascetics free from passion enter, desiring which they live the life of brahmacharya, that path I shall explain unto you briefly (8:11).

To die right takes a lifetime of purification and preparation. Only those can enter into God whose bonds of desire are broken. To this end they constantly practice brahmacharya–control of the senses and mind, which includes chastity/celibacy.

Going forth

> Closing all the doors of the body, confining the mind in the heart, drawing his prana into the head, established in yoga concentration, uttering Om, the single-syllabled Brahman, meditating on me, departing thus from his body, he attains the Goal Supreme (8:12-13).

It is important to remember here that "heart" means the core of our consciousness, and not the physical heart or heart chakra. Even more important, Krishna is not referring to some kind of strenuous breathing exercise, but rather, the natural and automatic rising of the life-force into the higher centers of the brain.

A resume

Krishna then recaps all he has said in this section with these words:

> He who thinks of me constantly, whose mind never goes else-where, for him, the constantly-united yogi, I am easy to attain. Coming to me, those great souls who have reached the high-est perfection do not incur rebirth in this world, which is the impermanent home of suffering. The worlds up to Brahma's realm are subject to rebirth's return, but for him who attains to me there is no more rebirth (8:14-16).

DAY, NIGHT, AND THE TWO PATHS

Within relativity, duality–positive and negative–is an absolute necessity for manifestation. Being alive, the cosmos requires that all things manifest this duality in a cyclic manner, that the positive and the negative polarities alternate in dominance. This can be seen in everything that lives. In fact, the more alive something is, the more evident are the alternating cycles. This principle manifests most obviously in the human body. The universe, being the body of God, also possesses this duality. Just as the image of God, the human being, breathes in and out to live, in the same way God breathes. The creation/manifestation of the universe is the exhalation of God, and its withdrawal/dissolution is the inhalation. Therefore Krishna says:

> **They know the true day and night who know Brahma's Day a thousand yugas long and Brahma's Night a thousand yugas long (8:17).**

I will not weary you–or me–with the mathematical basis for arriving at the numbers assigned to the ages, known as yugas. There are smaller ages within greater ages–wheels within wheels. Anyhow, some say that a "day of Brahma" lasts 4,320,000,000 years, and the "night" is of equal length.

However, Paramhansa Yogananda, whose guru Swami Sriyukteswar Giri was a foremost expert in these calculations, says in his *Autobiography of a Yogi*: "The universal cycle of the scriptures is 4,300,560,000 years in extent, and measures out a Day of Creation or the length of life assigned to our planetary system in its present form. This vast figure given by the rishis is based on a relationship between the length of the solar year and a multiple of Pi (3.1416, the ratio of the circumference to the diameter of a circle). The life span for a whole universe, according to the ancient seers, is 314,159,000,000,000 solar years, or 'One Age of Brahma.'"

Krishna continues:

> At the approach of Brahma's Day, all manifested things come forth from the unmanifest, and then return to that at Brahma's Night. Helpless, the same host of beings being born again and again, merge at the approach of the Night and emerge at the dawn of Day (8:18-19).

This is the situation of us all: compelled to manifest and compelled to return to unmanifestation in unending cycles. Will this ever end? Yes and No. It can end for those who wish it to end. For the rest, the coming and going will never end. Krishna will now show us how we can step off the ever-rotating wheel.

The Supreme Unmanifest

> But there exists, higher than the unmanifested, another un-manifested Eternal which does not perish when all beings perish. This unmanifest is declared to be the imperishable, which is called the Supreme Goal, attaining which they return not. This is my supreme abode (8:20-21).

Although the germs of the cosmos are unmanifest when withdrawn and invisible, there is another Unmanifest that is the Supreme Being behind both manifestation and dissolution. This is the ultimate source of all, eternal and changeless, untouched by the ever-changing condition of relative existence. It is the Reality behind the cosmic illusion-drama. To attain that state of being is the highest attainment possible for finite beings, for it is Infinity itself. Only those who reach that are freed from rebirth. For all the worlds from the highest to the lowest are subject to continual rebirth. The Unmanifest lies beyond all worlds, transcendent and changeless. And those who enter It become themselves transcendent and changeless.

> This is the Supreme Being [Parampurusha], attained by one-pointed devotion alone, within which all beings do dwell, by which all this is pervaded (8:22).

Bhakti, the word here translated as "devotion," means much more than mere emotion, but means devotion in the sense of being absolutely devoted–dedicated–to the endeavor to unite with God. As Swami Sivananda said: "Bhakti begins with two and ends in One." (He also said: "Devotion is not emotion.")

Yoga (union) in the highest sense must be the driving force of the aspirant's life, the point of reference around which he arranges his entire existence. Dabblers and fiddlers-around are not yogis, nor are those who are only intellectually intrigued by the possibility of divine union. The real yogis are those who live the words: "Arise, awake, and stop not till the goal is reached." God is the only Goal for them. And the search for God is their only life.

Two paths

> Now I shall tell you of the times in which the yogis, departing at the time of death, return or do not return (8:23).

We have already seen in the first part of this chapter that the state of mind and being in which we have habitually dwelt in life will determine the state we will attain at death. Here Krishna adds another factor, telling us that there are points in time that determine (or at least influence) whether or not the departing soul will return to earthly rebirth or pass on to evolve in higher worlds, perhaps even reaching the Absolute directly. Now he describes them:

> Fire, light, daytime, the bright lunar fortnight, the six months
> of the sun's north path: departing then the Brahman-knowers
> go to Brahman. Smoke, nighttime, the dark fortnight, the six
> months of the sun's south path: thereby attaining the lunar
> light, the yogi returns again. Truly these two light and dark
> paths the world thinks to be eternal. By one he goes to non-re-
> turn; by the other he returns again (8:24-26).

These paths, or bands of subtle energies on which the soul either ascends or descends, are spoken about in the Brihadaranyaka and Chandogya Upanishads. All commentators on the Upanishads and the Gita agree that these lists are symbolic of psychic energies or magnetism which draw the astral and causal bodies of the dying person upward or downward.

Various specific interpretations are possible. For example, light and fire represent clarity of consciousness, whereas night and smoke symbolize darkness and confusion of mind. The bright fortnight of the month and the northward movement of the sun refer to the upward orientation of the consciousness, and the dark fortnight and the southern solar movement indicate the habitual turning of the consciousness downward to materiality and ignorance. The moon is a symbol of the astral worlds in which earthly rebirth is inevitable, but the sun symbolizes those astral regions in which the soul is free of the compulsion to material re-embodiment and can move on to higher levels of existence for continued evolution.

Obviously the two paths or streams of energy and consciousness are being taken by each one of us right here in our present life, and will continue, then, after our subtle bodies are separated from the physical at the process we call death, though it is really a movement into a different mode of life. Therefore we should seriously analyze our life and see which stream we are moving in. For after death we only continue on just as we have been, although in the subtler realms the nature of our life becomes more evident.

In this world we can lie to ourselves and others, but not "over there." There the truth of things is revealed. Unless, of course, at the moment of death we merely fall into a psychic coma and know nothing until someone

311

whacks us on the backside at the time of our next birth. This happens to a large percentage of human beings. It takes a definite degree of evolution to go to either heaven or hell! As John Oxenham wrote: "The high soul climbs the high way, and the low soul gropes the low, and in between on the misty flats the rest drift to and fro" as spiritual sleepwalkers.

> No yogi who knows these two paths is confused. Therefore at all times be steadfast in yoga (8:27).

This implies that only the yogi follows the upward path to liberation. What about virtuous, sincerely religious people who are not yogis? We would assume that they, too, go the upward path, but Krishna concludes with these words:

> Whatever meritorious fruit is declared to accrue from study or recitation of the Vedas, sacrifice, tapasya, and almsgiving–beyond all these goes the yogi who knows the two paths; and he attains to the supreme, primeval Abode (8:28).

"Therefore, be a yogi!" (6:46).

THE SUPREME KNOWLEDGE

The Holy Lord said: To you who do not disbelieve I shall declare this most secret knowledge combined with realization, which having known you shall be free from evil (9:1).

What words! Yet they are purely wisdom, free from exaggeration or emotionality. The qualities of this great knowledge should be scrutinized by us who seek for it.

Most secret

Krishna calls this knowledge, not just secret (guhya), but most secret (guhyatamam). It is knowledge hidden from all but the knowers of Brahman, yet it can be spoken about to those who are approaching that knowledge. Essentially, Krishna is going to give us the knowledge that inevitably leads to that supreme knowledge. It is most secret because it is utterly incomprehensible and hidden to a consciousness that is not awakened and already purified to a marked degree. For regarding those not awakened and not purified it can justly be said: "They seeing see not; and hearing they hear not, neither do they understand" (Matthew 13:13).

Disbelief

False religions and false teachers demand faith in the sense of unquestioning acceptance of doctrines and dogmas. Or they require a person to accept all their statements. "Every word of the guru is a mantra." What outrageous, egomaniacal bunk!!! Krishna is nowhere near this kind of fakery. When he says "you who do not disbelieve" he is using the word *anasuyave*, which means to be free of contradiction or contention in the sense of willful contrariness–what in the American south is meant by the word "cussedness." Krishna is not blaming a sincere unacceptance of something, but rather a perversity and negativity of mind that causes a person to intentionally reject truth. It is a symptom of conscious evil, and a lot of people have it. That is why Saint Paul urged: "Take heed, brethren, lest there be in any of you an evil heart of unbelief" (Hebrews 3:12). This is not a matter of simple non-belief, as I have said. There is no wrong in not believing something, even if it proceeds from a limited understanding. It is the refusal to believe that is being spoken of here.

The same thing is found in the life of Jesus. We are told: "He did not many mighty works there because of their unbelief." Even: "He marveled because of their unbelief" (Matthew 13:58). It is evident that to Jesus unbelief was an actual psychic/spiritual force, not just a matter of ideas. The Greek word translated "unbelief" is *apistia*, which means to deliberately refuse to believe something from perversity of will, not sincerity of opinion. Such a crookedness of intention bars anyone from approaching the most secret knowledge.

Knowledge and realization

Krishna then tells us that this great knowledge is both intellectual knowledge (jnana) and the spiritual knowledge (vijnana) that comes from true spiritual experience. It is a knowing that is based on Being. In other words, it is the knowing of an adept yogi.

Liberation

Some people dearly love to know things, even if what they know has no practical use for them. But Krishna is not interested in mere intellectual curiosity which eventually will be seen as triviality of mind and heart. He is setting forth to us "this most secret knowledge combined with realization [understanding], which having known you shall be free from evil." Such knowledge has a very practical and perceptible effect: liberation of the spirit from the evil of compulsive rebirth. A liberated yogi may be born thousands of times after his liberation, but always through his liberated will. Nothing whatsoever constrains or compels him. This, and this alone, is freedom. Krishna continues:

> **Royal knowledge, royal secret, this the supreme purifier, readily understood, dharmic, pleasant to practice, eternal (9:2).**

Raja vidya, raja guhyam–royal knowledge and royal secret. This knowledge is royal because it enables those who possess it to become enthroned in the highest consciousness, giving them rulership over all that heretofore bound and compelled them. It is the supreme authority and power beyond and above which there is no authority or power, for it is a participation in the knowledge and power of God.

Supreme purifier

Such knowledge purifies us by dispelling all the shadows of ignorance, causing our mind to shine forth with–and in–the Light of God. We often see people who have engaged themselves with only the external disciplines and beliefs of religion come to a very bad end–a "fall" indeed. Many who have for decades "followed in the ways of righteousness" sink into a degradation undreamed of by them or those who know them. I myself have seen this sad phenomenon several times. In each case it was because, however sincere they may have been, they busied themselves with the externals of religion and did not gain inner, spiritual experience and knowledge. Thus, their inner disposition had never really changed. But the knowledge Krishna offers us is a transformative force, going far beyond "forgiveness of sins" and "getting right with God." It is a transmutation from the baseness of material, egoic consciousness into the gold of spirit-consciousness. And I do not mean consciousness of spirit as an object, but the Consciousness that *is* Spirit. A religion that does not lead us to this supreme purifier is a cruel mockery that can end only in grief and shame.

Plainly intelligible

This great knowledge has as a prime characteristic its perfect intelligibility. It is indeed subtle and deep and exalted, yet it is clearly comprehensible to those who have evolved to the point needed to put it into practice.

Discontented with the simplistic beliefs of the religion I was born into, when I looked afield I was appalled at the turgid meanderings of the labyrinth called "philosophy" in the West. The writings of renowned "thinkers" convinced me that they might be able to think, but they certainly could not speak or write clearly and to the point. It was obvious to me that they were adored just for their incomprehensibility that was mistaken for profundity. No thank you!

When after years of dissatisfaction I read the Gita I was awed by the clarity of its concepts and its mode of presentation. I was ready for more. Having read in *Autobiography of a Yogi* that Shankaracharya was the greatest of Indian philosophers, I approached his books in the Hollywood Vedanta Bookshop with caution. Surely such a sublime philosopher would be beyond my understanding. Nobody likes to risk being proved a dummy, but I took the chance and opened the first book at hand. Staggering revelation: it was beautifully comprehensible! More: it was gloriously simple, and equally profound. Happy amazement.

Although they should have been looked into before, I next turned to the Upanishads, the supreme heights of Indian thought. There I found profound clarity and profound simplicity that only eluded the ego-darkened mind. So I learned by this that those who really *know* can also communicate the clarity and purity of their knowing. This is because their knowledge comes from experience, not intellectual jugglings. Which is why in the Sanskrit original of this verse Krishna uses the expression *pratyakshavagamam*: that which is clearly seen by the eyes. Of course, in this case it is the inner eyes that are being spoken about.

Righteous

This knowledge is also *dharmyam*—according to the principles of righteousness, of dharma. This is a crucial point, for it is not unknown or even rare to come across scoundrels who claim that their spiritual realization has elevated them beyond or above the law of dharma. But Krishna tells us that the highest knowledge affirms dharma, not violates it.

Easy to practice

Next Krishna tells us that this great knowledge cannot only be put into practical expression, it is actually *susukham kartum*–easy to practice. Now that is the fact. If we find that it is not easy to practice or agreeable to us–for sukha also means pleasant and agreeable, even to the extent of giving us happiness–then something is very wrong. Either our "knowledge" is false or corrupt or *we* are false and corrupt. Or perhaps both. We need to figure out what is wrong and make it right. Those who inoculate themselves with the wisdom of the Gita will be secure from catching the diseases of adharma, of unrighteousness. And they will find that the way of dharma is for them a joyful and easy path.

Imperishable

The supreme truth is *avyayam*; it is imperishable in the sense that once attained it cannot be lost or eroded–it never fades away. Nor is it ever superseded or gotten beyond. It can never be lessened or changed. It is truly immortal. It is absolutely secure and abiding. On the other hand:

> **Those who have no faith in this dharma, without attaining me**
> **are reborn in the realm of death and samsara (9:3).**

Krishna uses an interesting word–*ashraddadhanah*, which means both not having faith and not giving faith. This second meaning refers to those who in their hearts know the truth but refuse to acknowledge and act upon it. This is a way of life for many people. But whichever it is–not having faith or refusing to act upon it (note the implication that faith and action are inseparable)–the result is failure to attain union with God and a return to earthly incarnation, "reborn in the realm of death and samsara."

We must resolve to nevermore tread that sorrowful path again.

UNIVERSAL BEING

Finite minds cannot really comprehend the Infinite. Yet, even a dim idea will be of inestimable value to them in their spiritual seeking. Krishna is now about to explain the fundamentals of Infinite Being in relation to finite creation and the finite beings within it.

All-pervading Being

> All this world is pervaded by me in my unmanifest aspect. All beings dwell within me, but I do not dwell within them (9:4).

It is a mistake to think of creation and Spirit as two layers or levels of reality like oil and water. Rather, Unmanifest Spirit (Avyakta) pervades everything. There is no point of existence where Spirit is not. On the other hand, there is the vast realm of Spirit in which there is nothing–or no thing–at all. Spirit pervades matter, but matter does not pervade Spirit. Nevertheless, there is an intimate connection between the two, for all relative existence exists within the Unmanifest.

The word translated "dwell" is *sthani*, meaning a place of residence. Krishna is saying that all beings abide in the Unmanifest, for It is the basis of their existence. Without the Unmanifest they would not exist. But the Unmanifest Spirit does not depend upon those beings–It would remain unchanged if they ceased to exist.

Krishna's purpose is to give us an order of priority. Spirit is not only first, it is all-encompassing. If we attain Spirit we will attain mastery over relativity. But if we only possess relative matter we will be nothing in the ultimate sense.

> **And yet beings do not dwell within me: behold my Divine Yoga. Sustaining beings and yet not dwelling in them, I myself cause all beings to come into manifestation (9:5).**

Krishna is giving a profound teaching here. Created things, including relative existence itself, never touch Spirit. In the same way, our energy bodies never touch our Self.

If that is so, then how does creation exist? For I have said that it not only exists, it exists within God (Brahman). Creation is also called Maya–Cosmic Illusion. Creation exists within Brahman as a mirage, an illusion. A mirage is real, but what is seen (water, buildings, etc.) is not. Maya is like a motion picture. The epic begins, unfolds, and ends, but really nothing has taken place. We were just watching images that were only light moving on a background. It was all an illusion. We could not see the motion picture if it was not projected onto a neutral background. We see the movie of Maya projected onto the background of Consciousness. Neither the background of the movie screen or that of Consciousness are in anyway really touched or affected by the images. But without the screens there would be no movie or creation.

Moving within the Unmoving

> **As mighty winds move everywhere, yet always dwell in the ether, know that even so do all beings dwell within me (9:6)**

Incredible as the continual changes in creation are, and the untold numbers of life-dramas perpetually unfolding with it, it all takes place within God, the sense of independence and separation being totally illusory. The realization of this frees us from all fear.

Relativity cannot exist without an infinite chain of dualities. Creation takes place in a series of manifestations and dissolutions. Krishna described this in the previous chapter. Referring back to this, he says about all sentient beings:

> At the end of a kalpa, all beings merge into my Prakriti: at the beginning of another kalpa, I myself send them forth (9:7).

At the end of a kalpa–Day of Brahma–all those remaining in relativity merge into the primordial matter, or prakriti, and enter a state of dreamless sleep. Then, when an equally long Night of Brahma has ended, they emerge from that sleep and continue on their evolutionary way.

> Resting on my Prakriti, I send forth again and again this entire multitude of beings, helpless under Prakriti's power (9:8).

This evokes the popular image of Shesh-Narayan (Vishnu) resting upon (sometimes rising from) the ocean of primal energy (prakriti) as the source of all worlds and the beings within them. All beings are "helpless" in this process because they have no will or choice in the matter, only the impetus of their karma from previous lives.

The divine actor

The Divine is at the root of all action, and without the Divine no action can take place. Yet Krishna says:

> And these acts do not bind me, sitting as one apart, indifferent and unattached in these actions (9:9).

The same is true of our immortal Self. Spirit is never touched, but is the silent, actionless witness of all that goes on.

How, then, do we have karma? We do not. But within the dream of Maya we experience it as such. Consider how in a dream you do so many things and undergo the consequences, yet it is only images, unreal. I have heard of people actually experiencing pain or nausea after awakening from dreams in which pain or nausea occurred. God has given us these dreams to teach us the truth about our greater span of life on earth. As Prabhava-nanda's very interpretive translation says: "Do not say: 'God gave us this delusion.' You dream you are the doer, you dream that action is done, you dream that action bears fruit. It is your ignorance, it is the world's delusion that gives you these dreams" (5:14).

Let us awake!

Maya–Its Dupes and Its Knowers

Maya does it all

> With me as overseer Prakriti produces both the animate and the inanimate; because of this the world revolves (9:10) .

Sankhya philosophy says that prakriti is inert by nature, but by the mere proximity of purusha–on both the cosmic and individual levels–prakriti moves and produces all that exist. So even though the spirit is the observer, and even in some ineffable way the controller, still the only "creator" is prakriti. Except for the spirits, prakriti is the sole source of all without exception. Both the living and the dead are made from the same substance. In fact, the differentiation is only one of movement or non-movement. The entire drama is the play of prakriti. When we realize this division we can begin to get a perspective on ourselves within this world and the process we are experiencing as life.

The blind, helpless, and hopeless

> The deluded despise me dwelling in human form, not knowing of my higher being as the Great Lord of all beings (9:11).

The foolish daily encounter divinity in themselves and in all that is around them. But, being blind, they stumble on by unaware, knowing nothing at all about themselves or others—and usually not caring, either, despising both themselves and others, and often denying the very existence of their true Self.

Cut off—at least in perception—from their own essential being, what can be their fate?

> Those of vain hopes, vain deeds, vain knowledge, without intelligence, abide in the delusive nature of rakshasas and asuras (9:12).

They are not just deluded—they are the source, the producer, of their delusion. Their hopes, actions, and seeming knowledge are vain because they are based on delusions. They live instinctually and sensually, unthinking. Their nature manifests the qualities of rakshasas and asuras. Rakshasas are cannibal demons, and we continually encounter people who devour life rather than live it. Asuras are willful dwellers in darkness. As Jesus said: "Men loved darkness rather than light, because their deeds were evil. For every one that doeth evil hateth the light, neither cometh to the light, lest his deeds should be reproved" (John 3:19, 20). But not all are like this. So Krishna says:

> But those great souls that abide in their divine nature, worship me single-mindedly, knowing me as the eternal Origin of beings... (9:13).

It is necessary to be good, but the good must then progress on to become godlike, to be a deva, a "shining one" filled with the Divine Light. Fixing their mind on God they make themselves living offerings. That is why the Manu Smriti (Laws of Manu) says that the greatest sacrifice is the offering of ourselves (purushamedha). And Patanjali says that samadhi is attained by offering our lives to God (Ishwarapranidhana). Such persons live in the awareness of God:

> Always glorifying me and striving with firm vows, bowing to
> me with devotion, always steadfast, they worship me (9:14).

This is a description of true devotion (bhakti), free from emotionalism and childish dependency.

Three views of God

But there is the approach of wisdom (jnana), which Krishna outlines thusly:

> And others, sacrificing by the sacrifice of knowledge, worship
> me as One and Manifold, variously manifested, omniscient
> (9:15).

This is very important because it has become the vogue to insist that only one way of viewing God is either right or the best. Krishna, however, states here that there are two legitimate ways the jnanis worship God: as absolute Unity and divine Diversity. Even those who prefer to look upon God as One will yet consider that the One has manifested in countless modes, omniscient and omnipresent in all. Both views are means to reach God. We must keep this in mind and not fall into the laziness of simplistic thinking in these matters.

God is all

> I am the ritual, I am the sacrifice, I am the offering, I am the
> herb, I am the mantra, I am the ghee, I am the fire, and the
> pouring out into the fire (9:16).

Over and over in the Gita it is pointed out that ritual is greatly inferior to yoga and wisdom. Yet, Krishna states that God is embodied in all those things, that they are the presence of God. They may be gone beyond, but they are not to be despised.

> I am the Father and Mother of this world, Establisher, Grand-
> father, the object of knowledge, the Purifier, the Omkara
> (Om), the Rig, Sama, and Yajur Vedas (9:17).

In relation to creation God has three aspects: one transcendent and two immanent. This is the basis for the doctrine of the Trinity as taught by Jesus, however far contemporary Christianity has drifted from the original understanding. God is immanent in creation as both the guiding intelligence and the creative energy–the divine Father and Mother. Transcending these two aspects is the Unmanifest Absolute which can symbolically be called the Great Father, *Pitamaha*. "Grandfather" is not really a very satisfactory equivalent since the connotations are just too human and folksy.

> I am the Goal, the Sustainer, the Lord, the Witness, the Abode,
> the Refuge, the Friend, the Origin, the Dissolution, the Foun-
> dation, the Treasure house and the Eternal Seed (9:18).

The Gita is absolutely perfect in expressing God through words.

> As the sun I radiate heat; I withhold and send forth rain; I am
> immortality and death; being and non-being am I (9:19).

Round trip ticket!

The eighteenth verse indicates that God is the ultimate Goal. Wanting to help us to attain that Goal, Krishna now speaks of the way that falls short of the Goal.

> The knowers of the three Vedas, the Soma drinkers, purified
> of sins, worshipping by sacrifices, seek the goal of heaven;
> they, the meritorious, attaining the world of Indra, enjoy di-
> vine, heavenly pleasures of the gods. Having enjoyed the vast
> heaven-world, with merit exhausted, they re-enter the world
> of mortals. Thus, carrying out the injunctions of the three Ve-

das, desiring objects of desire, going and coming from birth to birth, they obtain them (9:20-21).

Heaven is a trap, and the desire for heaven is the bait. For heaven keeps us from the only Goal: God. Those who go to heaven are the righteous, so Krishna says, but there is more for us than goodness, namely *Godness*. Since the Being of God transcends all relativity, so must we, and heaven is very much a matter of relative existence. As Krishna points out, heaven is desired only by those who hunger for sensory enjoyments, impelled by desire—and thereby hurled again and again into earthly rebirth. At the root of all is ego.

Eternal security

Those men who single-mindedly direct their thoughts to me, worship me. For them who are constantly steadfast I bestow what they lack and preserve that which they possess (9:22).

This last clause is not about earthly or heavenly possessions, but about spiritual attainments.

Those yogis who steadfastly fix their minds on God without wavering or slacking off, will find all their lacks being filled up and their present attainments preserved. They will remain with God forever, even if they should take up a human body for some higher purpose.

WORSHIPPING THE ONE

K rishna now states quite simply:

Even those who with devotion worship other gods also worship me, though with a mistaken approach (9:23).

The meaning is clear: there are no "other gods"–there is only the One who is being worshipped through all revealed names and forms.

"Even those who worship other gods with faith, also worship me, though they do so in ignorance" (Sargeant's translation). The word Sargeant translates as "in ignorance" is *avidhipurvakam*. It literally means "not according to the rules" or even "without/outside the rules." The idea is that these people do not know or understand how to worship God because they do not know or understand the nature of God. Other possible terms–ignorantly, incorrectly, mistakenly, improperly, inappropriately, inappositely, inaptly, ineptly, haphazardly, irregularly–either express a value judgment or add an extra meaning or attitude the Sanskrit does not include. This is good to keep in mind.

In very truth there is a Science of Religion, and that has been perfected in India. When those of other religions intuitively follow that science, things work exactly right and spiritual awakening and growth occur. However, since that science is just stumbled upon by the questing souls, and is not an integral part of those religions, the science is quickly, even instantly, lost. But since it is the bedrock foundation of Sanatana Dharma it endures through the ages, though often neglected by individuals. But once the eternal rules are followed, all is well.

The fine print

The paramount idea is that all are worshipping God–there is no one else to worship:

> Truly I am the Enjoyer and Lord of all sacrifices; but because they do not know me in truth they fall back into rebirth in this world (9:24).

This is not a matter of holding a mistaken intellectual conception of God, but of not directly perceiving God as he truly is. It is necessary for us to see God in his pure Being, for only then will we truly see our own Self and thereby be enabled to unite with God and attain total liberation in Spirit.

God sees all things "in truth" at all times. We do not, but it is necessary for us to do so, as explained in the previous sentence. Seeing God in truth is not an experience but a state of being, a state of identity with God. I am making such a point of this so we will not slip back into the dogmatizing and theologizing outlook of externalized religion.

The import of this verse is thoroughly mystical and thoroughly practical. Krishna is telling us that those who do not *know* God cannot *go* to God. No amount of reading sacred texts will help us, nor will all kinds of devotional and emotional effusions or multitudes of good deeds. We must ascend in consciousness to the heights of divine experience and be united forever with God. All the religiosity in the world is irrelevant here. Yoga–perfect union–alone is the means and the goal. Without yoga nothing is possible. It is not a matter of what religion or philosophy we hold, but a matter of evolution of consciousness. As the Gita says, we must become yoga-yukta–united to God through yoga. We must never lose sight of this fact.

Many paths–many goals

There are many paths and just as many goals. That is why Krishna says:

> Those who are devoted to the gods go to the gods. Those who are devoted to the ancestors [pitris] go to the ancestors. Those

who are devoted to the spirits [bhutas] go to the spirits. Those who are devoted to me surely come to me (9:25).

Three terms are used in this verse: devas, pitris, and bhutas. Devas are the demigods presiding over various powers of material and psychic nature. Pitris are ancestors or other departed human beings. Bhutas are non-human spirits of various sorts, some of them low-level nature spirits such as "elementals." Others are earthbound human spirits, and quite a few are beings of completely other streams of evolution–of other creations, even–that have somehow wandered into our universe and gotten trapped here. All of these may be either positive, negative, or neutral.

Those who occupy themselves with these beings will go to their astral regions after death and eventually return to earthly life. But those who orient their minds toward the Infinite will go to the Infinite. Even if they do not attain full union with God while here on earth, they will escape rebirth, graduate from the earth plane, and go to a higher world from which they will reach God after completing their evolutionary development. Alternately, they will come back to earth in a family of yogis and be impelled toward seeking union with God. "There he regains the knowledge he acquired in his former incarnation, and strives from thence once more toward perfection" (6:43).

We should step back to the fourth chapter of the Gita. There Krishna says: "In whatever way men resort to me do I thus reward them. It is my path which men follow everywhere" (4:11). Is this a contradiction to what he has now said regarding the worship of relative beings instead of the Absolute? No, because even that worship will eventually lead to something higher–even if only through disillusionment–until the questing soul learns to worship God alone.

GOING TO GOD

Instead of getting to heaven at last, I'm going all along!–Emily Dickinson

Turning the mind toward God

Since it is our nature to return to God it is a simple matter to do so. Fixing the mind on God is the essential thing. Therefore Krishna now outlines the way.

> Whoever offers to me with devotion a leaf, a flower, a fruit, or water, I accept that offering of devotion from him whose heart is pure. (9:26)

Devotion is the key to uniting our heart to God as the first step of The Way Back. It is usual in India to offer flowers, fruit, and water in worship, and Krishna recommends this. But there is much more to devotion than this, so he continues:

> Whatever you do, whatever you eat, whatever you offer in sacrifice, whatever you give, whatever tapasya you practice, do that as an offering to me (9:27).

The idea here is quite clear: *Everything in our life must be offered to God*, must be looked upon as steps in the pathway to God. If there is anything in our life that cannot be rightly offered to God, then it should be eliminated. This is an important guideline. So often people want to know what they should do to gain peace of mind, but rarely do they inquire as to what they should *stop doing* to gain peace of mind.

> **Thus shall you be freed from the bonds of actions producing both good and evil fruits. Steadfast in the yoga of renunciation and totally liberated, you shall come to me (9:28).**

The only karma we should have is God-karma! This will occur if we continually keep our mind immersed in the awareness of God.

God's favor?

Often in religious writings we find the idea that if we pay attention to God, he will pay attention to us; that if we are devoted to God, God will be concerned with us. In other words, we can control how God reacts to us. Not likely! It is true that God must hold a special place in our life, but that will not make us "special friends" of God. There is no You Be Nice To Me And I Will Be Nice To You bargains with God. Otherwise he would be as changeable and undependable as are we. To free us from these illusions Krishna next says:

> **I am the same to all beings. There is no one who is disliked or dear to me. But they who worship me with devotion are in me, and I am also in them (9:29).**

Samo'ham sarvabhuteshu, can equally mean "I am the same *to* all beings" and "I am the same *in* all beings." Both meanings are intended here, I feel sure, for one explains the other. God is the same to all beings because he is the unifying element within all beings. So all beings are equal in essence. Since God sees the potential in all beings, with the knowledge that all without exception shall realize that potential–and also that when the potential is realized all will be in exactly the same spiritual status–there can be no question of God looking differently on anyone. To start with, he sees himself within all. For him the beginning, middle and end of our evolutionary journey are simultaneous. There is no possibility of him reacting differently to different beings, nor even of acting differently to a particular being according to the stage of his journey at any moment.

"But they who worship me with devotion are in me, and I am also in them." Nevertheless there are differences between beings, but only from their side. Those who worship God in their hearts through an attitude of reverence and devotion are enabled to feel God within them and themselves within God. No one can ever be outside of God in actuality, but many are those who through delusion's darkness cannot perceive their existence within God and God's existence within them. In their consciousness there is no God, even though they are ever intimately known to God. Just as a person will starve with food right at hand if he does not know it is there, so these unhappy people live in a mental world devoid of God.

God is also manifested in the lives of the saints, who are living proofs of his reality, just as Hindu, Buddhist, and Christian saints prove the existence of Krishna, Buddha, and Jesus.

Sinner no more

> **If even an evildoer worships me single-heartedly, he should be considered righteous, for truly he has rightly resolved (9:30).**

There is an interesting and important implication here. Krishna is telling us that if an evil *doer* (for no one is evil by *nature*) resolves to fix his mind perpetually and undividedly on God, that person should be considered righteous. This is because we all are righteous in our inmost being, and those who resolve to conform their outer life to their inner nature are at that very moment righteous. Oh, yes, they will still have negative karmas and their minds and hearts will need to be cleared out and purified. But if they make that genuine resolve–not a whim of the moment or a reaction of fear of future misfortune–they will rise above the karmas and conditionings and manifest their atmic nature. We should respect and honor them, confident, as is Krishna, that they shall succeed.

They are like minors that one day shall enter into their inheritance—in a sense they are already wealthy.

> **Quickly he becomes a virtuous soul and goes to everlasting peace. Understand: no devotee of me is ever lost. Truly, those who take refuge in me even though they be from wicked origins, women, Vaishyas or Shudras, they also attain the Supreme Goal (9:31-32).**

Part of our problem is figuring out the intended meaning of *papa-yonayah*. Yoni is womb—that is easy. But papa means sin, degradation and—to make up a word—demeritorious. In other words, people either with unfortunate karma or without any particularly good karma are papayonayah.

Basically Krishna is saying that even those who have bad or unfortunate karma can attain Brahman as easily as those with good spiritual karma and a marked degree of spiritual development from previous lives. No one is left out of Krishna's call to higher consciousness. At the time of Krishna, and even today in India, some ignorant people, denying the truth of the Self, claim that only Brahmin males can attain liberation—and they have to be from "good" backgrounds. Krishna denies this.

It does not require much imagination to further realize that even now it is not such a good thing in Indian society to be of a low caste or a woman—and it was much, much worse before the twentieth century. Just consider how right now in south India when it is determined through ultrasound scanning that a child in the womb is female its death is cold-bloodedly planned either through abortion, poison, or even outright murder after her birth. Throughout the world women have lived in socially accepted slavery for thousands of years. The exceptions do not make the situation different.

Krishna—and Vyasa, the transmitter of his words—is telling us that since the Self is the same in all beings there are none that cannot attain the heights of God-realization. All that is needed is right resolve and dedication to spiritual life.

And now the pitch...

All the foregoing was the windup and now Krishna gives us the pitch.

> How much more easily, then, the holy Brahmins and devoted royal (kshatriya) sages. Having come to this impermanent and unhappy world, devote yourself to me. With mind fixed on me, devoted, worshipping, bow down to me. Thus steadfast, with me as your supreme aim, you shall come to me (9:33-34).

WISDOM AND KNOWING

The Holy Lord said: Once more hear from me the supreme word which I speak to you, who are beloved, with the desire for your welfare (10:1).

These opening verses of the tenth chapter hold very important truths, truths that must be assimilated before the Divine Glory can be perceived. To undo the conditioning of millions of births in subhuman forms and many human births is no simple thing. Just to get the idea requires that we hear the basic truths of rebirth, karma, and spiritual evolution over and over and over again. We already know these things, but the knowledge is buried so deeply beneath mountains of debris accumulated in past lives that it might just as well not even be there at all. So we have to start by being told it again and again. We continually need refresher courses in fundamental truths. (Which is why we must continually read the Gita.) Of course this becomes much easier the moment we become yogis and start digging ourselves out of the prison.

People rarely scrutinize their–or others'–motives in religion, and nobody thinks about what God's motives may be in communicating with humanity. But Krishna thinks this should be considered, so he tells us that God speaks to us not to express displeasure or pleasure, or to threaten or cajole us or to control us. God's sole motive is our welfare. He is ever the benevolent friend who counsels us, but never shouts or tries to influence us. A prime factor in our welfare is our free will, and he never transgresses there.

The originless Origin

> Neither the multitude of gods nor the great seers (rishis) know my origin. In truth I am the universal source of the gods and the great seers (10:2).

None of the highly-evolved beings who dwell in the higher astral and causal worlds, or the enlightened sages of earth, know the origin or beginning of God because he never had one. It is not just that such knowledge would be beyond the ken of the saints and angels, but rather that there is nothing to know. God is eternal. He is not just everlasting, he is without beginning. But we can know (not just believe) that God is *our* source or origin. Not in the sense that at some point of time we came into existence or were created by God, but in the sense that we have eternally existed within God, drawing our essential being from him. There never was a time when we did not exist, any more than there was a time when God did not exist. But God does not draw his being or existence from anyone, whereas we totally derive our being and existence from him. That is why in the second chapter of the Gita Krishna says to Arjuna: "Truly there never was a time when I was not, nor you, nor these lords of men—nor in the future will there be a time when we shall cease to be" (2:12). Whether the great beings in all the worlds look before or behind, they see only God—and themselves within God. This is the vision of immortality.

> He who knows me as birthless and beginningless, the mighty Lord of the world—he among mortals is undeluded and freed from all evils (10:3).

If we can attain the direct knowing of God's immortality and omnipotence, our sins and delusions will evaporate in that vision. For we will see God subjectively as one with our own Self. To see God is to become god.

The source of virtues

In the West we continually find the delusion that goodness can some-how be produced by thoughts and deeds, that virtue can be developed in us like seeds sown in a garden or steel can be tempered in a flame. But this is a great delusion. It is a matter of mystical experience, of union with God. For Krishna next says:

> Intelligence, knowledge, non-delusion, forbearance, truthful-ness, self-restraint, equanimity, happiness, suffering, birth, death, fear, and fearlessness, non-injury, impartiality, con-tentment, tapasya, almsgiving, both good repute and ill re-pute: these manifold conditions of beings arise from me alone (10:4-5).

This list is quite clear, but there are some nuances I think might be helpful to point out.

Intelligence=buddhi. Buddhi covers a great deal more than simple "intel-lect." It is understanding, reason, and intelligence. It is the thinking mind. The word buddhi itself is derived from the root verb *budh*, which means both to know something and be able to communicate what is known. In its highest sense, the buddhi is the faculty of enlightenment, which is why we have the word Buddha for an enlightened individual.

Knowledge=jnana. Jnana means knowledge in the sense of wisdom, of truly understanding something. It can also mean good sense, but in spir-itual texts it almost always means knowledge of Brahman, the Absolute.

Non-delusion=asammoha. Moha is delusive attachment or infatuation based on a completely false perception and evaluation of the object. Occa-sionally it has an almost magical connotation, as of a person being under a spell. The idea is that the person suffering from moha is bereft of reason and utterly overwhelmed by a passionate response to the object. Usually it is thought of as being directed to a person, but it can also be delusive obsession with a material object and even an aspiration or ambition for something or someone. Asammoha is complete absence of such obsession. So asammoha means levelheadedness and clearsightedness.

Forbearance=kshama. Forgiveness, patience, and forbearance–kshama is all of these.

Truthfulness=satyam. Satyam means truth, reality, truthfulness, and honesty.

Self-restraint=dama. Dama is self-control, self-restraint, and control of the senses.

Calmness [equanimity]=shama. Shama means calmness, tranquility, and control of the internal sense organs, including the mind. It can also mean being the same in all situations or in relation to others, being equal-minded at all times.

Happiness=sukham. Sukham is happiness and joy, also the state of being happy and joyful. It is the quality of being pleasant and agreeable, as also the mental condition of being pleasant or agreeable.

Suffering=dukham. Dukham is pain, suffering, misery, sorrow, grief, unhappiness, stress, or distress. Also that which is unsatisfactory or produces dukha.

Birth=bhava. Bhava is "becoming," from the verb "bhu" or "bhavh" which means to become or to exist. So it also means birth.

Death=abhava. Abhava means either to never exist or to go out of existence, so death is an implied meaning.

Fear=bhayam. Bhayam means fear or even terror.

Fearlessness=abhayam. Abhayam is "without fear," fearlessness, or a state of steadfastness in which one is not swayed by fear of any kind.

Non-injury=ahimsa. "Himsa" is injury, violence, or killing. Ahimsa, then, is non-injury in thought, word, and deed, non-violence, non-killing, and harmlessness.

Impartiality=samata. Samata is impartiality, equality; equanimity; and equalness. It is equanimity of outlook in the sense of making no distinction between friend and foe, pleasure and pain, etc.

Contentment=tushtis. Tushtis means contentment or satisfaction, especially satisfaction, contentment, or happiness with the status quo.

Tapasya=tapas. Tapas (tapasya) is austerity–practical (i.e., result-producing) spiritual discipline, or spiritual force. Literally it means the generation of heat or energy, but is always used in a symbolic manner, referring to spiritual practice and its effect, especially the roasting of karmic seeds, the burning up of karma.

Benevolence [almsgiving]=danam. Danam means giving, gift, charity, almsgiving, self-sacrifice, donation, or generosity.

Good repute=yashas. Yashas is fame, celebrity, and good repute.

Ill repute=ayashas. Ayashas is lack of fame, celebrity, or good repute, or actual disrepute or bad reputation.

All these things, and indeed all "the manifold conditions of beings [*bhavanti bhava bhutanam*]" are arising solely from the Supreme Being in response to their actions. The conditions are not imposed on those beings, but come as a result of their karmas created by their free will in the form of thoughts, words, and deeds.

The progenitors of humanity

In the past the ancient Seven Great Rishis and Four Manus, from whom have sprung these earthly beings, originated from me, born of my mind (10:6).

Krishna is telling us about the progenitors of the universe and the human race. First we have the Seven Rishis (Sapta Rishis), those seven great beings who exist at the top of creation and supervise it in all its aspects. For the production of humanity there were four great ones known as Manus, who produced and then guided humanity in its development both esoterically and through actual verbal instruction.

The Seven and the Four were "mind-born" sons of God. That is, when they awoke at the proper time in this creation cycle, they found themselves embodied in forms mentally created by Brahma. This is also true of the early humans. By the power of their creative thought these creators brought them into physical manifestation by merely willing them into embodiment.

Some believe that the Manus existed at the same time, and others consider that there was a succession of four extending over a huge span of time. Since there seems to be evidence that human beings appeared in different parts of the world at about the same time, the idea of them being contemporary with one another may be the right one, and may even explain racial differences. However that may be, all human beings are children of God, being children of the original sons of God.

I have concentrated on humanity, but Krishna makes it clear that all the forms of sentient beings ultimately come from these eleven co-creators. So there is one great family—not just of humans, but of all sentient beings.

The needful

He who knows in truth this my manifested glory and power, is united with me by unwavering yoga–of this there is no doubt (10:7).

The only way to know the power and glory of God is to directly perceive it through yoga and to even experience it within ourselves. Yoga enables us to see God, and the seeing establishes us in yoga–a perfect symbiosis. Krishna says this is beyond the possibility of any doubt.

The Brazilian healer, John of God, was asked how to meditate. He gave the cryptic answer: "Go back to before there was any creation." It is unlikely that anyone who heard or have read these words understands them, but the Gita makes them clear:

> **I am the origin of all; from me everything proceeds–thinking thus, the wise, endowed with meditation, worship me (10:8).**

In other words, John of God was telling them to erase all relative existence from their consciousness and "go back" to God alone. God himself is the bindu–the point–from which all beings began and extended into manifestation.

Here we see that when a yogi sees the truth of Brahman he does not become an impersonal, abstractionist intellectual, but rather becomes a worshipper of God.

> **With minds and lives intent on me, enlightening one another, and speaking of me constantly, they are content and rejoice in me. To them, the constantly steadfast, worshipping me with affection, I bestow the buddhi yoga by which they come to me (10:9-10).**

This is an accurate description of a real jnani, a true knower of Brahman. Also notice that verse nine implies that when we completely orient our lives toward God we will attract to ourselves other devotees with whom we will speak of divine things, each encouraging and assisting one another in the path to God-realization.

The lamp

> Out of compassion for them, I, abiding in their own Selves, destroy the darkness born of ignorance by the shining lamp of knowledge (10:11).

The Absolute in all its glory dwells as much in the heart of the ignorant as in the heart of the wise—it needs only to be perceived. In his mercy God shines, himself lighting the mind and heart, dispelling the darkness of ignorance.

GOING TO THE SOURCE

Krishna has already given a great deal of information regarding the nature of Brahman. Now we are going to be shown how much an embodied human being can comprehend of God, and how he should respond to that knowledge.

> Arjuna said: You are the Supreme Brahman, the Supreme Abode, the Supreme Purifier, the Divine Eternal Spirit, the First God, the Birthless and All-pervading. Thus do all the sages declare you: the Divine Sage Narada, Asita, Devala, and Vyasa. And you yourself say it to me (10:12-13).

Nearly all religion tries to reduce God to an all-powerful human being, rather than elevate human beings to the status of divinity. (I include much of Hinduism in this, as well.) Whatever we may be thinking intellectually, we tend to respond to the thought of God according to how much we have been conditioned by ignorant religion. But beyond all whittled-down and adjusted religion there is the Eternal Dharma which proclaims the truth about God, human beings, and their common essence. This dharma is most perfectly presented to us in the Gita. It is what Vyasa tells us we can know about God.

Supreme Brahman. Often the Upanishads speak of there being a higher and a lower Brahman, referring to the unmanifest and manifest aspects of Brahman. The word *param*–supreme, or higher–is used here to declare that we can know right here and now the Absolute Reality in its pure Essence, not in any lesser sense.

Supreme Abode. Brahman is That in which all things exist–have their being–so it is the ultimate abode of the Self. Right now we experience living far below this, though in reality we are always dwelling in Brahman. The Gita is telling us that even the embodied person can have the experience of dwelling in Absolute Consciousness.

Supreme Purifier. "Every man that hath this hope in him purifieth himself, even as he is pure" (I John 3:3). By baptizing–immersing–ourselves in God through yoga sadhana we become supremely purified. For *pavitram paramam* also can mean Supremely Pure.

Divine Eternal Spirit. Obviously Brahman is eternal, divine, and spirit, but these words have been put here as an indication that in the vision of God we will see that we, too, are eternal, and therefore always divine in nature. And that nature is pure spirit.

The First God. Not existing in time or space, there can be nothing prior to Brahman, or to us. *Adidevam*–literally the prime or first god–implies that there is a chain, a hierarchy of spiritual powers, of greatly evolved beings, devoted to the maintenance and evolution of the cosmos and those within it. These holy ones can rightly be called gods, but only Brahman is the primal God, the God of gods.

(Those who look upon the monotheism of the Bible in a simplistic and inflexible manner should consider these inspired statements of the prophet David: "God standeth in the congregation of the mighty; he judgeth among the gods" (Psalms 82:1). "For the Lord is a great God, and a great King above all gods" (Psalms 95:3). "O give thanks unto the God of gods: for his mercy endureth for ever" (Psalms 136:2).

Birthless and All-pervading. God never came into being, but has existed forever. Nor is God to be found in one place and not another, for he pervades all in eternal omnipresence.

All the sages. All the rishis, the seers, have known God–not just known about God–and they have said all the foregoing to be true. Arjuna says this because the worthy seeker-aspirant takes into serious account the words of those who have gone before him in the search for God. He will not be a slave of dogmatism or a blind believer, but he will provisionally accept the likelihood of the statements of Brahman-knowers until he comes to know for himself their truth and value.

You yourself. Not only have the sages told us the truth of Brahman, Brahman itself from deep within our consciousness has caused the intuition of these spiritual facts to arise into our minds and hearts. In this way, as Patanjali assures us, Brahman "is guru even of the ancients" (Yoga Sutras 1:26), and us, as well.

In a final declaration of faith Arjuna says:

> All this which you say to me I believe is true. Truly, Lord God (Bhagavan), neither the gods nor the demons know your manifestation (10:14).

Even highly evolved intelligences, whether positive or negative, can never know the full truth of God. Only those who have risen far higher and beheld God in a profound knowing that surpasses all other knowledge can truly *know.*

> For you alone know yourself by yourself, O you, the Purushottama: bestowing welfare on all beings, Lord of Beings, God of gods, Lord of the universe (10:15).

All these things, also, can be known by the persistent yogi, but the most significant thing is: "You alone know yourself by yourself." It is important because it is the truth about us, as well. Unless we open our inner consciousness we will know nothing–either about ourselves or about God.

Appealing to God

> Please describe completely your divine self-manifestations by which manifestations you pervade the worlds and abide in them. How may I know you, O Yogi, constantly meditating on you? And in what aspects of your Being are you to be

thought of by me, O Bhagavan? Explain to me further in detail your powers and manifestations. I am never satiated with hearing your amrita-like words (10:16-18).

God is not just behind all things, he is dwelling in all things as their ultimate Self. Since we are not beholding God directly in his essential Being, Arjuna asks to know what things in relative existence reveal the many aspects of God's Being.

The revelation

The Holy Lord said: Listen! I shall recount to you my truly divine self-manifestations–only the most prominent because there is no end to my extent (10:19).

Then, in twenty-three verses he give a long list of those things in which the divine power is most clearly manifest. Many of them deal with things that are themselves symbols of divine powers rather than objective realities. (The Glossary defines the many names and terms, so I will not do so here.) Krishna starts right at the top with the words:

I am the Self abiding in the heart of all beings; I am the beginning, the middle, and the end of all beings as well (10:20).

If he had stopped there he would have covered everything in those few words, words that by now I hope need no commentary or expansion. For much of what follows you may need to consult the Glossary.

Of the Adityas I am Vishnu; of luminaries the radiant Sun; of the Maruts I am Marichi; among the stars I am the Moon (10:21).

The sun is the source of the energies that make evolution–physical, mental, and spiritual–possible. When liberated beings leave their bodies they rise into and through the sun, passing into realms of existence beyond any need for further birth in the material plane. The Chandogya Upanishad says: "Even as a great extending highway runs between two villages, this one and that yonder, even so the rays of the sun go to both these worlds, this one and that yonder. They start from the yonder sun and enter into the nadis. They start from the nadis and enter into the yonder sun." (Chandogya Upanishad 8.6.2).

> Of the Vedas I am the Sama Veda; of the gods I am Indra; of the senses I am the mind; in all beings, I am consciousness (10:22).

The path to God, then, lies in the mind and in the awareness (consciousness) that lies behind the mind. Through meditation we experience that consciousness more and more until it encompasses Divinity itself.

> Of the Rudras, I am Shankara (Shiva); of the yakshas and rakshasas, I am Kubera; of the Vasus, I am Pavaka (Agni); and of mountains I am Meru. Of priests, know me to be the chief, Brihaspati; of commanders of armies I am Skanda; of bodies of water I am the ocean. Of the great Rishis I am Bhrigu; of words, I am Om [Ekakshara–the one-syllable]; of sacrifices, I am japa; of immovables, I am the Himalayas (10:23-25).

In this verse, "yakshas and rakshasas" refers to the benevolent, semi-divine beings.

> Of trees I am the ashwattha; of divine seers [deva-rishis], I am Narada; of the gandharvas I am Chitraratha; among the siddhas I am the sage Kapila (10:26).

Kapila was the formulator of the Sankhya philosophy on which the Yoga philosophy is based. The Gita itself is an exposition of Sankhya philosophy. Sankhya is mentioned specifically five times in the Gita, and the second chapter of the Gita is entitled "Sankhya Yoga."

> Of horses, know me to be Uchchaishravas who was produced from the amrita; of princely elephants, I am Airavata; and among men I am the king. Of weapons, I am the Thunderbolt of Indra; of cows I am Kamadhenu; of procreators, I am Kamadeva; of serpents I am Vasuki. Of Nagas, I am Ananta; of water beings, Varuna; of ancestors [pitris], I am Aryaman; of subduers I am Yama. Of Daityas, I am Prahlada; among measurers I am Time; of animals I am the lion; of birds I am Garuda. Of purifiers I am the wind; of warriors I am Rama; of sea creatures I am the dolphin; of rivers, I am the Ganges. Of creations I am the beginning, the middle and the end; of knowledge, the knowledge of the Self; of debaters I am logic (10:27-32).

Krishna says he is the knowledge of the Self, for to know the Supreme Self–Brahman–is to attain permanent union with It.

Of letters I am the letter A; of compounds I am the dual; I am infinite Time; I am the Sustainer, the Omniscient. I am all-devouring death and the origin of those events that are to be. Among feminine qualities I am fame, prosperity, speech, memory, mental vigor, courage and endurance. Of chants I am the Brihatsaman; of meters I am Gayatri; of months I am Margashirsha; of seasons I am Spring. I am the gambling skill of the fraudulent, the splendor of the splendorous; I am victory and effort; I am the sattwa of the sattwic. Of the Vrishnis I am Krishna; of the Pandavas I am Arjuna; of the sages I am Vyasa; of the poets I am Ushanas. I am the power of rulers, I am the strategy of the ambitious, of secrets, I am silence; the knowledge of knowers am I. Also I am that which is the seed of all beings. There is nothing that could exist without existing through me–neither animate nor inanimate. (10:33-39)

The Consciousness of God encompasses all.

The conclusion

There is no end to my divine manifestations. But this has been declared by me to exemplify the extent of my manifestations. Whatever is glorious or prosperous or powerful, in every instance understand that it springs from but a fraction of my radiant Power. But what is this extensive knowledge to you? I ever support this whole world by just one portion of myself (10:40-42).

Jaya Bhagavan!

FROM HEARING TO SEEING

Spiritual teaching, if it is authentic, always has a markedly practical effect. So here at the beginning of the eleventh chapter of the Gita Arjuna tells Krishna:

> **Arjuna said: As a kindness to me you spoke the Supreme Secret that is known as the Supreme Self. By this my confusion is gone (11:1).**

Amazing words! But nonetheless absolutely true.

First, knowledge about the Self and the Supreme Self come to the evolving spirit directly from God in a deeply personal manner, from Friend to friend. We must never lose sight of this. However high we may soar in ideas about the transcendent aspect of God, we must never lose sight of the fact that God is a Person relating to persons. Both God and we are fundamentally persons–purushas–and spiritual life must always be conducted in this perspective.

Second, the knowledge of God is the ultimate knowing. Beyond it there is nothing, for it embraces all things, God being infinite.

Thirdly, those who possess this knowing are freed absolutely from all delusion–it melts away like mist before the rays of the sun and is found no more.

Seeing comes from believing

It is exactly in the right order of things that after the seeker hears the truth and recognizes it by the intuition awakened by meditation, he would want to progress further by actually seeing/experiencing that which he now knows through intuition. For direct experience is the final step in our evolution. Therefore Arjuna now says:

> **The origin and dissolution of beings has been heard by me in detail from you, and your eternal greatness. Thus, as you have described yourself, O Supreme Lord, I wish to behold your Ishwara Form, O Purushottama. If you think it is possible for me to see it, O Lord of Yogis, then show to me your eternal Self [Being] (11:2-4).**

There is one point that is worthy of note in the fourth verse: "If you think it is possible for me to see it…." It has nothing to do with God's attitude toward us or a judgment as to our worthiness. It is simply a matter of capability. As Yogananda said in one of his talks, if you expand your consciousness sufficiently, "then God will automatically get into you." The English may be a bit novel, but the idea is clear. This is what yoga is all about: preparing us for the Divine Vision.

In response Krishna says:

> **Behold my forms a hundredfold—rather, a thousandfold—various, divine, and of many colors and shapes. Behold the Adityas, the Vasus, the Rudras, the two Ashwins, and the Maruts. Behold many wonders never seen before. See now present here in this my body the whole universe—both the animate and the inanimate—and whatever else you desire to see. But you are not able to see me with your own eyes. I give to you the divine eye: behold my Ishwara Power.**
>
> **Sanjaya said: Then, having thus spoken, O King, Krishna, the Great Lord of Yoga, showed unto Arjuna his supreme Ishwara Form: (11:5-9).**

As in the previous chapter, there is a tremendous amount of lists of things seen by Arjuna, many of them relating to Hindu cosmology. As before, I will only comment on those points that have a practical meaning for the yogi.

> With many mouths and eyes, with many wondrous aspects, with many divine ornaments, with many divine weapons up-raised, wearing divine garlands and clothing, with divine perfumes and ointments; embodying all wonders, the Infinite, Omniscient [Facing In All Directions]. If a thousand suns should rise together in the sky, such splendor would be like the brilliance of that Great Being. There, together in the body of the God of gods, Arjuna saw the entire universe present, though of many divisions.
>
> Then Arjuna, filled with astonishment and with his hair standing on end, bowing his head to the Divine Being, with joined palms said: O God, I behold all the gods and all kinds of beings together in your body: Lord Brahma seated upon the lotus, and all the rishis and celestial serpents. I see you in every direction in infinite form, with many arms, stomachs, faces and eyes. Neither end, nor middle, nor beginning of you do I see, O Lord of All, whose form is the universe. I see you crowned, armed with a mace and a discus; a mass of radiance shining everywhere, very hard to look at, all around blazing like burning fire and the sun—beyond measure. You are the Unchanging, the supreme object of knowledge, you are the ultimate resting-place of all; you are the imperishable defender of Eternal Dharma, you are the Primal Purusha, I now realize (11:10-18).

The new idea introduced here is that Brahman is itself the defender/protector/preserver of eternal dharma. This is because dharma is the very nature of Brahman. Sanatana Dharma is not a matter of the will or whim of a deity, but Reality in demonstration. This is how yoga can be the science of the Divine. Praying, praising, serving, believing, and all such—none of this has any ultimate reality. This should be no surprise, for all along we have known that Brahman alone is real.

"Armed with a mace and a discus" indicates the form of Vishnu, and Krishna as the incarnation of that aspect of God known as Vishnu.

You are without beginning, middle, or end, of infinite power, with innumerable arms; the sun and moon your eyes; blazing, consuming fire your mouth; consuming the universe with your brilliance. This space between heaven and earth, and all the directions are filled by you alone. Seeing this, your marvelous and awesome form, the three worlds are trembling, O Exalted One. There, truly, into you enter the throngs of gods, some of which extol you in fear with joined palms, crying "Hail!" The assemblages of great Rishis and Siddhas extol you with abundant praises. The Rudras, Adityas, Vasus, Sadhyas, and Vishwa-Devas, the two Ashwins, Maruts, Ushmapas, throngs of Gandharvas, Yakshas, Asuras, and Siddhas: all behold you, overcome. Having seen your great form with many mouths, eyes, many arms, many thighs and many feet, many stomachs, having many terrible tusks, the worlds are quaking, and so also am I. Truly, having seen you touching the sky, blazing, many-colored, with gaping mouths, with large and fiery eyes: I am trembling in my inmost heart, and find neither courage nor calm. Having seen your dreadful mouths, gaping with tusks, blazing like Pralaya-fires, I have no sense of direction or place of refuge. Have mercy, O Lord of Gods, Abode of the universe. And there all the sons of Dhritarashtra along with the throngs of kings, Bhishma, Drona, and Karna, with our chief warriors, enter precipitately into your mouths, terrible, gaping with tusks and fearful to behold. Some are found sticking in the gaps between your teeth, and some with their heads completely pulverized. As the torrents of many rivers flow towards the ocean, so these heroes of the world of men now enter into your flaming mouths. As moths precipitately rush into a blazing fire to destruction, in like manner so do these worlds also rush into your mouths to their destruction. You lick up and swallow all the worlds on every side with your flaming mouths. Filling the whole world with radiance, your fierce rays are consuming it, O Vishnu. (11:19-30)

I have been amazed through the years that this picture is not cited by the Christian missionaries as proof that the God of the Hindus is "the Devil." I am equally amazed by the fact that I, with only a fundamentalist

Protestant background, read this account and was thrilled by it, realizing that it was the nearest to an accurate description of the Divine in Its aspect as all-devouring Time as possible, a description of the indescribable. It all seemed normal to me, and still does.

Brahmacharini Mildred, one of Yogananda's disciples, told me: "Master said there is an aspect of God that would drive you insane if you saw it." I suspect he was referring to this aspect which Vyasa has so amazingly presented. I am glad to say that Vyasa's version "drove me sane" and made me a Sanatana Dharmi.

Aspiring to know

We have all heard that a little knowledge can be a dangerous thing, but lack of knowledge can be more dangerous, especially in spiritual life. So Arjuna tells Krishna:

> Tell me who you are: you of terrible form. Salutations to you, O Best of Gods, be merciful. I desire to comprehend you, O Primal One. I wish to understand your intent (11:31).

As much as we can, we need to intellectually grasp What/Who God is, and what is his "intention" or purpose for us. Otherwise we can never know what/who we are, and what we are supposed to be doing here, or anywhere, for that matter. True religion is not satisfied with groveling and slavish obeying: it seeks to turn unknowers into knowers, into worthy seers and siddhas.

> The Holy Lord said: I am mighty world-destroying Time, here made manifest to annihilate the worlds. Even without you, none of the warriors here arrayed within the hostile armies shall live. Therefore do you arise and acquire glory. Having conquered the enemies, enjoy thriving domain. These have already been struck down by me. Be merely an instrument. Drona, Bhishma, Jayadratha, Karna, and other battle heroes, already killed by me, do you kill. Do not hesitate. Fight. You shall conquer the adversaries in battle (32-34).

Worshiping God

Sanjaya said: Having heard this speech of Krishna, Arjuna with joined palms and trembling, bowing down, addressed Krishna in a faltering voice, overwhelmed with fear.

> Arjuna said: Rightly the world is delighted and rejoices in your renown. The demons, terrified, flee in all directions, and the throngs of siddhas bow to you in adoration (11:35-36).

Authentic reverence of God is not just sentimentality or begging. Rather, it strengthens and moves forward the machinery of the universe, purifying, elevating, and stimulating it. And it does the same to those who are the Godwards. But demons in human form revolt and flee when confronted with the Divine or what truly relates to or reveals the Divine. I have witnessed this many times. They also protest when anything of a spiritual nature is brought even peripherally into their environment. They howl in many ways: some quite sophisticated and intellectual, and some in overt hatred and spite. But the wellsprings are the same: inner evil. On the other hand, the Godwards joyfully reverence God, bowing down before him, thankful to be able to do so. This is a special trait of Eastern religion: Hindu, Taoist, Buddhist, and Eastern Christian. What joy they receive!

A new point

Now we move ahead:

> And why should they not bow to you, O Great One, Primal Creator greater than Brahma, Infinite Lord of Gods, Abode of the Universe, you the eternal, the truly existing, the non-existent, and That which is beyond both (11:37).

Here, too, there is one point that is relatively new to our study: "You... the truly existing, the non-existent, and That which is beyond both." It is not hard to figure that God encompasses all that exists, but how can Brahman also be what is not? "What is not" has three aspects: 1) what is not because it exists only in a potential form—as does the entire field of relative existence when it is withdrawn after a creation cycle; 2) that which has never so far existed, but which Brahman in its limitless creative power could bring into existence; and finally 3) everything that "is," simply because nothing relative ever really exists at any time, but is only an idea in the individual and the divine minds. Since "is" and "is not" is a dwandwa, a pair of dualities, it is obvious that for Brahman, being beyond duality, such distinctions cannot exist. That which transcends "is" and "is not" is Brahman itself. In this context, "is" is no more real than "is not."

Known/Knower

> You are the Primal God, the Ancient Purusha; you the su-preme resting-place of all this universe. You are the knower, that which is to be known and the supreme dwelling state of consciousness and being. By you is the whole universe pervaded, O you of infinite forms (11:38).

That which is known is also the knower. Such a concept seems beyond our comprehension until we realize that everything "known" is just an idea in our mind, and that is us. A perception is only a modification of the mind-substance (chitta) itself, and has no objective reality. So the object is really the subject all the time.

> You are Vayu, Yama, Agni, Varuna, Chandra, Prajapati, and the Great-grandfather, Brahma. I bow, yea, I bow to you a thousand times, again and again I bow, I bow to you. Salu-tation to you before and behind; salutation on every side, O All! You are infinite valor and boundless might. You pervade all—therefore you are All (11:39-40).

Those who see and know in the divine realms worship, bowing again and again with both body and mind. Krishna is showing us that jnana leads to bhakti, and bhakti leads to jnana. For they have the same object and purpose.

A reaction

History is filled with examples of people who have been kind or unkind to someone only to discover that the "someone" was a person of great prominence unrecognized by them. Arjuna finds himself in this situation. In India, to touch someone even unintentionally with the foot is considered great carelessness and rudeness. When that happens, the offender touches the feet of the person and begs their pardon. To touch them with the foot deliberately, and kick them (even gently) is a cardinal insult. Yet, very dear and close friends sometimes do such things in jest as sign of intimacy and camaraderie. We are told that often when resting together, if Krishna was lying near, Arjuna would push at him with his foot and tell him to move over. We are also told that if Krishna remarked that it was going to rain, and then it did not, Arjuna would say: "What a prophet you are! How wise! How all-knowing!" and mock him. He would also address him familiarly, leaving aside Krishna's royal and spiritual status. (Everyone knew Krishna was Yogeshwara, the Lord of Yoga).

Having now witnessed the real nature of Krishna as Infinite Being, Arjuna pleads:

> Whatever I have said impetuously as in ordinary friendship: "O Krishna, O Yadava, O Comrade," unconscious of your greatness, through ignorance though with affection, and, as if joking, disrespectfully treated you, in play, lying down, sitting or while eating, alone or with others, O Imperishable One, for that I ask pardon of you, O Boundless One. You are the Father of the world, of the animate and inanimate, you who are to be revered, you are the worshipful Guru. There is no one your equal in the three worlds. Who can excel you, O you of Incomparable Glory? Therefore, bowing down in prostration, I ask forgiveness of you, O Lord, who are worthy of honor. As a father to a son, a friend to a friend, a dear one to a beloved: O God, be merciful (11:41-44).

In *The Night of the Iguana*, one of the characters refers to "man's inhumanity to God." When we really grasp that all along we have been dealing with Absolute Divinity itself–ignoring, lying to, trying to fool, denying, and avoiding it—we are overcome with regret and dismay. How could we have done that? Like Arjuna we may try to find consolation in the idea that God is friend, father, and beloved, but in the long run that will not avail. Real peace will only come to us when we realize that God is our ultimate Self, that we are absolutely one with him—so how can he be either pleased or displeased with us? In fact, all those unworthy things we were doing to God we were really doing to our own selves as well.

But there is more. In the religious lore of the ages we find instances in which a face-to-face encounter with Reality virtually incapacitates the beholder, that it overstrains the still-evolving mind, as it is beyond its ability to take in and yet keep on functioning normally. God knows what he is doing. The eucharist of the Liberal Catholic Church speaks of "the limitations of time and space, wherewith it is Thy will to veil our earthly eyes from the excess of Thy glory," because at its present level of development the human mind cannot cope with its fullness. Arjuna experiences this, too, and therefore says:

> I am delighted at having seen that which has never before been seen, and yet my mind trembles with fear. Show me in mercy, O Lord, your previous form, O Lord of gods, abode of the universe. I want to see you as before: wearing a crown, armed with a mace, holding a discus. Appear in that four-armed form, O you of a thousand arms, who are embodied in all the forms in the universe (11:45-46).

Sometimes we have to settle for the veil rather than what is being veiled—at least for a while longer. In the same way, Arjuna asks to see the soothing form of Vishnu, the Preserver, in order to settle and reassure his mind.

How it comes about

What brings about the cosmic vision?

> The Holy Lord said: By my grace toward you this supreme Form has been shown to you by my own power: this form of

mine made of radiant splendor, universal, unbounded and primal, which has not been seen before by aught but you. Not by Vedic sacrifice or study, not by gifts, not by rites, nor by severe austerities can I be seen in such a form in the world of men, by any other than you. Be not afraid or bewildered, having seen this awesome form of mine. With your fears dispelled and with your heart gladdened, see once again this former form of mine.

Sanjaya said: Having thus spoken to Arjuna, Krishna showed once again his usual form. Thus the Great-souled One, having resumed his gentle, wondrous form, pacified the frightened one.

Arjuna said: Seeing your gentle human form, now I am composed and my mind is restored to normal (11:47-51).

The final assurance

Krishna sums up all the implications of Arjuna's experience in words that apply to us who seek the divine union:

> The Holy Lord said: Difficult to see is this form of mine which you have seen. Even the gods ever long to behold this form. Not by Vedic study, not by tapasya, not by charitable gifts, and not by sacrifice can I be seen as you have seen me. By single-minded devotion alone can I be known and truly seen in this manner and entered into. He who engages in action, holding me as the highest aim, devoted, abandoning attachment, free from enmity to all beings, comes to me (11:52-55).

May we pursue this without delay.

THE WISDOM OF
DEVOTION

Since the tenth and eleventh chapters of the Gita dealt with divine manifestations, and the eleventh described an actual vision of divinity as the cosmos, the next subject is how the yogi should think of–conceive of–God as he attempts to fix his mind upon him.

Saguna or Nirguna?

Through the ages a philosophical tug-of-war has gone on between those who prefer to consider God as possessing limitless, divine qualities, and those who prefer to think of God as being unthinkable, utterly beyond anything that can be conceptualized or spoken. These two aspects are called Saguna (with qualities) and Nirguna (without qualities). The yogi knows that both are true, but many philosophers insist on holding to one and rejecting the other, or declaring one to be higher or more accurate than the other. Consequently Vyasa has this twelfth chapter open with these words:

> Arjuna said: The constantly steadfast who worship you with devotion, and those who worship the eternal Unmanifest–which of them has the better understanding of yoga? (12:1).

Arjuna addresses Krishna as the Saguna Brahman, since he is communicating with Arjuna as a conditioned being.

> The Holy Lord said: Those who are ever steadfast, who worship me, fixing their minds on me, endowed with supreme faith, I consider them to be the best versed in yoga (12:2).

This is extremely clear, at least as far as the traits of those who have a better grasp of yoga is concerned. But why is their grasp better? Because they are able to focus their intention on a concept of the Divine that is not only within the scope of their intellect, it is a concept that inspires their seeking, for it is based on love which, as Swami Sriyukteswar points out in *The Holy Science*, is in its essential nature a magnetic force that unites the seeker with the object of the seeking. The path of devotion (bhakti) is as pragmatic as the path of knowledge (jnana).

The path of the formless

> But those who worship the Imperishable, the Undefinable, the Unmanifested, the All-pervading, Inconceivable, Unchanging, Unmoving, the Constant– (12:3).

None of these qualities are within the range of our experience, not even from eternity. So how can we begin to conceive of them? For example, in the West it is thought that "eternal" means that which is without end, but in reality it means that which has neither beginning nor end–that which is absolutely outside the realm of time, space, or relativity. Can we think the unthinkable? Can we conceive the inconceivable? Of course not–its very nature makes it impossible for us. So how, then, can Nirguna Brahman be approached, much less known? Krishna tells us.

> Controlling all the senses, even-minded everywhere, happy in the welfare of all beings–they attain to me also (12:4).

The final clause is heartening, but consider what is required of those that really seek the formless and qualitiless Absolute.

Controlling all the senses. Samniyamyendriyagramam means both sub-duing and controlling–that is, disciplining–the senses and powers of the body and mind (indriyas). Asceticism is the key trait of those that seek God, either saguna or nirguna. But they do not consider themselves as being in any way self-denying. Just the opposite: they see their way of life as real freedom from the bondages so avidly sought and cherished by the world. They do not grin and bear it; they rejoice with thankful hearts that they have found the key to a wider and freer life.

In *The Scent of Water*, Elizabeth Goodge wrote about a medieval thief who reformed and became a hermit. He helped build a church and did all the woodcarving. At the back of the church in an obscure place he carved his self-portrait showing himself wearing a crown of thorns. But the obser-vant saw that there was a gap between the thorns and the surface of the carving, and when they put their fingers inside, by touch they could tell that beneath the crown of thorns he was really wearing a crown of roses. That was his secret. The world saw him as penitent and self-denying, but in reality he was crowned with joy.

Even-minded everywhere. Sarvatra samabuddhaya means everywhere and at all times to be even-minded, undisturbed by anything–neither repelled nor attracted, but ever centered in the unmoving, witnessing consciousness that is the Self.

Happy in the welfare of all beings. Sarvabhutahite ratah means to be rejoicing in the welfare of all beings–not just human beings, but every living thing. It is very important that Krishna lists this trait, as jnanis are usually thought to be antiseptic, uncaring, and outright incompassionate people who are indifferent to the world and all that goes on in it. Rather, as Krishna has already said in the sixth chapter regarding the jnani: "He who is steadfast in yoga [yoga-yukta] at all times sees the Self present in all beings and all beings present in the Self. He who sees me everywhere, and sees all things in me–I am not lost to him, and he is not lost to me. He, established in unity, worships me dwelling in all things; whatever be his mode of life, that yogi ever abides in me. He who judges pleasure or pain by the same standard everywhere that he applies unto himself, that yogi is deemed the highest" (6:29-32).

What a marvelous, positive picture. I can tell you this is no abstract ideal, but a very accurate picture of a Brahman-knower, for I have seen it myself in the great yogis I met in India, especially Swami Sivananda of Rishikesh. Every saint I met in India was lovingly intent on the welfare of others–and I do not mean they were obsessed with promoting an organization or traveling around gathering admirers (and contributors). In fact, nearly every holy person I encountered usually stayed in one place and devoted their life to the upliftment of those who came seeking refuge from the fire of this haywire, material world. They lived in tranquility as Krishna says, and true hearts were drawn to them as the bee to the fragrant flower. They were always available, for their life, like that of God, was one of loving service to all.

This is indeed a beautiful image, yet Krishna goes on to say:

> **Greater is the effort of those whose minds are set on the Unmanifest, for the Unmanifest as a goal is truly difficult for the embodied ones to reach (12:5).**

Actually, I have already explained the "why" of this.

The way of Form (Saguna Brahman)

Now Krishna expounds the way of those who devote themselves to the attainment of Saguna Brahman.

> **But those who, renouncing all actions in me, intent on me as the highest goal worship me, meditating on me with single-minded Yoga–of those whose consciousness has entered into me, I am soon the deliverer from the ocean of mortal samsara (12:6-7).**

This, too, merits close scrutiny.

Renouncing all actions in me. There are many people wandering around India pretending to be monks and excusing their indolence and worthlessness as "renunciation of action." But Krishna indicates that renunciation must only take place in the state of God-consciousness–that mere absten-tion from action to supposedly free or purify the mind is meaningless and worthless, a delusion based on ignorance and laziness. It is utterly mistaken to think that withdrawal from action will free our minds to seek God. That is getting the order completely turned around. First we must establish ourselves in at least a practical degree of spiritual awareness before we can think of stopping action.

Sri Ramakrishna said: "There is a kind of renunciation called 'monkey renunciation.' A man tormented by the troubles of the world goes to Benares wearing an ocher robe. No news of him for days. Then comes a letter, 'You should not worry. I have got a job.'" In the same way when people do not get a job for a long time or feel intimidated by the thought of steady work, want out of a difficult financial sit-uation, are discontented with their family life or faced with another year of a college education, they begin making noises about taking up monastic life and write to us inquiring as to whether we have "room for a hermit" in our ashram. In other words, they want to come and sit around in one place with no obligations until they get bored and get the revelation that they can serve God better in the world–as if they would have ever left it!

Intent on me as the highest [goal]. This has two aspects: 1) regarding God as the Supreme to such a degree that nothing else occupies our mind or is valued by us, and 2) regarding Saguna Brahman as the Absolute–not a lesser or lower aspect of God. For there is only Brahman; the distinction of saguna and nirguna is from our side alone.

Worship me, meditating on me with single-minded Yoga. Unwavering meditation on God is the worship of God. This really should be kept in mind whenever in the Gita we are told to worship God. When Krishna was speaking to Arjuna there was no such thing as a Hindu temple in the entire world. Followers of Vedic religion only adopted image worship and temple ritual after having been influenced by the Greeks who settled in Kashmir. It is the same with Buddhism. For centuries in India there were no images or temples of Buddha, only dharma halls with a dharma chakra (wheel of dharma) on the front wall.

Whose consciousness has entered into me. The consciousness must not just be directed to God or concentrated on God—it must *enter* into God. The yogi's consciousness must be merged into the Consciousness that is God.

I am soon the deliverer from the ocean of mortal samsara. It will not take dozens of lives. Those who are real yogis will soon arrive at the goal. For them the heaving sea of constant birth and death is no more.

Keep your mind on me alone, causing your intellect to enter into me. Thenceforward, without doubt, you shall dwell in me (12:8).

That is certainly clear. It is a simple matter of cause and effect. Those who keep their minds absorbed in God already begin living in God and shall become perfectly united with God both in this world and in the next.

The alternative

> **If you are unable to fix your mind on me steadily, then seek to attain me by the constant practice of yoga. Even by performing actions for my sake, you shall attain perfection. If you are unable to do even this, then relying upon my yoga power, relinquishing all the fruits of action, act with self-restraint. Knowledge is indeed better than practice; meditation is superior to knowledge; renunciation of the fruit of action is better than meditation; peace immediately follows renunciation (12:9-12).**

This does not mean that yoga is not necessary, but rather that sometimes we have to work backwards. Tyaga, the word translated "renunciation" literally means "abandonment," and in the Gita means the relinquishment of the fruit of action. Anxiety about results can torment even the yogi, so at the very beginning we must put aside any motives but devotion to God. Actually, God must be the only aim of our life, not just our formal yoga practice. As the prophet Isaiah said: "Thou wilt keep him in perfect peace, whose mind is stayed on thee" (Isaiah 26:3).

RIGHT CONDUCT

He who hates no being, is friendly and compassionate, free from "mine," free from "I," the same in pain and pleasure, patient, the yogi who is always content, self-controlled and of firm resolve, whose mind and intellect are fixed on me, who is devoted to me–he is dear to me. He who agitates not the world, and whom the world agitates not, who is freed from joy, envy, fear and distress–he is dear to me. He who is indifferent, pure, capable, objective, free from anxiety, abandoning all undertakings, devoted to me–he is dear to me. He rejoices not, he hates not, he grieves not, he desires not, renouncing the agreeable and disagreeable, full of devotion–he is dear to me. The same to enemy and to friend, the same in honor and disgrace, in heat and cold, pleasure and pain, freed from attachment, the same in blame and praise, silent, content with anything whatever, not identifying with any place or abode, steady-minded, full of devotion–this man is dear to me (12:13-19).

Learning to behave

Somewhere a very long time ago (over half a century) I read in an article by Paramhansa Yogananda that his guru, Sri Yukteswar, said to him at the beginning of their association: "Learn to behave." Yogananda commented that this was the most important teaching he ever received from

Sri Yukteswar. I admit that it puzzled me because I was so conditioned by the "You behave yourself!" rebukes from parents to unruly children. Nevertheless, something seeped into my consciousness, because when two years later I went to India I immediately realized that the major thing I needed to do there was learn to behave. Part of the Aryan Eightfold Path taught by Buddha was Right Conduct.

It is a wonderful thing to discover yoga, a spiritual methodology that works according to precise principles, having nothing to do with the ups and downs, highs and lows, of haphazard religious endeavors. There are no hit-or-miss random payoffs or the whims of a pleased or displeased deity in the life of a yogi. The results are very real and very exact. If the aspirant has learned yoga that will lead to realization of the Self, a determined resolve to gain higher awareness and the will power needed to practice the yoga faithfully and skillfully is all that is needed. Leaving behind the Master/Slave syndrome of ignorant religion (along with that of false yoga and false gurus and their attendant toxic guru/disciple enslavement), the yogi moves onward to the revelation of his divine Self as an integral and eternal part of God.

But there are very definite and necessary qualifications for the aspiring yogi, and Krishna is about to explain them to us. So to I am going to divide the above verses into a "yogi list."

A yogi:

hates no being
is friendly and compassionate
is free from attachment to possessions
is free from egotism
is indifferent to pain and pleasure
is patient
is always contented and balanced in mind
is self-controlled
is one whose conviction is firm
is one whose mind and intellect are fixed on God
is devoted to God

does not agitate [trouble] the world

is not agitated [troubled] by the world

is freed from joy

is freed from envy

is freed from fear

is freed from distress [anxiety]

is free from wants

is pure

is capable

is disinterested

is free from anxiety

has abandoned all undertakings

neither rejoices nor hates

grieves not

desires not

has renounced the pleasant and the unpleasant

is alike toward enemy and friend

is the same in honor and dishonor [disgrace]

alike [indifferent] in cold and heat

alike in pleasure and pain

freed from attachment

indifferent to blame or praise

is silent

is content with anything whatever

is homeless [in his heart, abiding only in God]

is steady-minded

Five times in these verses Krishna comments that such a one "is dear to me." It is easy to see why.

To conclude the subject Krishna says:

> **Those who honor this immortal dharma just described, endued with faith, deeming me the Goal Supreme, devoted—they are exceedingly dear to me (12:20).**

The only comment needed here is for me to point out that the wisdom taught by Krishna is not philosophy or theology but a way of life. We should always keep this in mind.

THE FIELD AND ITS
KNOWER

The question

The opening words of the Gita are *Dharmakshetre Kurukshetre*–The field of Dharma, the field of the Kurus. The entire discourse takes place on the battlefield of Kurukshetra in North India. Naturally the Gita is considered symbolic as well as literal and historical. The first symbol to be considered is "field." The thirteenth chapter of the Gita is all about that. It opens with a question.

> Arjuna said: Prakriti and Purusha, the Field and the Knower of the Field, knowledge, and that which should be known–I wish to know this, O Krishna.

This verse is not found in all texts of the Gita. As pointed out before in this commentary, the Gita is really an exposition of Sankhya philosophy, the original philosophy of the upanishadic sages. The prime concept of Sankhya is that of the divine duality of purusha and prakriti—matter and spirit, energy and consciousness. This concerns every person looking to understand his present situation and his potential attainment. It is not without significance that in his question Arjuna puts Prakriti before Purusha. Being a yogi, he knows that we must deal with the material-energy side of things before we can hope to know about spiritual matters. Also, he implies the threefold mystery: knower, knowing, and known. Separating them into their true boundaries is essential for us.

The overview

Krishna begins with an overview of the question.

> **The Holy Lord said: This body is called the Field, and he who knows this is called the Knower of the Field–so say the knowers of these things (13:1).**

This is very clear. Because we sow seeds of action in it, and reap their fruits, the body is our field, and we, as the experiencer of both sowing and reaping, of karma, are the knower of the field, though we often fail to understand what we perceive.

> **And know me also to be the Knower of the Field in all fields. The knowledge of the Field and the Knower of the Field I consider to be *the* knowledge (13:2).**

Know me also to be the Knower of the Field in all fields. It is great wisdom to know that we are an immortal, unchanging consciousness that is witnessing the drama of the mortal and ever-changing field–both the little field of our own body and life-sphere and the greater field of the cosmos and the cycles of creation/dissolution. And it is greater wisdom to know that God is the Knower of all fields, small and great–that God is experiencing our life right along with us. This a great wonder. And so:

The knowledge of the Field and the Knower of the Field I consider to be the *knowledge.*

It is not enough to know the Knower, we must also know the Known. Self-knowledge is not enough; that which is not the Self must also be known. Awareness of the not-Self (*anatma*) must also be there, as Buddha pointed out. We must learn what is not us and what is, so when we encounter the bewildering vagaries of the field we can be at peace and say: "That is not 'me.'" Identification with the body is one of our greatest errors–it must be seen as the phantom it really is. This is why yoga has so much to say about the field. We must recognize and master it so the knower-Self can fully manifest within and through it.

> **The Field—what it is and of what kind, what its modifications are, whence they come and what are the Knower's powers, that hear from me in brief. This has been sung many times by the rishis in many sacred chants, in passages about Brahman [Brahma Sutras], full of convincing reasoning (13:3-4).**

This great knowledge is completely traditional, and Krishna is reminding Arjuna of this fact. There is no "new yoga for a new age." Rather, there is eternal yoga for the eternal spirit. That is what the Gita is all about.

The field

> **The great elements, the consciousness of "I" [ahankara], intellect and the unmanifest, the ten senses and one, and the five fields of actions of the senses, desire, aversion, pleasure, pain, the whole organism, consciousness, stability—thus is the Field briefly described, and its aspects (13:5-6).**

This is certainly complex, but it is also very clear. Basically everything we know in a objective manner is the field. If we can perceive, recall, and name anything, it is part of the field and should be known as such and never identified with. All Krishna has listed is anatma: not-Self.

Preparation for knowledge

There is no need for Krishna to talk about the knower of the field at this point, for it would be mere theory. Instead we must prepare our minds for such knowledge. So Krishna continues:

> **Absence of pride, freedom from hypocrisy, harmlessness [ahimsa], fortitude, rectitude, approaching a teacher, purity, constancy and self-control,**

detachment from the objects of sense, absence of egotism, keeping in mind the evils of birth, death, old age, disease, and pain, non-attachment, absence of clinging to son, wife, home and suchlike; constant even-mindedness in desired and undesired events, unswerving devotion to me with single-minded yoga, living in secluded places, having distaste for association with many people, establishment in the knowledge of the Supreme Self, keeping in mind the goal of knowledge of the truth—this is said to be true knowledge. The contrary is ignorance (13:7-11).

How simple—and what a lifetime project to fulfill! Whatever goes contrary to this is ignorance and must be ruthlessly ejected from our lives and minds.

The knower of the field

Krishna now will describe the cosmic Knower in all fields, but in reading it we must not forget that everything he says applies also in a finite degree to our individual Self.

I shall explain that which must be known, knowing which one attains immortality: the beginningless, Supreme Brahman, which is said to be neither being nor non-being [existent nor non-existent] (13:12).

"Existent" and "non-existent" are terms proper only to relative existence with its constant change, including the great changes of birth and death. To be eternal is not to exist forever, but to be completely beyond the possibility of either existence or non-existence in relativity. Absoluteness is the goal.

With hands and feet everywhere, eyes, heads and faces everywhere, with ears throughout the universe—THAT stands, enveloping everything (13:13).

"Having ears everywhere" is a translation of *sarvatahshrutimal loke*—"having hearing in all the world." Immediately there comes to mind the meaning of Avalokiteshvara or Kuan Yin: "Hearing the Sounds of the

World." God hears not just the prayers but the words and thoughts of all human beings and the cries of all animals and even plants. This is because God pervades the world and is within all things as their Knower.

> **Having the appearance of all the qualities of the senses, yet free of all the senses, unattached yet maintaining all, free from the gunas, yet experiencing the gunas (13:14).**

Part of divine omniscience is the experiencing of all things. God is separate, yet he fully experiences everything through everyone. Every sentient being is a door of his perception. He experiences the internal and external sensations and impulses of all sentient beings. Great yogis reflect this to some degree. In the thirty-fifth chapter of his autobiography Yogananda narrates the following about Yogiraj Lahiri Mahasaya:

"The master's omnipresence was demonstrated one day before a group of disciples who were listening to his exposition of the *Bhagavad Gita*. As he was explaining the meaning of *Kutastha Chaitanya* or the Christ Consciousness in all vibratory creation, Lahiri Mahasaya suddenly gasped and cried out:

"'I am drowning in the bodies of many souls off the coast of Japan!'

"The next morning the chelas read a newspaper account of the death of many people whose ship had foundered the preceding day near Japan."

Yogananda experienced this himself on a small scale, as he relates in Chapter Thirty of *Autobiography of a Yogi*:

"I sat one morning in my little attic room in Father's Gurpar Road home. For months World War I had been raging in Europe; I reflected sadly on the vast toll of death.

"As I closed my eyes in meditation, my consciousness was suddenly transferred to the body of a captain in command of a battleship. The thunder of guns split the air as shots were exchanged between shore batteries and the ship's cannons. A huge shell hit the powder magazine and tore my ship asunder. I jumped into the water, together with the few sailors who had survived the explosion.

"Heart pounding, I reached the shore safely. But alas! a stray bullet ended its furious flight in my chest. I fell groaning to the ground. My whole body was paralyzed, yet I was aware of possessing it as one is conscious of a leg gone to sleep.

"'At last the mysterious footstep of Death has caught up with me' I thought. With a final sigh, I was about to sink into unconsciousness when lo! I found myself seated in the lotus posture in my Gurpar Road room."

> Outside and inside beings–the animate and the inanimate–incomprehensible because of its subtlety, far away and also near, undivided, yet remaining as if divided in beings, this is to be known as the sustainer of beings, their absorber and generator (13:15-16).

All this is done for the sake of sentient beings–for their evolution in consciousness. Even our bodies are really produced by God for us to inhabit. It is true, however much the philosophically "sophisticated" may sneer: *We are the center of the universe, its purpose for existing.* Of course "we" includes all sentient beings, and everything is potentially sentient. From this we see that God is not just Father and Mother, he is also Companion and Servant. Blessed are those that give this God his due: their entire heart and life.

> Also this is said to be the light of lights, beyond all darkness; knowledge, the to-be-known, the goal of knowledge seated in the heart of all (13:17).

He is the reality of everything internal and external–the "one thing real" that alone is worthy of our involvement.

> Thus Field, knowledge and that which must be known has been briefly stated. Comprehending all this, my devotee approaches my state of being (13:18).

So we see how essential this knowledge is, and nothing, including religion, can be substituted for it.

INTERACTION OF PURUSHA AND PRAKRITI

Before continuing, we should first be reminded that what is said of Brahman and Prakriti is also to be applied to the individual spirit, the purusha, and its individual energy levels or prakriti.

Beginningless source

> **Know that both Prakriti and Purusha are beginningless; and know that the modifications and the gunas arise from Prakriti (13:19).**

This verse is quite pivotal for our correct understanding. First of all, both prakriti and purusha are eternal–without beginning, and therefore without end. This means that prakriti is not a dream or mirage, something that will cease to exist when realization is attained, though our mistaken ideas about prakriti will melt away. Prakriti is like the screen in a theatre. The movie will end, but the screen will remain. Next, all things originate in prakriti, and so do their modifications; for the gunas, the primal building blocks of manifestation, themselves are prakriti. (The next chapter will be about the three gunas.)

Two important ideas come into play here: 1) Nothing ever comes from spirit (purusha) or is done by spirit. 2) As Poe said: "All that we see or seem is but a dream within a dream"–namely, prakriti, the creative energy.

Therefore, although we must never forget our essential nature as spirit, everything in our experience–in the field–is an objectification of mula-prakriti, the root-energy from which all things are formed. For this reason yoga is very much a matter of prakriti, for it is prakriti that needs to be refined and evolved to become a perfect reflection of the purusha. That alone is liberation. So yogis pay great attention to such things as diet and health. Meditation practice itself entails certain necessary elements, which is why Patanjali lists asana, pranayama, pratyahara, and dharana as prerequisites for meditation.

To cultivate a false, abstract "spiritual-mindedness" that denies or ignores prakriti is to be in error. For:

> **Prakriti is declared to be the cause of that which is to be done, the instrument and the doer. The Purusha is declared to be the cause in the experiencing of pleasure and pain (13:20).**

This verse is extremely difficult to translate. The idea is that prakriti is the source of both action and the instrument of action, but purusha is the source of the internal experiences and internal reactions, our experience of pleasure and pain that result from the movements of prakriti. Consciousness is an attribute of the purusha. The more conscious we are–the more we identify with consciousness itself rather than objects of consciousness–the more "real" we are.

The knower in the field

> **The Purusha abiding in Prakriti experiences the gunas of Prakriti; attachment to the gunas is the cause of its birth in good and evil wombs (13:21).**

This is really rather simple. We experience the different modes (gunas) of materiality, and our reaction to them–whether positive or negative–intensely attaches our awareness to prakriti. The character of our attachment/aversion determines the kind of birth we will have. Most translators employ the expression "good and evil wombs," and Prabhavananda has "pure or impure," but the Sanskrit says *sadasadyonijanmasu*–birth in real (sat) and unreal (asat) wombs, or birth in true/real or false wombs. This is a purely psychic/spiritual expression.

Sentient beings within prakriti exist in a vast scale, from totally ignorant and basically unconscious up to subtle and expanded consciousness that approximates and reflects the Consciousness that is Brahman. It is this degree of reflection of the divine consciousness that determines how real or unreal the birth and body will be. The closer to God we are, the more real we are, and the further away we are, the more unreal we are.

This is completely psychological, not spatial. Nevertheless it should make us think carefully about every aspect of our life, including those we associate with. How real are we, and how real is our life? If we wish to approach Reality and unite with it, this is a basic requisite. A sure sign that an aspirant will fail in spiritual life is his neglect of this crucial scrutiny. It is an extension of the adage: If You Fail to Plan, You Plan to Fail.

A bit of reflection. It is so common for spiritual aspirants to say that they are different from their families, that they feel alien to them, etc. But this cannot be true. We are only born in families of people with whom we have a deep affinity. True, that affinity may be more subconscious than conscious, but it is there and is a force to be reckoned with. We have no doubt all known people who denounced their parents or family for traits which they themselves possessed. I knew a scrupulously honest young man who was born into a family of low-level criminals. It would have been wisdom for him to realize that criminality was latent in him and watch his mind carefully to guard against it. Again, we all know people who rebelled and cut the cord and got away only to return after some years and become exactly like their parents. Look at the militant hippies of the sixties. Most of them became more bourgeois than their parents. Jane Fonda became a Cub Scout den mother! "Sadhu, beware" is always wise counsel.

We have really completed the subject of Prakriti, though it will be mentioned again, so now I would like to make a summation of the subject. To do this we must consider the very common concept of Shiva-Shakti. Shiva is Consciousness and Shakti is Energy. They are Unity seeming to be

Duality. Shiva is Shakti, and when there is no more need for manifestation/creation whatsoever, Shakti merges in Shiva—or rather, is revealed as Shiva. As Sri Ramakrishna frequently pointed out, Brahman and Shakti are like fire and its power to burn.

We need to understand the actions and effects of Prakriti-Shakti, especially as it affects us, but always keeping in mind that Shiva alone exists. I am making a point of this because some teachers in India maintain that Prakriti is just a kind of inert lump that exists coeternally with Brahman and becomes shaped into moving manifestations when Brahman "enters" Prakriti as Ishwara. This is an impossibility. Only Purusha, either infinite or finite, really exists. Prakriti/Shakti is only the thought, the dream, of Brahman/Shiva. We have to talk about it because we are presently in the net woven of creative energy by the will of the Weaver: Brahman/Ishwara.

Many facets

> The Supreme Spirit in this body is called the witness and the consenter, the supporter, the experiencer, the Great Lord, and also the Supreme Self (13:22).

Let us take this a bit at a time.

The Supreme Spirit [Parampurusha]. These are all titles of the One who is incarnate in the universe and in all bodies. These major titles reveal its function within matter. We are considering the Absolute here, not any intermediary or secondary aspect or secondary form-manifestation of the Supreme or our own spirit. All is under the direct control of God, and of us, as well. *Ishwara* means the ruler, the controller. Just as God is the Great Ruler, so are we on the individual level. We are in total control of our personal life-sphere. True, that control depends on the supreme control of God, but it is none the less absolute, though finite.

In this body. In its essential nature, Purusha is beyond any designation or discussion, but when it enters into embodiment—the Supreme Purusha as the cosmos or the individual purusha as a relative, incarnate being—then we can speak about it.

The witness. *Upadrashta* means that the purusha perceives everything–nothing is left unknown to it. This applies both macrocosmically and microcosmically. But equally important is its implication that the purusha is always observing, but itself is never the actor nor does it become somehow transmuted into what it witnesses. In no way does it become part of what it sees. This eternal objectivity is a prime trait of the spirit.

The consenter. *Anumanta* is a very interesting word. It means someone who consents, permits, and even approves something. The idea is that both God and the individual spirit have agreed to the process of evolutionary creation. We did not just get dumped here by a deity who gave us no choice. We decided to enter into relative being, and on the strength of that act of will we did so. We have agreed to everything that has happened to us, from when we were manifesting as an atom of hydrogen and all along up the scale to right now. You are only reading these words because you have already decided to in your higher mind. And your reaction to them will be determined accordingly. Now please understand that consent is not approval and enjoyment. We see just by looking back in this life that we have done things that did not merit approval, that we should not have desired. For example, revenge may be sweet for some temperaments, but it is never right or worthy of us. Yet, when we agreed to come onto the playing field we were aware of what might befall us.

We allow everything that happens to us, because it is necessary for our learning. We have always, from a long time ago and far beyond this world, permitted the whole thing. We are not being helplessly carried along, though the ego-mind thinks so. Yes, we even approve of all the past, present, and future, for ultimately it will lead to our perfection in God. The little steps along the way may be miserable and even contemptible, but however mucky or chancy the rungs of the ladder may be, they get us to the top, and once we step off into freedom it will all be seen as well worth the doing

The supporter. Nothing exists without the substratum of Spirit. It supports and bears up all that is. So it is called *bharta.*

The experiencer. This is very interesting. We have already been told that spirit is seeing everything, but now the word *bhokta* tells us that it also *feels*

it as well as sees it objectively. So the spirit is both objective and subjective, both transcendent and immanent, yet without really becoming anything other than what it eternally is. This is a crucial insight. Further, it tells us that ignorance, indifference, or numbness in relation to the world is not spiritual but degraded. We see this in the saints. They are more conscious, more reactive and more involved than anyone else, yet they remain ever what they truly are, and never forget it at any time. They are both "here" and "there," just as is God.

What a storehouse of deepest wisdom is the Bhagavad Gita! You can see how necessary it is to delve into the Sanskrit text. Learning Sanskrit as an additional language is a herculean labor, but with a few good dictionaries and word-for-word translations (especially Sargeant's) you can mine the treasures for yourself.

Transcending rebirth

> He who thus knows the Purusha and Prakriti along with the gunas, whatever be his state of evolution, he shall never be born again (13:23).

This means that anyone who turns toward knowledge of the Self, of Spirit, can come to that knowledge and be free from rebirth in the material plane. This does not mean that a person can live in any vile or foolish manner, then get religious and escape the consequences of his actions. Nevertheless it is true, as Krishna has said, that even the worst person who resolves to purify himself can succeed, but that is a coping with evil, not a jumping over it or a circumventing of the moral law. This is, certainly, a statement of great hope and optimism. No matter what our present degree of evolution may be, whatever our present situation, if we go directly to the heart of things and experience and manifest the Self, then there will be no more need for birth in this lowest of worlds. Consequently this subject of the field and the knower of the field is vital for us.

Ways of gaining this knowledge

In the next two verses Krishna is going to give a broad outline of the ways in which we can come to know the field and its knower.

> Some perceive the Self in the Self by the Self through meditation, others by Sankhya yoga, and still others by karma yoga (13:24).

The first half of this is an explanation of what authentic meditation really is. All that glitters is not gold, and all that is called meditation is not really meditation. Krishna will help us determine what is real meditation.

Meditation is the process by which we "perceive the Self in the Self by the Self." We both start and end with the Self. We do not bother with anything that is not the Self. Meditation is direct, immediate experience of the Self. Just as it takes a while to take in a vista reaching from horizon to horizon, in the same way it can take time to fully see the Self in its infinity, but still we start out perceiving it, even if only in the form of the peace and stillness that is a trait of the Self.

How is the Self the means by which we perceive the Self? When you eat salt you know what salt is. Nothing else will give you an idea of the nature of salt. Nothing is needed to lead up to the experience of salt except salt itself: just taste it. It is the same with meditation that reveals the Self. First we must take hold of the Self as an instrument of perception.

Krishna then tells us that by jnana yoga, study of the Sankhya philosophy along with pondering on its principles, the seeker can also gain glimpses of the truth of the Self. This is because "thoughts are things," and the Sankhya philosophy is the thought of the sage Kapila, about whom Krishna has already said: "Among the siddhas, I am the sage Kapila." When we study the teachings of Kapila we will absorb some of the power of his enlightenment that lies behind his words. It is a matter of vibration. And the same is true of the Gita, which is why we should read it every day till the end of our lives.

Also Krishna says that the Self can be intuited by those that engage rightly and wholeheartedly in karma yoga–acting with the consciousness that the Self alone is real while dedicating each action to God, the Supreme Self.

In the next verse Krishna says:

> **Others, also, not knowing thus yet hearing from others, worship. They also cross beyond death, devoted to what they have heard (13:25).**

Krishna is not talking about just any kind of teaching, but rather the teaching of the ancient sages. If we carefully study them, learning from those that have understood them, and apply them as best we can, we shall rise above the death of material consciousness and enter into spiritual awareness that in time will bring us into complete understanding and the capacity for liberating yoga practice. It is all in the doing.

SEEING THE ONE WITHIN THE ALL

The One in all

Krishna now concludes the subject of the field and the knower of the field, pointing out the results of seeing their nature and their union.

> Know this: whatever is born, the animate or the inanimate, know it to be resulting from the union of the Field and the Knower of the Field (13:26).

All that exists within the field of relativity, even if only momentarily, has arisen from the interaction of the field (prakriti) and the knower of the field (purusha), that are really one and the same. For "creation" is a dream of the purusha, though infinitely more stable and lasting than our nightly dreams.

Regarding those who wake from the cosmic dream, Krishna says:

> He who sees the Supreme Lord existing in all beings equally, not dying when they die–he sees truly (13:27).

What a glorious vision! And Krishna uses the term Parameshwara–Supreme Lord–for he is speaking of a very personal seeing of God, not some abstract metaphysical Principle. God is indeed Principle, but so much more besides. To ever see God, to not have the world be a veil but a window, is possible to the yogi, a sublime possibility. For such a one: "Death is swallowed up in victory" (I Corinthians 15:54).

The One in him

> Truly seeing the same Lord existing everywhere, he injures not the Self by the lower self. Then he goes to the Supreme Goal (13:28).

Unpleasant as the fact may be, people live in continual violation of their spirit-nature. Daily they outrage their divine Self in a multitude of ways, all of which have the single effect of burying, even suffocating, their Self, of dethroning and degrading it–at least within this plane of relative existence, even though the Self can never be diminished or harmed in the transcendental realm. The way human beings live is a kind of constant attempted murder of their own deathless being. This is a terrible mode of life, and the world around us reveals the results.

Although nearly all of the world continues to repeat the same deadly folly, we as individuals need not do so. We can make our heart and our home a haven of peace, an abode of Consciousness. It is all a matter of refining and elevating our usual state of mind through japa and meditation, of thus "truly seeing the same Lord existing everywhere" around us. Freed from the lie of ego, we come to know who and what we really are, and our eternal relationship with God.

> He who himself sees thus: that all actions are performed exclusively by Prakriti, and perceives that therefore he is himself not the doer–he sees truly (13:29).

In the midst of "change and decay all around I see," the yogi is undisturbed, because he knows that prakriti alone is moving, changing, breaking up, and recombining–that the Self is untouched by all that, the unmoving witness of it all. As Yogananda continually reminded his students, "this is all just movies." The movie is not ultimately real, but the movie-viewers are. And when the show is over they will leave the theater and go home where they belong without a backward look.

> **When he perceives the various states of being as resting in the One, and their expansion from that One alone–he then attains Brahman (13:30).**

First we see the truth of the individual Self, and then we are enabled to know the Supreme Self. All states and forms of existence come from Brahman and ever remain within Brahman. The entire cosmos is a great ritual of Consciousness. As the fourth chapter says: "Brahman is the offering, Brahman is the oblation poured out by Brahman into the fire of Brahman. Brahman is to be attained by him who always sees Brahman in action." This being so:

> **This eternal Supreme Self, without beginning and devoid of gunas, even though dwelling in the body, does not act, nor is it tainted. As the all-pervading ether because of its subtlety is not tainted, so the Self seated in the body is not tainted at any time in any situation. As the sun alone illumines this entire world, so the Lord of the field illumines the entire field. Those who know through the eye of knowledge the distinction between the Field and the Knower of the Field, and the liberation of beings from Prakriti–they go to the Supreme (the Highest) (13:31-34).**

This is no intellectual exercise, but "knowledge combined with realization" (9:1). Once we know the difference between purusha and prakriti, and how to distance ourselves from the prakriti-dream, we are on the way to freedom from bondage in this or any other world.

THE THREE GUNAS

In chapter three the subject of the gunas was introduced. They were briefly mentioned in chapter four, and now this fourteenth chapter is devoted to them. The first two verses are reminiscent of others we have encountered already:

Highest wisdom

> The Holy Lord said: Again I shall explain to you the highest of knowledges, the best of all knowledge, having known which all the sages attained to the highest perfection. Resorting to this knowledge they attain identity with me. At creation they are not born, nor do they tremble at its dissolving (14:1-2).

Simplistic, linear, two-dimensional thinking characterizes Western thought, including religion. In some instances the entire range of ordinary religious beliefs can be summed up in a moderate-sized paragraph. Neatly tied up theological and philosophical packages are the delight of the Western mind. As I. K. Tamini points out in *The Science of Yoga*, there is little interest in the reality of the theories as long as they hang together, are logical, and sound right. The competing Western ideologies are mostly empty packaging, hollow boxes whose appeal lies only in their external impression. As the prophet said: "A wonderful and horrible thing is committed in the land; the prophets prophesy falsely, and the priests bear rule by their means; and my people love to have it so" (Jeremiah 5:30-31).

In contrast we have the rich, multilevel, and wide-embracing philosophies of the East, philosophies that are demonstrable, whose esoteric principles are proven by the observable changes in those that fulfill them. Much of the time they appear inconsistent, even contradictory, but that is a characteristic of reality itself. They often say the same thing about differing subjects. For example, in Hinduism all the sahasranamavalis (collections of one thousand titles) addressed to various deities declare each of them to be the only true deity, and a great deal of the same titles are attributed to them all. It is, furthermore, usual for a Hindu to recite several of these over a period of time without any unease whatsoever. I have known yogis who would say: "The one thing you need is…," and then name differing things at different times. Of course. Sanatana Dharma does not "make sense," it *is* sense, and it makes the adherent sensible.

More than once already, Krishna has stated his intention to give us the highest wisdom. And has spoken differently each time. Now he does it again, but giving us an understanding of what true wisdom really does for the wise.

Beyond this wisdom there is simply nothing more to be known, because Wisdom and Brahman are the same. That is, Truth is not a set of intellectual ideas, but Reality itself. When someone asked Shankara: "What is Truth [Satya]?" he answered: "There is no such thing as Truth, there is only The True [Sat]." This is because Shankara was a yogi, not a mere philosopher, and he knew that "knowledge combined with realization, which having known you shall be free from evil" (9:1), was the only thing that really mattered.

Knowledge (jnana) must be sought for. True, it is already inside us, but what value is that to us who are blind to it? We must open our eyes or remove the debris that separates us from it. In the newborn infant are all the faculties and powers of the adult. Yet that means nothing to the infant. In time the inner seeds will manifest and adulthood be gained. It is the same with us. There is a necessary search for Truth, but that search must be an inner search, the practice of yoga.

The Supreme Perfection attained by the sages is Brahman, Infinity itself. It is not mere freedom from fault or a plenitude of good attributes.

It is a transcending of the condition in which good or bad, vice or virtue, can exist–a transcendence in which there is not even the possibility of their existence.

United with Brahman, the Brahman-nature was living through the sages, for it *was* them. "This is the divine state; having attained this, he is not deluded. Fixed in it even at the time of death, he attains Brahmanirvana" (2:72).

"At creation they are not born, nor do they tremble at its dissolving." Having no longer any need for the cosmic school, they have graduated from the plane of relativity. They are not compelled to take birth in a future creation cycle, nor are they dispossessed of a body-dwelling when the universe dissolves. They have moved beyond all such cycles into Original Being. They experience the fulfillment of Jesus' prayer: "O Father, glorify thou me with thine own self with the glory which I had with thee before the world was" (John 17:5).

Prakriti: the originating womb

For me great Brahma is the womb, and in that do I place the seed. The origination of all beings comes from that. Whatever be the forms produced within all wombs, the great Brahma is their womb, and I the seed-casting Father (14:3-4).

Brahma is the creator of the three lower levels of the seven-level creation. Since creation is really only a dream, the egg or seed of that dream is placed within his consciousness, and all develops from there. Creation is often spoken of as an egg (garbha) in Sanskrit texts. And that egg is prakriti, so that subject is being continued here. Just as an egg is warmed in order for it to hatch, so Brahma focuses his consciousness on the prakriti-egg, and its potentials are realized. So both Brahma and prakriti are the wombs of all things.

Prakriti is the great field of creative energy, but the seeds planted therein are the individual spirits who are evolving through the vast span of creation cycles. Thus, Prakriti is our mother and Brahma is our father–the only real parents we will ever have, all others being but temporary reflections of these divine archetypes. We need to realize that we are divine in origin, and that our purpose in being here is to manifest our innate divinity. We must also keep in mind that since there is only One, Prakriti is really Purusha, that what we mistake for matter is really Spirit. Although there appear to be many separate beings, in essence they are one in Brahman.

All forms within Prakriti are really only modifications and combinations of the three gunas. So Krishna continues:

> **Sattwa, rajas, and tamas–these gunas born of Prakriti bind fast in the body the imperishable embodied one (the Atman) (14:5).**

The gunas are not three things, but qualities of the energy that is Prakriti. They are modes or functions of energy. The primal energy moves in three different ways. So the gunas are not things of themselves, only appearances. But very significant appearances.

The three gunas are called sattwa, rajas, and tamas. When we experience them as real, they bind and limit us to body consciousness, making us undergo change and death, even though we are unchanging and immortal. So the three gunas are the basic forces of illusion. It is interesting that there are three primary colors whose combinations make all other colors. Without these three we would never see any colors.

The next thirteen verses deal with the gunas, moving back and forth between them. To make it much easier to understand their differences, I will first give the thirteen verses relating to them, and then separate the verses into three sections so we can look at one guna at a time in depth.

The three gunas

Of these, sattwa is stainless, luminous, and health-giving; it binds by attachment to happiness and by attachment to knowledge. Know rajas' nature is passion arising from thirst and attachment; it binds fast the embodied one by attachment to action. Know indeed that tamas is born of ignorance, deluding all embodied ones. It binds by distraction, laziness and sleep.

Sattwa causes attachment to happiness, rajas causes attachment to action; and tamas, veiling knowledge, causes attachment to delusion.

Sattwa prevails over rajas and tamas; and rajas prevails over sattwa and tamas; and tamas prevails over sattwa and rajas.

When the light of knowledge shines in all the gates of the body, then it should be known that sattwa is dominant. Greed, activity, undertaking of actions, restlessness, and desire–these arise when rajas is dominant. Darkness, inertia, heedlessness and delusion–these arise when tamas is dominant.

When the embodied one dies when sattwa is dominant, then he enters the stainless realms of the knowers of the Highest. Dying in rajas, he is born amid those attached to action. Dying in tamas, he is born from the wombs of the deluded.

They say the fruit of action performed well, is sattwic and without fault; but the fruit of rajas is pain, and the fruit of tamas is ignorance.

From sattwa arises knowledge; and from rajas arises greed; from tamas arises heedlessness, delusion and ignorance.

Those established in sattwa go upward; the rajasic remain in the middle; the tamasic, abiding in the lowest guna, go downward. (14:6-18).

Sattwa

Of these, sattwa is stainless, luminous, and health-giving [salubrious]; it binds by attachment to happiness and by attachment to knowledge. From this we know that sattwa is free from impurity–from any element that obstructs higher consciousness from functioning on any level. Further, sattwa illuminates the mind and whatever the mind is fixed upon. Understanding and practical knowledge arise naturally in the sattwic mind. Sattwa is free from any defect, either mental or physical. Nevertheless, sattwa is as much an element of bondage as rajas or tamas. It binds us through attachment to happiness and ease of heart and to the pursuit of spiritual wisdom. When these are sought as attributes of the Self, such seeking frees us. But if they are sought under the influence of sattwa, they are sought for their short-term benefits, only for our personal well-being and understanding. The motive is tainted, albeit only as the faintest shadow, by egoic motive.

Sattwa, too, must be shed by the ascending spirit, for: *Sattwa causes attachment to happiness.*

Sattwa prevails over rajas and tamas. Sattwa is a force of positive introversion, of keen awareness of inward states, a condition essential for proficiency in meditation. It is psychic sensitivity, an awareness of subtler realms of being. This is because sattwa is fundamentally an orientation toward spiritual ascension which results from the dissolving of all lower things. The ultimate sattwa (shuddhasattwa) is a melting away of all that is not spirit.

When the light of knowledge shines in all the gates of the body, then it should be known that sattwa is dominant. Those in whom sattwa predominates are not bewildered by life and its experiences. Rather, the sattwic person is ever gaining in understanding, being taught by life itself. The sattwic person "sees" in the fullest sense.

When the embodied one dies when sattwa is dominant, then he enters the stainless realms of the knowers of the Highest. Being himself a knower, at the time of death he ascends to the pure worlds of those established in the highest consciousness, his state of mind being in harmony with theirs.

They say the fruit of action performed well (well done), is sattwic and without fault (taint). Action that increases the quality of sattwa in us is the only truly good action. This is a necessary lesson for us who seek the Highest, for: *From sattwa arises knowledge.*

And as has been said: *Those established in sattwa go upward.* But he must *abide* in sattwa, be established in sattwa, not just having occasional bouts or flashes of sattwa. Sattwa must be a steady condition.

Rajas

Know rajas' nature is passion arising from thirst and attachment; it binds fast the embodied one by attachment to action. Rajas produces fevered desire in us, whatever the object might be. Fundamentally it makes us crave enjoyment and possession of the objects of enjoyment. It literally addicts us to action–the shackles of rebirth and karma.

Rajas causes attachment to action. Pity the person who says: "I am a doer, not a thinker," who considers himself "a man of action," and thinks it is an enviable virtue.

Rajas is a consuming monster, for: *Rajas prevails over sattwa and tamas.* The individual's will is wiped out, at least for the moment. In the third chapter Arjuna asks: "By what is a man impelled to commit evil, against his own will, as if urged by [some] force?" (3:36). And Krishna answers: "This [force] is desire, it is anger, that is born of the rajo-guna: great consumer and of great evil; know this to be the enemy" (3:37).

Greed, activity, undertaking of actions, restlessness, and desire–these arise when rajas is dominant. And we are the slaves!

The following are self-explanatory: *Dying in rajas, he is born amid those attached to action. The fruit of rajas is pain. From rajas [arises] greed. [After death,] the rajasic remain in the middle.*

Tamas

Know indeed that tamas is born of ignorance, deluding all embodied ones; it binds by distraction, laziness and sleep[iness]. Tamas, veiling knowledge, causes attachment to delusion (negligence). When this is seen in anyone or anything, tamas is prevailing and enslaving, for Krishna says: *Tamas prevails over sattwa and rajas.*

Darkness, inertia, heedlessness and delusion–these arise when tamas is dominant. Dying in tamas, he is born from the wombs of the deluded. Commentators say this means that the tamasic person is born either to parents of utter stupidity and torpor, or that they may even sink to rebirth in a subhuman form.

The fruit of tamas is ignorance. Negligence and delusion arise from tamas, and ignorance too; from tamas arises distraction (heedlessness; delusion; confusion) and ignorance. That is clear to any but the tamasic.

[After death] the tamasic, abiding in the lowest guna, go downward. Again, this means either birth among the stupid or the subhuman (whatever the form, human or animal); and it can also mean sinking into the regions of darkness known as hells.

The three doers

> When the beholder sees no doer other than the gunas, and
> knows that which is higher than the gunas, he attains to my
> being (14:19).

Of course, it is really Prakriti alone that does all things, the gunas simply
being modes of the Primal Energy. Yogananda usually elucidated these
concepts by the example of a motion picture. The picture itself is Prakriti,
with its colors and forms being the gunas, and the white undifferentiated
light is the Purusha, the Infinite. (Sometimes he likened Prakriti to the
screen.) So everything that happens or that we perceive are merely joinings
and disjoinings of the gunas. The gunas alone do anything. Realizing this we
should be stimulated to look beyond the gunas to the transcendent Spirit
which is absolute Unity. Through yoga we can enter into that Oneness
and be free from the illusions of the gunas.

The conqueror

> When an embodied being rises above these three gunas, which
> are the source of the body, freed from birth, death, old age and
> pain, he attains immortality (14:20).

This makes it clear that we do not need some kind of mastery or control
over the gunas, but rather we require a metaphysical transcendence, an
awakening that will take us beyond their reach. What to the ignorant are
unbreakable bonds then become nothing more than cobwebs–not even
that: mere illusions.

The gunas are not only the source, the material of the body, they are
also the forces that impel us into imprisonment in the body. When the
poet wrote: "Change and decay all around I see," he was speaking of
the gunas. But when he continued: "O thou that changest not," he was
addressing the Self.

Freed from the gunas, and therefore from the body, "released from
birth, death, old age, and pain, he attains immortality." That is, he knows
who he really is and dreams no more dreams of the gunas.

Arjuna said: By what marks is he known who has gone beyond the gunas? What is his conduct, and how does he go beyond these three gunas? (14:21).

How do we know when the gunas are transcended?

He neither detests the presence nor desires the absence of illumination [prakasha] or activity [pravritti] or delusion [moha](14:22).

This is an important point. We want to transcend the gunas, yet we are to be indifferent to their presence or their absence (actually, in this verse, the *effects* of their presence or absence.) Non-interaction with them is the secret. But the even greater secret is the will and the desire to reach God Who is beyond the gunas. Finding God is the real secret. The idea that it is wisdom to just remain in the world and wander "skillfully" through the maze is absurd. (Like the silly idea that being able to make holograms of match-boxes in your mind is a preparation for meditation.) God must be the central focus of our consciousness and our life.

We will do well to never forget Krishna's description of the true yogi: "He who is steadfast in yoga [yoga-yukta] at all times sees the Self present in all beings and all beings present in the Self. *He who sees me everywhere, and sees all things in me–I am not lost to him, and he is not lost to me*" (6:29, 30).

The next three verses are so perfect they need no comment beyond our embodying of them.

He who sits apart, indifferent to and unmoved by the gunas, realizing: "the gunas are operating," stands firm and is un- wavering. The same in pain or in pleasure, self-contained, to whom a clod of earth, a stone, and gold are alike; to whom the liked and the unliked are the same, steadfast, to whom blame and praise of himself are equal, indifferent in honor and dishonor, impartial toward the side of friend or enemy, renouncing all undertakings–he is said to be beyond the gunas (14:23-25).

How it is done

I have given my ideas about getting beyond the gunas, but these words of Krishna far exceed them:

> And he who serves me with the yoga of unswerving devotion, going beyond the three gunas, is fit for absorption in Brahman. For I am the abode of Brahman, the immortal, immutable, abode of everlasting dharma and of absolute bliss (14:26-27).

Om Tat Sat Om.

THE COSMIC TREE

There are certain symbols that are common to many cultures, especially in their distant past. One such is the Cosmic Tree. Devotees of Wagner's music will well remember the *Welt-Atem*, the World Ash, that grew through the center of the earth, and how in *Die Walkure* Sigmund draws out the great sword *Nothung* (Needful) that had been thrust into it by Wotan, his father.

India, too has this symbol:

> **The Holy Lord said: They speak of the eternal ashwattha tree with roots above and branches below, its leaves the Vedic hymns; he who knows it is a knower of the Vedas (15:1).**

This has both a macrocosmic meaning and a microcosmic one.

The cosmos, physical, astral, and causal, is rooted above in the Supreme Consciousness, in Brahman. Everything has originated in Brahman, has Brahman for its essential Being. That which is "below" is a manifestation of Brahman.

It is usual to say that the leaves of the tree are the hymns of the Veda, but this verse conveys a vital point of the character of relative existence. The word *chhandamsi* means poetic meter or rhythm. The meaning is that every thing is simply a mode of vibration, an energy-pattern, a variation on the single note of Om, of Mulaprakriti, the Primal Energy. Om, the Shabda (Sound) Brahman, is the Root Sound of which creation is a series of permutations. Those who know this–which implies knowledge of Purusha and Prakriti and their relationship–are knowers of the true Knowledge, the eternal veda/vidya.

We are rooted in our own Self and in Brahman, the Self's Self. All that we identify with as us are the modes of Prakriti, of Creative Energy–which is Brahman in extension. All things are "songs" of God, incarnations of Om, the Pranava.

Now we get more on the individual trees:

Below, above, its branches spread afar, nourished by the gunas. Its buds are the sense-objects; and in the world of men below its roots engender action (15:2).

The universal ashwattha tree, like the earthly banyan tree, puts down roots from its branches, making the one tree into many dependent trees–an apt symbol of Brahman and us. The three gunas are the elements which make up the universal and individual trees. The objects of the senses are the buds of the trees which, tending downward, make fresh roots in the world. These roots are karmas, both action and the results of action.

Its form is not perceptible here in the world, not its end, nor its beginning, nor its foundation [that which enables it to continue in existence]. Cutting this firm-rooted ashwattha tree with the strong axe of non-attachment, (15:3).

As long as our consciousness is centered in this world, in relative existence, in the experience of the body, mind, and senses, we cannot possibly comprehend the true nature and life of the world and our embodiment within it. Therefore we must transfer our consciousness to the Spirit-self which is eternally rooted in Brahman. Then here and now we will comprehend everything. Just as the kernel of a seed or nut when it ripens pulls away from the shell, in the same way as we ripen through the practice of meditation we shall become detached from all that is of the world. The resulting illumined consciousness (prajna) will be the axe by which we can cut through the subsidiary roots of the earthly ashwattha tree.

Writing of this, Dr. I. K. Taimni observed: "According to the yogic philosophy it is possible to rise completely above the illusions and miseries of life and to gain infinite knowledge, bliss, and power through enlightenment *here and now* while we are still living in the physical body.... No vague promise of an uncertain postmortem happiness this, but a definite scientific assertion of a fact verified by the experience of innumerable yogis, saints, and sages who have trodden the path of yoga throughout the ages."

This being absolutely so, Krishna concludes:

> Then that place is to be sought to which, having gone, they do not return again: "In that Primeval Purusha from which streamed forth the ancient Power, I take refuge" (15:4).

The second half of this verse should be our constant aspiration.

FREEDOM

The great bondage

> Without pride or delusion, with the evil of attachment con-
> quered, constantly dwelling in the Self, with desires dispelled,
> freed from the pair of opposites known as pleasure and pain,
> the undeluded reach the eternal Goal (15:5).

This is the state of moksha–of freedom.

It is possible to waste a lot of time and struggle on things that prove
impossible to accomplish because we are going about it in the wrong way.
This first sentence gives us invaluable information about dealing with ego
and delusion. "How can I get rid of ego?" is a constant refrain of those
who realize how deadly it can be. According to the Gita, pride (ego) and
delusion are side-effects of ignorance. So we need to work on ridding
ourselves of that. Furthermore, once ignorance is gone, so is attachment
to the dream-illusions of this world. For our eyes see clearly both the truth
and the untruth of things.

The most important characteristic of the liberated yogi is living in
conscious, unbroken union with Spirit, individual and infinite. This is the
goal of all those within the field of relativity. Illuminated consciousness is
total fulfillment, therefore within it all desire has melted away. In the same
way the experiences of the senses no longer control or produce delusive
reactions. There is an important implication here: the liberated person still

experiences the external world—it does not vanish—but without identifying with it or being influenced by it. This is true mastery. Such a state is beyond all change. It cannot be lessened or obscured, for it is Reality itself.

> **There the sun, moon or fire illuminate not; going whither they return not, for that is my Supreme Abode (15:6).**

Eternal spirit

How is it that what the Gita says about us and our infinite destiny can be true when it seems so beyond anything we know of ourselves? That is because we have no idea of our own nature as part of that Infinite Life that is God. This is why the Gita should be our daily study: to keep us reminded. Now Krishna will explain how we are in a sense incarnations of Divinity.

> **Merely a fragment of myself, becoming an eternal jiva in this world of jivas, draws to itself the senses, and the mind as the sixth sense, abiding in Prakriti (15:7).**

Every sentient being is rooted in Infinite Being and is in an incomprehensible way a part of that Being. Our presence is the Presence of God, however much we keep that divine aspect of ourselves covered up. At no time are we other than eternal beings free within God, but the dream of duality and delusion has overcome us. We think we are cut off from God because we have put on the costume of the material body with the five outer senses and the inner sense of the mind.

There are really two persons inhabiting each body: the individual spirit and the Supreme Spirit. Krishna keeps speaking of the Lord (Ishwara) so we will not lose sight of that fact, and also so we will realize that the Infinite Will is always in control, however the dream may seem otherwise.

> **When the Lord takes on a body, and when he leaves it, he takes the senses and the mind and goes, like the wind takes the scents from their seats, the flowers and herbs (15:8).**

Nothing is really lost to us by death. We take all that matters with us, and we bring it back with us in the next birth to continue our evolutionary path. Each life affects us, and we take those influences along with us. Because they are so subtle they are symbolized as fragrances. But they are none the less real for that.

According to the Upanishads and the Gita, Ishwara lives in the heart, the core, of every human being, and experiences all which they experience. Therefore Krishna underlines that both the incarnating jivatman and the Paramatman enter and depart from the body together. The manner of this is incomprehensible.

> Presiding over hearing, sight, touch, taste and smell as well as the mind, this Ishwara experiences the objects of the senses (15:9).

Both we and God are witnesses through the senses and mind of all our experiences as we incarnate in the many mansions of creation. We seem to undergo those experiences–which we do, but as in a dream. God experiences all that we do–this is a manifestation of our oneness with God. God knows it is a dream, but we do not and so we suffer.

Two kinds of human beings

> Whether departing, remaining or enjoying, accompanied by the gunas, the deluded do not see him. Those with the eye of knowledge see him (15:10).

There are two basic divisions in this world: those that do not see God and those that do. And those that see God and their own Self never lose sight of those divine realities whether incarnate, dying, or experiencing the modes (gunas) of Prakriti. The others never see anything–but in time they will, for that is the destiny of all sentient beings.

Who sees God?

Who are those that see God? Not the merely religious or virtuous, for Krishna continues:

> The yogis, striving, behold him dwelling within the Self; but the undeveloped and unintelligent, even though striving, see him not (15:11).

Only the adept yogis who have entered into their own spirit-consciousness beyond the tossing waves of samsara—including their own gross and subtle bodies—see God. And they do not see him outside themselves, but at the very core of their being, pervading their own consciousness.

Who does not see?

When the scriptures of authentic dharma speak of the ignorant and describe their dilemmas, it is never to condemn or despise them, but to inform us who seek to be wise. In this verse two words are used to describe those that cannot possibly see God, and they tell us much.

The first word is *akritatmano*, which means one who is unprepared and unperfected. Now this is important, for Krishna is not talking of bad or unworthy people, but of those who have not evolved sufficiently and therefore are unprepared for the Divine Vision—actually incapable of it. This is not a fault, but a stage on the way in which all but a fraction of sentient beings presently find themselves. But we are hereby told what we need: to prepare ourselves and strive to be more complete in mastery of our energy levels and more centered in the consciousness that we really are. We need to become steady practicers of yoga.

The other word is *acetasah*—the unthinking. This includes both those that are simply unaware and those that refuse to be aware. There are people that live heedlessly throughout life after life, never considering the deeper implications of their existence. Even though they have an intellectual belief in God, they do not live life in the perspective of that truth. Only those who ponder deeply on the eternal mystery of God, man, and life are open to understand and move onward from mere thinking about it to actually walking the Way.

THE ALL-PERVADING REALITY

Light

> That light which resides in the sun, which illumines the whole world, which is in the moon and in fire–know that light to be mine (15:12).

In chapter thirty of his autobiography Paramhansa Yogananda has written the following:

"Among the trillion mysteries of the cosmos, the most phenomenal is light. Unlike sound-waves, whose transmission requires air or other material media, light-waves pass freely through the vacuum of interstellar space. Even the hypothetical ether, held as the interplanetary medium of light in the undulatory theory, can be discarded on the Einsteinian grounds that the geometrical properties of space render the theory of ether unnecessary. Under either hypothesis, light remains the most subtle, the freest from material dependence, of any natural manifestation....

"'Fiat lux! And there was light.' God's first command to his ordered creation (*Genesis* 1:3) brought into being the only atomic reality: light. On the beams of this immaterial medium occur all divine manifestations. Devotees of every age testify to the appearance of God as flame and light. 'The King of kings, and Lord of lords; who only hath immortality,

403

dwelling in the light which no man can approach unto.' (I Timothy 6:15-16)

"A yogi who through perfect meditation has merged his consciousness with the Creator perceives the cosmical essence as light; to him there is no difference between the light rays composing water and the light rays composing land. Free from matter-consciousness, free from the three dimensions of space and the fourth dimension of time, a master transfers his body of light with equal ease over the light rays of earth, water, fire, or air. Long concentration on the liberating spiritual eye has enabled the yogi to destroy all delusions concerning matter and its gravitational weight; thenceforth he sees the universe as an essentially undifferentiated mass of light."

Everything is light, for everything is God, who is Light (I John 1:5).

Power

> Entering the earth, I support all beings with my energy. Having become the watery moon, I cause all plants to thrive (15:13).

Ojas means vitality, vigor, luster, splendor, and energy, including spiritual energy. It is the power which accomplishes all things in the cosmos. It is even the power within the light of the moon, the power that governs the growth of plants. It is not just Divine Power, it is Divinity itself, for God is also Power.

Fire

> Becoming the digestive fire, I abide in the body of all living beings. Joined with prana and apana, I digest the fourfold food (15:14).

God is Vaishvanara, Cosmic Fire, which includes all forms of manifested fire, including digestive fire in the bodies of sentient beings. Fire is the most precious external element that human beings possess. In our technological age we cannot image how essential fire is, and how necessary it used to be to preserve fire. The scratch of a match, the flick of a gas-powered lighter, or a turn of a knob produces this vital thing. Now the only time we even see fire is when we cook or make fire for our amusement. It has become as disregarded and taken for granted as God, whose manifestation it is.

In ancient times fire was worshipped or honored as a gift of God and an extension of God's being. This was true even in early Christianity. Even now in India fire is saluted when kindled for either cooking or light, and devout Hindus in the cities salute the electric light when it is first turned on in the evening.

The all-encompassing Being

What a profound state of consciousness it is to see God in all things at all times–to understand that "in him we live, and move, and have our being" (Acts 17:28). To underline this Krishna says:

> **Seated within the hearts of all, from me come memory and knowledge and their loss: I alone am to be known by all the Vedas; I am the Author of the Vedanta, and the Knower of the Vedas (15:15).**

Brahman is in our hearts as the inmost Indweller, the source of our consciousness and life. Since everything comes to us from God; so also does their departure. Knowledge (understanding) and memory of experience from which reason arises, as well as knowledge and memory of our self-nature, come and go, originating in and returning to God. For he is the eternal Antaryamin: indweller, inner guide, inner ruler, the "witness" who dwells within every living being.

What is found as subject in the writings and discourses of the wise– that is Brahman. For there is none other of which to speak. He originates Wisdom, teaches Wisdom, and is the Knower of the end of Wisdom: his own Self, Brahman.

The immortal

> There are two purushas in this world–the perishable and the
> imperishable. All beings are the perishable, and Kutastha is
> called the imperishable (15:16).

It is not the spirit that is perishable, but its wrappings, the various
sheaths or bodies. Yet, the spirit is "perishable" in its experience of those
bodies until it awakens to its true nature. In this verse Brahman is called
Kutashtha, which means changeless, immutable, and "dweller in the
height," or "on the summit." Unlike Brahman, we dwell in the bottom
lands and undergo suffering and change.

> But there is also the Highest Purusha, called the Supreme Self,
> the eternal Ishwara, Who pervades all the three worlds and
> sustains them (15:17).

Brahman has two aspects–transcendental and immanent. The previous
verse is speaking of the immanent, the personal Ishwara aspect of God.
The perishable purushas live within Ishwara and can communicate with
him. But our association with the personal aspect of God is meant to end
when we ourselves become transcendental and can pass from all relative
worlds into that Absolute beyond all relativity.

> Since I transcend the perishable and am also above the imper-
> ishable, so in this world and in the Veda I am known as the
> Supreme Purusha [Purushottama] (15:18).

The impersonality of Brahman can seem barren, even antiseptic, to us
who are so used to the realm of Ishwara, so Krishna then says:

> He who, undeluded, thus knows me as the Supreme Purusha,
> he, knowing all, worships me with his whole being (15:19).

When we truly know Brahman in its transcendent aspect the response is intense devotion–wholehearted worship. Sri Ramana Maharshi is a perfect example of this. Though uncompromisingly non-dual in his ways and words, he was deeply devotional, often shedding tears of love when hearing the lives and words of saint-devotees of God. How important it is for us to have this perspective as well is seen by Krishna's closing words in this chapter:

> **This most secret teaching has been imparted by me; awakened to this, a man becomes wise and all his duties are fulfilled (15:20).**

THE DIVINE AND THE
DEMONIC

Divine and demonic

In every religious tradition we have the idea of two ways to live in this world or two kinds of people to be found in this world. And in each tradition there are several forms of this classification. So now in this sixteenth chapter we find what is no doubt the oldest recorded form of this approach. Vyasa postulates that human beings are divided into two types: divine and demonic. He uses two Sanskrit words: *daivim* and *asurim*–devic and asuric.

Deva literally means "shining one." Though it is usually applied to highly evolved astral beings, in this chapter it refers to people who live in the light of spiritual consciousness which illumines their outer life as well. These people were called *Arya* in more ancient writings and in the teachings of Buddha. Devim, or devic, is the inner and outer state of such shining ones, and indicates that they are progressing toward liberation.

Asura means one who is without light (sura), without spiritual consciousness, who has a darkened consciousness, even preferring dark to light. Such persons are asuric (asurim), turned away from divinity within and without and moving further into degradation of consciousness and life.

This is a grave subject, especially since we often see divine and demonic traits in the same person. Such a one must discriminate clearly and eliminate the demonic and foster the divine. So in considering this we must not think that if we have a preponderance of devic qualities it assures us that all is well. Even the presence of a single demonic quality or tendency is of great danger to us lest it draw us away from the light into the dark. On the other hand, if in a predominantly demonic person we find one or more divine traits we can encourage them to move more into the light. For no one ever stands still: we are either moving upward or downward. Yet at all times we must remember that the Self of both the daivic and the asuric is fundamentally divine.

The divine personality

> **The Holy Lord said: Fearlessness, purity of being, stead-fastness in knowledge and yoga, almsgiving, self-control, sacrifice, self-study [swadhyaya], tapasya, and straightfor-wardness, non-violence, truthfulness, absence of anger, re-nunciation, tranquillity, without calumny, compassion for beings, uncovetousness, gentleness, modesty, absence of fickleness, vigor, patience, fortitude, purity, absence of ha-tred, absence of pride–they are the endowment of those born to a divine state (16:1-3).**

Since this is self-explanatory, I am going to give you the Sanskrit terms and the full definitions of the words that have more than one meaning, taken from *A Brief Sanskrit Glossary*.

Fearlessness. Abhaya(m): "Without fear;" fearlessness; a state of steadfastness in which one is not swayed by fear of any kind; absence of fear.

Purity of being. Sattwasamshuddhi: Purity of being; purity of heart; purity of feeling; increase of light and purity; purification of one's existence.

Almsgiving. Danam: "Giving;" gift; charity; almsgiving; self-sacrifice; donation; generosity.

Self-control. Dama: Self-control; control of the senses; restraint; taming; domination.

Sacrifice. Yajna: Sacrifice; worship; offering; sacrificial ceremony; a ritual sacrifice; usually the fire sacrifice known as agnihotra or havan.

Self-study. Swadhyaya: Introspective self-study or self-analysis leading to self-understanding. It can also mean study of scriptures and spiritual texts, especially those pertaining to the Self.

Austerity. Tapasya: Practical (i.e., result-producing) spiritual discipline; self-denial; spiritual force.

Straightforwardness. Arjava: honesty; rectitude; righteousness; simplicity.

Non-violence. Ahimsa: Non-injury in thought, word, and deed; non-violence; non-killing; harmlessness.

Truthfulness. Satya(m): Truth; the Real; Brahman, or the Absolute; truthfulness; honesty.

Renunciation. Tyaga: Literally: "abandonment." Renunciation.

Tranquility. Shanti: Peace; serenity; calm; tranquility; contentment.

Without calumny. Apaishunam: Absence of calumny, slander, or fault-finding.

Uncovetousness. Aloluptwam: Freedom from desire, lust, or greed.

Gentleness. Mardava(m): Gentleness; kindness; mildness; tenderness.

Modesty. Hri: Modesty; bashfulness; absence of pride.

Absence of fickleness. Achapalam: Determination; absence of fickleness; absence of change; immovability; fixedness, firmness; steadiness; steadfastness.

Vigor. Tejas: Vigor; strength; radiance.

Patience. Kshama: Patience, forgiveness; forbearance.

Fortitude. Dhriti: Determination; determined; steadfast; constant; attraction; sustaining effort; firmness; patience; endurance; fortitude; courage; strength.

Purity. Shaucha: Purity; cleanliness (of mind and body).

Absence of hatred [malice]. Adrohas: Without malice; absence of hatred.

Absence of pride. Atimanita: Without excessive pride; high honor.

They are the endowment of those born to a divine state. Fortunately we do not have to possess all of these to be yogis, but we should work toward it. This is a valuable checklist and can reveal who is a real spiritual aspirant destined to get somewhere. No one is beyond it. This I can tell you: Swami Sivananda of Rishikesh (Divine Life Society) embodied every one of these virtues to the maximum possible degree. So it can be done.

Birthright

We bring into this world only what we have accumulated in past lives. This is our inheritance, so to speak. God has absolutely nothing to do with it, nor does anyone else or any factors whatsoever other than our own previous action. It is our destiny as determined by us–none other and nothing other.

> **Hypocrisy, arrogance, conceit, anger, harshness and ignorance are the endowment of those born to a demonic state (16:4).**

Those who spontaneously exhibit these traits are demonic in nature. We see this even in children and it increases as the years go along. The environment of the demonic reflect their nature–those around them have the same traits as individuals and as a society in general.

> **The divine state is deemed to lead to liberation, the demonic to bondage. Do not grieve: you are born for a divine state (16:5).**

If we cultivate those qualities on the deva list and root out those qualities on the demon list our liberation is assured in time, just as increased bondage is certain for those who persist in the ways of the demons. It is interesting to see the modesty of Arjuna and his awareness of human frailty, for Krishna sees that he fears lest he be of demonic destiny. This is how it always is on this earth: the unworthy feel worthy and the worthy feel unworthy. There is a healthy self-doubt and self-mistrust.

More about the demons

> **There are two types of beings in this world: the divine and the demonic. The divine has been described at length. Hear from me of the demonic (16:6).**

The Gita is a very positive and spiritually optimistic book, so why are we being shown the way of demons? For a very positive reason: so we will detect demonic ways in ourselves and counteract them, and so we will discern whether those we encounter are divine or demonic. For the wise yogi avoids the demonic and seeks out the divine. If he finds demonic persons already in his life he eliminates these associations. Usually when he meditates and changes his vibration they fade out of his life, but if not then he must himself terminate the association as gently and diplomatically as possible.

Demonic men know not what to do or refrain from; purity is not found in them, nor is good conduct, nor is truth (16:7).

This is so true that it takes the breath away. The demonic not only do not know what they should or should not do, they hate the very idea of knowing, because then they would have to face their corruption. And they hate anything that would somehow make the truth plain to them. They are opponents of truth, purity, and right action. And that includes those who contentedly (often smugly) say: "I am an agnostic." As Jesus told Nicodemus: "This is the condemnation, that light is come into the world, and men loved darkness rather than light, because their deeds were evil. For every one that doeth evil hateth the light, neither cometh to the light, lest his deeds should be reproved. But he that doeth truth cometh to the light, that his deeds may be made manifest, that they are wrought in God" (John 3:19-21).

"The world," they say, "is without truth, without a basis, without God, produced by mutual union, with lust for its cause–what else?" (16:8).

This is certainly a picture of those that today consider themselves the intellectual, academic and political elite.

Aparaspara is translated "mutual union" by many translators into English, but it literally means "not one by the other," or "not by a succession." In his translation Judge has: "not governed by law," and Aurobindo: "a world of chance." It seems to me that the idea is denial of both cause and effect and the manifestation of the universe in an orderly and hierarchical manner according to exact laws. We are all familiar with the atheistic-materialistic ideas about the universe being without meaning, purpose or even order. It seems to me that Vyasa is indicating that such a view of the world without either God or cosmic order is demonic.

> **Holding this view, these lost souls, small-minded and of cruel deeds, arise as the enemies of the world, bent on its destruction (16:9).**

This verse has some interesting aspects that need looking into. Two words are used to describe these demons:

Nastatmanas. This word means those whose souls are lost, in the sense of a condition of being lost, and those who have lost touch with their souls. It is amusing to think how annoyed many yogis get when Fundamentalist Christians ask them if they are "saved," but here we have the same concept in the Gita! Those away from God are lost and those that have been rescued from that state are saved. The souls wandering in illusion from life to life are certainly lost–to themselves. When we begin practicing meditation we see how lost we are to ourselves. Fortunately, this is only a mental condition that can be corrected by our own effort. For we are always one with God and completely in charge in the highest levels of our being.

Alpabuddhayas. This means those of small intelligence–both those who because of lack of evolution are limited in intelligence, and those who willfully choose to narrow their intelligence, to make their minds small in scope.

The actions of such people are cruel, greedy, and selfish–in other words: egocentric. They come into this world as its enemies, because its purpose is evolution and eventual liberation, and they loathe anything that uplifts and enlightens and will do anything to destroy it. To destroy spiritual knowledge and life is to strike at the very root of the world: its divine purpose. All like them are enemies of humanity, for true humanity is that which leads to divinity.

> Attached to insatiable desires, full of hypocrisy, arrogance and intoxication, having accepted false ideas through delusion, they act with foul purposes (16:10).

Enslaved not just to the objects of desire, but to desire itself, these addicts of degradation are yet filled with pride, reveling in falsehood and illusion, bullying anyone who dares to not conform to their degraded ways. Believing their own madness they rush onward, increasing the pollution of their hearts.

> Clinging to boundless cares ending only in death, with gratification of desire as their highest aim–convinced that this is all– (16:11).

These demons live in hell, even on earth, clinging to their fears and anxieties. We see this all the time in the way people love conflict and their own misfortunes. How many times do we see people that can easily be freed from their miseries, but aggressively defend them and repulse any means of alleviation.

> Bound by a hundred snares of hope, given over to desire [lust] and anger, they seek to gain by unjust means accumulation of wealth to gratify their desires (16:12).

Sounds like the ideal modern "consumer."

> "Today this has been acquired by me. This I shall also obtain. This is mine, and this gain also shall be mine (16:13).

This is the pursuit of the dream of most people that is really a nightmare.

> "That enemy has been slain by me, and I shall slay others, too, for I am the Lord, I am the enjoyer, I am successful, powerful and happy (16:14).

This is certainly the philosophy of most of the world's governments, and of the big business that controls and motivates them.

> "I am wealthy and high-born," they say, "Who else is equal to me? I shall sacrifice, I shall give, I shall rejoice." Thus, they are deluded by ignorance (16:15).

If this is not a picture of contemporary mankind, then what is? See how they "get religious" and give thanks to God for his "goodness"? And worse: they are the target of their own delusions.

> Led astray by many imagined fancies, caught in a net of delusion, addicted to the gratifying of desire, they fall into a foul hell (16:16).

And that hell is their own foul mind.

> Self-conceited, stubborn, filled with the intoxication of wealth, they sacrifice in name only, for show, not according to the prescribed forms (16:17).

Religion is no sign of virtue, as this verse shows. The religion of such persons has themselves as its center and its measure of worth. And the worst are those that "make up my own religion," disregarding the ways and the words of the wise.

> Clinging to egotism, power, haughtiness, desire and anger, these malignant people hate me in their own and in others' bodies (16:18).

They do not mind parroting the "You Are God And I Am God" cliche, but they hate the manifestation of the divine Self in the form of moral purity and spiritual discipline as outlined by Patanjali:

1. Ahimsa: non-violence, non-injury, harmlessness
2. Satya: truthfulness, honesty
3. Asteya: non-stealing, honesty, non-misappropriativeness
4. Brahmacharya: sexual continence in thought, word and deed as well as control of all the senses
5. Aparigraha: non-possessiveness, non-greed, non-selfishness, non-acquisitiveness
6. Shaucha: purity, cleanliness
7. Santosha: contentment, peacefulness
8. Tapas: austerity, practical (i.e., result-producing) spiritual discipline
9. Swadhyaya: introspective self-study, spiritual study
10. Ishwarapranidhana: offering of one's life to God

They are masters of The Big Talk, but these ten virtues will be definitely missing from their minds and lives. You and I cannot change such people, but we can do one good thing: *avoid them altogether.*

> **These malicious evildoers, cruel, most degraded of men, I hurl perpetually into only the wombs of demons here (16:19).**

Our environment–especially our family–is a reflection of our inner mind, otherwise we would have been born elsewhere.

> **Entering the demonic wombs, and deluded birth after birth, not attaining to me, they fall into a progressively lower condition (16:20).**

The implication is that such persons sink so low that they become inwardly subhuman and and may even begin being born in animal bodies. This is a terrible thought, but more than one person has told me of seeing animals that seemed to be degraded humans. Yogananda once brought a cat to Brahmacharini Radhalila and asked her to care for it, saying that it had been a human being. "I won't tell you what it did in its previous life to be born as a cat, because if I told you, you would hate it and would not take care of it."

She believed what he told her, because the cat had human eyes, not the eyes of a cat, and whoever it looked at would feel it instantly and get the shivers.

The demon doors

As we saw at the beginning of this chapter, the truly worthy often question their worth and are very aware of the possibility of their going astray. The demons, on the other hand, are completely assured of their worth and goodness. (Bishop Fulton Sheen tells in his autobiography of being called to the deathbed of a very old woman who said to him: "I am the worst woman in New York City." "No you aren't," he told her. "If you were the worst woman in New York you would claim to be the best woman in New York.") So, since Krishna's message will only be heard by those of divine tendency, he tells us how to ensure that we will not fall into demonic consciousness:

> **Triple is the gate of this hell, destructive of the Self: desire, anger and greed. Therefore one should abandon (renounce) these three (16:21).**

Kama, krodha, and lobha are the three Sanskrit words used here.

Kama is desire in any form. It is harmful because it overshadows the intelligence and will power and impels us to worthless or negative actions. So whether it is a mild force or a volcanic passion, desire must be resisted and eliminated, and lust is the greatest destroyer of all. Rather than desires we should have intelligent decisions backed up by the enlightened will.

Krodha is anger in all its shades of intensity. Anger is really frustrated egotism. As Krishna explains: "For a man dwelling on the objects of the senses, attachment to them is born; from attachment desire is born; and from [thwarted] desire anger is born. From anger arises delusion; from delusion, loss of memory; from loss of memory, destruction of intelligence [buddhi]: from destruction of intelligence one is lost" (2:62-63).

Lobha is greed, which includes envy and covetousness. Of the three it is the most obviously egotistical. It is both ego-worship and a demand that others worship our ego, too. Any force of "I want" is greed.

The truth is, these three doors to hell of the mind and body are mixed together. When you have one you are sure to have the other two, as time will prove. This being so, Krishna assures us that:

> **A man who is liberated from these three gates to darkness does what is best for him, and thus goes to the Highest Goal (16:22).**

This is one of the most important teachings of the Gita. *Tamodvarais* can mean either "gates to darkness" or "gates to tamas." In this instance I think it does mean the first, but it is instructive to realize that desire, anger, and greed, although rajasic, if indulged in will lead us down into tamas.

He who casts aside the injunctions of the scriptures, following the impulse of desire, attains neither perfection nor happiness, nor the Supreme Goal (16:23).

The need to follow the path outlined by the sages can hardly be exaggerated. Otherwise we follow our ego-whims, claiming to be intuitive and following our inner wisdom. Only those in the blinding grip of ego think that they can ignore the counsels of the enlightened and manage. But in most instances they really do not plan to manage. Rather, they plan to fall and then feel justified in abandoning any semblance of spiritual life altogether: "I used to be a yogi;" "I used to be a vegetarian;" "I used to be celibate;" "I used to be religious;" and worst of all: "I used to be a monk (or nun)." As Yogananda often said: "People are so skilled in their ignorance."

> **Therefore the standards of the scriptures should be your guide in determining what should be done and what should not be done. Knowing what the scriptural injunctions prescribe, you should perform action here in this world (16:24).**

This is the only sensible conclusion, one that will lead all who heed it to Eternal Wisdom.

FAITH AND THE THREE GUNAS

We have no way of knowing if Vyasa divided the Gita into chapters and verses. It is likely he did not, because the demarcation between the chapters is not always detectable, as is the case in this chapter. The first verse is a logical continuation of the last two verses of chapter sixteen. Without them as context, it lacks logic and relevance to some degree. So here they are. Krishna says:

"He who casts aside the injunctions of the scriptures, following the impulse of desire, attains neither perfection nor happiness, nor the Supreme Goal. Therefore the standards of the scriptures should be your guide in determining what should be done and what should not be done. Knowing what the scriptural injunctions prescribe, you should perform action here in this world" (16:23-24).

Sacrifice and faith

Now we are ready to begin chapter seventeen. In response to the two verses just cited:

> Arjuna said: Those who cast aside the prescriptions of the scriptures, doing sacrifice with faith, what is their condition: sattwa, rajas or tamas? (17:1).

Two words here need defining: Yajna and Shraddha. In this chapter yajna means not just ritualistic offering (sacrifice) but any kind of worship or spiritual action. Shraddha always means faith, but in the sense of an intuition-based conviction, not just a mere unquestioning belief. So Arjuna is presenting us with the picture of a person who believes wholeheartedly in the efficacy of spiritual action or practice, but who disregards the principles of spiritual tradition as set forth in the scriptures or teachings of the enlightened ones. Such a one simply goes ahead and does what he thinks is the best way to approach spiritual life, picking and choosing what he does and how he does it. This is not what Krishna has been saying to do. So Arjuna wants to know if faith, or belief that the actions will produce the desired effect, will compensate for the disregard of the shastras (scriptures). In other words, he is thinking of the type of person that in this century claims to be "spiritual, not religious." Can that really work, Arjuna wants to know. What is the guna (quality) of such faith?

Inner quality

Krishna has already said that: "One acts according to one's own prakriti—even the wise man does so" (3:33). He expands on that in this connotation:

> The Holy Lord said: Threefold is the embodied ones' faith inherent within their nature: the sattwic, the rajasic and the tamasic. So hear of this (17:2).

So faith does not determine the quality of the person—the person's interior character (swabhava) determines the type of faith he has. That may seem obvious, but for some reason in the West we continually reverse cause and effect, so I want to make a point of it.

Krishna has more to say about this:

> The faith of each one is according to his nature. A man consists of his faith—he is what his faith is (17:3).

Shraddhamayo 'yam purusho—a person is made/formed of faith. *Yo yacchraddhah sa eva sah*—what his faith is: he is. And if he has no faith? He is nothing. So we can determine the basic character of a person by his faith. Krishna will now tell us how.

The worshipped

The sattwic worship the gods; the rajasic worship yakshas and rakshasas; the others, the tamasic men, worship the spirits of the departed and hosts of nature spirits [bhutas] (17:4).

Several types of beings are mentioned here and should be defined. We will rely on our old friend, *A Brief Sanskrit Glossary*.

Devas are "shining ones;" in the evolutionary hierarchy they are semi-divine or celestial beings with great powers, and therefore "gods." Sometimes they are called demi-gods. Most devas are the demigods presiding over various powers of material and psychic nature.

Yakshas are of two kinds: semidivine beings whose king is Kubera, the lord of wealth; or a kind of ghost, goblin, or demon. The rajasic worship the first kind to gain material advantage, and worship the second kind to get them to harm those standing in their way of material gain.

Rakshas are also of two kinds: semidivine, benevolent beings, or cannibal demons or goblins, enemies of the gods. The rajasic worship them for the same reasons as they worship the yakshas.

Pretas are ghosts–spirits of the dead. Sometimes these are just wandering earthbound "tramp" souls, but they may be famous people or one's own ancestors.

Bhutas are of two types: some are subhuman nature spirits or "elementals," but some are earthbound human spirits: ghosts. Bhutas may be either positive or negative.

Ganas are usually part of groups of spirits that wander together–mostly of various types. The term is also used as a kind of "miscellaneous" category for entities that have not otherwise been identified. A gana may be benevolent or malevolent, but is usually disorderly, chaotic, and wild in the sense of untamed or unruly, and potentially dangerous (hazardous). A gana's appearance is usually deformed, repulsive, or frightening.

Although Krishna speaks of "worship" in connection with these beings, it means any kind of intentional supernatural involvement or contact. This should be kept in mind.

It is not enough to just move into the world of the invisible; we must know where we are going to end up in that world. And we will certainly end up in the worlds of the kind of beings we habitually have contact and interchange with. Inconceivably vast as the physical universe is, the astral world is inconceivably larger than the physical plane. Not all beings in the astral realms can be contacted by human beings, but innumerable ones of numberless classifications or levels of evolution can be—often to the detriment or destruction of the human. Yet, since each one of us acts according to his dominant nature, so it will be in our supernatural involvement.

The sattwic

Since their very nature orients them toward higher realms of consciousness and impels them to evolve upward into and even beyond those realms, Krishna tells us that the sattwic worship the devas, whose nature is light. From deva we get the word "divine." In its highest sense it means God the Absolute. In a secondary sense it means all who consciously dwell in and reflect the divine light as "partakers of the divine nature" (II Peter 1:4). These include the various forms of God that are manifestations of the infinite divine attributes as well as the beings known as gods who wield divine powers for the assistance of those beneath them on the evolutionary ladder. Such beings include angels, saints, departed masters, and a host of other holy helpers. Since their entire will and consciousness is focused on God, interchange with them will elevate our consciousness toward the Divine as well. Communion with them will strengthen our aspirations toward God-realization.

The rajasic

The rajasic are quite different. Hungering for material things (including power) which they regard as the only source of happiness, pleasure, or fulfillment, they resort to gods and spirits that are ego- and greed-oriented like themselves. Such gods demand offerings of various kinds and, though they conceal this fact from their devotees, at the time of death those who worship or traffic with them will be taken into their worlds and made their servant-slaves. Some will be quickly shunted back to earthly rebirth to again become their devotees and supply them with what they want, but they can be kept imprisoned in those worlds for ages, as well. The awful thing about this is that most of the time these gods really have little power, and it is the offering of their worshippers that gives them their power. So in reality it is the gods that are dependent on the worshippers, not the other way round, however it may seem.

The yakshas and rakshas are divided into higher and lower types, but all are in bondage to ignorance and rebirth in some form, and contact with them can never really work to the ultimate good of the human who does so. The higher yakshas and rakshas are much more evolved than humans and can do things for them on a mundane level. They have good will, but still look upon humans as servants and demand offerings of some kind. They are never altruistic, and do not consider that they should be. They look upon themselves as merchants or suppliers of services. They can be angered and refuse to give the requested help, and often (very often) wreak vengeance on those who anger them or refuse them something. They can make life miserable or even terminate it–all according to the karma incurred by their petitioners. And this is how it is with the "positive" ones!

Some yakshas and rakshas are degraded, demonic beings, avid for worship, gifts, and power, lying and deceitful, always scheming to injure and deceive those who approach them, though for a while they seem benevolent in order to ensnare their devotees. Their only intention is to delude and plunder. Filled with pride they despise those that approach them and from the initial contact intend to lie and loot them. These, too, will harm and destroy those that offend them. Both these types, higher and lower, are the gods worshipped by greedy, egoic religionists of all types–some quite openly deal with such beings while others do so in a secret or deceitful form. And of course these entities continually introduce themselves as gods, saints, and great masters. And frankly, a large percentage of "gurus" are very like yakshas and rakshas.

The tamasic

The tamasic naturally gravitate to the pretas and bhutas. The pretas are the spirits of the dead. Ancestor worshippers and spiritualists openly seek out these spirits. Besides the pretas are the bhutas that range from earthbound ghosts to elementals and subhuman nature spirits. Some of these are deluded, evil, or just plain stupid. Some of them, being completely outside the stream of human evolution, do not really know what is going on, but play with humans the way tame animals would. Nothing good can come of any of this.

Many of these spirits demand offerings of all sorts and they have a very real power to do harm, and a predisposition to do so. Some even kill human beings, not realizing that they are doing so. Air elementals often urge people to jump out into the air, thinking they will fly with them. Water elementals urge swimmers to keep swimming further and further from shore until they become exhausted and drown–though that is not the elementals' intention. Fire elementals urge people–and especially children–to play with fire in hopes of a conflagration, though destruction is not their purpose. Earth elementals urge people to continually go underground and often try to keep them there by cave-ins and other mishaps. Again, they have no concept of death, so the elementals have no malicious intent. They just want to be friends.

There is no use warning the rajasic and tamasic away from their playmates. It is their nature to interact with them. Krishna is just giving us this information so if we have any pockets of rajas or tamas lingering in us we will be warned and not indulge them. Mostly he is wanting to show us how we can determine the guna of a person or a religion by scrutinizing their supernatural contact. What about those that have no supernatural contact of any kind? We should consider them non-existent, spiritually speaking.

Demonic asceticism and discipline

As just pointed out, negative and foolish spirits demand many kinds of sacrifice, some of them being insane forms of asceticism that destroy body, mind, and soul. Hating their dupes, and knowing that the body is meant to be an instrument of enlightenment, they urge them to harm this invaluable gift of God. Besides that, many demonic people are filled with self-loathing and express it through destructive asceticism. Finally, there are those of whom Krishna has said: "These malignant people hate me in their own and in others' bodies" (16:18).

It is with this in mind that Krishna continues:

> Those who practice extreme austerities not ordained by the scriptures, accompanied by hypocrisy and egotism along with the force of desire and passion, senselessly torturing in the body the entire aggregates of the elements, and me within the body, know them to be of demonic resolves (17:5-6).

In every religion we find this in some form, and almost always it is praised and considered a proof of sanctity, although it is actually evidence of delusion and psychosis. This is rampant in India, so much so that I do not even know where to begin or end in recounting it. Since I hope none of you will develop mental illness and become deluded yogis of this type, I will not bother you with further exposition.

But since part of the next chapter of the Gita deals with food, I will name some of the foolish and harmful dietary ideas enjoined by contemporary Indian yogis who should know better, especially in the climatic conditions of India.

Prohibition of salt. Salt is essential to correct brain function. Lack of salt produces mental and physical debility, which is why sensible employers supply salt tablets to workers who perspire a great deal while at their job. One hellish summer I was in Benares and feeling terrible, hardly able to think. I had gone to visit the publishers of the Chowkhamba Sanskrit Series, whose main office was in a sweltering attic. As I sat there feeling like I could die and afraid I was going to pass out, I came to the conclusion that I should leave my fellow travelers in India and return to America and check into a hospital for tests. I really felt that bad. Mercifully there popped into my mind the matter of salt tablets used by workers during extremely hot weather or working conditions. Upon leaving there, I went directly to a drugstore and bought some. That night before sleeping I took several, and awoke in the morning feeling completely well and mentally alert. So from then on I kept salt tablets with me when traveling in India.

Nothing can justify the prohibition of salt except in special medical cases such as high blood pressure, and then it should be made by a qualified medical practitioner. Yet this moronic dictum is to be found in many books on yoga.

Prohibition of chillies. Anywhere in the world, but particularly in a tropical climate like that of India, intestinal parasites are an inevitable problem. And few things are more helpful in eliminating them than chili peppers, especially fresh green ones. Chillies contain a natural form of quinine that is very cleansing for the digestive tract and helps in warding off malaria, another tropical danger. To tell yogis to never eat chillies in any form is irresponsible as well as ignorant.

Prohibition of garlic. Equally nonsensical and irresponsible is the prohibition of garlic. Garlic is the best antibiotic nature has to offer. It cures many ills and destroys intestinal parasites and cleanses the intestines. Large amounts of garlic can be of supreme help at the onset of colds, flu, and other troubles. It is also very beneficial in high blood pressure and insomnia.

Prohibition of onions. Onions purify the blood and tone up the digestive tract. They also enable a person to endure hot weather (raw onions are especially good for this). They are beneficial in every climate, but in India they are especially so. Not only did Sri Ramana Maharshi consider prohibition of onions and garlic silly, he actually wrote a satirical song about his mother's exaggerated aversion to even touching them. Since one of his disciples, Annamalai Swami, was in charge of building in the blistering hot weather, he had him eat so much onions that he reeked of onion and consequently became known in the ashram as "Onion Swami."

Prohibition of all spices or flavorings. This is utterly silly. The spices and other flavorings used in traditional Indian cooking have genuine health benefits. For example, Sri Anandamayi Ma formulated a recipe her devotees called "Anandamayi Kitchuri." For flavoring it contained turmeric, ginger, anise seed, fenugreek seed, cumin seed, plenty of chilis and salt. This was eaten by those who practiced intense sadhana under her direction. Each of those ingredients has a medicinal value, and Ma said that if this was eaten daily as the major item in the diet, they would not become ill. I have eaten some of the food that Ma herself ate daily, and it was hot! Those who had eaten Ma's cooking told me the same. Sri Ramakrishna used to tell those who were cooking for him: "Put in enough spices to make a pig squeal!"

There are those in India that call their food prohibitions "eating sattwic," but Krishna will say in just a few verses that tamasic people like and recommend tasteless food. The idea that the yogi's life is to be bland and boring does not come from real yogis. And that applies to food, as well. Krishna will also point out that sattwic people like flavorful food. As one famous yogi told me: "Boring people like boring food and interesting people like interesting food."

FOOD AND THE THREE GUNAS

The food also liked by each one is threefold, as is sacrifice, tapasya, and almsgiving. Hear the distinction of them (17:7).

It is interesting that these three things are major indicators of the dominant guna of an individual.

Sattwic food

Foods increasing life, purity, strength, health, happiness, cheerfulness, flavorful, smooth, firm and substantial are liked by the sattwic (17:8).

Since we are seeking to become increasingly sattwic, we should look at each point of this verse so we can improve our diet and increase our sattwa, remembering that food becomes mind according to the Chandogya Upanishad. "Food when eaten becomes threefold, its coarsest portion becomes the faeces; its middle (portion) flesh, and its subtlest (portion) mind... Thus, my dear, mind consists of food" (6.5.1, 4). "Of the curd, my dear, when churned, that which is subtle moves upwards, it becomes butter. In the same manner, my dear, of the food that is eaten, that which is subtle moves upwards, it becomes mind. Thus, my dear, mind consists of food" (6.6.1,2, 5).

Ayus–food that actually increases the span of life. In other words, truly healthy food that protects the body and fosters it. The problem is that everybody has their own idea about what kind of food is healthy. I recommend that you read Dr. Neal Barnard's books on diet, starting with *Food For Life*. Also T. Colin Campbell's *The China Study*. But the absolute best books on diet and health are *How Not To Die* and *How Not To Diet,* by Dr. Michael GregerMost people are slowly killing themselves with wrong diet. If they do not shorten their life, they make sure that they are sick for years at the end of their life. Ayus also means what increases life force.

Sattwa–food that increases the quality of sattwa, which also implies food that promotes virtue, both in the sense of strength and in the sense of goodness. It is food that lightens and promotes health of body and mind, food that is actually spiritual in its effect. This is purely vegan food, free of both animal and chemical elements.

Bala–food that imparts strength to the body and mind.

Arogya–food that strengthens the immune system so the body can resist or rid itself of disease.

Sukha–food which is easy for the body to digest and which produces ease and comfort in the body.

Priti–food that truly satisfies the body nutritionally, and therefore the mind. It need not be eaten like medicine. In fact, priti is that which gives actual pleasure in the eating.

Rasyas–food which has abundant good flavor, that has plenty of taste.

Snigdhas–food which contains sufficient oil, which is smooth and pleasant to eat.

Sthiras–food which is substantial.

Hridyas–food which is hearty, satisfying and pleasant-feeling in the stomach.

This is a valuable checklist to help us eat truly sattwic food.

Rajasic food

> Foods that are pungent, sour, salty, excessively hot, harsh, astringent and burning, producing pain, grief, and disease are liked by the rajasic (17:9).

Kata–food that is extremely acrid, pungent, or sharp–that is virtually caustic to the mouth.

Amla–food that is very acidic, sour, or vinegary.

Lavana–food that is very salty or briny (containing pickle-type fluid). This is hard on the kidneys and raises the blood pressure.

Atyushna–food that is excessively hot. The problem here is deciding what is excessive, for the more people eat hot food the more tolerance they develop, until what will be painfully burning hot to others will be mild to their taste. I knew a man who would sit and eat jalapeño peppers whole like a snack. When I asked if they were hot, he said No. So I bit into one. Volcano!

Tikshna–food that is harsh, fiery, and acid, especially in the stomach.

Raksha–food that is astringent, and also rough and dry, the kind of things that cut the roof of your mouth or even your esophagus as it goes down.

Vidahinas–food that is burning and scorching.

The results

This kind of food is productive of:

Duhkha–pain and discomfort or stress.

Shoka–misery: that regret so many feel and which makes anti-acid manufacturers rich, and which contributes to ulcers.

Amaya–sickness in the sense of malfunction and disease produced by the harming it does to the body.

Next to its harmful effects, the more unfortunate aspect of this kind of food is its addicting nature. So rajasic food is the most difficult kind to give up.

Tamasic food

> That which is stale, tasteless, putrid, leftover to the next day, uchchishta [the remnants of food eaten by others; actual leavings from someone's plate] and impure, is the food the tamasic like (17:10).

Yatayamam–food that is leftover, stale, and even spoiled. A lot of people eat this kind of food just from laziness or lack of initiative–both traits of tamas. Most chain restaurant food is unfit for human consumption, what to say about the "deli" food from big grocery stores. No one knows how old that is. Fast food chains pack their food–especially meat–in bags of formaldehyde and other horrors. Some people will cook a large amount of food and then eat it for a week or more. I have known people that would scrape off the mold and eat away. Much canned food is another offense to humanity. The willingness to eat stale food–and sometimes the inability to tell it is stale–is more psychological than physical, and we must not let misapplied thrift get us into the habit of eating this devitalized food. Since there was no refrigeration in ancient India, no food was considered fit to eat if it sat overnight. However, now that we can refrigerate and even freeze food, the eating of leftovers is not always detrimental.

Gatarasam–food that is tasteless, devoid of flavor. This description applies to a lot of "sattwic" food cooked by those that think they are spiritual or even yogis. It is flavorless and insubstantial, and often has a displeasing color and texture. And on top of it all they give people a little dab, commenting: "This is really pretty rich [or heavy] and you mustn't eat too much." Some chance! The last time I had to eat in the home of such dedicated, grim and rote people, the amount served for eight people would only have sufficed for three normal human beings. Their tasteless and insufficient food reflected their philosophy and their minds.

Puti–food that is putrid, stinking, and fetid. How many times have you seen restaurant signs or ads boasting that they serve aged steaks? It is the custom of "gourmets" to "hang" birds and let them decay a bit before cooking them. I read of one restaurant that would "hang" grouse until they bred maggots, which they would wash off before cooking. One evening a group of customers called for the chef and rhapsodized over the delicious "stuffing" that had been in the grouse. At first the chef was bewildered, and then realized that the maggots had not been removed, but had been baked in the grouse! This is a clear example of how tamasic food perverts the palate.

Meat itself is rotting flesh. And what of the moldy and "stinky" cheese so beloved to many? Think of the awful smell fish and seafood emit when being cooked, what to say of the stench in oriental markets that stock them dried? Delight in such things is distinctly abnormal. Do I need to mention such ghastly things as "hundred year old" eggs and suchlike?

Uchchistam–food that has been eaten on by another person. This is a favorite of many. They grab off the plates of others, plop things from their plates on others' plates, say: "Give me a taste of that" and take a bite off whatever someone has been eating (often a body part of an animal). Eating another's spit! In modern times when we know about germs and communicable diseases, it makes no difference to them. "Give me a sip of that... tear off a hunk of that for me... let me have a little bite of your...." This is the way they feed. It is also a way they take the life energies of others and give to them their unhealthy or diseased energies.

Drink

The description of tamasic food applies to drink, as well, the rajasic and tamasic loving fermented, alcoholic liquids, and being addicted to every form of poisonous soft drink.

A missing element

At the time of Krishna refined sugar in any form was unknown, so it is not on the list. It may be disguised as rajasic in elaborate and ingenious forms of sweet things, but its destructive nature makes it tamasic, though there is a good case for arguing that it should not even be listed as food, but poison.

Even more

These principles can be applied to every aspect of our life, not just to food. Society, religion, personalities, modes of life–just about everything can be classified with the traits of the food Krishna has described. We really *are* what we *eat*, and *eat* what we *are*, even metaphysically speaking.

RELIGION AND THE THREE GUNAS

Whenever the word "sacrifice" is used in the Gita it covers the entire range of spiritual practice and spiritual life in general. In the following verses ritualistic worship–and no doubt the fire sacrifice–is certainly referred to, but it applies in the wider sense, as well.

Sattwa

> Sacrifice which is offered, observing the scriptures, by those who do not desire the fruits, concentrating the mind only on the thought: "This is to be offered;" that is sattwic (17:11).

Sattwa alone leads to liberation, so it is wise to order our spiritual life according to its traits as listed here.

First, we are told that sattwic spiritual life is lived according to the principles of the scriptures. This includes the teachings and counsels of those who have attained higher consciousness. It is necessary for us who have not traveled the path to consider the advice of those who have successfully traversed it. We need not be slavish or idolatrous about any scripture or teaching, but we need to seriously consider the words of those who have been inspired from within to lead humanity toward higher life. Mary Baker Eddy very aptly called such persons Way-Showers. This implies a very practical attitude toward them: they are not gods or absolute authorities, but they show the way to succeed in spiritual life. They are not interested in imparting a philosophy, but in showing us how to attain the highest consciousness.

Just as a person experienced and skilled in something can teach others, so do they. It is always a clear matter of cause and effect. It either works or it does not. Belief, obedience, or "surrender" have absolutely nothing to do with it. At all times it is according to the judgment of the seeker. Sometimes we have to follow a path to find out for ourself if it works. And nothing is sadder than those who spend years getting nowhere, yet clinging to a worthless discipline because they have committed themselves to it or, even worse, have entered into some pathological personal compact (including a supposed guru-disciple relationship) that enslaves them and blinds them to the evidently valueless character of that path or association. Most unfortunate of all are those who are bound and blinded by "love" for the teacher or group that is stagnating and devastating their lives and hearts. "Loyalty" and "attunement" is the slave-collar about their neck.

Next we are told that spiritual life is not engaged in for personal gain in the external sense, but rather as an offering to the Divine both within and without. Such a way of life is not engaged in for any other motive than being in harmony with the cosmic order the ancient sages of India called *Ritam*. Truly spiritual people live a spiritual life because it is according to their true nature. They are expressing their inmost being. They are not trying to become something, but are moving out of darkness into the light so they can know what they really are: to behold their eternal Self, that which Buddhists call the Original Nature. Real spiritual life is not loading ourselves with an array of spiritual paraphernalia, but divesting ourselves of all that is not us.

Rajas

> But sacrifice which is offered with a view for the fruit and for the purpose of ostentation, know that to be rajasic (17:12).

This pretty well describes nearly all the religious or spiritual life of human beings. Those who are interested in the good will or admiration of man and God, and hope to receive whatever they desire in return for their religiosity, are in the grip of the rajasic ego. Ultimately it leads nowhere but back to more rebirth and confusion.

Tamas

> Sacrifice devoid of faith, disregarding the scriptures, with no food offered, without mantras, without gift or fee is declared to be tamasic (17:13).

Sometimes we have to pay attention to ignorance to figure out the ways of wisdom. And that is the case here regarding tamasic religion. This is a very full picture of deluded and confused "spirituality," and we need to look at it so we can avoid it.

Sacrifice devoid of faith. The first quality of tamasic religion listed is *shraddhavirahitam*–devoid of faith or having abandoned faith. To really understand this, we must remember that as mentioned before shraddha is not mere intellectual belief, but an interior, intuitive conviction that arises as an enlivening of the inner intelligence of an individual. In other words, a religion of shraddha is a religion that is spiritually alive, and therefore inwardly perceptive. In the sixth chapter of the Gita we have this description of one who has this divine shraddha: "The yogi... having become one with Brahman,... easily touching Brahman,... I am not lost to him, and he is not lost to me" (6:27-28, 30). This is the religion we should seek, realizing that it can be hinted at outwardly, but can only be achieved inwardly. As Jesus said (Luke 17:21): "The kingdom of God is within you"–actually *is* you.

Contrary to the scriptures. The word used here is very interesting: *vidhi-hinam*–which means both "lacking scriptures" and "discarding scriptures." Krishna is implying here that scriptures are necessary for real spiritual life. However, in the East any book that contains wisdom is considered a scripture, even if it was written this morning. So Krishna is speaking of the wisdom of enlightened teachers that have been put into words and set down for our help in pursuing spiritual life.

He is also referring to a spiritual tradition—not narrow and sectarian, but a tradition, nonetheless. In the West we tend wisely to shy away from tradition because of the deadly ignorance in the West of those who boast of being traditional. But in the East tradition is always subject to intelligent scrutiny and is never a matter of "the book says it, so I believe it." Most important, authentic spiritual tradition is understood to be verifiable by each seeker for himself. In the West many are satisfied with intellectual jugglery and argumentation, but in the East it is practical experience that is sought. Whenever I quote a scripture in my writings I certainly think of it as lending authority to what I have to say, but I also use quotations simply because the scriptures say it so much better than I can.

Tamasic religion is that which has no authentic scripture(s), no viable tradition(s). It may either be the shallow and flimsy "make up my own" whimsical kind, or a religion burdened with fantasy and lies claiming to be God's latest revelation to the world. Either way, its characteristic is the darkness, confusion, and delusion of tamas.

On the other hand, some tamasic religion may have a great deal of scriptures in which true wisdom is to be found, but the leaders and adherents prefer to ignore the wisdom and subvert the teaching to suit their own fancy. So while adulating the scriptures they really cast them aside. Consider the way nearly every religion manages to condone spiritually poisonous behavior and thought, wresting the scriptures to not only approve, but often to advocate them. Almost no religion is free from this, as anyone with open-eyed experience and observation will know. Often the divine light of holy wisdom is completely covered by the evil and untruth of a religion's popular form.

Finally, *vidhihinam* can also simply mean "without knowledge (vidya)" or "discarding (ignoring) knowledge." In other words, ignorant and ineffectual religion that boasts of its "faith" since it has no substance or reality. Today we find many religious currents in the world that were born in ignorance, and went on from there to greater ignorance. There are also religions that started out with authentic spiritual knowledge, with true spiritual revelation, but turned away from it in order to gain power and wealth. This is especially the case with state religions, or those that used to be state religions. Having remodeled their spiritual structure to suit their governing patrons, they lost their original value and often the patronage, as well. Christianity is the latest and most blatant example of this.

With no food offered. Asrishtannam means food that is either not offered, or is not shared out after the offering. This is an important part in Eastern religion of whatever kind. There is always offering of food which is then distributed to those present—usually in the form of an abundant feast. But the selfish refuse to do so, and their religion becomes one of taking but not giving. This is the mark of any cult—old or new.

Without mantras. First, there is the mantra known as the *sankalpa* which is recited at the beginning of any ritual, stating its purpose and dedication. Its absence would indicate religion that is vague, even purposeless, performed in a rote way simply for the doing of it, or religion whose real purpose is not at all grasped, and is therefore meaningless. But *mantrahinam* is like *vidhihinam*; it has the dual meaning of "without mantra" or "disregarding mantra." This indicates religion that is without order or legitimacy, and especially religion that is without power, for power (effectiveness) is the fundamental characteristic of mantra. So we are looking at a religion that never had any spiritual power, or has come to discard and even deny that power. It can also be applied to the adherents of a religion that does have power and knowledge, but regarding which they are either ignorant or indifferent.

Without gift [given to the officiants]. Adakshinam simply means "without fee" or voluntary offering. This means a religion in which the members engage in take-but-not-give policy, the obverse side of the type where the religion itself only demands and takes. Such religion is proud of the fact that it expects nothing of its adherents, and they are proud of that, too. "Our religion is democratic," they boast. "You don't need to do anything you don't want to." They confuse democracy with anarchy. It is certainly true that in worthy religion the members are not coerced or cajoled in any way. But people that want to avoid all involvement, commitment, or investment of time and thought are unworthy of such a religion and will never benefit from it until they change their outlook.

Such religion often denies the fact of priesthood or hierarchical realities, refusing to recognize that some people may be more spiritually skilled or knowledgeable than others. Such religion revels in a kind of egalitarianism that suppresses anything but lock-step standardization and mediocrity. "The priesthood of all believers" sounds nice, but it often masks ineffectiveness and repression.

Adakshinam also indicates a kind of selfish materialism that hates expenditure of time, effort, or even money on religion. My great-aunt Lou Maxey not only never put anything in the collection plate, she would grimly shake her head No whenever it came by her! But she was one of the first to head to the back of the church to get a free copy of the weekly church magazine. Deadbeat religion is nothing new.

At the opposite pole are the saints–that is why they *are* saints. As Mirabai, the great poet/musician saint of India wrote: "I have sold everything in the marketplace of this world and bought my Khanaia (Krishna). Some laugh at me and say the price was too great, and some say that the price was too small. But Mira only knows that it was everything she had."

Tamasic religion really has no genuine perception at all–it is only obscurity and confusion. However, there are degrees of tamas (as with the other gunas, as well), and we can encounter people who have no faith in their religion because they dimly intuit that it is nonsense. But, being tamasic–one quality of which is inertia–they stay with it and go through the motions although knowing it means nothing. Here, too, we find religions that once had a mystical aspect, but jettisoned it for material gain or from spiritual blindness resulting from impurity and dullness of heart. There are individuals that are the same. For whatever reason, they blind themselves to the insights they once had and become wanderers in the fog along with so many others. I have seen people do this for various reasons, but the result was always the same: inner death. And I have never seen one regain what they willfully cast aside. Rebirth alone will restore it to them, and after how long a struggle?

The whole subject of tamasic religion is certainly gloomy, but spiritual adults know they have to acknowledge a lot of facts that are not pretty or pleasant, just as in material life unpleasant realities must be faced. The up side of the whole thing is that having given careful consideration to the matter we can avoid slipping into its ways and ourselves losing our inner vision.

The wise traveller knows both the right and the wrong roads.

Tapasya and the Three Gunas

Tapasya is practical (i.e., result-producing) spiritual discipline. Literally it means the generation of heat or energy, referring to spiritual practice and its effect, especially the roasting of karmic seeds, the burning up of karma. It also refers to the heat necessary for the hatching of an egg. Without tapasya there is no significant spiritual progress. So Krishna tells us of three levels of tapasya as well as its characterization according to the dominant guna of the persons engaging in tapasya.

Tapasya of the body

> **Reverence for the gods, the twice-born [dwijas], teachers and the wise; purity, straightforwardness, brahmacharya and non-injury: these are called tapasya of the body (17:14).**

Reverence (pujanam) is internal, so why does it come first in the list of physical tapasya? Because Krishna is not thinking of mere philosophizing or abstraction–empty words. He is thinking of action, of kriya, which creates positive karma in the form of purification and enlightenment. Puja is the word usually translated worship, and some translators use it rather than reverence. Worship in Krishna's view is not mere verbal praise or glorification, but a living out of the interior attitude of reverence. As Jesus once asked: "Why call ye me, Lord, Lord, and do not the things which I say?"

(Luke 6:46) So to reverence a spiritual authority is not to flatter, grovel, and promote them or shower them with money and gifts. Rather, it is faithfully and seriously applying their teachings. Krishna speaks of four kinds who deserve our reverence: gods, twice-born, teachers, and wise men.

Devas are gods–not the Supreme God, but highly evolved beings who can affect our life. We might think of them as angels or saints, bodiless beings that interact with humans and help them in many ways. All viable religions have some form of devas.

The dwijas are the "twice-born." Often this term applies to those who have undergone the upanayanam ritual and received the sacred thread (yajnopavita) and instruction in the Gayatri mantra, but here a wider sense is meant. The twice-born are those who have awakened inwardly, whose consciousness has been quickened and is continuing to expand. Such persons may not be perfectly enlightened, but if they are ahead of us in evolution they deserve our respect and can benefit us by their experience.

Teachers have even more experience and are qualified to give spiritual instruction and guide their students in their spiritual practice and development. These are valuable, indeed.

But most valuable are the sages (prajna), those that are fully awakened, totally conscious, knowing themselves and the Absolute. To be with them is to be with God and to receive the bounty of God. To find such a rare being is the highest good fortune if his company is cultivated and his teaching scrupulously followed.

Now here is an interesting question: Since the list ascends in spiritual excellence, why were devas/gods at the bottom of the list? Because there is no substitute for contact with living, breathing human beings that are examples of the ideals we should pursue. More importantly, it is easy to fantasize and believe we are in contact with high spiritual beings when it is all a projection of our minds. Even worse, we can be duped by the entities known as tramp souls or astral trash that are always ready to show up and claim to be everyone from our grandfather, to Abraham Lincoln, to Krishna, Buddha, or Jesus. It is important to have as teacher an honest human being that will be truthful to us regarding whether or not we are practicing correctly and progressing as a consequence. The ego may not like it, but the spirit will be liberated. That is why Vyasa, the greatest sage of India, sent his son Sukadeva to King Janaka of Mithila for spiritual instruction, rather than teaching him himself. This was necessary so the father and son egos could not intrude themselves and prevent absolute honesty from prevailing.

Krishna has presented us with four disciplines that are necessary for physical tapasya: purity (shaucha), rectitude (arjavam), celibacy (brahmacharya), and non-violence (ahimsa). Here is how *A Brief Sanskrit Glossary* defines them:

Arjavam: Straightforwardness; honesty; rectitude (from the verb root rinj: "to make straight."

Ahimsa: Non-injury in thought, word, and deed; non-violence; non-killing; harmlessness.

Shaucha: Purity; cleanliness.

Brahmacharya: Continence; self-restraint on all levels; discipline.

We must realize that Krishna is presenting us with a total package. To lack a single one of the elements listed in this verse is to lack in physical tapasya.

Tapasya of speech

> Speech which causes no distress or vexation, truthful, pleasant, beneficial, instruction in the knowledge of the Self: these are called tapasya of speech (17:15).

Anudvegakaram vakyam, has three meanings: 1) speech that does not cause distress; 2) speech that does not overawe; 3) speech that does not cause apprehension. And it means all three.

First, it is speech that does not cause the hearer to feel anxious or coerced, to feel that he must do what he is told or dire things will result. Such speech makes him feel that doom is hanging over him, and that the speaker–or his ideas–alone can avert disaster. Such speech disturbs the hearer's peace of mind, making him feel pressured.

Second, it is speech that does not make the hearer feel minimized, disempowered, and insignificant. It does not make him feel that the biggers and betters know what is right, not him, and that if he does not do what they say is right then he is bad, even evil. He does not dare to contradict or deny what they say. Often, he does not even question or rebel against such bullying, but bows his head and complies and conforms.

Third, it is speech that does not cause fear. Sadly, fear and greed are the prime motivators of most human beings. So fear is used on all sides by those that intend to make profit from the duped person, whether it be advertising, medicine, politics, ecology, health, religion or social pressures. The many-headed monster of fear has been shaping humanity from its beginning.

Of course, this all overlaps. The three aspects cross-pollinate one another. As I have mentioned, in the final analysis negative speech is a form of coercion, of bullying. And it comes into every aspect of our life, though it is popular and safe to attribute it to religion exclusively.

Satyam is speech that is absolutely true, both from a factual standpoint and from the reality of things. Satyam leads to ultimate truth when practiced uncompromisingly. Satyam reveals the truth of things, and never implies anything false or veiled. Satyam is plain and straightforward.

Priya is speech that is agreeable and pleasant, even kindly and endearing.

Hitam is that which is beneficial and wholesome. So it is informative and improves the status of its hearers–if they listen. It is not trivial chitchat and small talk. It makes the hearer better for the hearing.

Swadhyayabhyasanam is the practice of study of oneself (self-analysis). This is not imposed on the aspirant, it is a voluntary thing altogether. It must be altogether self-motivated, coming from no other source than an awakening consciousness

All of this is tapasya of speech–speech that includes the exercise of thought and intelligence.

Tapasya of mind

> Tranquility of mind, kindliness, silence, self-control and purity of the mental state: these are called tapasya of the mind (17:16).

Sri Ramakrishna often said: "the mind is everything," so this is of extreme importance.

Manaprasada means a mind that is peaceful, clear, calm, and of a positive disposition towards others.

Saumyatwam, means gentleness, benevolence, and mildness.

Maunam is silence in the sense of stillness, or absence of mental chatter. In such positive silence intuition manifests and dominates, imparting a knowing that is beyond mere talk.

Atmavinigraha, is self-restraint, self-control. It is not mere discipline, but real mastery of the mind—and therefore of the entire being.

Bhavasamshuddi is purity of the state of being, including the entire state of mind and heart.

What Krishna describes is a state, a condition, of the mind, not a veneer of speech and action that may mask just the opposite of what he describes. As my beloved friend, Swami Sivananda, put on the wall of the satsang hall as a motto and had printed on pencils he gave out: BE good; DO good. First we must be what we aspire to; then we can act truthfully and positively. In the West we continually get cause and effect reversed, thinking that if we act and speak in a certain way it will make us what we appear to be. That is terribly wrong. We must get to the root of things, to the consciousness of which the mind is an instrument. We must practice tapasya of mind.

Sattwic tapasya

> **This threefold tapasya practiced with the highest faith by those without desire for fruits and steadfast, is considered to be sattwic (17:17).**

There are some key words we should look at in this verse to appreciate its profound meaning.

Shraddhaya paraya, highest faith, means *mumukshutwa*: intense desire or yearning for liberation (moksha). This is the sole basis for sattwic tapasya, the primary trait of a sattwic spiritual aspirant.

Although tapasya accomplishes many things in the life and mind of a tapaswin (one who engages in tapasya), not the least of them is intense purification and opening of higher faculties of awareness. All those aspects of sattwic tapasya are but the means to the single end: liberation of the spirit. Thus it is called *aphalakankshibhir*–without desire for personal gain (fruit) in the egoic sense, though of course moksha is the supreme attainment (paramartha).

Such an aspirant is then described as *yuktaih*–always "in yoga," through the continual fixing of the mind upon the Highest.

Such are the sattwic, and such is sattwic tapasya.

Rajasic tapasya

Tapasya which is practiced with hypocrisy to gain acceptance, honor and reverence, is declared to be rajasic, unstable, and transitory (17:18).

Three words are used in the first line:

Satkara, which means honor, reverence, favor, or hospitality. Literally, it means "good-doing," so it implies that the rajasic tapaswin wants to be thought well of in general, which of course will result in the four meanings just listed. *Mana*, which means honor and respect. *Puja*, which usually is translated as "worship," but can also mean reverence akin to worship. In India they basically go together. Guru puja is quite common, and almost as common is the claim of disciples that their guru is really an avatar, a divine incarnation. This is carried to absurd lengths all the time. Contrary to Buddha's assertions, many contemporary Indian teachers are fingers pointing to themselves–not to the goal of nirvana.

Dambhena means fraudulent and hypocritical. Such people supposedly engage in extreme ascetic actions and continually have the most exalted experiences. But when you look closer it is all puff and patter. They do nothing but sit around being adored and toadying to the rich and the influential, occasionally emitting a string of platitudes whose banality is astonishing–but not as amazing as the mindless plaudits of their admirers.

Swami Sri Yukteswar, the guru of Paramhansa Yogananda, continually cautioned people to never believe the claims made about yogis, especially the claims made by their disciples. Rather, he counseled them to carefully examine matters for themselves. As a young man he heard of a yogi who always slept in a state of levitation. So he hid under the yogi's bed and waited. Nothing but snores. So he crawled from under the bed and said in a loud voice: "I don't see any levitation—only sleep!" The yogi woke up, and to cover himself shouted: "I wondered why I did not levitate tonight as usual. You were spying on me!" The young Priya Nath merely laughed and went his way, not impressed by the declaration.

Pious hypocrisy is common coin of the crowd-pleaser. It is a favorite ploy in India to claim that you spent decades doing intense tapasya in the Himalayas. I personally know one Big Baba of Bengal who claims he spent over twenty years in the Himalayas, when investigation easily shows that he was a building contractor in Calcutta all the time! Swami Sivananda humorously wrote some instruction for these people. First, he said, rent a little house (kutir) in Rishikesh or Hardwar for six months. Arrange to have your food brought to you, and never be seen by anybody. Sit around inside and do what you like, including a lot of sleep. During that time write two or three "trash leaflets" (his expression) and a couple of bad devotional songs (bhajans). Then at the end of the six months go down to the plains and put it out that you have been living in silence (mauna) for many years way up in the Himalayas, even beyond Uttar Kashi. Arrange for yourself a few meetings where you will talk aimlessly, sing your bad songs, and give out your worthless leaflets. In no time at all you will be a sought-after guru, and maybe even an avatar.

This is no idle allegation. Once in Rishikesh I was stopped and grilled by a fairly well-educated "sadhu" who begged me to tell him how to get to America and make a splash. On another occasion in holy Naimisharanya a monk told me that if I would spend a few hours with him each day for a week, "I will show you how to get the people of America in the palm of your hand." And he even held up the palm of his hand as he said it. That is how these people think. Rajasic is too nice a word for it.

Krishna winds up the subject by saying that rajasic tapasya, besides its obvious flaws, is worthless because it is *chalam*—unsteady and wavering—and *adhruvam*—impermanent, infirm, and unfixed. This is because rajas by its nature is restless and changing. A rajasic person does not hold single-mindedly to anything for long. Therefore any tapasya will be impermanent, especially because it is not oriented toward the unchanging and ever-existent Absolute, but rather toward the ever-changing and unsteady ego-dream.

Tamasic tapasya

> Tapasya which is practiced with deluded notions of the Self, and self-torture, or for the purpose of harming another, is declared to be tamasic (17:19).

There is a lot to look at here, and all unpleasant. But the result will be positive.

Mudhagrahenatmano means with deluded or confused understanding or concept of the Atman, the Self. This is a crucial point. For if there is no right understanding of the nature of our Self, we will do a great deal of foolish and pointless things. This is true of religion in general. In Sanatana Dharma alone is there a clear understanding of the Atman-Self. And if you do not even know who or what you are, how can you even live life in a sensible manner? Most people do not. What kind of religion can we have if we have no clue as to what we really are? Any discipline will be as mistaken as our ideas about ourself. This is why most religion is destructive, as are the disciplines—or lack thereof.

When people mistake their physical and psychic makeup for their Self, they cannot help but misunderstand what is really needed for spiritual life, and will waste their time to no purpose, ultimately harming themselves. Such persons will often engage in *padaya*—torture or torment. They will torture the body with strenuous and painful actions, even mutilating it or hastening its death by injury to its health. Ritual mutilation is often practiced on their own bodies by those engaged in negative ascesis. Or just the opposite: they will harm the body through deluded indulgence and lack of discipline or purification. But most of all they will torment their Self by burying it beneath ignorant ideas and actions, clouding and distorting their minds so there is no hope of comprehending true spiritual matters or disciplines. They will live a life contrary to their real spirit-nature, and thus bring nothing but suffering to themselves and others.

Finally, tamasic tapasya is sometimes engaged in as a kind of evil magical practice whose intention is to gain the power to harm another, or to placate negative entities who will do the harming on behalf of the tapaswin. I am sorry to say that this is found in India even to this day. I know of a "sadhu" who lives in a temple in Kerala and does incredibly complex and strenuous disciplines to get such power. This man was once hired to bring about the death of a friend of mine, supposedly through placation of a "deity." Fortunately a letter from this evil man to the one hiring him was missent to my friend, who spiritually armed himself and came to no harm.

The expression used for this in the text is *parasyotsadanartham*, which means the destruction of another, but it can also mean for the overturning or defeat of another. This is often the aim of such tapasya: either the unseating of a person in authority or advantage, or the bringing about of his loss of money, position, or reputation.

Sometimes tapasya is engaged in just to be thought "more ascetic than thou" in relation to others engaged in spiritual discipline. A kind of ascetic one-upmanship and rivalry is often found among monastics of all religions. This was especially the case in Christian monasticism in the Egyptian desert during the third century (and after) when enough time had lapsed for the Church to have greatly forgotten what Jesus had really taught about spiritual life and discipline. Regarding this, in his book, *Benedictine Monachism*, Dom Cuthbert Butler wrote:

"The spirit, the dominating principle of this monachism, may be thus characterized. It was a spirit of individualism. Each worked for his personal advance in virtue; each strove to do his utmost in all kinds of ascetical exercises and austerities, in prolonging his fasts, his prayers, his silence. The favorite name to describe any of the prominent monks was 'great athlete.' And they were athletes, and filled with the spirit of the modern athlete. They loved to 'make a record' in austerities, and to contend with one another in mortifications; and they would freely boast of their spiritual achievements. One who had seen them describes the Nitrian monks as 'surpassing one another in virtues, and being filled with a spirit of rivalry in asceticism, showing forth all virtue, and striving to outdo one another in manner of life.' But it is in Palladius' account of Macarius of Alexandria that this spirit shows itself most conspicuously: 'If he ever heard of any one having performed a work of asceticism, he was all on fire to do the same;" and Palladius illustrates it by examples. Did Macarius hear that another monk ate nothing but one pound of bread a day? For three years he ate each day only what broken bread he could extract in a single handful through the narrow neck of a jar. Did he hear that the monks of Pachomius' monastery ate nothing cooked by fire throughout Lent? He did the same for seven years. Did he hear that their observance was ""great""? He did not rest satisfied till he had gone to see, and had beaten them all.' Thus the practice of asceticism constituted a predominant feature of this type of Egyptian monachism. Their prolonged fasts and vigils, their combats with sleep, their exposures to heat and cold, their endurance of thirst and bodily fatigue, their loneliness and silence, are features that constantly recur in the authentic records of the lives of these hermits, and they looked on such austerities as among the essential features of the monastic state." Much more crazy things were (and are) done, but this is sufficient for us to get the idea–and hopefully avoid it.

In conclusion

Krishna has given us all this information so we can determine the type and quality (guna) of our personal spiritual practice. This alone would make the Gita unparalleled in value for those who seek the higher life. And it contains so much more.

All glory be to Sri Vyasadeva, the supreme guide of all who aspire to liberation!

CHARITY AND THE THREE GUNAS

The Bhagavad Gita is a digest and clarification of the Upanishads, and is essentially inseparable from them. In the Brihadaranyaka Upanishad it says that once the Creator, Prajapati, spoke a single syllable, "Da," to his human disciples. "Then he said: 'Have you understood?' They answered, 'Yes, we have understood. You said to us, ""Datta–Be charitable."'" 'Yes,' agreed Prajapati, 'you have understood.'" (Brihadaranyaka Upanishad 5:2:2) So *Dana*, which means: giving, gift, charity, almsgiving, self-sacrifice, donation, and generosity, is both an action and an attitude. Krishna considers this an important factor in spiritual life, one which we will profit from understanding. Once more he analyzes a subject from the aspect of its guna-quality.

Sattwic Dana

> That gift which is given with the thought: "It is to be given," to a worthy person, one who has done no prior favor to the giver, in a proper place at a proper time: that gift is considered sattwic (17:20).

This is extremely relevant to us, since at the present time good works and social action are becoming the refuge of the morally and spiritually bankrupt as a cover for their inner deficiency. As is to be expected, ignorant people who think that outer action equals inner quality, are enthusiastically embracing and applauding this fraud. Yogis, too, from both their good will and the sincerity–often simplicity–of their hearts may unsuspectingly run in this track as well. For discrimination (viveka) is often mistaken for cynicism, and is sure to be denounced by the deceivers and the deceived. Delusion is always favored by the deluded. Krishna's outline of sattwic dana will not at all be compatible with their fantasies–and that will be a pretty good indication that it is true and worthy of our attention.

Given with the thought: "it is to be given." This implies that it is not only right to give in a moral sense, but that it is a requisite for acting in harmony with cosmic law. It is not an option, but a necessity–at least for those seeking to climb up the evolutionary ladder through cooperation with universal law. This has many aspects, not the least being that charity is a powerful antidote to negative karmas accrued through past greed, selfishness and hard-hearted refusal to help others. It also heals the mind scarred by callous and cruel indifference to the needs of others.

Given to a worthy person. Patre means someone who is worthy or competent, a person who is deserving and capable of benefiting from the gift or assistance. Sattwic charity itself must be worthy and competent. That is, it must be intelligent and effective, helping people not just for the moment, but for the future. Sattwic charity is not just "need driven" on the surface, but must take into account the entire situation and be very focused on the quality of the recipients and the ultimate results. For example, it is silly to provide roller skates for poor children when they do not have any shoes. Just recently I heard a brag ad on radio about many teenagers working hard to provide cosmetic surgery for poor people. While people are starving and wandering the streets homeless, this is absurd. It is like dropping candy bars to people in the desert that are dying of thirst. Get them out and give them water. This is the sattwic way. Of course, sattwic charity requires personal contact and care, something that so many are not willing to provide. They want it all done by agencies to which they contribute.

At a proper place. The environment of the recipient must be taken into careful consideration. It would be silly to give aid to someone living on an island where atomic testing is scheduled, and not help them to relocate.

Sattwic charity is much more than the equivalent of impulse buying that is the vogue right now.

In all religious traditions, dana is considered a powerful spiritual, mental, and even physical therapy. A perfect example of this is in the life of Saint John Regis. He transformed the lives of countless thousands through the spiritual counseling he gave in the confessional. Once he had been invited to an out-of-the-way place, and even though deep snow had fallen he insisted on traveling on foot to keep his promise to the people there. On the way he fell and broke his leg. Finding a stick to help him move, and holding to the shoulder of a fellow-traveller, he actually went on and kept his appointment. Upon arrival he immediately went to the church and into the confessional, despite the protests from those around him. Many hours later, after having uninterruptedly heard confessions, he agreed to be examined by a doctor, who found that the leg was perfectly healed!

Rajasic dana

> But that gift which is given with the aim of recompense, or with regard to the giving's fruit, or is given reluctantly, is considered rajasic (17:21).

One of the major determinants in religion is disposition of heart. God told the prophet Samuel: "The Lord seeth not as man seeth; for man looketh on the outward appearance, but the Lord looketh on the heart" (I Samuel 17:21). Therefore Krishna points out in this and the next verse that the inner attitude of the giver reveals the predominant quality (guna) of the act. To give grudgingly or unwillingly is a rajasic attitude. A great deal of religion is not done willingly, but out of fear, greed, or other egoic motives. Since rajas is the guna of action for gain of some kind, he then says that any gift that is made with the purpose of getting some personal benefit, looking for the final result, is of rajas.

As a consequence it would not be amiss to wonder if the giving described in the previous verse as sattwic is not really rajasic? For doing the right also produces a benefit which is surely desired by the sattwic individual. The answer is both yes and no. Certainly the sattwic person wants to attain and maintain the "to be done" attitude which tends toward his personal liberation, but the focus of such a desire is the transcendent Self, whereas the focus and motivator of the rajasic desire is the transient ego. So they are of vastly differing quality. Further, the sattwic person is thinking of the persons to be helped, but the rajasic is thinking of himself. The sattwic man is unselfish, the rajasic man is selfish. They are poles apart.

Another form of rajasic dana is that which is done to control the recipients. Religions often engage in this to buy converts. Missionaries, Christian and Moslem, do this in all third world countries quite shamelessly, even proudly.

Tamasic dana

> The gift which is given at the wrong place or time, to unworthy persons, without respect or with disdain, is declared to be tamasic (17:22).

An unworthy person is someone who will not benefit from the gift (or assistance), either because of innate incapacity or perverse attitude, or who will deny being benefitted, or who demands something different or more. We all have seen this to some extent. An unworthy person is also one who does not even need the gift, but pretends to. So is one who is quite capable of helping himself, but sees no need to if someone will do it for him.

It is virtually impossible to expand on what is meant by "the wrong place" and "the wrong time," since each individual situation determines—and often reveals—that.

"Without paying respect, or with contempt" can be either hidden or obvious. I have personally known people involved in welfare programs that thoroughly despised the people they were distributing bounty to, and as a result being adored by them as their personal great White Father or Mother. How ironic. I have heard people make utterly contemptuous remarks about the people they were going to go out and "make nice" to, even getting tearful with fake "caring" for those they denigrated. On the other hand, many tamasic people are overtly disdainful of those they are helping. This is particularly true of religious charities, especially the Protestant ones. I do not say this out of prejudice, but from a lifetime of observation. Those involved in Catholic charities are consistently kind and truly interested in those they help. Protestants, being the proud originators of "the work ethic," are usually just foremen, herding "the rabble" and obviously just "cleaning up the mess." Again, I have seen this myself, especially in "rescue mission" endeavors. Just as jailers consider all inmates guilty and deserving of little but a hard time, so these people consider their charges nothing but lazy nuisances who really deserve being booted out onto the street and allowed to suffer or else rounded up as vagrants and put in jail.

Something greater

God and our Self are beyond the three gunas, and so are those who even while living in this world have ascended enough in consciousness to have attained or be very near liberation from the compulsion of birth and death (on the earth, at least). So Krishna is describing their action, a fourth degree beyond even sattwa. First he introduces a mantra that should accompany all good action.

> "Om, Tat, Sat;" this is known as the triple designation of Brahman. By this were created of old the Brahmanas, Vedas, and Sacrifice (17:23).

"Created" is a rather weak translation of *vihitas*, which means "constituted" in the sense of ordained, apportioned, arranged, or determined. This is an important distinction, because according to the Upanishads and Gita nothing is created in the way Western religions mean by the word. Rather, everything is *manifested* from the ever-existent Being of Brahman.

Om, Tat, and Sat have various levels of meaning. Paramhansa Yogananda explained that they indicate the real meaning of the Christian Trinity: Sat, "the Real, the True," is the transcendental Absolute, the "Father;" Tat, "That," is the immanent Consciousness in all things, the

"Son," that possesses attributes and can therefore be spoken about and indicated (as "That"); Om is the Cosmic Vibration, the "Holy Spirit," which *is* all things within which the Son dwells as the Knower and Controller.

Om is the object; Tat is the subject; and Sat is the substratum of existence and consciousness by and in which the first two exist or consist.

Om is the substance and action of sacrifice; Tat is intelligence and knowledge (Veda); and Sat is the illumined consciousness of the knowers of Brahman–for it is itself Brahman.

All this is implied by a thoughtful and intentional invocation of "Om Tat Sat." So Krishna continues:

> Therefore the acts of sacrifice, gift and tapasya prescribed by the scriptures are always begun uttering "Om" by the Brahmavadins (those who walk the path to Brahman). Uttering "Tat" without interest in fruits, acts of sacrifice, tapasya and the various acts of gift are performed by the seekers of liberation. "Sat" is used in its meaning of Reality and Goodness; so also the word "Sat" is used in the sense of an auspicious act (17:24-26).

This needs no comment.

> Steadfastness in sacrifice, tapasya and gift is called "Sat." And action in connection with these is designated as "Sat" (17:27).

The highest form of action not only leads to Brahman, it *is* Brahman in an incomprehensible manner. So those that continually engage in such action are living in Brahman as manifestations of Brahman. This is the supreme level of Karma Yoga.

> Whatever is sacrificed, given or done, and whatever tapasya is practiced without faith, is called "Asat" [Unreal]. It is naught here or hereafter (after death) (17:28).

Such an act is not condemned or fulminated against with declarations that God despises or even hates it. Not at all: it simply does not exist in the world of the Real. And whatever our apparent status, that is the world (loka) in which the real part of us, the Self, ever exists.

SANNYASA AND TYAGA

Although the Gita covers all aspects of the spiritual aspirant, it is primarily psychological, showing us the states of mind needed for the successful pursuit of Brahmanirvana, the realization of God. Now in this closing chapter Krishna will be enunciating truths that are indispensable to the sadhaka. First, Arjuna himself asks about two key concepts:

Arjuna said: I desire to know separately the essential nature of sannyasa and tyaga (18:1).

Dictionary definition

Sannyasa literally means total [*san*] throwing away [*as*], absolute rejection. In contemporary usage, sannyasa always means formal renunciation, formal monastic life. But in the Gita it is the mental state of thoroughgoing renunciation, of uncompromising abandonment of all that is unfit and unworthy, of intense dispassion toward the things of the world, both internal and external.

Tyaga literally means "abandonment," the turning from all that hinders the realization of the Self. In the Gita, tyaga means renunciation in the sense of the relinquishment of the fruit of action. Sri Ramakrishna said "What is the message of the *Gita*? It is what happens when you repeat it ten times. If *Gita* is repeated ten times it comes to sound like *tagi* [tyagi–one who renounces]. This is the teaching of the *Gita*–'Oh man, try to realize God by giving up everything.' Be he a holy man [sadhu] or a worldly man, he has to give up all attachment from the mind." Again we see that this is primarily psychological. One of the saddest sights in India are the many men who thought that they need only wander around in gerua clothes to be sannyasis–tyagis. Now they have found it is not so, but are trapped and go here and there intent on nothing but food and shelter, becoming daily more and more materialistically minded. What their next life will be, who can say? But this one will likely not be a step up.

Philosophical definition

Now Krishna begins the answer to Arjuna's query:

> **The Holy Lord said: The renunciation of actions arising from desire the sages understand as sannyasa. The abandonment of the fruits of all action the wise declare to be tyaga (18:2).**

Sannyasa in this chapter, then, simply means the giving up of all action motivated by *kama*, by egocentric desire or emotion (passion). Other actions are permitted the seeker, as are other kinds of desire. For example, mumukshutwa, which is intense desire or yearning for liberation (moksha), is permitted, for it arises from the Self, not the ego. Action which maintains the body, such as eating or taking medicine with the desire for continued life and good health, is also acceptable, if life and health are desired so sadhana can be continued. So also is any action based on a desire to help others. It is important to understand this, because many unripe aspirants get the mistaken idea that any desire whatsoever is detrimental, and that monks or dedicated yogis cannot engage in any action–something that is impossible for the living.

Sannyasa, then, is external, even though based on internal disposition. Tyaga, however, is completely mental, a state of both thought and attitude. It is perfect dispassion toward the results of any action–not from disinterest or indifference, but because all actions engaged in are "to be done" in and of themselves. Even if no overt result comes, it does not matter. It is the simple doing that matters. Of course, even then there is a positive result from having acted in consonance with the cosmic order: Ritam.

Vyasa presents these two to us because total consistency is necessary for success in spiritual pursuit. As Jesus said in aphorism twenty-two of the Gospel of Thomas: "When you make the inside like the outside and the outside like the inside, and the above like the below,... then will you enter the kingdom."

Making it practical

Now we come to a section that cannot be ignored if we would intelligently and effectively lead the yoga life. Let us be sure to now have the "ears to hear" of which Jesus so emphatically spoke.

> **Some men of wisdom declare that all action should be abandoned as an evil, while others declare that sacrifice, gift and tapasya should not be abandoned. Hear from me the conclusion regarding tyaga. Tyaga has been designated to be of three kinds. Acts of sacrifice, gift and tapasya should not be abandoned, but should be done. Sacrifice, gift and tapasya are purifiers of the wise (18:3-5).**

This is so reasonable that it seems impossible that anyone could see it otherwise. But it is not so. In India yogis and monks that engage in social service and spiritual education are usually looked upon as second-rate, if not downright deluded or hypocritical. I cannot count the number of times I have heard that my beloved Swami Sivananda of Rishikesh was "not a real sadhu, just a karma yogi." His overflowing love and solicitude, his mammoth caring heart, caused many to say: "Oh, he is not a sannyasi, he is more like someone's grandfather!" The nobly sacrificing sadhus of Ramakrishna Mission, because they have hospitals in which they care for the sick and dying, are contemptuously referred to as "bedpan swamis."

A nurse once saw a man severely injured and lying in a busy road. When she tried to pull him to safety, she found he was too heavy for her to manage. Two sadhus were sitting nearby on a bridge watching unconcernedly. She begged them to help her, and got the answer: "We are sadhus; we can't do things like that." But Krishna makes it clear that no one is exempted from doing what is right and good. After all, what else does God do eternally? Who is above God?

Not surprisingly, Krishna says that renunciation can be tamasic, rajasic, or sattwic.

> But renunciation of obligatory action is not proper. Abandonment of these from delusion is declared to be tamasic. (18:7).

Moha (delusion) means mistaken attachment or aversion.

> He who abandons action from fear of trouble or of pain, does not obtain the fruit of that renunciation; he performs rajasic renunciation (18:8).

Dukham (pain) means stressful or unpleasant. The final clause literally means: "Having performed rajasic tyaga, he cannot attain to (real) fruit-renouncing tyaga."

> When work is done because it is a duty (ought to be done), disciplined, having abandoned attachment and the fruit as well, that renunciation is considered sattwic (18:9).

Perfect attitude

> The man of renunciation, wise, filled with sattwa, with doubt eliminated, does not dislike disagreeable work, nor is he attached to agreeable work. Truly, embodied beings are not able to give up actions entirely; but he who relinquishes the fruit of action is called a man of renunciation (18:10-11).

Three kinds of fruit

> For those who have not renounced, the fruit of action is three-fold when they depart this world: undesired, desired and mixed; but for the renouncers there is none whatever (18:12).

"Undesirable" and "desirable" are of course according to the non-renouncer's ego, binding him even more by his evaluation/reaction to them.

This second clause is a powerful truth: It is possible to act and accrue no karma whatsoever. It is a matter of consciousness.

DEEPER INSIGHTS ON ACTION

We are in the final chapter of the Gita, so Vyasa, assuming that we have listened and learned the basic facts regarding action, now goes into the subject on a more detailed level, intending that when we have assimilated these teachings we will be ready to successfully engage in life's actions like Arjuna.

Five factors of action

> Learn from me these five factors for the accomplishment of all actions, declared in the Sankhya (18:13).

This is one of those verses wherein those that adhere to philosophies other than Sankhya put in words more to their liking such as "the scriptures" or "the wise." But the word is *Sankhya. Karana,* which can be translated "factor," also means an instrument or a cause. All three meanings apply in this verse. Now here are the five:

> The body, the doer, the functions of various kinds, the various distinct activities, and the divine overseer as the fifth. Whatever action a man performs with his body, speech, or mind–either right or wrong–these are its five factors (18:14-15).

So every single action involves five elements. An analysis of them will reveal the extremely complex nature of any action, and how it can be that the simplest action can bind us with the bonds of karma.

1. The *adhishthanam*, the seat or abode–of what? Of all the subtle bodies, including the mind and intellect, and ultimately the abode of the Self. This being so, far more than the physical body is involved here. Five bodies come into the picture, in fact.

2. *Karta*, the Doer. Since we are consistently told by the Gita that the Paramatman and the jivatman never engage in action, it is the ego-sense that is the real doer.

3. *Karanam*: Bodily "instruments" such as the hands, feet, etc., by which the body itself acts in relation to outside objects or situations.

4. *Vividhashcha prithakcheshta,* the many actions or functions of the pranas within the physical and subtle bodies. Also anything that takes place internally.

5. *Daivim:* In the Upanishads the devas are said to preside over the senses, even to control them. This idea has doubtless come about through considering the individual body as a reflection or model of the Cosmic Body in which the gods are the controlling powers. However that may be, Krishna (Vyasa) does not say devas, but daivim–that which is of the *quality* or *capacity* of the devas. Since "deva" literally means "shining one," the idea of daivim in this verse is that which illumines the experiences of the body, in other words, the senses–both as instruments and as powers of perception.

No wonder we are bound up in the net of our actions–even the simplest and most innocent ones! There are no small or insignificant acts. Since every single deed involves a tremendous amount of instruments, it also produces effects on those instruments, which include our mind and heart. Is it any wonder, then, that Krishna has already said: "This divine illusion [maya] of mine made of the gunas [gunamayi] is difficult to go beyond" (7:14)?

The dream and the dreamer

> This being so, he who sees himself as the actual doer does not
> really see, because he does not have a perfect (complete) un-
> derstanding (18:16).

Akritabuddhhitvan means to have an incomplete, imperfect, or unperfected understanding. An important implication here is that the individual
is capable of perfecting his understanding, and therefore he must. But
until he does so, he will misunderstand himself and the world around him.
For him, all his experiences and those involved in them are only a dream.

The dreamlike nature of the world is perceived the world over, though
it is a doctrinal principle only in Sanatana Dharma–a revealing fact. Even
poets such as Edgar Allan Poe ("All that we see or seem is but a dream
within a dream.") and Shelley ("Lift not the painted veil which those who
'live' call 'Life.'") wrote about the dream-nature of the world.

As long as we are asleep and dreaming we cannot really see the truth
about action. But we can listen to those who are awake and receive their
understanding and act accordingly. Even more, the truly awake can show
us the way to our own awakening, the way of yoga. It is only through meditation that our understanding can truly be perfected, for in their highest
reaches understanding and intellect (buddhi) are purely consciousness. And
only yoga works with consciousness. All other things, however beneficial,
affect only the lesser parts of our being.

The purified consciousness

> He whose state of mind is not egoistic, whose intellect is not
> tainted, even though he slays all these people, he does not slay,
> neither is he bound (by karmic consequences) (18:17).

He who transcends the condition of forming karmic bonds is one
whose very state of being–bhava, consciousness, outlook, attitude, and
interior disposition–is *nahamkrito*, not partaking of ego (ahankara) in

any way. That is, he is established in the Self which is eternally free from ego. It is important to realize that he did not rid himself of ego; rather, he established himself in his true swabhava of the divine Atman that has never even been touched by ego. Having gone beyond the ego, he had no need to do anything in relation to it, for it was always only a shadow, only a false appearance.

The intelligence/intellect (buddhi) of such a person is *na lipyate*–not tainted. Lipyate means "befouled" or "besmeared." But he is not even slightly touched by egoism. He no longer dreams that he acts as an entity separate from Brahman or that, separate from Brahman, he reaps the consequences of those acts. After his enlightenment, Buddha was walking down the road and met a Brahmin who asked him: "Who are you?" He simply answered: "I am awake," and kept on walking. Krishna is speaking of one who, like Buddha, has awakened into the reality of the Self, leaving the mirage of ego far behind.

Having abandoned the realm of ego, or relative existence seemingly separate from Brahman, he neither acts nor is bound by action. He cannot be, any more than Brahman can. It is a matter of true nature.

The three inciters to action

We have been told about the five factors of all action. Now we are going to be told about the three things that move us to action–or to the dream of action–and the three things that carry out the motivation.

> Knowledge, the known and the knower are the threefold impulse to action. The instrument, the action and the doer are the threefold constituents of action (18:18).

Perception, perceiving, and the perceiver–these three incite to action. It is all in the realm of objective consciousness. Perception impels us to action mostly from the impulse to avoid unpleasant experience and to gain pleasant experience. Perception is also internal, so there is also the avoidance of unpleasant feelings and the desire for pleasant feelings. It is very much the same with the objects of perception for which we have an attraction (raga) or aversion (dwesha). The perceiver meant here is not the ultimate perceiver, the Self, but the mind/intellect which also acts on the pleasure/pain, like/dislike, good/bad principles, and other dualities.

The three basics of action listed here are *karanam, karma,* and *karta.* Karanam is the instrument or means of action. This has been covered in detail in the previous section. Karma is the act itself, used here to mean *doing*–the expenditure of will and energy to accomplish something. Karta means the agent, or doer–again, in this instance meaning the whole body/mind/ego complex, and not the ultimate Self.

Just see what is involved in understanding karma. What then to say of Karma Yoga? No wonder that Swami Sivananda Hridayananda ("Doctor Mother") told a group that came to see her at the Sivananda Yoga Vedanta Center in Chicago: "I have known only one real karma yogi: Swami Sivananda."

No surprise to us who have come this far in the Gita!

KNOWLEDGE, ACTION, DOER, AND THE THREE GUNAS

Understanding the three gunas and their application in life is obviously very important to Krishna. Right away in his instructions to Arjuna that begin in the second chapter, he introduces the subject of the gunas in verse 45, saying: "The Vedas are such that their scope is confined to the three gunas; be free from those three gunas." Scattered throughout the Gita are teachings on the gunas, and now here in the closing chapter he takes up the subject.

> It is said in the doctrine of the three gunas (the Sankhya Philosophy) that knowledge, action and the doer are of three kinds: hear them also duly (18:19).

Sattwic knowledge

> That by which one sees the one indestructible Being in all beings, undivided in the divided (many)–know that knowledge to be sattwic (18:20).

Notice: real knowledge is a matter of *seeing*, not merely thinking or believing. And the true seeing is the vision of Unity. Simple, but not easy.

Rajasic knowledge

But that knowledge which sees in all beings different beings of various kinds, know that knowledge to be rajasic (18:21).

This is a very problematical viewpoint, whether taken socially, religiously, or personally. To conceive of oneself as a isolated point in space, absolutely separate from everything, a spirit separate from the mind, the body, the surrounding world, all other sentient beings, and even God, is a terrible seed that grows into the multi-headed monster of dual consciousness: a through ticket to constant rebirth and accumulating ignorance. The suffering inherent in such a view is potentially colossal. The only view more unfortunate is that of tamas, whose description Krishna now gives.

Tamasic "knowledge"

But that knowledge which clings to a single effect as if it were the whole, and without reason, without basis in truth and trivial—that is declared to be tamasic (18:22).

Since the world of humanity is in the death-grip of tamas, we need to analyze this, for we have become so used to it that we often miss the awful implications in such a view.

Clings to a single effect as if it were the whole. This is a constant in modern society. People are absolute idolators of their mentally lazy clichés—whether social, political, religious, scientific, or personal. There is only one right way to do a thing, or to think, worship, eat, behave, etc., etc. "My way is the only way" is the fundamental principle. "All the ills of the world will vanish if everyone thinks and acts like me," is the doctrine. Often a single thing is chosen and harped on constantly, as if there is no wider picture. Simplistic is the watchword. Simple, lazy, and stupid—that sums it all up. A refusal to learn anything new is necessary for the maintenance of this tamasic condition.

Without reason. "The [insert name of scripture] says it and I believe it!" The same with prophets, teachers, parents, and whoever has put a thumbprint in their brain. No need to think: they have been *told*. Religion and science–including medicine–are the two major offenders, working untold harm. Put a label on it and that is what it is! Deny its existence and it ceases to be. No need for facts or intelligent consideration, they only confuse us and make trouble....

Without basis in truth. One of the first things I observed about people was their utter purposelessness because they had no grasp of the truth, the reality, of things and situations. Even when only a few years old, I saw that the people around me were learning nothing, doing nothing, and being nothing. I realized that when they died it would be as though they had not even been born. And the whole society was set up to produce and perpetuate this state of pointlessness. I had no intention of being caught in the net. I had no idea what I was going to do, but I knew it would not be what they were doing.

This trait also implies living or thinking in a manner that simply leads nowhere. "Ever learning, and never able to come to the knowledge of the truth" (II Timothy 3:7), is how Saint Paul described it. Most people are just running in the hamster wheel made for them, thinking that they are living and going somewhere.

Trivial. Small-mindedness is a requisite for contemporary life. The absurd popularity of trivia books, games, and suchlike demonstrates this. People hardly read books, and when they do they are unbooks–books of trivia facts, the first of which was the bestseller *The Book of Lists*. It is considered an advantage if a book need not be read completely, but just picked up and grazed in at random. As Dietrich von Hildebrand, the great Catholic philosopher, pointed out in his writings, modern people suffer from what he called "discontinuity," the inability to sustain anything that requires more than minimal thought or will. So of course the previously-cited traits apply to them. It is as though everyone has ADD. For this reason society is run by those whose greed and lust for power (and often simple dedication to evil) motivate them and enable them to sustain their intentions and endeavors. The loonies and racketeers really have taken over the asylum because the staff is sleepwalking through life.

Sattwic action

> Action which is ordained and free from attachment, done
> without attraction or aversion [raga-dwesha], with no desire
> to obtain the fruit–that action is said to be sattwic (18:23).

Having come this far in the Gita, on the surface this verse needs no
comment, but there are some points it will be good to look at. The word
niyatam, here translated as "ordained," literally means controlled or subdued, the idea being that sattwic action is that which is done as discipline,
as a symptom of mastery of the lower levels of being. Although sattwic
action is done without attachment, *sangarahitam* also means "without
clinging [sanga]" as well as without attachment. A sattwic person can let
go of his actions, let what is done be done and the past truly be the past
and move onward. This is no small capability.

Rajasic action

> But that action done with desire for the fulfillment of desires,
> with self-centeredness, or furthermore is done with much ef-
> fort, is considered rajasic (18:24).

Krishna is not saying that everything should be easy, but that "busyness" is rajasic. I think we all know people who are always running
around doing things (often undefined) and talking about how rushed
they are, but we see little results. This is the mental trait of rajas
manifesting externally: people always "on the go" but staying in one
place. I once saw a sign that said: "Would you rather work smarter or
harder?" Rajasic people prefer to work harder. Their inner nervous-
ness and instability manifest this way. Change for the simple sake of
change is an aspect of this, as is the constant insistence of things being
new or up to date. On many levels of our American society this is an
obsessive compulsion.

Disorganization is also a trait of rajas.

Tamasic action

> That action which is undertaken because of delusion, without regard to the consequences of loss, injury or one's own ability–that is said to be tamasic (18:25).

This is quite clear, so I only want to say: Blessed are they that know what they can do and what they cannot do, and act accordingly. It is tamasic to underestimate or overestimate our abilities.

The other traits listed need no comment since they are going on around us all the time. We just need to watch out and not suffer the consequences of others' foolish action and inaction.

Sattwic doer

> A doer free from attachment, non-egoistic, endowed with steadfastness and resolution, and unaffected by success or failure, is said to be sattwic (18:26).

Anahamvadi (non-egoistic) means "free from talk of oneself" or "free from self-speaking," "self" here being *aham*, the ego. This is not just bragging; it is continually talking about oneself, whether complimentary, derogatory or trivial. This is a major trait of spiritual fakes, whatever the type. No matter what the subject is, it somehow always gets around to them and sticks there. I have some tapes of various disciples of renowned gurus that are supposedly their remembrances of the gurus. In one tape that is over an hour in length the guru is spoken about only once, and then for only about four minutes. In another tape it is the same, but only two minutes. I also have some videotapes made of disciples that are some hours in length, and it is the same story. Sometimes an incident with the guru is briefly cited, followed by at least half an hour's philosophical disquisition that is filled with incidents from the speaker's life. A very famous Buddhist teacher in Europe is known for the fact that he never speaks of philosophy or spiritual texts, but talks on and on about himself, usually with very little point.

Rajasic doer

A doer that is passionate, desiring to obtain action's fruits, greedy, violent-natured, impure, easily elated or dejected, is declared to be rajasic (18:27).

Ragi (passionate) means someone in the grip of raga–passionate desire for something.

Lubdhas (greedy) means someone who is consumed with desire for material things.

Himsatmakas (violent-natured) is someone whose very nature is violent and bent on the injury of others.

Ashucis (impure) is someone who is both impure and polluted.

Harshashokanvitah karta (easily elated or dejected) means one who is continually filled with happiness and misery–bouncing back and forth from one to the other, and often both simultaneously, so confused and unstable is such a person. So is the rajasic person, and so is rajasic religion!

Tamasic doer

An agent that is unsteady, vulgar, obstinate, false, dishonest, lazy, despondent and procrastinating, is said to be tamasic (18:28).

Ayuktas means a person who is both undisciplined and unaware of others, acting as though he is the only person around that counts.

Prakritas, means vulgar, ostentatious, and vain.

Naikritikas means dishonest as well as generally vile.

Vishadi means despondent, but also someone who is depressed and continually distressed. This is the way of life for a lot of people who have no real reason to be so. Many people are professional gloom-and-doom nay-sayers. They are so negative, literally, that they prefer misery to happiness, both for themselves and others. They love bad news or the threat of disasters.

Dirghasutri means not just procrastinating or dilatory, but someone who never really acts, however much he may talk. Those who do nothing because they are so convinced they can only fail, also are numbered among the tamasic.

There is not much inspiration in all this, is there? But Krishna wants us to intelligently understand what is going on with ourselves and others. "For none of us liveth to himself, and no man dieth to himself" (Romans 17:7).

THE THREE GUNAS:
INTELLECT AND FIRMNESS

Now hear the three kinds of intellect and steadfastness according to the gunas, set forth completely and severally (18:29).

This is an interesting juxtapositioning: intellect and will-power. For what good is intelligence without the will to act upon it, and what use is a strong will with no intelligence to guide it? Again we see how perfect the Bhagavad Gita is, and how unique in the world.

We have considered buddhi quite a bit, but it is good to remember that buddhi is intellect, understanding, and reason–the thinking, analytical mind. Dhrita has not been covered before. *A Brief Sanskrit Glossary* defines it as "steadfastness; constancy; sustained effort; firmness; patience; endurance." Basically, it is the exercise of the will. And in this verse it means the will itself.

Sattwic intellect

That intellect which knows the paths of work and renunciation, when to act and when not to act, what ought to be done and what ought not to be done, what is to be feared and what is not to be feared, bondage and liberation, is sattwic (18:30).

Intelligence and just plain good sense is the trait of a sattwic intellect. This embraces both mundane and spiritual matters. A sattwic individual always knows what is appropriate action, inaction, speech, and silence. He is keenly aware of both the practical and the ethical aspects of acting and not acting–and of the character and value of both. He lives according to an inviolable code that of necessity is elaborate and subtle–though to him it is simplicity and clarity itself because he grasps the underlying principles of thought and conduct.

The sattwic person knows when to fear and when not to fear, what is rightly feared and what is rightly disregarded. This is a profound thing, for human beings are continually being influenced by those around them as well as the conditions in which they live. Knowing what to be wary of and what to regard lightly is a secret of great happiness and freedom from stress. Pressures are exerted on us continually from both internal and external sources. Understanding what merits our conformity and what has no real claim on us is wisdom beyond price.

But the most important knowledge is that of bondage and liberation–not just the philosophical concepts of bandha and moksha, but those things which either produce or abrogate them.

We see from this that the sattwic person is in total charge of his internal and external life–not by mere will power but by insight into the truth of himself and all he encounters.

Rajasic intellect

> **That intellect which incorrectly understands dharma and adharma, what should be done and what should not be done, is rajasic (18:31).**

This does not mean being wrong all the time, but being right sometimes and wrong sometimes, sometimes on the beam and sometimes off. This is the experience of nearly everyone: you win a few and you lose a few. This is because our understanding is imperfect and also because it can be clouded by various mental factors, not the least of which is simple ignorance. At the root of this condition is fluctuation of the very mind-substance, the chitta, so it cannot perfectly intuit the nature of objects and actions. Desires and fears flaw our judgment.

Tamasic intellect

> That intellect enveloped in darkness, regarding adharma as dharma, and seeing all things pervertedly (turned backward: that is, seeing all things completely opposite to their true nature or state), is tamasic (18:32).

The key to this state is the word *viparitan*, which Sargeant translates "perverted," but which actually means "contrary" or "turned backward." The idea is that the mind is in a state of continual reversal that sees things opposite to what they really are. The mind has become like a photographic negative: what is really light is dark, and what is really dark is light. This is the habitual state of a tamasic intellect. Everything is consistently false, contrary to reality. This is the state of literal negativity. It is a terrible thing.

The only positive thing about it is that when we know such a person we can tell the nature of anything by their reaction to it. If they like something then it is harmful or evil. If they dislike something it is beneficial and good. I have known several people like this and I often used them as a kind of aberrant oracle. I would present something to them and see how they reacted. They were one hundred percent trustworthy in their response–if they liked something I knew it was poisonous, and if they detested something I knew it was truly good. Even in the field of religion I found them to have an unerring accuracy, as long as I took everything opposite to their opinion, of course. In relation to religion, politics, people, even health matters, and especially morality and ethics, they are perfect judges. They can be trusted to always see (or claim they see) things opposite to what they really are.

Sattwic firmness (steadfastness)

> That firmness of intellect or purpose by which through yoga the functions of the mind, the vital force (prana) and the senses are restrained, is sattwic (18:33).

Another, equally legitimate translation is: "The firmness by which, *through the unswerving practice of yoga*, one holds fast the functions of the mind, vital force and the senses—that firmness is sattwic." Of course, the core idea of both versions is that sattwic firmness is produced by the practice of yoga. For only through yoga can there be any appreciable or permanent control of the mind, prana, or senses. The key word is *avybhicharinya*, which does mean "unswerving," but also means "not going astray" in the sense of not departing from the right practice of yoga. I say this because most that is called yoga either does nothing or harms and confuses the mind, whereas the Upanishads, the Gita, and the Yoga Sutras all agree on the right yogic process. The sadhaka who studies those texts and holds steadfastly to what he learns there will unerringly reach the Goal.

Rajasic firmness

> But that firmness by which one holds to dharma, enjoyment and wealth from attachment and desire for the fruits of action, is rajasic (18:34).

Besides desire for the fruits of action, this verse includes desire for what is brought to a person by the possession of duty, pleasures, and wealth. Since the dharma of a rajasic person is based on self-interest, on the ego itself, it cannot be real dharma, and cannot produce the positive effects of dharma. Rather, it compounds the enslavement to the demands of ego. It is adharma: "not dharma."

Tamasic firmness

> That firmness by which a stupid person does not abandon sleep, fear, depression and arrogance, is tamasic (18:35).

Obviously we all need sleep to live normally, but Krishna mentions *swapna* (sleep) here to indicate being asleep in the mind, whatever the bodily state. At the same time it is true that tamasic people sleep too much, and are continually dropping off the moment they sit still. Many of them take refuge in sleep so they will not have to face the mess they have made of their life. I have known negative people that would fall asleep the moment they came into a positive spiritual atmosphere. It was their way of blotting it out.

Krishna is not speaking of those that have a physical problem which saps their vitality. Such people are not tamasic but ill and need the assistance of professional health care. For example, I knew a woman who, when asked how she was, invariably answered: "Oh, I am so *tired*...." Much later it was discovered that she was suffering from leukemia. Anemic people have this symptom as well.

Anyhow, tamasic people will not give up "lazing around" mentally or physically. Even more, they are addicted to fear (often in the form of worry), and grief (often in the form of discontent and generally being "out of sorts"). They love to blame and they love to brood and they love to be "hurt" and "wronged." Their depression (*vishadam*) is a wallowing in self-pity and blame of others. It often takes the form of pessimism and distrust of others.

Vishadam also can mean a kind of lassitude, and "what's the use?" lack of motivation. Although such people are as boring and tiresome as possible, Krishna says another trait is *madam*, which means pride and conceit to the level of virtual intoxication of ego. You would not expect this of dreary, "poor me" people, but I have seen it to be true. The more tamasic, the more inwardly arrogant and proud, even to the point of psychosis. Such a person is called *durmedha*, which means dull-witted as well as outright stupid. A lot of tamasic people I have known were not mentally limited–some were quite intelligent–but they were dull, dreary, and boring *by choice*. And they were all steadfast in their tamasic slough.

This study may have been a bit tedious, and certainly not very inspiring, but it is necessary for us to know all this.

THE THREE KINDS OF
HAPPINESS

Now hear from me of the threefold happiness that one enjoys through practice and by which one attains to the end of pain (18:36).

I t is said that everyone wants to be happy, but happiness is not the same to everyone. So Krishna now takes up that subject, for people differ greatly in "the pursuit of happiness" owing to the predominance of one of the three gunas.

Sattwic happiness

That happiness which is like poison at first, but like amrita in the end, born of the light of one's own Self [atmabuddhi], is declared to be sattwic (18:37).

Sri Ramakrishna often remarked that rock sugar (not refined sugar) is a cure for certain liver ailments, but to those with such disorders sugar tastes bitter, so they avoid it. The same thing is true of certain other substances. A naturopath once gave me a cup of warm liquid to drink. I swallowed it down and remarked that it tasted good. "If you had said it was nasty tasting, I would have known that you have liver trouble," he said. It is the same with those (us?) who have spiritual disorders: that which cures them seems distasteful to them and they avoid it. This is a very problematical situation. People have to pervert their bodies to develop addictions to poisonous substances, and in time their addictions seem normal and even healthy, and abstinence seems miserable and harmful. It is the same with the mind and heart.

A friend of mine once spoke with a young man who was utterly addicted to immorality and alcohol. When he pointed out the misery those things caused, the man countered with: "Living like you do would be like living in a prison!" He had no idea how free the other man was, and how content as a result of his abstinence and spiritual outlook. Krishna is speaking of this here. In the beginning that great happiness and fulfillment which is *atmabuddhiprasadajam*–arising from the tranquility, purity, and brightness of the union of the buddhi with the Atma–seems like a pipe dream or even death. But those who pursue it will find it is the joy of immortality.

Nevertheless, an important principle is set forth in this verse. In the beginning it is normal for spiritual practice to be boring or even annoying. But at the end it will be all sukha: happiness and ease. For it never really is poison, but only seems so to the distorted mind-mirror of those bound in ignorance.

Rajasic happiness

> That happiness arising from the contact of the senses with their objects, which in the beginning is like amrita but changes into that which is like poison, is declared to be rajasic (18:38).

Here we have the opposite of the previous verse. Those things that to the ignorant seem like the nectar of immortality ("This is really living!" "This is the way to live!" "I like it: give me more!") will in time be seen as deadly poison, but then it is often too late. That is why the Bible says: "Remember now thy Creator in the days of thy youth, while the evil days come not, nor the years draw nigh, when thou shalt say, I have no pleasure in them" (Ecclesiastes 12:1). The happiness of rajas is simply fool's gold.

An interesting point: In this and the previous verse the word *pariname* is found. It means "when transformed," the idea being that in time the two kinds of happiness transmute or ripen into either amrita or poison. Actually, they reveal their inner nature–they do not really change, but it seems so to the sadhaka.

Tamasic happiness

> That happiness which in the beginning and as a result is delusive of the Self, arising from sleep, indolence and heedlessness, is declared to be tamasic (18:39).

Krishna describes tamasic happiness as *mohanam*–deluding, addicting, and confusing–arising from spiritual "sleep" (*nidra*), idleness and outright spiritual laziness (*alasya*), and negligence and confusion (*pramada*). Notice that, unlike sattwic and rajasic happiness, tamasic happiness does not transform into anything other than what it is at the beginning. It does not lead to anything, but remains utterly inert. Sattwic and rajasic happiness leads to conclusions about their merit or demerit. Tamasic happiness, on the other hand, simply lies there and wallows in its own inertia. It goes nowhere.

There is a lesson for us here. We need not worry about sattwic people because they will become increasingly established in sattwa. We need only wait for rajasic people to wake up and move up to sattwa. And we need not even give a second thought to the tamasic: they are going to stay right where we see them. The essence of this is that sensible people do not go around trying to change others. The sattwic are already what they should be, the rajasic are moving toward sattwa, and the tamasic are simply that: tamasic. They "come from the nowhere and go to the no-place." (I am only speaking of the present birth. They, too, progress in time, but very slowly and it takes a great deal of time for them to crawl out into even half-light.) The wise bless others and keep on working on themselves. Certainly they will encourage those with them on the path and even assist them, but they cannot put anyone on the path or keep them there. Experience proves this over and over.

We are all in it together

> There is no being either on earth, nor yet in heaven among the gods, that can exist free from these three gunas born of Prakriti (18:40).

There we have it. All are caught in the net woven of the gunas. However, sattwa leads to liberation from that net, to the state known as *trigunatita*–"beyond the three gunas." But until that state is reached we will live according to the guna dominant in us. This is the real basis of authentic caste, and Krishna now takes up that subject:

> Of the Brahmins, the Kshatriyas and the Vaishyas, as also the Shudras, the duties are distributed according to the qualities of their swabhava (18:41).

In this section of verses, "duty" is the usual translation of "actions" (karma), and cannot be objected to. But in these verses it also means the actions that will be done by the different castes, impelled by their innate nature (swabhava). In other words, these are the things that will be done, and the qualities revealed, spontaneously by the various castes. Caste is not determined by action, but action is produced by the innate caste-nature, the swabhava.

The brahmins

> Tranquility, self-restraint, tapasya, purity, patience, uprightness, knowledge, realization [vijnana], belief in God–these are the duties of Brahmins, born of their swabhava (18:42).

It is time for vocabulary-building and review.

A brahmin is one striving for brahmajnana, so we must cultivate the qualities listed for them assiduously if we really plan to succeed in our spiritual quest. Here they are:

Shama is calmness, tranquility, and control of the internal sense organs.

Dama is self-control, control of the senses, and restraint.

Tapas (tapasya) is austerity, practical (i.e., result-producing) spiritual discipline; spiritual force.

Shaucha is purity and cleanliness, including physical and mental purity. Physical shaucha involves purity of diet—abstinence from meat, fish, eggs, alcohol, nicotine, and any mind-altering drugs.

Kshama is forgiveness, patience, and forbearance.

Arjava is straightforwardness, honesty, and rectitude.

Jnana is knowledge, especially knowledge of (or about) Reality or Brahman, the Absolute.

Vijnana is the highest knowledge, beyond mere theoretical knowledge. It is transcendental knowledge or knowing, a high state of spiritual realization in which all is seen as manifestations of Brahman. It is final knowledge of the Self.

Astikyam is piety and belief in God.

What is to be noted about these traits is the fact that they are the prerequisites for spiritual life–they are not spiritual life itself, which is something even higher, the state of *yogayukta*, of continual uniting of the consciousness with God through yoga. It is sad to see that in most religions the things needed for being a beginner are considered the highest attainments.

Most important is the fact that these traits are not artificial or imposed modes of thought and deed, but are a manifestation of the brahmin's *swabhava*–his inherent state of mind, his state of deep inner being. A brahmin is not one who acts like a brahmin, but who *is* a brahmin and therefore acts accordingly.

The kshatriyas

> Valor, splendor, steadfastness, skill, not fleeing in battle, generosity and lordliness of spirit are the duties of Kshatriyas, born of their swabhava (18:43).

These are traits needed by us, too, for as a person passes from lower to higher caste he retains his positive qualities. So we should consider the qualities of all the castes as necessary for us.

Sauryam is heroism, valor, and strength.

Tejas is radiance and brilliance of mind and spirit.

Dhriti is the quality of being steadfast, constant, firm, patient, and endurant. It also means one possessed of the ability to engage in sustained effort.

Dakshyam is skill, virtuosity, and dexterity. One who is *daksha* is expert, intelligent, wise, and able.

Apalayanam is not fleeing battle or trying to avoid conflict.

Danam is generosity, charity, and a giving disposition, as well as self-sacrifice.

Ishwarabhava is a lordly disposition or spirit; nobility and dignity.

All these reveal the swabhava of a kshatriya.

The vaishyas and shudras

> Agriculture, cow-herding and trade are the duties of the Vaishyas, born of their swabhava, and the Shudras' duty is doing service, born of their swabhava (18:44).

This is quite straightforward. It is interesting that only physical actions are listed, whereas both the brahmins and kshatriyas require many psychological factors. Obviously vaishyas and shudras require ethical principles as much as anyone else. In fact, all that has been said in the previous chapters of the Gita applies to all the castes.

Everyone–swakarma

Krishna now speaks of humanity in general, saying:

> Satisfied in his own duty, a man attains perfection. Hear how he who is happy in his own duty [swakarma] finds perfection. By worshipping with his swakarma him from whom all beings

have their origin, by whom all this universe is pervaded, a man
[manava: human being] finds perfection (18:45-46).

We have already encountered swabhava and swadharma—the inmost
disposition of the Self and the dharma (usually translated "duty") that
reveals the Self or makes attainment of the Self possible. In these two
verses we meet the word *swakarma*: action that reflects or manifests the
Self—at least in its present state of evolution. To follow or engage in our
swakarma is to worship God, for spiritual, evolutionary principles are not
to be merely ascribed to or discussed, *they are to be lived*. That is how we
evolve, and evolution is the sole purpose of creation.

Swakarma is an inseparable part of swadharma, so Krishna continues:

**Better is one's own swadharma, though imperfect, than an-
other's duty, though well performed. Performing the duty
prescribed by one's own nature (swabhava) produces no fault
(18:47).**

We are not talking here of "God's will" in the negative, fear-filled way
of Western religion. We are talking of our own nature, which has been put
into our hands and which we alone can perfect. If we violate our nature by
work alien to that nature, however good it may appear or how much it may
be praised by others, we incur evil, for we sin against ourself. Therefore:

The duty to which one is born should not be abandoned, although faulty,
for all undertakings are enveloped by defects as is fire by smoke (18:48).

Two expressions in this verse are very important: *sahajam karma* and
dosha. Sahaja means that which is innate, actually inborn. Karma is action.
So sahajam karma is that kind of action, that way of life, which is a natural
expression of our innate character, of our deep mind. This must be engaged
in, even though, as Krishna points out, all relative existence and action are
obscured to a greater or lesser degree by dosha—dosha being imperfection,
blemish, fault, or shortcoming. This is because of the innate nature of
relativity itself, which fundamentally is Maya, or illusion.

We do the best we can with what we have. The reward is infinite.

FREEDOM

The supremely free

> He whose intellect (buddhi) is unattached, whose lower self
> is subdued, from whom desire has departed, by renunciation
> attains the supreme state of freedom from action (18:49).

Sometimes detachment is mistaken for a kind of emotionless or flat
state of mind devoid of response or reaction. I have known yogis who
tried to maintain a zombie-like state they thought was detachment. Some
even refused to show their children or one another affection because they
feared becoming attached. But this is a misunderstanding, and the word
asakta clears it up. For it means "not-clinging," letting things simply pass
on without trying to hold on to them. I have lived with great yogis who
greatly loved music and beauty, but they never formed an attachment or
addiction to them. They enjoyed them while keeping their awareness centered in the Self and free from identification or grasping after them. They
had great hearts that rejoiced in the good fortune of others and grieved
at their misfortune.

One time in Delhi a great yoga-siddha came to the home of some
of my friends. My friends were dedicated yogis and invited some other
sadhakas to come meet the saint. Among the group was an aged woman
in great anguish of heart. When she told her sorrow to the saint, to my
amazement he began to shed tears in sympathy—and so did all the others

present. This was a great lesson to me, one that my yogi-friends back in the West needed as well. For detachment is not indifference. Throughout the world for over two thousand years people have honored both Buddha and Jesus more for their compassion and caring than even for their wisdom.

Without self-mastery there is no hope of freedom. The self referred to here is the lower self, the appendages of the true Self that are usually mistaken for It. And that must be conquered, so there must be a battle–which is what the Gita is all about.

Vigatasprihah merits a looking into. *Sprihas* means deep desire, intense longing for something, as well as envy at its possession by someone else. *Vigata* means "gone away" or "completely disappeared." In the freed individual sprihas is not present and suppressed, or even latent, but rather has been completely banished and dissolved permanently. This is an exalted state, but one we all can–and must–attain.

Anyone can physically turn from something or rid their external life from it, but only the yogi can truly renounce: that is, renounce it mentally in his heart. This is the renunciation Krishna is speaking of. When one has attained that, then he is *nishkarmyasiddhim*–perfect in non-action. For his mind no longer acts, only his lower self which is the instrument of his enlightenment. This is a supreme (paramam) state, as he says.

Attaining Brahman

> Learn from me in brief how one who has attained perfection also attains Brahman, that supreme state of knowledge (18:50).

Krishna is not saying that union with Brahman is a kind of secondary side-effect of non-attachment and non-action, but he is indicating that Brahmajnana is so abstract and exalted that those who attempt to reach it may fail. But if they turn inward and work with their own consciousness they will remove the obstacles to Brahmajnana–and thus attain it. The wise work with what is at hand. It is like pulling on a rope to bring something closer to us and into our grasp. We only reach the top step of a stair by stepping on the lower ones in between. It seems obvious, but the ego has a way of blinding us to such simple truths.

Qualifying for knowing Brahman

Now we encounter another list of necessary traits, this time the requisites for knowing Brahman. They come at the end of the Gita because it is so crucial for us to know about them and to strive for them single-mindedly.

> Endowed with a supremely pure intellect, controlling the lower self by firmness, turning from the objects of the senses, beginning with sound, casting off attraction and aversion, dwelling in a solitary place, eating lightly (what is easily digested), with speech, body and mind controlled, constantly devoted to yoga meditation, taking refuge in vairagya, forsaking egotism, force, pride, desire, anger, possessiveness, freed from the notion of "mine" and peaceful–he is fit for union with Brahman (18:51-53).

Buddhya vishuddhaya yukto means "united to a totally purified intelligence [buddhi]," the idea being that the yogi's awareness must at all times be united with his highest intelligence. It can also mean "with a totally purified intelligence in a state of yoga"–in union with the consciousness that is the Self. As in most Sanskrit texts, all possible meanings are intended. Yoga the practice is the way to yoga the state of union.

Dhrityatmanam niyamya means "controlling [or subduing] one's self with firmness [or determination]." It can also mean "steadily [i.e., continuously] controlling one's self." Mastery is the meaning here–perpetual mastery.

Shabdadin vishayans tyaktva means "having abandoned [or left behind] the objects [or spheres] of the senses, beginning with sound." This is a profound yogic principle. By means of sound all the other sense-objects or sensory mental levels can be transcended. This if course refers to the subtle sound of japa within meditation.

Ragadveshau vyudasya means "casting aside [or rejecting, abandoning] raga-dwesha" the alternating cycles of attraction and repulsion, liking and disliking, loving and hating.

Viviktasevi means "living in solitude" or "frequenting isolated places." The first is both external and internal. The truth is, a person can live in a high-rise apartment complex and still live in solitude if he keeps to himself and maintains inward awareness. But it is helpful if the yogi can live in a quiet, uncrowded place, even outside a city. This is ideal, but the ideal cannot always be obtained. The second meaning would apply to someone who simply cannot live in solitude. He should go as much as possible to quiet, isolated places and stay there as long as possible. Sri Ramakrishna continually advised this. His great disciple, Mahendranath Gupta ("M"), the author of *The Gospel of Sri Ramakrishna*, followed this assiduously. He had several secret places, some in Calcutta and some outside, where he would disappear for a day or more, or he would stay in those places but return home for meals. Sri Ramakrishna said this was absolutely necessary to gain–and retain–one's spiritual progress.

Krishna is not telling the yogi to be completely anti-social, but he definitely means for us to live mostly to ourselves. Even satsang should be limited.

Laghvashi means two things: "eating lightly" and "eating things that are easily digested." Both are needful to good health, yet we must not interpret "eating lightly" as starving ourselves. So a yogi should do his best in these matters, always keeping good sense in mind.

Yaktavakkayamanasah means "whose speech, body, and mind are controlled [disciplined]."

Dhyanayogaparo nityam means "constantly [ceaselessly] devoted to yoga meditation" and "constantly holding yoga meditation as the highest object." The yogi does not merely tincture his life with yoga, making it a kind of "yoga cooler," but rather constantly practices meditation–which in this instance includes constant japa–and considers it the supreme commitment and factor of his life. This is rare, and so are realized yogis, for that very reason.

Vairagyam samupashritah means "taking refuge in dispassion [vairagya]" and "supported by dispassion." The first meaning indicates that we do not wait for the virtue of vairagya to arise of its own accord as a result of spiritual practice, but rather that we take hold of ourselves and deliberately turn from troubling objects or situations, refusing to permit them in our lives, and cutting off all responses to them. We also expel from our minds and lives (including our environment) all things and situations that destroy dispassion. That is why we have a free will: to be used to eliminate that which erodes it. It is a necessary foundation for our spiritual peace and safety.

Now we are given a list of things the yogi relinquishes. The word *vimuchya* does not mean a mere laying aside or a temporary cessation, but total abandonment, either getting it away from us, or ourselves away from it. Here is what Krishna says we eliminate from our life (including our minds and hearts):

Ahankara–egotism and ego-consciousness.

Balam–force, in the sense of coercion or bullying of others. This is a facet of ahimsa, actually. But I would like to point out that if this word was spelled with a long first "a" instead of a short one, the word would mean "childishness," and would equally apply as a requisite for successful yoga practice. Considering that the ego is a monstrous child, this may be the intended word. In *Dracula*, Dr. Van Helsing speaks of the fact that Dracula is really a cunning and powerful infant, and speaks of "his so-great child mind," because over the centuries he has become increasingly infantile as his greedy and demanding ego has consumed everything else about him.

Darpam–arrogance and pride, both traits of a childish, egoic mind.

Kamam–desire and longing for things.

Krodham–anger and wrath directed towards others.

Parigraham–grasping after things, taking them, seizing them either legally or illegally. This includes hoarding and constant adding to one's possessions.

That is what we give up. What do we acquire?

Nirmanas–unselfishness, for the word literally means "not mine." It, too, implies not acquiring things just for the getting of them.

Shantas–tranquility, calmness, being completely at peace.

All those–and only those–who fit this entire list are *brahmabhuyaya kalpate*: fit (qualified) for oneness with Brahman. Others have done it, and so can we. Yet, we see from this how few yogis there really are. And why.

THE GREAT DEVOTEE

We tend to think of union with Brahman as a result of jnana, of being a perfect jnani. And this is so, certainly, otherwise Adi Shankaracharya would not have written so much on the subject of jnana. But perhaps we mistake bhakti–devotion–for something much less. As Swami Sivananda was wont to comment: "emotion is not devotion." Bhakti means dedication, a strong affinity for something–so strong that it brings us to the object of our devotion, or brings it to us. (Usually it is a combination of both.)

Sri Ramakrishna is unique among India's spiritual teachers for many reasons, but one of the most remarkable is his ability to make clear in a sentence what others would take a multitude of words to make only slightly more comprehensible. Whenever he prefaced something with the words: "Do you know what it is like?…" a gem of astounding wisdom would follow–and so simple that anyone could understand easily. He formulated a whole system of spiritual life that is unequaled for its simplicity and profundity. He defined bhakti and jnana in a sentence apiece. Here they are:

"Jnana is knowing 'The world is unreal; Brahman alone is real.'"

"Bhakti is feeling: 'God is the Master and I am the servant.'"

Obviously a sensible person ascribes to both propositions. Only the accomplished yogi is really a jnani or a bhakta. Consequently Krishna says:

Absorbed in Brahman, with Self serene, he grieves not nor desires, the same to all beings, he attains supreme devotion unto me (18:54).

Well, there we have it. Bhakti and Brahmajnana are inseparable. Actually bhakti is the fruit of realization. Yet bhakti is both cause and effect, for he continues:

> By devotion to me he comes to know how great I am in truth, then having known me in truth, he forthwith enters into me (18:55).

Literally, part of this verse says: "He comes to realize how great and Who I am." It also equally means: "He comes to realize the extent of my Being"–the infinity of God. Having known this in truth–not just in theory or "on faith"–such a one straightaway enters Brahman.

> Doing all actions, always taking refuge in me, by my grace he attains the eternal, immutable state [abode] (18:56).

Madvyapashrayah literally means both "trusting in me" and "taking refuge in me." This is a natural result of those who have understood that their seemingly separate existence independent of God is an illusion, that God is in very truth their All in All. Thus he becomes their "eternal, imperishable abode," and they themselves are revealed as eternal and imperishable.

Now for some practical instructions:

Reaching the Eternal Abode

> Mentally renouncing all actions in me, holding me as the highest goal, resorting to buddhi-yoga, constantly fix your mind on me (18:57).

It has already been said in the Gita that it is impossible for anyone to remain without acting at any time. For even when sitting still, the body is acting at a tremendous degree, and that is all under the direction of the subconscious mind. So we are thinking and acting all the time–otherwise we would die. For this reason Krishna makes a point of saying that all actions must be renounced *chetasa*–mentally. But he is not advocating just pulling back the mind and being indifferent and feeling separated from the action, just being an observer. For that would be mere mental isolation. Instead, he says: "Mentally renouncing all actions *in me.*" That is something completely different. He is telling us that by the constant remembrance of God and awareness that we are living in God, that all is God, we should do all actions in the awareness that it is ultimately the divine power that is acting, that we are witnesses, but not passive witnesses. Rather, we are intent on following the counsel: "Stand still, and consider the wondrous works of God" (Job 37:14).

Though Sargeant has "yoga of discrimination," the Sanskrit is *buddhiyogam*, the yoga of the intellect in the sense of the yoga of our highest and subtlest levels and spiritual faculties. Yoga that does not reach to these rarefied levels is not any yoga at all, but a muddling around in the lower levels of our being that will confine our awareness to those levels.

Certainly discrimination will result from our tapping into those supreme levels of our existence, but buddhi yoga is so much more. Krishna says: "Constantly fix your mind on me."

How to lose your way

> Fixing your mind on me, you shall by my grace surmount all obstacles; but if from egotism you will not hear me, then you shall perish (18:58).

Sometimes to succeed we need to know the way to fail. *Ahamkarat* literally means "I making," the assertion and empowering of the ego. The result of this is *vinankshyasi,* which means both "you shall be lost" in the sense of losing your way and wandering aimlessly and fruitlessly, and "you shall perish" in the sense of utter failure.

You will!

> If, filled with egotism, you think: "I will not fight," this your resolve shall be in vain, for your nature [prakriti] will compel you (18:59).

Krishna here warns Arjuna (and us) against being in the state of *ashritya na*, which literally means "not depending on" or "not taking refuge in." Only when we think we are separate from God and capable of being independent do we think we can contravene the divine law–which is the Divine Will. We actually think we can circumvent God and do as we please. Basically, we plan to make a fool of God, not realizing that we are only making a fool of ourselves. Our very existence depends on God, and if we are wise we take refuge in God–not in the manner of a pygmy groveling at the feet of the master, but by entering into God and reclaiming our eternal and irrevocable unity with God. This is the only viable refuge open to us.

If we think we can avoid acting in accordance with the divine plan, *manyase mithya*: "you think falsely," or: "you imagine in vain–hopelessly." Is it any wonder the world is in the terrible mess we see all around us? People are trying any way they can to avoid their only possible destiny. See how they scramble after mirages, disdaining the glorious realities open to them, making pathetic excuses for their pathetic lives. Yogananda said that during his early years in Boston he was once walking in a neighborhood when suddenly God showed him that the houses were just like chicken coops and the people inside were like chickens that pecked, scratched, laid and hatched eggs, and ended up fried chicken. God then asked him if he would like to become fried chicken; and he replied: "No, Lord. I came with Thee and I will go with Thee." A wise resolve.

How many people ignorantly say: "It is my life; I will live it as I please;" "It is my body, I will do with it what I want." Even after two thousand years, who really understands or even believes the divine words: "Whosoever will save his life shall lose it: and whosoever will lose his life for my sake shall find it. For what is a man profited, if he shall gain the whole world, and lose his own soul? or what shall a man give in exchange for his soul?" (Matthew 16:25-26). So they pass from life to life in confusion and suffering. Awakening does not come easily to such people. So Krishna is warning us to not be one of them.

Yes, we like Arjuna must fight, must engage in the struggle with the unreal so the Real can be gained. And if we think we will not, we are very wrong, for even our material nature–our prakriti–will compel us. For no matter how we distort our presence in this world, it has a single purpose: the return to God. And return we shall, though the longer we delay the longer and more demanding will be the battle. It is not a matter of whether or not we will become seekers of God–only when. But as I say, by delaying we make the struggle much more ferocious and fraught with fear.

Many make the excuse of not being "ready" for spiritual life, but the moment we attained human form we were ready and equipped with all we needed. We all have delayed, and that is all the more reason to stop it right now before we make things worse for us. Bad things happen to good people because of what they did when they were themselves bad people. That is the law.

Krishna drives the message home, saying:

> **What you do not wish to do, through delusion, you shall do against your will, bound by your karma born of your own nature [swabhava] (18:60).**

Arjuna did not really have a choice; he had come to the point of evolution where only the right thing could be done by him. Let us hurry up and get to that point, too.

The ultimate Determiner

> **The Lord dwells in the hearts of all beings, causing them by his maya to revolve as if mounted on a machine (18:61).**

The purpose of this revolution through birth, life, death, and endless repetitions of these cycles, is evolution of consciousness. It is Maya because it is a projection of appearances only, what Yogananda called "the cosmic motion picture."

> **Fly unto him alone for refuge with your whole being. By that grace you shall attain supreme peace and the eternal abode (18:62).**

The key words here are "whole being." Spiritual life is not a condiment to be sprinkled in our life to somehow make it better. Spiritual life is just that: *life*; and it requires the totality of our being to be successful. It is a continual, uninterrupted endeavor. For it is our total being that must be transformed in order for us to enter the Eternal. Anything less fails.

THE FINAL WORDS

We are approaching the end of the marvelous Bhagavad Gita. Krishna's final words are now to be given to us who, like Arjuna, on the battlefield of life seek wisdom.

> **Thus has the knowledge that is more secret than all that is secret been expounded to you by me. Having reflected on this fully, act in the way you wish (18:63).**

Nothing like this second sentence can be found in any other scripture of the world. This is why the Gita merits our highest valuation and our conformity to its glorious message. Krishna respects the free will of Arjuna and knows that ultimately it is all Arjuna's decision. To interfere with that will by promises, threats, warnings, and cajolings will only produce a temporary conformity to Krishna's words. Only when it arises from within Arjuna's illumined understanding can he rightly engage in battle. Nor can we live the yoga life if it is not based on our own impulse to divine realization and our full awareness of all that it implies. Krishna tells Arjuna to give full consideration to what he has been told and then act—not out of faith in Krishna, respect for Krishna, or love for Krishna, *but because he knows it is the truth, having understood it for himself.* It is the same for us.

The secret of love

Hear again my highest teaching, most secret of all, because you are dearly loved by me; therefore I shall tell you what is for your good (18:64).

Krishna's teachings are not *sarvaguhyatamam*—most secret of all—because God is hiding these truths from us, but because we, through our perverted intuition, are hiding them from ourselves! How many times have we heard people say: "Don't tell me that!" about something they know is true? And we all grew up with: "What you don't know won't hurt you," the idea being that what we don't know will not obligate us. Wrong! For in the depths of our being we do know the truth, even if our whole life is a denial of it. That is why God says in the Bible: "Ye are gods; and all of you are children of the most High. But ye shall die like men, and fall like one of the princes" (Psalms 82:6-7). The Septuagint renders it: "But you die like men and are laid in the grave like animals." It is our choice, but it is a conscious choice, at least on the inner levels where it counts.

We babble about love, love, love, but love is truth—truth that is loved. Only the saints really love, being one with the God who *is* love. And they are always truthful with us. Even more, they only love the true part of us and oppose the false part. They are never the friend of our ego, nor will they ever accommodate it. And they will not force or demand us to follow the right way. That is all in our hands. Yet they speak only for our welfare. Those who act otherwise are not holy but unholy, slaves of their own "sacred" egos, and uninterested in our genuine welfare.

The mind

Fix your mind on me, be devoted to me, sacrifice and bow down to me. In this way you shall truly come to me, for I promise you—you are dear to me (18:65).

Remember that the "me" of Krishna is both the Supreme Self (Paramatman) and the individual Self (jivatman). So we are devoted to Spirit and spirit. The word *manmanas* is rightly translated "fix your mind on me," but it literally means "me-minded." That is, our mind is to be a perfect reflection of Spirit, so that with Saint Paul we can say: "We have the mind of Christ" (I Corinthians 2:16). "Let this mind be in you, which was also in Christ Jesus" (Philippians 2:5). And Saint Peter said to the followers of Christ: "Arm yourselves likewise with the same mind" (I Peter 4:1).

Krishna and the Apostles speak like this because we are the divine Self: "Christ in you, the hope of glory" (Colossians 1:27). It is too bad that Christians do not believe the words of Saint Paul: "God, who commanded the light to shine out of darkness, hath shined in our hearts, to give the light of the knowledge of the glory of God in the face of Jesus Christ" (II Corinthians 4:6).

We must be Krishna-minded and Christ-minded, for that is to be God-minded. And we are dear (priya) to God.

Refuge

Abandoning all duties, take refuge in me alone; then I shall free you from all demerits, do not grieve (18:66).

Everything must be the way to God to us. Even right action is not to be valued for itself, but because it leads to God. The same is true of all spiritual and material deeds. We must be able to say with Swami Sivananda: "Only God I saw!" Krishna does not mean that we need not follow the ways of dharma, only that we must keep looking at God and not at them as we follow them. God must be the sole purpose of our life, the sole means and the sole goal. This is "abandoning all duties" in God, as God, for God, "that God may be all in all" (I Corinthians 15:28).

When our consciousness is so fixed on God, so merged in God that it becomes God, then all evils shall fall away like the shadows they are, and we shall live in the Light as that Light. Where then, shall grief be? Krishna brings up this subject because it was Arjuna's grief that sparked the entire discourse. So we have come full circle with him.

Tell not this secret to...

> **This should not be spoken of by you at any time to one who is without tapasya, nor to one who is not dedicated, nor to one who does not desire to listen, nor to one who speaks evil of (mocks) me (18:67).**

Two words here need a good look.

Ashushrushave means "one who does not desire to hear (listen)" and "the non-obedient." This is both those who just do not want to be bothered and those who are not unaware of spiritual teaching but do not follow it, for whatever reason or excuse.

Abhyasuyati means "he speaks evil of," "he shows indignation toward," or "he sneers at." That pretty well covers the reactions of negative people toward truth: they decry it as evil, unnatural, cultish, repressive, superstitious, harmful, scary, and suchlike. They love to say: "that frightens me" about anything they hate. They are righteously indignant about it for the previous reasons cited, as well as charging it with being false and a way to control others or profit from them. And they also sneer for the same reasons, as well as mocking and despising truth as stupid or worthless, backward, primitive, naive, simplistic, etc. They all entail rejection for one reason or another.

This implies that we must look carefully at a person before we waste our time. As Jesus said: "Give not that which is holy unto the dogs, neither cast ye your pearls before swine, lest they trample them under their feet, and turn again and rend you" (Matthew 7:6). Before that Solomon said: "Speak not in the ears of a fool: for he will despise the wisdom of thy words" (Proverbs 23:9). I am aware that good and true souls naturally assume that others are as interested and sincere as they, but after some experience they come to know differently. Experience is still the best teacher.

We must not waste time or degrade precious truth by speaking with unfit persons. We should just say something diplomatic or neutral and change the subject or leave.

It is obvious from this that Krishna would never countenance forcing wisdom on anyone, or trying to convert them or change their views.

On the other hand

> He who with supreme devotion to me teaches this supreme secret unto my devotees shall doubtless come to me (18:68).

Abhidhasyati means to present and to explain. To teach the worthy is the highest devotion to God, for "inasmuch as ye have done it unto one of the least of these my brethren, ye have done it unto me" (Matthew 25:40). Those who illumine the path of their worthy fellow-seekers shall themselves go unerringly to God.

> And no one among all men shall do more pleasing service to me, nor shall there be another on the earth dearer to me than he. And he who will study this dharmic dialogue of ours, by him will I have been worshipped through the sacrifice of knowledge; such is my conviction. Even the man who hears this, full of faith and not scoffing, he also, liberated, shall attain the happy worlds of those of righteous deeds (18:69-71).

Let us take these words to heart. The Gita is an open door to the highest consciousness and life.

What will you do?

All the hearing in the world is pointless if it does not result in a resolve, in a conclusion of some sort. So Krishna asks Arjuna (and us):

> Has this been heard by you with a one-pointed mind? Has the delusion of your ignorance been destroyed? (18:72).

There are those who listen with the ears on their head, but not the ears of their mind and heart. Krishna indicates here that those who truly listen with an intent mind will have their ignorance and delusion dispelled by their intelligent attention.

The right answer

> Arjuna said: My delusion is destroyed, and I have regained my knowledge through your grace; I am firm and my doubts are gone. I will act according to your word (18:73).

No need to comment on this—just "Go, and do thou likewise" (Luke 10:37).

The narrator speaks

> Sanjaya said: Thus have I heard this wondrous dialogue of Krishna and the great-souled Arjuna, which causes the hair to stand on end. By the grace of Vyasa have I heard this supreme and most secret yoga directly from Krishna, Yoga's Lord, himself declaring it. O King, remembering again and again this marvelous dialogue between Krishna and Arjuna, I rejoice again and again. And remembering again and again that most marvelous form of Krishna, great is my wonder, O King, and I rejoice again and again (18:74-77).

And us

If we, too, will remember again and again, without ceasing, this supreme scripture of enlightenment, wondering at the wisdom-grace of Krishna and the readiness of Arjuna to follow the Way pointed out to him, then we will join our voices with Sanjaya's and say with total certainty and understanding:

Wherever there is Krishna, Yoga's Lord, wherever is Arjuna the bowman, there will forever be splendor, victory, wealth and righteousness: this is my conviction (18:78).

OM. Peace. Peace. Peace.

GLOSSARY

Abhyasa: Sustained (constant) spiritual practice.

Abhyasa Yoga: Yoga, or union with God, through sustained spiritual practice.

Adharma: Unrighteousness; demerit, failure to perform one's proper duty; unrighteous action; lawlessness; absence of virtue; all that is contrary to righteousness (dharma).

Adhibhuta: Primal Being; pertaining to the elements; the primordial form of matter.

Adhidaiva: Primal God.

Adhiyajna: Primal Sacrifice; Supreme Sacrifice.

Adhyatma: The individual Self; the supreme Self; spirit.

Adityas: Solar deities, the greatest of which is Vishnu.

Agni: Fire; Vedic god of fire.

Ahankara: Ego; egoism or self-conceit; the self-arrogating principle "I," "I" am-ness; self-consciousness.

Ahimsa: Non-injury in thought, word, and deed; non-violence; non-killing; harmlessness.

Airavata: The white elephant of Indra that was produced by the churning of the ocean.

Amrita: That which makes one immortal. The nectar of immortality that emerged from the ocean of milk when the gods churned it.

Ananta: Infinite; without end; endless; a name of Shesha, the chief of the Nagas, whose coils encircle the earth and who symbolizes eternity, and upon whom Vishnu reclines.

Anarya(n): Not aryan; ignoble; unworthy. See Aryan.

Apana: The prana that moves downward, producing the excretory functions in general; exhalation.

Aparigraha: Non-possessiveness, non-greed, non-selfishness, non-acquisitiveness; freedom from covetousness; non-receiving of gifts conducive to luxury.

Arjava(m): Straightforwardness; simplicity; honesty; rectitude of conduct (from the verb root *rinj*: "to make straight"); uprightness.

Arjuna: The great disciple of Krishna, who imparted to him the teachings found in the Bhagavad Gita. The third of the Pandava brothers who were major figures in the Mahabharata War. His name literally means "bright," "white," or "clear."

Arya(n): One who is an Arya–literally, "one who strives upward." Both Arya and Aryan are exclusively psychological terms having nothing whatsoever to do with birth, race, or nationality. In his teachings Buddha habitually referred to spiritually qualified people as "the Aryas." Although in English translations we find the expressions: "The Four Noble Truths," and "The Noble Eightfold Path," Buddha actually said: "The Four Aryan Truths," and "The Eightfold Aryan Path."

Aryaman: Chief of the Pitris.

Ashwattha: The pippal (sacred fig) tree, in the Bhagavad Gita, the eternal tree of life whose roots are in heaven. The "world tree" in the sense of the axis of the earth and even of the cosmos.

Ashwins: Two Vedic deities, celestial horsemen of the sun, always together, who herald the dawn and are skilled in healing. They avert misfortune and sickness and bring treasures.

Astikyam: Piety; belief in God.

Asura: Demon; evil being (a-sura: without the light).

Asuric: Of demonic character.

Bhagavan: The Lord; the One endowed with the six attributes, viz. infinite treasures, strength, glory, splendor knowledge, and renunciation; the Personal God.

Bhrigu: An ancient sage, so illustrious that he mediated quarrels among the gods.

Bhuta: A spirit. Some bhutas are subhuman nature spirits or "elementals", but some are earthbound human spirits–ghosts. Bhutas may be either positive or negative.

Brahma: The Creator (Prajapati) of the three worlds of men, angels, and archangels (Bhur, Bhuwah, and Swah); the first of the created beings; Hiranyagarbha or cosmic intelligence.

Brahmachari(n): One who observes continence; a celibate student in the first stage of life (ashrama); a junior monk.

Brahmacharya: Continence; self-restraint on all levels; discipline; dwelling in Brahman.

Brahman: The Absolute Reality; the Truth proclaimed in the Upanishads; the Supreme Reality that is one and indivisible, infinite, and eternal; all-pervading, changeless Existence; Existence-knowledge-bliss Absolute (Satchidananda); Absolute Consciousness; it is not only all-powerful but all-power itself; not only all-knowing and blissful but all-knowledge and all-bliss itself.

Brahmana: A Vedic liturgical text explaining the rituals found in the Vedic samhitas (collection of hymns). A guidebook for performing those rites.

Brahmanirvana: The state of liberation (nirvana) that results from total union with Brahman.

Brahmavada: The Path to Brahman; the way to supreme enlightenment.

Brahmavadin: Literally "one who walks the path of Brahman." One who advocates that there is one existence alone–Parabrahman.

Brahmin (Brahmana): A knower of Brahman; a member of the highest Hindu caste consisting of priests, pandits, philosophers, and religious leaders.

Brihaspati: The guru–priest and teacher–of the gods.

Brihatsaman: A hymn to Indra found in the Sama Veda.

Buddhi: Intellect; intelligence; understanding; reason; the thinking mind; the higher mind, which is the seat of wisdom; the discriminating faculty.

Buddhi Yoga: The Yoga of Intelligence spoken of in the Bhagavad Gita which later came to be called Jnana Yoga, the Yoga of Knowledge.

Car-warrior: See Maharatha.

Caste: See Varna.

Chandra: Presiding deity of the moon or the astral lunar world (loka).

Chitraratha: The chief of the gandharvas.

Daityas: Demons who constantly war with the gods. Sometimes "races" or nationalities who acted contrary to dharma and fought against the "aryas" were also called demons (daityas or asuras); giant; titan..

Deva: "A shining one," a god–greater or lesser in the evolutionary hierarchy; a semi-divine or celestial being with great powers, and therefore a "god." Sometimes called a demi-god. Devas are the demigods presiding over various powers of material and psychic nature. In many instances "devas" refer to the powers of the senses or the sense organs themselves.

Dharma: The righteous way of living, as enjoined by the sacred scriptures and the spiritually illumined; characteristics; law; lawfulness; virtue; righteousness; norm.

Dharmic: Having to do with dharma; of the character of dharma.

Dhrita: Steadfastness; constancy; sustained effort; firmness; patience; endurance.

Dukha(m): Pain; suffering; misery; sorrow; grief; unhappiness; stress; that which is unsatisfactory.

Dwesha: Aversion/avoidance for something, implying a dislike for it. This can be emotional (instinctual) or intellectual. It may range from simple non-preference to intense repulsion, antipathy and even hatred. See Raga.

Dwija: "Twice born;" any member of the three upper castes that has received the sacred thread (yajnopavita).

Gandharva: A demigod–a celestial musician and singer.

Ganga: See Ganges.

Ganges (Ganga): The sacred river–believed to be of divine origin–that flows from high up in the Himalayas, through the plains of Northern India, and empties into the Bay of Bengal. Hindus consider that bathing in the Ganges profoundly purifies both body and mind.

Garuda: A great being who can assume bird form, and therefore considered the king of birds. Often depicted as an eagle, he is the vehicle of Vishnu.

Gayatri Meter: A meter found only in the Rig Veda, consisting of three lines of eight syllables each. It is considered especially appropriate for mantric invocation of deities before worship.

Ghee: Clarified butter.

Guna: Quality, attribute, or characteristic arising from nature (Prakriti) itself; a mode of energy behavior. As a rule, when "guna" is used it is in reference to the three qualities of Prakriti, the three modes of energy behavior that are the basic qualities of nature, and which determine the inherent characteristics of all created things. They are: 1) sattwa–purity, light, harmony; 2) rajas–activity, passion; and 3) tamas–dullness, inertia, and ignorance.

Guru: Teacher; preceptor; spiritual teacher or acharya.

Indra: King of the lesser "gods" (demigods); the ruler of heaven (Surendra Loka); the rain-god.

Ishwara: "God" or "Lord" in the sense of the Supreme Power, Ruler, Master, or Controller of the cosmos. "Ishwara" implies the powers of omnipotence, omnipresence, and omniscience.

Janaka: The royal sage (raja rishi) who was the king of Mithila and a liberated yogi, a highly sought-after teacher of philosophy in ancient India. Sita, the wife of Rama, was his adopted daughter.

Jiva: Individual spirit.

Kalpa: A Day of Brahma–4,320,000,000 years. It alternates with a Night of Brahma of the same length. He lives hundred such years. Brahma's life is known as Para, being of a longer duration than the life of any other being, and a half of it is called Parardha. He has now completed the first Parardha and is in the first day of the second Parardha. This day or Kalpa is known as Svetavarahakalpa. In the Day of Brahma creation is manifest and in the Night of Brahma is it resolved into its causal state.

Kamadeva: God of beauty and love; the Vedic Cupid who shoots a bow with flowers instead of arrows.

Kamadhenu: Wish-fulfilling cow produced at the churning of the milk ocean.

Kamadhuk: See Kamadhenu.

Kandarpa: See Kamadeva.

Kapila: The great sage who formulated the Sankhya philosophy which is endorsed by Krishna in the Bhagavad Gita. (See the entry under Sankhya.)

Karma: Karma, derived from the Sanskrit root *kri*, which means to act, do, or make, means any kind of action, including thought and feeling. It also means the effects of action. Karma is both action and reaction, the metaphysical equivalent of the principle: "For every action there is an equal and opposite reaction." "Whatsoever a man soweth, that shall he also reap" (Galatians 6:7). It is karma operating through the law of cause and effect that binds the jiva or the individual soul to the wheel of birth and death. There are three forms of karma: sanchita, agami, and prarabdha. Sanchita karma is the vast store of accumulated actions done in the past, the fruits of which have not yet been reaped. Agami karma is the action that will be done by the individual in the future. Prarabdha karma is the action that has begun to fructify, the fruit of which is being reaped in this life.

Karma Yoga: The Yoga of selfless (unattached) action; performance of one's own duty; service of humanity.

Karma Yogi: One who practices karma yoga.

Karmakanda: The ritual portion of the Veda. The philosophy that Vedic ritual is the only path to perfection.

Kshatriya: A member of the ruler/warrior caste.

Kubera: The god of wealth.

Kusha: One of the varieties of sacred grass (darbha) used in many religious rites. Because of its insulating qualities, both physical and metaphysical, it is recommended as a seat (asana) for meditation, and as mats for sleeping (it keeps the sleeper warm).

Kutastha: Immutable; absolutely changeless; not subject to change; literally: "summit abiding" or "on the summit." He who is found without exception in all creatures from Brahma or the creator down to ants and Who is shining as the Self and dwells as witness to the intellect of all creatures; rock-seated; unchanging; another name for Brahman.

Mahapralaya: The final cosmic dissolution; the dissolution of all the worlds of relativity (Bhuloka, Bhuvaloka, Swaloka, Mahaloka, Janaloka, Tapaloka, and Satyaloka), until nothing but the Absolute remains. There are lesser dissolutions, known simply as pralayas, when only the first five worlds (lokas) are dissolved.

Maharatha: "A great-car-warrior," a commander of eleven thousand bowmen as he rode in his chariot.

Manava: Man; a human being; a descendant of Manu.

Manava dharma: The essential nature of man; religion of man; the duties of man.

Manu: The ancient lawgiver, whose code, The Laws of Manu (Manu Smriti) is the foundation of Hindu religious and social conduct.

Manus: Progenitors of the human race who were also its lawgivers and teachers.

Margashirsha: A lunar month, roughly the latter half of November and the first half of December. This is the time of ideal weather in India.

Marichi: The chief of the Maruts.

Maruts: The presiding deities of winds and storms.

Maya: The illusive power of Brahman; the veiling and the projecting power of the universe, the power of Cosmic Illusion. "The Measurer"–a reference to the two delusive "measures," Time and Space.

Meru: The mountain, of supreme height, on which the gods dwell, or the mountain on which Shiva is ever seated in meditation, said to be the center of the world, supporting heaven itself–obviously a yogic symbol of the spinal column or merudanda. The name of the central bead on a japa mala (rosary).

Moha: Delusion–in relation to something, usually producing delusive attachment or infatuation based on a completely false perception and evaluation of the object.

Naga: Snake; naked; a kind of powerful spirit-being worshipped in some areas of India, possessing great psychic powers and the ability to appear and communicate with human beings; one order of Sadhus, who are nude.

Narada: A primeval sage to whom some of the verses of the Rig Veda are attributed.

Om: The Pranava or the sacred syllable symbolizing and embodying Brahman. See the book *Om Yoga Meditation.*

Pandavas: The five sons of King Pandu: Yudhishthira, Bhima, Arjuna, Nakula, and Sahadeva. Their lives are described in the Mahabharata.

Pandus: See Pandavas.

Papa(m): Sin; demerit; evil; sinful deeds; evil deeds.

Parigraha: Possessiveness, greed, selfishness, acquisitiveness; covetousness; receiving of gifts conducive to luxury.

Pavaka: Agni.

Pitamaha: Grandfather; Great Father; titles of Brahma, the Creator.

Pitri: A departed ancestor, a forefather.

Prahlada: A daitya prince who rejected his daitya heritage and became a devotee of Vishnu. His father, the evil Hiranyakashipu, tortured him and attempted his life because of his devotion and his speaking to others of divine matters, yet he remained steadfast.

Prajapati: Progenitor; the Creator; a title of Brahma the Creator.

Prakriti: Causal matter; the fundamental power (shakti) of God from which the entire cosmos is formed; the root base of all elements; undifferentiated matter; the material cause of the world. Also known as Pradhana. Prakriti can also mean the entire range of vibratory existence (energy).

Pralaya: Dissolution. See Mahapralaya.

Prana: Life; vital energy; life-breath; life-force; inhalation. In the human body the prana is divided into five forms: 1) Prana, the prana that moves upward; 2) Apana: The prana that moves downward, producing the excretory functions in general. 3) Vyana: The prana that holds prana and apana together and produces circulation in the body. 4) Samana: The prana that carries the grosser material of food to the apana and brings the subtler material to each limb; the general force of digestion. 5) Udana: The prana which brings up or carries down what has been drunk or eaten; the general force of assimilation.

Preta: Ghost; spirit of the dead.

Purusha: "Person" in the sense of a conscious spirit. Both God and the individual spirits are purushas, but God is the Adi (Original, Archetypal) Purusha, Parama (Highest) Purusha, and the Purushottama (Highest or Best of the Purushas).

Purushottama: The Supreme Person; Supreme Purusha; the Lord of the universe. (See Purusha.)

Raga: Blind love; attraction; attachment that binds the soul to the universe. Attachment/affinity for something, implying a desire for it. This can be emotional (instinctual) or intellectual. It may range from simple liking or preference to intense desire and attraction. Greed; passion. See Dwesha.

Rajas: Activity, passion, desire for an object or goal.

Rajasic: Possessed of the qualities of the raja guna (rajas). Passionate; active; restless.

Rajoguna: Activity, passion, desire for an object or goal.

Rakshasa: There are two kinds of rakshasas: 1) semidivine, benevolent beings, or 2) cannibal demons or goblins, enemies of the gods. Meat-eating human beings are sometimes classed as rakshasas.

Rama: An incarnation of God–the king of ancient Ayodhya in north-central India. His life is recorded in the ancient epic Ramayana.

Rishi: Sage; seer of the Truth.

Rita(m): Truth; Law; Right; Order. The natural order of things, or Cosmic Order/Law. Its root is ri, which means "to rise, to tend upward." It is said to be the basis for the Law of Karma.

Rudras: "Roarers;" Vedic deities of destruction for renewal, the chief of which is Shiva; storm gods.

Sadhyas: A group of celestial beings with exquisitely refined natures thought to inhabit the ether.

Sama Veda: A collection of Rig Veda hymns that are marked (pointed) for singing. It is sometimes spoken of as the "essence" of the Rig Veda.

Samsara: Life through repeated births and deaths; the wheel of birth and death; the process of earthly life.

Sankalpa: A life-changing wish, desire, volition, resolution, will, determination, or intention–not a mere momentary aspiration, but an empowering act of will that persists until the intention is fully realized. It is an act of spiritual, divine creative will inherent in each person as a power of the Atma.

Sankhya: One of the six orthodox systems of Hindu philosophy whose originator was the sage Kapila, Sankhya is the original Vedic philosophy, endorsed by Krishna in the Bhagavad Gita (Gita 2:39; 3:3,5; 18:13,19), the second chapter of which is entitled "Sankhya Yoga." *A Ramakrishna-Vedanta Wordbook* says: "Sankhya postulates two ultimate realities, Purusha and Prakriti. Declaring that the cause of suffering is man's identification of Purusha with Prakriti and its products, Sankhya teaches that liberation and true knowledge are attained in the supreme consciousness, where such identification ceases and Purusha is realized as existing independently in its transcendental nature." Not surprisingly, then, Yoga is based on the Sankhya philosophy.

Sannyas(a): Renunciation; monastic life. Sannyasa literally means "total [san] throwing away [as]," absolute rejection.

Sannyasi(n): A renunciate; a monk.

Sapta Rishis: "Seven Sages." Great Beings who exist at the top of creation and supervise it.

Sarva(m): All; everything; complete.

Sattwa: Light; purity; harmony, goodness, reality.

Sattwa Guna: Quality of light, purity, harmony, and goodness.

Sattwic: Partaking of the quality of Sattwa.

Shankara: "The Auspicious One." A title of Shiva.

Shudra: A member of the laborer, servant caste.

Siddha: A perfected–liberated–being, an adept, a seer, a perfect yogi.

Skanda: Subramanya; the god of war and son of Shiva and Parvati; Skanda.

Soma: A milkweed, *Ascelpias acida*, whose juice in Vedic times was made into a beverage and offered in sacrifices; the nectar of immorality; a name of Chandra, the presiding deity of the moon.

Sudarshana Chakra: The invincible weapon of Lord Vishnu which is able to cut through anything, and is a symbol of the Lord's power of cutting through all things which bind the jiva to samsara. Thus it is the divine power of liberation (moksha).

Swabhava: One's own inherent disposition, nature, or potentiality; inherent state of mind; state of inner being.

Swadharma: One's own natural (innate) duty (dharma, based on their karma and samskara. One's own prescribed duty in life according to the eternal law (ritam).

Swakarma: Action, duty, business or occupation determined by (according to) one's own innate nature.

Tamas: Dullness, darkness, inertia, folly, and ignorance.

Tamasic: Possessed of the qualities of the tamo guna (tamas). Ignorant; dull; inert; and dark.

Tapasya: Austerity; practical (i.e., result-producing) spiritual discipline; spiritual force. Literally it means the generation of heat or energy, but is always used in a symbolic manner, referring to spiritual practice and its effect, especially the roasting of karmic seeds, the burning up of karma.

Tyaga: Literally: "abandonment." Renunciation–in the Gita, the relinquishment of the fruit of action.

Tyagi: A renouncer, an ascetic.

Uchchaishravas: The name of Indra's horse (or the horse of the Sun god, Surya), that was born of the amrita that was churned from the ocean by the gods. The name means "high-sounding" and refers to the power of mantra.

Uchchishta[m]: The remnants of food eaten by others, the actual leavings from someone's plate, considered extremely unclean physically and psychically. (This does not apply to food left in a serving dish or cooking vessel unless someone ate from it rather than serving it on their own dish.)

Ushanas: An ancient seer and poet.

Ushmapas: A class of ancestors (pitris) which live off subtle emanations or vapors.

Vairagya: Non-attachment; detachment; dispassion; absence of desire; disinterest; or indifference. Indifference towards and disgust for all worldly things and enjoyments.

Vaishya: A member of the merchant, farmer, artisan, businessman caste.

Varna: Caste. (Literally: color.) In traditional Hindu society there were four divisions or castes according to the individual's nature and aptitude: Brahmin, Kshatriya, Vaishya, and Shudra.

Varuna: A Vedic deity considered the sustainer of the universe and also the presiding deity of the oceans and water. Often identified with the conscience.

Vasava: A name of Indra.

Vasudeva: "He who dwells in all things"–the Universal God.

Vasuki: The king of the serpents. He assisted at the churning of the milk ocean.

Vasus: Eight Vedic deities characterized by radiance.

Vayu: The Vedic god of the wind; air; vital breath; Prana.

Vedas: The oldest scriptures of India, considered the oldest scriptures of the world, that were revealed in meditation to the Vedic Rishis (seers). Although in modern times there are said to be four Vedas (Rig, Sama, Yajur, and Atharva), in the upanishads only three are listed (Rig, Sama, and Yajur). In actuality, there is only one Veda: the Rig Veda. The Sama Veda is only a collection of Rig Veda hymns that are marked (pointed) for singing. The Yajur Veda is a small book giving directions on just one form of Vedic sacrifice. The Atharva Veda is only a collection of theurgical mantras to be recited for the cure of various afflictions or to be recited over the herbs to be taken as medicine for those afflictions.

Vedic: Having to do with the Vedas.

Vijnana: The highest knowledge, beyond mere theoretical knowledge (jnana); transcendental knowledge or knowing; experiential knowledge; a high state of spiritual realization–intimate knowledge of God in which all is seen as manifestations of Brahman; knowledge of the Self.

Vishnu: "The all-pervading;" God as the Preserver.

Vishuddha: Supremely pure; totally pure.

Vishwa devas: A group of twelve minor Vedic deities.

Vrishnis: The clan to which Krishna belonged.

Vyasa: One of the greatest sages of India, commentator on the Yoga Sutras, author of the Mahabharata (which includes the Bhagavad Gita), the Brahma Sutras, and the codifier of the Vedas.

Yadava: "Descendant of Yadu" an ancient Indian king; the Yadavas, a clan of India, were descended from King Yadu; a title of Krishna, since he was part of the Yadava clan. Swami Bhaktivedanta, founder of the Hare Krishna movement in the West, as well as some anthropologists, believed that the Yadava clan, who disappeared from India shortly after Krishna's lifetime, emigrated to the middle east and became the people we know today as the Jews, Abraham having been a Yadava.

Yajna: Sacrifice; offering; sacrificial ceremony; a ritual sacrifice; usually the fire sacrifice known as agnihotra or havan.

Yaksha: There are two kinds of yakshas: 1) semidivine beings whose king is Kubera, the lord of wealth, or 2) a kind of ghost, goblin, or demon.

Yama: Yamaraja; the Lord of Death, controller of who dies and what happens to them after death.

Yoga: Literally, "joining" or "union" from the Sanskrit root yuj. Union with the Supreme Being, or any practice that makes for such union. Meditation that unites the individual spirit with God, the Supreme Spirit. The name of the philosophy expounded by the sage Patanjali, teaching the process of union of the individual with the Universal Soul.

Yogamaya: The power of Maya, of divine illusion. It is Maya in operation, the operation/movement rising from the presence (union–yoga) of God (Ishwara) within it, and therefore possessing delusive power.

Yogeshwara: Lord of Yoga; a name of Lord Krishna.

Yogi(n): One who practices Yoga; one who strives earnestly for union with God; an aspirant going through any course of spiritual discipline.

Yuga: Age or cycle; aeon; world era. Hindus believe that there are four yugas: the Golden Age (Satya or Krita Yuga), the Silver age (Treta

Yuga), The Bronze Age (Dwapara Yuga), and the Iron Age (Kali Yuga). Satya Yuga is four times as long as the Kali Yuga; Treta Yuga is three times as long; and Dwapara Yuga is twice as long. In the Satya Yuga the majority of humans use the total potential–four-fourths–of their minds; in the Treta Yuga, three-fourths; in the Dwapara Yuga, one half; and in the Kali Yuga, one fourth. (In each Yuga there are those who are using either more or less of their minds than the general populace.) The Yugas move in a perpetual circle: Ascending Kali Yuga, ascending Dwapara Yuga, ascending Treta Yuga, ascending Satya Yuga, descending Satya Yuga, descending, Treta Yuga, descending Dwapara Yuga, and descending Kali Yuga–over and over. Furthermore, there are yuga cycles within yuga cycles. For example, there are yuga cycles that affect the entire cosmos, and smaller yuga cycles within those greater cycles that affect a solar system. The cosmic yuga cycle takes 8,640,000,000 years, whereas the solar yuga cycle only takes 24,000 years. At the present time our solar system is in the ascending Dwapara Yuga, but the cosmos is in the descending Kali Yuga. Consequently, the more the general mind of humanity develops, the more folly and evil it becomes able to accomplish.

ABOUT THE AUTHOR

Abbot George Burke (Swami Nirmalananda Giri) is the founder and director of the Light of the Spirit Monastery (Atma Jyoti Ashram) in Cedar Crest, New Mexico, USA.

In his many pilgrimages to India, he had the opportunity of meeting some of India's greatest spiritual figures, including Swami Sivananda of Rishikesh and Anandamayi Ma. During his first trip to India he was made a member of the ancient Swami Order by Swami Vidyananda Giri, a direct disciple of Paramhansa Yogananda, who had himself been given sannyas by the Shankaracharya of Puri, Jagadguru Bharati Krishna Tirtha.

In the United States he also encountered various Christian saints, including Saint John Maximovich of San Francisco and Saint Philaret Voznesensky of New York. He was ordained in the Liberal Catholic Church (International) to the priesthood on January 25, 1974, and consecrated a bishop on August 23, 1975.

For many years Abbot George has researched the identity of Jesus Christ and his teachings with India and Sanatana Dharma, including Yoga. It is his conclusion that Jesus lived in India for most of his life, and was a yogi and Sanatana Dharma missionary to the West. After his resurrection he returned to India and lived the rest of his life in the Himalayas.

He has written extensively on these and other topics, many of which are posted at OCOY.org.

Light of the Spirit Monastery

Light of the Spirit Monastery is an esoteric Christian monastic community for those men who seek direct experience of the Spirit through meditation, sacramental worship, discipline and dedicated communal life, emphasizing the inner reality of "Christ in you the hope of glory," as taught by the illumined mystics of East and West.

The public outreach of the monastery is through its website, OCOY.org (Original Christianity and Original Yoga). There you will find many articles on Original Christianity and Original Yoga, including *Esoteric Christian Beliefs*. *Foundations of Yoga* and *How to Be a Yogi* are practical guides for anyone seriously interested in living the Yoga Life.

You will also discover many other articles on leading an effective spiritual life, including *The Yoga of the Sacraments* and *Spiritual Benefits of a Vegetarian Diet*, as well as the "Dharma for Awakening" series–in-depth commentaries on these spiritual classics: the Upanishads, the Bhagavad Gita, the Dhammapada, and the Tao Teh King.

You can listen to podcasts by Abbot George on meditation, the Yoga Life, and remarkable spiritual people he has met in India and elsewhere, at http://ocoy.org/podcasts/

READING FOR AWAKENING

Light of the Spirit Press presents books on spiritual wisdom and Original Christianity and Original Yoga. From our "Dharma for Awakening" series (practical commentaries on the world's scriptures) to books on how to meditate and live a successful spiritual life, you will find books that are informative, helpful, and even entertaining.

Light of the Spirit Press is the publishing house of Light of the Spirit Monastery (Atma Jyoti Ashram) in Cedar Crest, New Mexico, USA. Our books feature the writings of the founder and director of the monastery, Abbot George Burke (Swami Nirmalananda Giri) which are also found on the monastery's website, OCOY.org.

We invite you to explore our publications in the following pages.

Find out more about our publications at
lightofthespiritpress.com

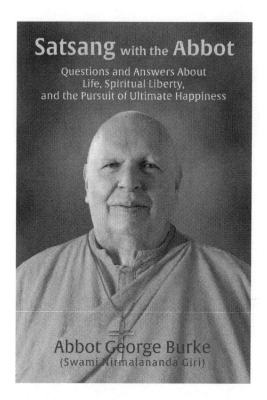

Satsang with the Abbot

Questions & Answers about Life, Spiritual Liberty, and the Pursuit of Ultimate Happiness

Grounded in the perspective of classic Indian thought, directly taught by such luminaries as Swami Sivananda of Rishikesh and Sri Anandamayi Ma, and blessed with the clarity and originality of thought that can only come from years of spiritual practice (sadhana), Abbot George Burke's answers to inquirers' questions are unique, fresh, and authoritative.

The questions in this book range from the most sublime to the most practical. "How can I attain samadhi? " "I am married with children. How can I lead a spiritual life? " "What is Self-realization? "

In Abbot George's replies to these questions the reader will discover common sense, helpful information, and a guiding light for their journey through and beyond the forest of cliches, contradictions, and confusion of yoga, Hinduism, Christianity, and metaphysical thought.

What Readers say:

"Abbot George speaks as one who knows his subject well, and answers in an manner that conveys an effortlessness and humor that puts one at ease, while, at the same time, a wisdom and sincerity which demands an attentive ear. "—*Russ Thomas*

The Christ of India
The Story of Original Christianity

"Original Christianity" is the teaching of both Jesus of Nazareth and his Apostle Saint Thomas in India. Although it was new to the Mediterranean world, it was really the classical, traditional teachings of the ancient rishis of India that even today comprise Sanatana Dharma, the Eternal Dharma, that goes far beyond religion into realization.

In The Christ of India Abbot George Burke presents what those ancient teachings are, as well as the growing evidence that Jesus spent much of his "Lost Years" in India and Tibet. This is also the story of how the original teachings of Jesus and Saint Thomas thrived in India for centuries before the coming of the European colonialists.

What Readers say:

"Interpreting the teachings of Jesus from the perspective of Santana Dharma, The Christ of India is a knowledgeable yet engaging collection of authentic details and evident manuscripts about the Essene roots of Jesus and his 'Lost years'. ...delightful to read and a work of substance, vividly written and rich in historical analysis, this is an excellent work written by a masterful teacher and a storyteller." –*Enas Reviews*

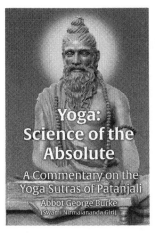

Yoga: Science of the Absolute
A Commentary on the Yoga Sutras of Patanjali

In *Yoga: Science of the Absolute*, Abbot George Burke draws on the age-long tradition regarding this essential text, including the commentaries of Vyasa and Shankara, the most highly regarded writers on Indian philosophy and practice, as well as I. K. Taimni and other authoritative commentators, and adds his own ideas based on half a century of study and practice. Serious students of yoga will find this an essential addition to their spiritual studies.

What Readers say:

"Abbot George has provided a commentary that is not only deeply informative, making brilliant connections across multiple traditions, but eminently practical. More importantly he describes how they can help one empower their own practice, their own sadhana." —Michael Sabani

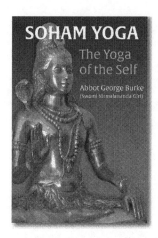

Soham Yoga
The Yoga of the Self

An in-depth guide to the practice of Soham sadhana.

Soham (which is pronounced like "Sohum") means: I Am That. It is the natural vibration of the Self, which occurs spontaneously with each incoming and outgoing breath. By becoming aware of it on the conscious level by mentally repeating it in time with the breath (*So* when inhaling and *Ham* when exhaling), a yogi experiences the identity between his individual Self and the Supreme Self.

The practice is very simple, and the results very profound. Truly wondrous is the fact that Soham Yoga can go on all the time, not just during meditation, if we apply ourselves to it. The whole life can become a continuous stream of liberating sadhana. "By the mantra 'Soham' separate the jivatma from the Paramatma and locate the jivatma in the heart" (Devi Bhagavatam 11.8.15). When we repeat Soham in time with the breath we are invoking our eternal being. This is why we need only listen to our inner mental intonations of Soham in time with the breath which itself is Soham.

What Readers say:

"The more I read this book, study it and practice Soham meditation and japa, the more thrilled I am to find this book. It is a complete spiritual path of Yoga."—*Arnold Van Wie*

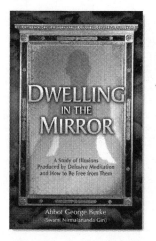

Dwelling in the Mirror
A Study of Illusions Produced by Delusive Meditation and How to Be Free from Them

"There are those who can have an experience and realize that it really cannot be real, but a vagary of their mind. Some may not understand that on their own, but can be shown by others the truth about it. For them and those that may one day be in danger of meditation-produced delusions I have written this brief study." –Abbot George Burke

In *Dwelling in the Mirror* you will learn:

• different types of meditation and the experiences they produce, and the problems and delusions which can arise from them.

• how to get rid of negative initiation energies and mantras.

• what are authentic, positive meditation practices and their effects and aspects.

• an ancient, universal method of meditation which is both proven and effective.

What Readers say:

"I totally loved this book! After running across many spiritual and self-help books filled with unrealistic promises, this little jewel had the impact of a triple Espresso."—*Sandra Carrington-Smith, author of Housekeeping for the Soul*

The Dhammapada for Awakening
A Commentary on Buddha's Practical Wisdom

The Dhammapada for Awakening brings a refreshing and timely perspective to ancient wisdom and shows seekers of inner peace practical ways to improve their inner lives today.

It explores the Buddha's answers to the urgent questions, such as "How can I find find lasting peace, happiness and fulfillment that seems so elusive?" and "What can I do to avoid many of the miseries big and small that afflict all of us?".

Drawing on the proven wisdom of different ancient traditions, and the contemporary masters of spiritual life, as well as his own studies and first-hand knowledge of the mystical traditions of East and West, Abbot George illumines the practical wisdom of Buddha in the Dhammapada, and more importantly, and make that makes that teaching relevant to present day spiritual seekers.

What Readers say:

"In this compelling book, Abbot George Burke brings his considerable knowledge and background in Christian teachings and the Vedic tradition of India to convey a practical understanding of the teachings of the Buddha. ...This is a book you'll want to take your time to read and keep as reference to reread. Highly recommended for earnest spiritual aspirants" *–Anna Hourihan, author, editor, and publisher at Vedanta Shores Press*

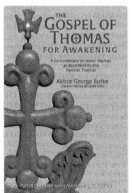

The Gospel of Thomas for Awakening
A Commentary on Jesus' Sayings as Recorded by the Apostle Thomas

"From the very beginning there were two Christianities." So begins this remarkable work. While the rest of the Apostles dispersed to various areas of the Mediterranean world, the apostle Thomas travelled to India, where growing evidence shows that Jesus spent his "Lost Years," and which had been the source of the wisdom which he had brought to the "West."

In *The Gospel of Thomas for Awakening*, Abbot George shines the "Light of the East" on the sometimes enigmatic sayings of Jesus recorded by his apostle Saint Thomas, revealing their unique and rich practical nature for modern day seekers for spiritual life.

Ideal for daily study or group discussion.

What Readers say:

"An extraordinary work of theological commentary, *The Gospel of Thomas for Awakening* is as informed and informative as it is inspired and inspiring".—*James A. Cox, Editor-in-Chief, Midwest Book Review*

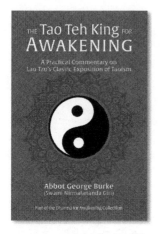

The Tao Teh King for Awakening
A Practical Commentary on Lao Tzu's Classic Exposition of Taoism

With penetrating insight, Abbot George Burke illumines the the wisdom of Lao Tzu's classic writing, the Tao Teh King (Tao Te Ching), and the timeless practical value of China's most beloved Taoist scripture for spiritual seekers. With a unique perspective of a lifetime of study and practice of both Eastern and Western spirituality, Abbot George mines the treasures of the Tao Teh King and presents them in an easily intelligible fashion for those wishing to put these priceless teachings into practice.

Illumined with quotes from the Gospels, the Bhagavad Gita, Yogananda and other Indian saints and Indian scriptures.

What Readers say:

"Burke's evident expertise concerning both Western and Eastern spirituality, provides readers with a wide-ranging and intriguing study of the topic. For those who seek spiritual guidance and insight into Lao Tzu's wisdom, this work offers a clear pathway." – *Publisher's Weekly (BookLife Prize)*

The Bhagavad Gita for Awakening
A Practical Commentary for Leading a Successful Spiritual Life

With penetrating insight, Abbot George Burke illumines the Bhagavad Gita's practical value for spiritual seekers. With a unique perspective from a lifetime of study and practice of both Eastern and Western spirituality, Abbot George presents the treasures of the Gita in an easily intelligible fashion.

Drawing from the teachings of Sri Ramakrishna, Jesus, Paramhansa Yogananda, Ramana Maharshi, Swami Vivekananda, Swami Sivananda of Rishikesh, Papa Ramdas, and other spiritual masters and teachers, as well as his own experiences, Abbot Burke illustrates the teachings of the Gita with stories which make the teachings of Krishna in the Gita vibrant and living.

What Readers say:

"This is not a book for only "Hindus" or "Christians." Anyone desiring to better their lives mentally, emotionally, and spiritually would benefit greatly by reading this book."— *Sailaja Kuruvadi*

The Upanishads for Awakening
A Practical Commentary on India's Classical Scriptures

With penetrating insight, Abbot George Burke illumines the Upanishads' practical value for spiritual seekers, and the timelessness of India's most beloved scriptures. With a unique perspective of a lifetime of study and practice of both Eastern and Western spirituality, Abbot George mines the treasures of the Upanishads and presents them in an easily intelligible fashion for those wishing to put these priceless teachings into practice

The teachings of the Upanishads are the supreme expressions of the eternal wisdom, the eternal vision of the ancient rishis (sages) of India. The truths embodied in the Upanishads and their inspired digest-summary, the Bhagavad Gita, are invaluable for all who would ascend to higher consciousness.

What Readers say:

"It is always a delight to see how he seamlessly integrates the wisdom of the West into the East."
–Roopa Subramani

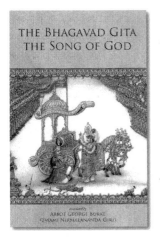

The Bhagavad Gita–The Song of God
A new translation of the most important spiritual classic which India has produced.

Often called the "Bible" of Hinduism, the Bhagavad Gita is found in households throughout India and has been translated into every major language of the world. Literally billions of copies have been handwritten and printed.

The clarity of this translation by Abbot George Burke makes for easy reading, while the rich content makes this the ideal "study" Gita. As the original Sanskrit language is so rich, often there are several accurate translations for the same word, which are noted in the text, giving the spiritual student the needed understanding of the fullness of the Gita.

For those unable to make a spiritual journey to India, a greater pilgrimage can be made by anyone anywhere in the world by simply reading The Holy Song of God, the Srimad Bhagavad Gita. It will be a holy pilgrimage of mind and spirit.

Robe of Light
An Esoteric Christian Cosmology

In *Robe of Light* Abbot George Burke explores the whys and where-fores of the mystery of creation. From the emanation of the worlds from the very Being of God, to the evolution of the souls to their ultimate destiny as perfected Sons of God, the ideal progression of creation is described. Since the rebellion of Lucifer and the fall of Adam and Eve from Paradise flawed the normal plan of evolution, a restoration was necessary. How this came about is the prime subject of this insightful study.

Moreover, what this means to aspirants for spiritual perfection is expounded, with a compelling knowledge of the scriptures and of the mystical traditions of East and West.

What Readers say:

"Having previously read several offerings from the pen of Abbot George Burke I was anticipating this work to be well written and an enjoyable read. However, Robe of Light actually exceeded my expectations. Abbot Burke explicates the subject perfectly, making a difficult and complex subject like Christian cosmology accessible to those of us who are not great theologians."—*Russ Thomas*

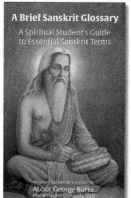

A Brief Sanskrit Glossary
A Spiritual Student's Guide to Essential Sanskrit Terms

This Sanskrit glossary contains full translations and explanations of many of the most commonly used spiritual Sanskrit terms, and will help students of the Bhagavad Gita, the Upanishads, the Yoga Sutras of Patanjali, and other Indian scriptures and philosophical works to expand their vocabularies to include the Sanskrit terms contained in them, and gain a fuller understanding in their studies.

What Readers say:

"If you are reading the writings of Swami Sivananda you will find a basketful of untranslated Sanskrit words which often have no explanation, as he assumes his readers have a background in Hindu philosophy. For writings like his, this book is invaluable, as it lists frequently used Sanskrit terms used in writings on yoga and Hindu philosophical thought.

"As the title says, this is a spiritual students' guidebook, listing not only commonly used spiritual terms, but also giving brief information about spiritual teachers and writers, both modern and ancient.

"Abbot George's collection is just long enough to give the meanings of useful terms without overwhelming the reader with an overabundance of extraneous words. This is a book that the spiritual student will use frequently."—*Simeon Davis*

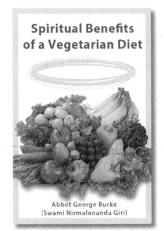

Spiritual Benefits of a Vegetarian Diet

The health benefits of a vegetarian diet are well known, as are the ethical aspects. But the spiritual advantages should be studied by anyone involved in meditation, yoga, or any type of spiritual practice.

Although diet is commonly considered a matter of physical health alone, since the Hermetic principle "as above, so below" is a fundamental truth of the cosmos, diet is a crucial aspect of emotional, intellectual, and spiritual development as well. For diet and consciousness are interrelated, and purity of diet is an effective aid to purity and clarity of consciousness.

The major thing to keep in mind when considering the subject of vegetarianism is its relevancy in relation to our explorations of consciousness. We need only ask: Does it facilitate my spiritual growth–the development and expansion of my consciousness? The answer is Yes.

A second essay, *Christian Vegetarianism,* continues with a consideration of the esoteric side of diet, the vegetarian roots of early Christianity, and an insightful exploration of vegetarianism in the Old and New Testaments.

Available as a free Kindle ebook download at Amazon.com.

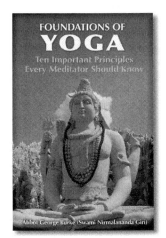

Foundations of Yoga
Ten Important Principles Every Meditator Should Know

An in-depth examination of the important foundation principles of Patanjali's Yoga, Yama & Niyama.

Yama and Niyama are often called the Ten Commandments of Yoga, but they have nothing to do with the ideas of sin and virtue or good and evil as dictated by some cosmic potentate. Rather they are determined on a thoroughly practical, pragmatic basis: that which strengthens and facilitates our yoga practice should be observed and that which weakens or hinders it should be avoided.

It is not a matter of being good or bad, but of being wise or foolish. Each one of these Five Don'ts (Yama) and Five Do's (Niyama) is a supporting, liberating foundation of Yoga. An introduction to the important foundation principles of Patanjali's Yoga: Yama & Niyama

Available as a free Kindle ebook download at Amazon.com, as well as in paperback.

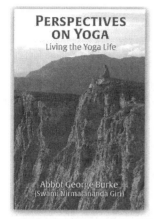

Perspectives on Yoga
Living the Yoga Life

"Dive deep; otherwise you cannot get the gems at the bottom of the ocean. You cannot pick up the gems if you only float on the surface." Sri Ramakrishna

Many people come to the joyous and liberating discovery of yoga and yoga philosophy, and then dive no deeper, resting on their first understanding of the atman, Brahman, the goal of yoga, and everything else the classic yoga philosophy teaches about "the way things are."

In *Perspectives on Yoga* author Abbot George Burke shares the gems he has found from a lifetime of "diving deep." This collection of reflections and short essays addresses the key concepts of the yoga philosophy that are so easy to take for granted. Never content with the accepted cliches about yoga sadhana, the yoga life, the place of a guru, the nature of Brahman and our unity with It, Abbot George's insights on these and other facets of the yoga life will inspire, provoke, enlighten, and even entertain.

What Readers say:

"Abbot George eloquently brings the eastern practice of seeking God inwardly to western readers who have been taught to seek God outwardly."—*Bill Braddock*

May a Christian Believe in Reincarnation?

Discover the real and surprising history of reincarnation and Christianity.

A growing number of people are open to the subject of past lives, and the belief in rebirth–reincarnation, metempsychosis, or transmigration–is becoming commonplace. It often thought that belief in reincarnation and Christianity are incompatible. But is this really true? May a Christian believe in reincarnation? The answer may surprise you.

Reincarnation-also known as the transmigration of souls-is not just some exotic idea of non-Christian mysticism. Nor is it an exclusively Hindu-Buddhist teaching.

In orthodox Jewish and early Christian writings, as well as the Holy Scriptures, we find reincarnation as a fully developed belief, although today it is commonly ignored. But from the beginning it has been an integral part of Orthodox Judaism, and therefore as Orthodox Jews, Jesus and his Apostles would have believed in rebirth.

What Readers say:

"Those needing evidence that a belief in reincarnation is in accordance with teachings of the Christ need look no further: Plainly laid out and explained in an intelligent manner from one who has spent his life on a Christ-like path of renunciation and prayer/meditation."—*Christopher T. Cook*